A New Star-Rating System
& Other _____
from _____

D0006016

In our continuing effort to _____ e, and most appealing travel guides available, we've added some great new features.

Frommer's guides now include a new **star-rating system.** Every hotel, restaurant, and attraction is rated from 0 to 3 stars to help you set priorities and organize your time.

We've also added **seven brand-new features** that point you to the great deals, in-the-know advice, and unique experiences that separate travelers from tourists. Throughout the guide, look for:

Finds	Special finds—those places only insiders know about
Fun Fact	Fun facts—details that make travelers more informed and their trips more fun
Kids	Best bets for kids—advice for the whole family
Moments	Special moments—those experiences that memories are made of
Overrated	Places or experiences not worth your time or money
Tips	Insider tips—some great ways to save time and money
Value	Great values—where to get the best deals

We've also added a **"What's New"** section in every guide—a timely crash course in what's hot and what's not in every destination we cover.

Here's what the critics say about Frommer's:

Other Great Guides for Your Trip:

Frommer's®

Philadelphia & the Amish Country

12th Edition

by Jay Golan

Wiley Publishing, Inc

About the Author

Jay Golan has been writing about travel in Europe, Asia, and the United States since college. Educated at Harvard, Oxford, and Columbia Universities, he has worked for major cultural institutions in Boston and New York for 20 years, most recently at Carnegie Hall. He and his young family live in New York City and frequently visit relatives and friends in Philadelphia. This edition is dedicated to his two most reliable critics, Emma and Sophie, and to Barat.

Published by:

Wiley Publishing, Inc.

909 Third Ave.
New York, NY 10022

ISBN 0-7645-6747-0
ISSN 0899-3211

Editor: Liz Albertson
Production Editor: Donna Wright
Cartographer: John Decamillis
Photo Editor: Richard Fox
Production by Wiley Indianapolis Composition Services

Front cover photo: Society Hill © Bob Krist Photography
Back cover photo: Amish Hats on Rack © Kim M. Koza/Corbis

For information on our other products and services or to obtain technical support, please contact our Customer Care Department within the U.S. at 800-762-2974, outside the U.S. at 317-572-3993 or fax 317-572-4002.

Wiley also publishes its books in a variety of electronic formats. Some content that appears in print may not be available in electronic formats.

Manufactured in the United States of America

5 4 3 2 1

Contents

List of Maps

An Invitation to the Reader

In researching this book, we discovered many wonderful places — hotels, restaurants, shops, and more. We're sure you'll find others. Please tell us about them, so we can share the information with your fellow travelers in upcoming editions. If you were disappointed with a recommendation, we'd love to know that, too. Please write to:

Frommer's Philadelphia & the Amish Country, 12th Edition
Wiley Publishing, Inc. • 909 Third Ave. • New York, NY 10022

An Additional Note

Please be advised that travel information is subject to change at any time — and this is especially true of prices. We therefore suggest that you write or call ahead for confirmation when making your travel plans. The authors, editors, and publisher cannot be held responsible for the experiences of readers while traveling. Your safety is important to us, however, so we encourage you to stay alert and be aware of your surroundings. Keep a close eye on cameras, purses, and wallets, all favorite targets of thieves and pickpockets.

New! Frommer's Star Ratings & Icons

Every hotel, restaurant, and attraction listing in this guide has been ranked for quality, value, service, amenities, and special features using a star-rating scale. In country, state, and regional guides, we also rate towns and regions to help you narrow down your choices and budget your time accordingly. Hotels and restaurants in the Very Expensive and Expensive categories are rated on a scale of one (highly recommended) to three stars (exceptional). Those in the Moderate and Inexpensive categories rate from zero (recommended) to two stars (very highly recommended). Attractions, towns, and regions are rated according to the following scale: zero stars (recommended), one star (highly recommended), two stars (very highly recommended), and three stars (must-see).

In addition to the rating system, we also use seven icons to highlight insider information, useful tips, special bargains, hidden gems, memorable experiences, kid-friendly venues, places to avoid, and other useful information:

(Finds (Fun Fact (Kids (Moments (Overrated (Tips (Value

The following abbreviations are used for credit cards:

AE	American Express	DISC	Discover	V	Visa
DC	Diners Club	MC	MasterCard		

FROMMERS.COM

Now that you have the guidebook to a great trip, visit our website at **www.frommers.com** for travel information on nearly 2,500 destinations. With features updated regularly, we give you instant access to the most current trip-planning information available. At Frommers.com, you'll also find the best prices on airfares, accommodations, and car rentals—and you can even book travel online through our travel booking partners. At Frommers.com, you'll also find the following:

- Online updates to our most popular guidebooks
- Vacation sweepstakes and contest giveaways
- Newsletter highlighting the hottest travel trends
- Online travel message boards with featured travel discussions

What's New in Philadelphia

Maybe because it's originally William Penn's "greene countrie towne" and has such an illustrious past, Philadelphia has to plan especially well to keep alive the best and most attractive of the past 3 centuries, while constantly striving to keep pace with the future. One thing's for sure — there's no lack of imagination here.

PLANNING YOUR TRIP The Philadelphia International Airport has completed new terminals, an airport Marriott, a shopping complex, and a new commuter runway; look for the 4-level terminal A West with 13 new wide-body international gates, 60 ticket counters and 11 new restaurants. A project to develop shops and offices alongside the handsome but lonely Amtrak Penn Station at 30th Street looks like it's lifting off.

ACCOMMODATIONS The building boom of the 1990s may have slowed down, but the result is 20,000 beds in the region, many of them being sold at deep discount these days. The major new hotel is the **Hyatt Regency Philadelphia at Penn's Landing,** 201 S. Columbus Blvd. (✆ **215/928-1234**) on the Delaware waterfront, with Keating's restaurant on the riverbank terrace and immediate access to I-95. The two really spectacular rehabs since 2000 are **The Ritz-Carlton Philadelphia,** 10 Avenue of the Arts (S. Broad St.), (✆ **215/ 523-8000**), in a Pantheon-like historic bank next to City Hall, and the **Loews Philadelphia Hotel,** 1200 Market St. (✆ 215/627-1200), in a classic 1932 Art Deco skyscraper

opposite the Convention Center. See chapter 5, "Where to Stay," for more details.

DINING Philadelphia is a wonderful dining city — 7th in the country says John Mariani of *Esquire Magazine* — but it's light on glamour. So top restaurateurs are starting to adopt the Yankee strategy of paying top dollar to import talent like Masaharu Morimoto at **Morimoto,** 723 Chestnut St. (✆ **215/413-9070**) and Douglas Rodriguez at **Alma de Cuba,** 1623 Walnut St. (✆ **215/988-1799**). Exploration of multicultural fusion cuisine continues with spots like Guillermo Pernot's romantic **Pasion!,** 211 S. 15th St. (✆ **215/875-9895**). The theatrical restaurant experience is exemplified at the retro-futuristic **Pod,** 3636 Sansom St. in West Philadelphia (✆ **215/387-1803**), and the shimmering and very chic **Buddakan,** 325 Chestnut St. (✆ **215/ 574-9440**). Plus, both of these restaurants have cuisine that stands up to the surroundings. Chefs move around a lot and recent shifts are re-energizing the classic **Le Bec-Fin,** 1523 Walnut St. (✆ **215/567-1000**) and the new Tuscan bistro **Avenue B** opposite the new Kimmel Center for the Performing Arts, 260 S. Broad St. (✆ **215/ 790-0705**). See chapter 6, "Where to Dine," for complete details.

SIGHTSEEING The old is new again. To make the Liberty Bell's current home, and the stretch of city that was cleared to the north of it, less of an eyesore, the city and the National Park Service are carrying out a $130 million renovation plan, adding beautiful walkways and landscaping. The new **Independence Visitor Center** at Market and 6th streets (℃ **215/965-7676**) is already smoothing the way, and the **Liberty Bell** is in a new larger pavilion near the corner of 6th and Chestnut streets, right near a new interpretive center. Within a block, the new **National Constitution Center,** 525 Arch St. (℃ **215/923-0004**) is opening on July 4, 2003, to provide an entertaining exploration of this amazing document, the root of America's achievements. The stretch of Broad Street south of City Hall has been renamed the **Avenue of the Arts,** and its crowning glory is the majestic glass enclosed **Kimmel Center for the Performing Arts,** opened at Broad and Spruce streets in 2001 and joining the Academy of Music a block north as one of the nation's leading performing arts complexes (℃ **215/893-1999** for tickets). The **Philadelphia Museum of Art,** 26th Street and the Ben Franklin Parkway (℃ **215/763-8100**) just celebrated its 125th anniversary by acquiring a huge insurance headquarters across the street, so look for more gallery and office space. The gardens around the museum are being restored. The beautiful classic **Waterworks** along the Schuylkill River will house a terraced restaurant by summer 2003.

For fans who make the journey to South Philadelphia for professional sports, the 1971 Veterans Stadium is being replaced. The Eagles will play in the new 66,000-seat Lincoln Financial Field starting in the fall of 2003, and the Phillies will occupy a more intimate and modern ballpark, seating 43,000, from April 2004. The latter has cool features such as an open-air concourse and an open steel seating bowl, so that the city outside can catch glimpses of the field and vice versa. See chapter 7, "Exploring Philadelphia," for complete details.

SHOPPING The lack of tax on clothing here attracts shoppers, and the top news is yet more expansion in size and increased quality at the **King of Prussia Court and Plaza** (℃ **610/265-5727**), a 450-store behemoth near the junction of suburban routes 202 and I-276. It's got top national chain restaurants, movie theaters, and even simulated rock climbing for the kids. The **Old City** neighborhood, just north and east of Independence Hall, has become a mecca for contemporary and 20th century crafts, art, and specialty services. **Rittenhouse Row,** especially the stretch of Walnut Street just east of Rittenhouse Square, is looking spiffy again, with stores like **Burberrys, Joan Shepp Boutique, Knit Wit,** and **Lagos** jewelry. Chapter 9, "Shopping," has complete details.

AFTER DARK Look to the **Avenue of the Arts** as the local capital of classic performances. You'll find The Philadelphia Orchestra in the cello-shaped **Verizon Hall** of the **Kimmel Center** (℃ **215/893-1999**), and great theater at the restored movie palace now known as the **Harold Prince Music Theater,** 1412 Chestnut St. (℃ **215/972-1000**). The blocks of **Old City** contain small bars and great pubs like **Silk City Lounge,** 5th and Spring Garden Street (℃ **215/592-8838**), but the major nightclubs are right on the Delaware waterfront piers. Take a taxi or water taxi in summer to visit places like **Maui Entertainment Complex, Rock Lobster,** and **KatManDu.** See chapter 10, "Philadelphia After Dark," for details.

The Best of Philadelphia

Philadelphia today is an inseparable mix of old and new. Scratch the surface of William Penn's "green countrie towne" and you'll find both a wealth of history and plenty of modern distractions.

Philadelphia has the largest surviving district of original colonial homes and shops in the country, with dozens of treasures in and around Independence National Historical Park. It boasts the most historic square mile in America, the place where the United States was conceived, declared, and ratified — and the city and federal governments are investing heavily to show this area off and teach its lessons. Philadelphia offers some of the best dining values and several of the finest restaurants in America. The city is a stroller's paradise of restored Georgian and Federal structures integrated with smart shops and contemporary row house courts to create a working urban environment. It's a center of professional and amateur sports, with more than 9,800 acres of parkland within the city limits. It's a city filled with art, crafts, and music for every taste, with boulevards made for street fairs and parades all year long. From row-house boutiques to the Second Continental Congress's favorite tavern, from an Ivy League campus to street artists and musicians, from gleaming skyscrapers to Italian marketplaces, Philadelphia is a city of the unexpected.

The earlier colonial view of Philadelphians as reflective, sophisticated, and tolerant has been replaced by the brash, good-hearted "Rocky" stereotype. Philadelphia is "The place that loves you back," as the current marketing campaign puts it. Of course, both characterizations have some grain of truth to them. There's a tremendous diversity among the 1.5 million residents of this city, spread over 129 square miles — there's the opportunity to sink into the plush seats at the new Kimmel Center and sample gourmet cuisine in the dining room of Zanzibar Blue, and there's also the chance to perch in the bleachers of Veterans Stadium.

Geographically, Philadelphia sits pretty. Some 60 miles inland, it's the country's busiest freshwater port, controlling the Delaware Valley. Philadelphia occupies a tongue of land at the confluence of the Delaware — one of the largest U.S. rivers feeding into the Atlantic — and the Schuylkill (*school*-kill) rivers. The original settlement, and the heart of Center City today, is the band of solid ground about 5 miles north of the junction's marshland. Since then, of course, the city has drained and used the entire tongue to the south and has exploded into the northeast and northwest. The city is a natural stopping place between New York and Washington, D.C., with easy access to both by rail and road. And the casinos and beaches of Atlantic City, the Revolutionary War sites of Valley Forge and Brandywine, the great Du Pont family mansions, and Pennsylvania Dutch country all lie within 90 minutes of the city.

1 Frommer's Favorite Philadelphia Experiences

- **Taking Afternoon Tea at the Swann Lounge:** The quintessential luxury tea is found at the Four Seasons, overlooking one of the city's finest squares, with fountains on both sides. See p. 67.

- **Visiting the Barnes Foundation:** The Barnes Foundation Gallery in Merion houses the most important private collection of Impressionist and early French modern paintings in the world, displaying more Cézannes than all the museums of France put together. The museum is bankrupt and may need to make significant changes, so try to schedule a visit in advance around its open hours from Friday to Sunday (or Wed–Fri in summertime). See p. 118.

- **Wandering Through Fairmount Park:** It would take dozens of outings to fully explore the 100 miles of trails in this 8,900-acre giant of an urban park — some of them are virtually unchanged since Revolutionary times. We'll settle for gazing at the hundreds of flame azaleas that bloom behind the Art Museum in spring, and the dozen Georgian country mansions, kept in immaculate condition, that pepper the park. See p. 136.

- **Shopping on First Friday:** On the first Friday of every month, the galleries, stores, and studios of Old City — just above Independence National Historical Park — remain open with refreshments and artists on hand until 9pm. Wander along the cobblestone streets, stopping into one of the many coffee bars or bistros. See "The Shopping Scene" in chapter 9.

- **Stepping Back in Time in Historic Philadelphia:** Everyone knows about the miraculous reclamation of this country's colonial capital, from work on the Liberty Bell to renovation on hundreds of row houses, with their distinctive brickwork and 18th-century formal gardens (and welcoming benches). But the new tours (especially the nighttime "Lights of Liberty" show, see p. 118), the costumed town criers with free maps, and the Revolutionary War–era street theater bring the experience even closer. Just wander; they'll find you. See "National Historical Park: America's Most Historic Square Mile" in chapter 7.

- **Snacking on Pretzels, Hoagies, and Philly's Famous Cheesesteaks:** Philadelphia has a rich tradition of cuisine from haute (as in the shad roe from fish caught in the Delaware River each Apr) to hot (the warm, soft, salty pretzels served slathered with mustard at stands all over town). The hoagie is something else — cold cuts, lettuce, and onions layered with oil and vinegar — along with its cousin the cheesesteak, also served on an enormous elongated bun. See "Local Favorites: Cheesesteaks, Hoagies & More" in chapter 6.

- **Strolling Around Independence Square at Night:** The combination of history, elegance, and proportion among the three main buildings that contained America's first government always induces a sense of wonder at this country's good fortune in its founding citizens. You might even feel the urge to jump aboard one of the horse-drawn carriages lined up nearby (security concerns have shut down Chestnut Street traffic in front). See "National Historical Park: America's Most Historic Square Mile" in chapter 7.

The Eastern Seaboard

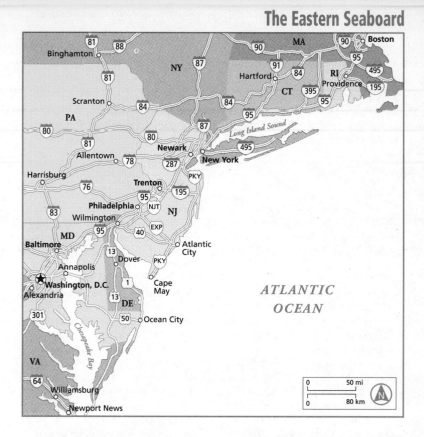

- **Enjoying the Lights at Night:** The William Penn statue atop City Hall, the Ben Franklin Bridge, and seven Schuylkill River bridges are permanently lighted, joining the pinlights that outline the boathouses along the Schuylkill River. Sheer magic.
- **Listening to Hot Jazz and Blues:** There are at least half a dozen clubs with world-class, down-home, accessible, and affordable American music any night you're in town, very possibly with local sons like Grover Washington Jr. and Christian McBride. See "Jazz & Blues Clubs" in chapter 10.
- **Touring an Open House:** If you're in the city at the right time, don't miss the tours of restored

mansions in Society Hill, Ritten-house Square, or Fairmount Park for a delightful lesson in interior design and Americana. The open houses are scattered throughout the year, but I especially love the ones during pre-Christmas season. See the "Philadelphia Calendar of Events" in chapter 2.

- **Breathing Deeply at the Philadelphia Flower Show:** In early March, the scent-sational Flower Show — the largest and

---

Fun Fact A Central City

Thirty-eight percent of the nation's population lives within a 4½-hour drive from Philadelphia.

most prestigious indoor exhibition of its kind in the world — descends on the Pennsylvania Convention Center. See p. 16.

- **Exploring the Philadelphia Museum of Art:** It has a stupendous collection of masterpieces, period rooms, and crafts, and is becoming one of the hottest museums in the country for special exhibitions. Look for more blockbusters like the recent van Gogh and Cézanne exhibitions. The late Wednesdays and Fridays have become one of the city's trendiest social scenes. See p. 119.

- **Cheering the Regattas Along the Schuylkill:** On any spring weekend, stand along Boathouse Row just north of the Philadelphia Museum of Art, and get ready to cheer. Crews race each other every 5 minutes or so, with friends along the riverbanks rooting them on. See p. 146.

- **Stocking Up at the Reading Terminal Market:** From Bassett's ice cream to Bain's turkey sandwiches to the food of the 12th Street Cantina, this is the century-old mother lode of unpackaged, fresh, honest-to-goodness provisions. Amish farmers come every Thursday through Saturday to sell their custards and scrapple (a kind of herbed pork casserole held together with cornmeal and fried before serving, either hot or cold). And what could be more convenient than the market's location right underneath the Convention Center? See p. 108.

- **Exploring South Philly:** Exuberant attitude punctuates every interchange you'll have, whether you're on a stroll (with ample tastings) through the Italian Market or wandering farther south to seek out the area's great pizzas, cannoli, or famed cheesesteaks. See p. 54 for a description of the neighborhood and p. 100 for info on where to eat.

- **Dining on Walnut and Sydenham Streets:** This particular corner near Rittenhouse Square has more world-class restaurants within mere feet of each other — Le Bec-Fin, Circa, Striped Bass, Brasserie Perrier, Susanna Foo, and Alma de Cuba — than any other spot anywhere in the world. Whatever your taste or price range, you should try one of them. See chapter 6 for descriptions of and information on all of these restaurants.

2 Best Hotel Bets

- **Best Historic Hotel:** Well, it's only the "lite" version of what it used to be, when Thomas Edison designed the fixtures and the ballroom virtually defined swank. But the top floor of the **Park Hyatt Philadelphia at the Bellevue,** Broad and Walnut streets, or 1415 Chancellor Court, between Walnut and Locust streets (© **800/ 223-1234**), with its occasionally oddly proportioned rooms, carries traces of a century's worth of history. See p. 68.

- **Best for Business Travelers:** I'm partial to the new **Hotel Sofitel,** 120 S. 17th St. (© **800/SOFI TEL**). This upscale chain with a French accent is incredibly convenient, and the rooms are large and elegant, with easy access to plugs and modem jacks at a handsome desk. You'll find personal voice mail, also. The service staff is efficient and courteous. See p. 67.

- **Best for a Romantic Getaway:** Some people like a slick, cosmopolitan suite in the clouds for romance. But I'll take the **Penn's View Hotel,** Front and Market streets (℡ **800/331-7634**), any day. Even at the noisy corner of Front and Market streets, the upper floors feel like an exquisite club, with views over the Delaware River. And how could you not like what the *New York Times* hails as "the mother of all wine bars" downstairs? See p. 65.

• **Best Hotel Lobby for Pretending You're Rich:** There's no place like the cool, plush **Four Seasons Hotel,** 1 Logan Sq. (℡ **800/332-3442**), for rubbing elbows with the moneyed elite (it's also a great place to stay if you *are* the moneyed elite). The Swann Lounge overlooking Logan Circle is a constant stream of chic outfits, custom suits, and the frequent black tie. See p. 67.

• **Best for Families: The Inn at Penn,** in West Philadelphia at 3600 Sansom St. (℡ **800/445-8667**), is a crosstown ride from the historical sights, but offers the whole family space to roam among spacious corridors, ever-present fruit to munch on and tea to sip in a comfortable library lounge, plus TV for children to watch while parents exercise. Also, the campus of U. Penn. across the street is perfect for throwing a Frisbee or playing tag. See p. 75. Slightly tattered but more moderately priced is the **Embassy Suites Center City,** 1776 Benjamin Franklin Pkwy. at Logan Square (℡ **800/362-2779**), with cute little open-air balconies (yes, the railings are sturdy), and an opulent buffet breakfast at the TGI Friday's at street level. It's 5 minutes to the premier children's museums and Logan Circle. And all the rooms are suites, so parents can have their privacy. See p. 71.

• **Best Moderately Priced Hotel:** The **Hawthorn Suites Philadelphia at the Convention Center,** adjacent to the Convention Center at 1100 Vine St. (℡ **800/527-1133**), is the best choice in its price range. A suite with two double beds and a sofa bed in the living room goes for $179 but can often be had for less. Full breakfast and afternoon hors d'oeuvres are included, along with in-room microwaves, refrigerators, and coffeemakers. See p. 74.

• **Best B&B:** Many, many more B&Bs are listed through **A Bed & Breakfast Connection/Bed & Breakfast of Philadelphia** (p. 61) than are listed independently. My favorite among the latter is **Shippen Way Inn,** 418 Bainbridge St. (℡ **800/245-4873** or 215/627-7266), a tiny row house in Queen Village built around 1750 and lovingly maintained. You might also try **Ten Eleven Clinton,** 1011 Clinton St. (℡ **215/923-8144**), an elegant 1836 Federal town house on a quiet tree-lined street. See both on p. 68.

• **Best Service:** The training process set up by the Ritz-Carlton group's C.O., Horst Schulze, for every employee of every **Ritz-Carlton** hotel is legendary, and the staff at the hotel at 10 Avenue of the Arts (℡ **800/241-3333**) is no exception. Guests pay top prices (though weekend packages are actually quite affordable) to be pampered. It's a fantasyland of amenities; service attendants earn points for thinking of extras like both foam and down pillows in the closets and bookmarks in the *TV Guides.* See p. 69.

• **Best Location:** Assuming we're visitors who have come to see Independence Park, why not wake up looking at it through the floral chintz curtains at the **Omni Hotel at Independence Park,** 4th and Chestnut streets (© **800/843-6664**)? All 155 guest rooms have views of the Greek Revival Second Bank of the U.S. and a half-dozen of America's Georgian jewels. And the clip-clopping of horses and carriages below maintains the sense of history. See p. 64.

• **Best Health Club:** The **Wyndham Philadelphia at Franklin Plaza,** 17th and Race streets (© **800/996-3426**), with 758 rooms — second only in quantity to the Convention Center Marriott — has the best facilities for hotel guests, including a 45-foot indoor pool, a track, three racquetball courts, three squash courts, outdoor handball, and two tennis courts — all on the third-floor lobby roof. Weights and Nautilus machines round out the picture inside. See p. 73.

• **Best Hotel Pool:** I'm actually cheating a tiny bit here, but part of the garage complex of the **Park Hyatt Philadelphia at the Bellevue** (see "Best Historic Hotel," above) is the Sporting Club, with its four-lane, junior Olympic pool. Only hotel guests and local members can use the pool and the other 2 acres of health facilities. See p. 68.

• **Best Views:** Many of the hotel listings in chapter 5 specify one side or another as preferable. In Center City, rooms at **Rittenhouse Hotel,** 210 W. Rittenhouse Sq. (© **800/635-1042**), are on floors five to nine, and all have wonderful views of the Philly landscape, from the colorful park below on the east to the western view of the Schuylkill and the Parkway. See p. 69. The new **Hyatt Regency Philadelphia at Penn's Landing,** on the Delaware River waterfront at 201 S. Columbus Blvd. (© **800/228-3360**), commands spectacular views; I prefer surveying all of Center City to the west and Camden to the east from this hotel. See p. 61.

• **Best Hotel Restaurant:** The Zagat guide to local restaurants listed the **Fountain Restaurant** in the **Four Seasons** (see "Best Hotel Lobby for Pretending You're Rich," above) as one of the country's top 50 dining spots — and many other publications have concurred. Natural light streams over fresh flowers, tapestries, and wide armchairs. It's virtually flawless, with high prices to match the high quality. See p. 67.

3 Best Restaurant Bets

• **Best Spot for a Romantic Dinner:** The appropriately named **Pasion!** 211 S. 15th St. (© **215/875-9895**) recently doubled in size but kept its intimate, glowing ambience, along with its terrific South American fusion cuisine. Warm and exotic. See p. 93.

• **Best Spot for a Business Lunch:** The **Fountain** at the Four Seasons Hotel, 1 Logan Sq. (© **215/963-1500**), fulfills every requirement: It's quiet, the tables are well spaced, the decor and service are impressive, and the cuisine — top-of-the-line steak, chops, and fish — is elegantly presented. Magnificent windows overlook the gardens of Logan Circle, casting a glow on the Georgian and mahogany paneling. See p. 89.

• **Best Spot for a Celebration:** If you have a special occasion to celebrate — even if it's just being in Philadelphia — the newly redecorated **Le Bec-Fin,** 1523 Walnut

St. (© **215/567-1000**), is the clear choice. The cuisine, under chef Georges Perrier, has an international reputation, and the opulence of the fixed-price meal is staggering. And those dessert carts — unforgettable! Advance reservations are a must. See p. 90.

- **Best Decor:** This is necessarily a personal evaluation, but I figure if you're visiting Philadelphia, you're interested in a sense of history and old-style elegance. If so, head for the **Paris Bar and Grille,** in the stunning rotunda of the recently renovated bank now housing the Ritz-Carlton Hotel at 10 Avenue of the Arts (© **215/735-7700**), in the center of town. Surrounded by the soaring dome and windows, the American organic cuisine has high expectations to fill but seems to be up to the task. See p. 69.

- **Best View:** Crowds make the **Chart House,** 555 S. Columbus Blvd. (formerly Delaware Ave.) at Penn's Landing (© **215/625-8383**), the Convention Center of the Philadelphia restaurant world. The food is amazingly good given the size of this place, and the views of the Delaware River from the restaurant's own pier are spectacular. Not cheap, though. See p. 81. Speaking of price, one of the city's great chefs has just re-emerged with **Lacroix at The Rittenhouse** (© **215/546-9000**), on a second-floor gallery overlooking elegant Rittenhouse Square. See p. 69.

- **Best Wine List:** I can't resist mentioning two, since they're only a block apart and owned by the same people. **La Famiglia,** 8 S. Front St. (© **215/922-2803**), offers one of the finest wine cellars in the world according to *Wine Spectator* magazine. One block north, the **Ristorante Panorama,** in the Penn's View Inn at Front

and Market streets (© **215/922-7800**), is a charming Italian trattoria that reportedly has the largest single wine-dispensing machine in the world, with 120 different bottles available by the glass ($2.75–$30 per 5-ounce glass). What's really fun is to order a "flight" — five glasses grouped around a theme. Flights fall in the $14 to $50 range. See p. 81 for La Famiglia, and p. 88 for Ristorante Panorama.

- **Best Value:** For its unbeatable central location and elegant surroundings (in a retro-fitted bank), I'm always happy to dine at **Circa,** 1518 Walnut St. (© **215/545-6800**). Most dinner entrees are less than $20, and lunch is even cheaper. Stick around for the great dance club action after 10pm on weekends. See p. 94.

- **Best Value Fixed-Price Meal:** On the high end, there's nothing like **Le Bec-Fin's** $38 lunch at 1523 Walnut St. (© **215/567-1000**) for classic French. For $24, you'll get a tasty, 3-course, pre-theater dinner at Philly's hottest jazz spot, **Zanzibar Blue,** 200 S. Broad St. (© **215/732-5200**). (See p. 90 for Le Bec-Fin and p. 97 for Zanzibar Blue.

- **Best for Kids:** If your kids are like mine, they like the broad selection and energy that a mall-type food court gives them. **The Food Court at Liberty Place,** between Chestnut and Market streets and 16th and 17th streets, has old city stalwarts like Bain's Deli and Bassett's Original Turkey, along with out-of-towners like Sbarro and Mentesini Pizza. It's spotless, large, and steps away from the city's best urban mall. See p. 109.

- **Best Date Restaurant:** I'd pick two relative newcomers here. For a classy bistro with contemporary fare in Old City, I would go for **Fork,** 306 Market St. (© **215/625-9425**). See p. 86. My wife and I have always loved relaxing at **Friday Saturday Sunday,** 261 S. 21st St. (© **215/546-4232**), which is slightly funky and boasts terrific, consistent fare, glowing lighting, and great value. See p. 92.

- **Best American Cuisine: Twenty 21,** 2005 Commerce Square, between 20th and 21st Street (© **215/851-6262**) looks corporate, but the young trio who recently reclaimed and renamed this high-ceilinged, comfortable spot serve inventive American dishes, from Nebraska beef to pastas of all ethnicities. See p. 96.

- **Best Chinese Cuisine:** A reserved former librarian, born in inner Mongolia and raised in northern China and Taiwan, Susanna Foo quietly built up a national reputation with her eponymous **Susanna Foo,** 1512 Walnut St. (© **215/545-2666**). Her innovative mix of East and West relies on reductions rather than on dashes of soy sauce and ginger, and skillets and saucepans rather than a wok. The dim sum — appetizer-sized portions — is a city favorite. See p. 95.

- **Best Continental Cuisine:** The **Fountain** at the Four Seasons Hotel, 1 Logan Sq., between 18th Street and Franklin Parkway (© **215/963-1500**), is consistently rated best in town for understated, complex versions of classic continental dishes. Since the food is so uniformly excellent, my advice is to go with the chef's choices on the fixed-price menu. See p. 89.

- **Best French Cuisine:** Most Frenchmen have never tasted a meal as good as what Georges Perrier prepares at **Le Bec-Fin** (see "Best Spot for a Celebration,"

above). A meal here may well be one of the food events of your lifetime. See p. 90.

- **Best Italian Cuisine:** Philadelphia must have 1,000 Italian restaurants, but I especially like **The Saloon,** 750 S. 7th St. (© **215/627-1811**), the type of dignified, elegant place that draws everyone in town sooner or later. See p. 100.

- **Best Seafood:** As you would expect, Philadelphia has a superb reputation for fish houses, and the best in town is **Striped Bass,** 1500 Walnut St. (© **215/732-4444**), located on the most chic dining block in the city. The dinner scene in *The Sixth Sense* was filmed here. Chef Terence Feury continues to create a menu that is breathtaking in its unusual treatment of fish and seafood. See p. 93.

- **Best Steakhouse:** Philadelphia has always been more of a seafood and pasta town than a steak town. The top choice is **The Prime Rib,** 1701 Locust St. (© **215/772-1701**), offering great porterhouse served with fresh shredded horseradish. The ambience is that timeless 'special occasion' place — jazz combos and formally-clad waiters included. See p. 93.

- **Best Burgers and Beer:** In this case, bigger is better. The **Independence Brew Pub,** at 1150 Filbert St., right under Reading Terminal Headhouse (© **215/922-4292**), has hundreds of seats, all happily occupied with diners chowing on delicious thin-crust pizzas and spectacular sundaes. An on-site brewery produces six different ales, porters, and lagers fresh each day. No reservations for parties under six. See p. 98.

- **Best Pizza: Marra's,** 1734 E. Passyunk Ave., between Morris and Moore streets (© **215/463-9249**), in South Philadelphia, has pies with thin crusts and delicious, spicy traditional toppings, baked in brick ovens; enjoy them in those old wooden booths. See p. 100.

- **Best Desserts:** Apart from the dessert cart at **Le Bec-Fin** (see "Best Spot for a Celebration," above), the best sweet show in town is to be found at **Painted Parrot Café,** 211 Chestnut St. (℃ **215/922-5971**) in the heart of the historic district; choices range from a harlequin mousse tart and other chocolate delights to fruit. Wednesday brings a $7.95 "all-you-can-savor dessert buffet" (a dangerous concept!) starting at 5pm. See p. 87.

- **Best Breakfast:** The **Down Home Diner** at Reading Terminal Market (℃ **215/627-1955**), open from 7am, has wonderful blueberry pancakes, fresh eggs with garlic grits, and a breakfast "pizza" with sausage biscuits, smoked cheddar, and tomato. All ingredients are fanatically organic, from small-scale producers wherever possible. Lunch has its charms too, with meatloaf, black-eyed pea and ham-hock soup, and pecan pie. The vintage jukebox plays great old American tunes. See p. 97.

- **Best Brunch:** Nearly every restaurant offers Sunday brunch, ranging from standard bagels with spreads to a full brunch menu. The **White Dog Café,** 3420 Sansom St. (℃ **215/386-9224**), in West Philadelphia, swings both ways, offering everything from simple breakfast dishes to elaborate late-morning feasts in a completely comfortable, unpretentious environment. See p. 102.

- **Best People-Watching:** No place is hotter than **Morimoto,** 723 Chestnut St. (℃ **215/413-9070**)

where the "Iron Chef" of TV fame holds sway amid cool booths and a sea of changing colors. See p. 81. If you want to spot a celebrity, head for another of the Stephen Starr-owned operations such as **Buddakan,** 325 Chestnut St. (℃ **215/574-9440**), where a huge gilded Buddha presides over a trendy crowd. See p. 81. Or head for hip Manayunk, halfway between Center City and Bryn Mawr, where the window seats at **Sonoma,** 4411 Main St. (℃ **215/ 483-9400**), are great for watching thousands of people stroll by, hour after hour, between noon and midnight. See p. 106.

- **Best Afternoon Tea:** The advent of true luxury hotels in Philadelphia has brought with it exquisite afternoon teas served all over town. I love the Cassatt Lounge at the **Rittenhouse Hotel,** 210 W. Rittenhouse Sq. (℃ **215/546-9000**), for its cheery decor, tucked-in garden, and for Mary Cassatt's drawings commemorating her brother's house, which once stood on the site. See p. 69. For a more solid, English burgher version of afternoon tea, try **The Dark Horse,** 421 S. 2nd St. (℃ **215/928-9307**), in Head House Square. See p. 85.

- **Best for Pretheater Dinner:** It's had some ups and downs recently, but I'm partial to **Toto,** 1407 Locust St. (℃ **215/546-2000**), just steps from the Academy of Music and the Merriam. It has always looked spectacular, and now serves a simpler, less over-the-top Italian menu with a grill-almost-anything-at-anytime angle. See p. 94.

- **Best Outdoor Dining:** In the historic district, the back garden of **City Tavern,** 138 S. 2nd St., near Walnut Street (℃ **215/413-1443**), belongs to Independence

National Historical Park, and diners are surrounded by century-old trees and Federal-style landmarks while they imbibe their strong ale or punch, and dine on a historically faithful 18th-century–recipe potpie. See p. 85. In Center City, head for 18th Street along Rittenhouse Square, between Walnut and Locust streets: Anywhere you park among **Devon Seafood Grill, Rouge, Potcheen** or **Bleu** (the last has the best cuisine) on that block is great. See p. 189.

- **Best Late-Night Dining:** When it's after midnight, I head for Chinatown. **Shiao Lan Kung,** 930 Race St. (© **215/928-0282**), while not very impressive in its decor, has wonderful hot pot dishes, and you can order fresh sea bass from the tank. See p. 105.

- **Best Ice Cream: Bassett's Ice Cream** (© **215/925-4315**), an original 1892 tenant of Reading Terminal Market, has long claimed supremacy for its rich, smooth flavors. Plus they make a terrific milkshake. A second location, at the Food Court at Liberty Place, carries the same quality ice cream but lacks that turn-of-the-century soda fountain ambience. See p. 96 for a description of Reading Terminal Market and p. 109 for a description of the Food Court at Liberty Place.

2

Planning Your Trip to Philadelphia

1 Visitor Information

TOURIST OFFICE The **Independence Visitor Center,** 6th and Market streets, Philadelphia, PA 19107 (© **800/537-7676,** 215/965-7676, or 215/636-1666), opened in late 2001 as a collaboration between public and private sectors, is a great one-stop introductory destination. It offers a wealth of publications, from seasonal calendars of events to maps for the city and region, along with a cafe, book and gift shop, and a first-class exhibition on Philadelphia's place in history. Knowledgeable volunteers staff the phones and counters. Definitely ask for the "Official Visitors Guide," a seasonal compendium of exhibitions, events, and the like. The Center also offers an increasing number of package tours combining special museum exhibitions, concerts, or sporting events with discount hotel prices, free city transit passes, and Amtrak discounts. Once you're in town, note that many bus tours, historic trolley rides, and walking tours start from here.

WEBSITES For the growing number of visitors who have access to the Internet, there are a number of websites that you'll find helpful. The Independence Visitor Center site is at **www.independencevisitorcenter.com**. Other sites include: **www.digitalcity.com/philadelphia**, which contains a great deal of user feedback and opinions along with excellent and pithy summaries of events, sighs, and restaurants; **www.gophila.com**, run by the city's tourism marketing bureau and very up to date; the private **www.phillyvisitor.com**, driven by paid advertisers and hotlinks; **www.cityspin.com/Philadelphia**; and **http://philadelphia.citysearch.com**. Contact **http://reservation.nps.gov** to reserve tickets in advance to the historic landmarks.

2 Money

Except for truly deluxe experiences, you will find moderate prices in Philadelphia less than those in New York and on a par with, or slightly above, those in Washington, D.C.

Minimal cash is required, since credit cards are accepted universally and ATMs linked to national networks are strewn around the airport, tourist destinations, and increasingly within hotels. It's a good idea to exchange at least some money — just enough to cover airport incidentals and transportation to your hotel — before you leave home, so you can avoid the less-favorable rates you'll get at airport currency exchange desks. Check with your local American Express or Thomas Cook office or your bank. American Express cardholders can order foreign currency over the phone at © **800/807-6233.**

> **Tips** **Destination: Philadelphia — Red Alert Checklist**
>
> - Booking in advance: If you're planning on going to a **Kimmel Center** performance by groups such as **The Philadelphia Orchestra**; eating at one of the country's great restaurants such as **Le Bec-Fin;** or staying at a hotel such as **The Ritz-Carlton**, you should reserve in advance. The wonderful but quixotic **Barnes Foundation** in Merion, one of the world's great Impressionist art collections, has limited hours and attendance, so be sure to reserve ahead.
> - On the historical side, **Independence National Historical Park** and some government sites such as the **U.S. Mint** have gotten much more security-conscious since September 2001. You can — and in some cases, must — call ahead for reserved time slots to visit **Independence Hall,** or the new **Liberty Bell Pavilion.** Many scheduled tours, festivals, and special events have also been changed, so call ahead for opening and closing hours.
> - Did you bring your ID cards that could entitle you to discounts such as AAA and AARP cards, student IDs, and so on?
> - Did you bring emergency drug prescriptions and extra glasses and/or contact lenses?
> - Do you have your credit card PINs?
> - If you have an E-ticket, do you have documentation?
> - Did you leave a copy of your itinerary with someone at home?

It's best to exchange currency or traveler's checks at a bank, not a currency exchange, hotel, or shop.

ATMS

ATMs are linked to a network that most likely includes your bank at home. **Cirrus** (© 800/424-7787; www.mastercard.com) and **PLUS** (© 800/843-7587; www.visa.com) are the two most popular networks in the U.S.; call or check online for ATM locations at your destination. Be sure you know your four-digit PIN before you leave home and be sure to find out your daily withdrawal limit before you depart. You can also get cash advances on your credit card at an ATM. Keep in mind that credit card companies try to protect themselves from theft by limiting the funds someone can withdraw away from home. It's therefore best to call your credit card company before you leave and let them know where you're going and

how much you plan to spend. You'll get the best exchange rate if you withdraw money from an ATM, but keep in mind that many banks impose a fee every time a card is used at an ATM in a different city or bank. On top of this, the bank from which you withdraw cash may charge its own fee.

CREDIT CARDS

Credit cards are invaluable when traveling. They are a safe way to carry money and provide a convenient record of all your expenses. You can also withdraw cash advances from your credit cards at any bank (though you'll start paying hefty interest on the advance the moment you receive the cash.) At most banks, you don't even need to go to a teller; you can get a cash advance at the ATM if you know your PIN. If you've forgotten yours, or didn't even know you had one, call the number on the back of your credit card and ask the bank to send it to

> **_Tips_ Small Change**
>
> When you change money, ask for some small bills or loose change. Petty cash will come in handy for tipping and public transportation. Consider keeping the change separate from your larger bills, so it's readily accessible and you'll be less of a target for theft.

you. It usually takes 5 to 7 business days, though some banks will provide the number over the phone if you tell them your mother's maiden name or pass some other security clearance.

WHAT TO DO IF YOUR WALLET GETS STOLEN

Be sure to block charges against your account the minute you discover a credit card has been lost or stolen. Then be sure to file a police report.

Almost every credit card company has an emergency 800-number to call if your card is stolen. They may be able to wire you a cash advance off your credit card immediately, and in many places, they can deliver an emergency credit card in a day or two. The issuing bank's 800-number is usually on the back of your credit card — though of course, if your card has been stolen, that won't help you unless you recorded the number elsewhere.

Citicorp Visa's U.S. emergency number is ⓒ **800/336-8472.** American Express cardholders and traveler's check holders should call ⓒ **800/ 221-7282.** MasterCard holders should call ⓒ **800/307-7309.** Otherwise,

call the toll-free number directory at ⓒ **800/555-1212.**

Odds are that if your wallet is gone, the police won't be able to recover it for you. However, it's still worth informing the authorities. Your credit card company or insurer may require a police report number or record of the theft.

If you choose to carry traveler's checks, be sure to keep a record of their serial numbers separate from your checks. You'll get a refund faster if you know the numbers.

If you need emergency cash over the weekend when all banks and American Express offices are closed, you can have money wired to you from **Western Union** (ⓒ **800/325-6000;** www.westernunion.com). Most of the time, you need to present valid ID to pick up the cash at the Western Union office. Be sure to let the sender know in advance if you don't have ID. If you need to use a test question instead of ID, the sender must take cash to his or her local Western Union office, rather than transferring the money over the phone or online.

3 When to Go

Philadelphia is great to visit any time, although given the city's seasonal popularity and the constant flow of conventions, you'll find the best deals in the fall and winter. Concert and museum seasons run from early October to early June, and July 4th is obviously a huge crowd scene at Independence Hall.

The city has four distinct seasons with temperatures ranging from the

90s (30s Celsius) in summer to the 30s in winter (around 0 Celsius) (Below-zero temperatures normally hit only one out of every four winters.) Summers, the height of tourist season, can get swelteringly humid. In the fall, the weather becomes drier. Spring temperatures are variable; count on comfortable breezes.

Average Temperatures & Precipitation in Philadelphia

	Jan	Feb	Mar	Apr	May	June	July	Aug	Sept	Oct	Nov	Dec
High °F/C	40/4	41/5	50/10	62/17	73/23	81/27	85/29	83/28	77/25	66/19	54/12	43/6
Low °F/C	26/-3	26/-3	33/1	43/6	53/12	63/17	68/20	66/19	60/16	49/9	39/4	29/-2
Precip. in days	11	9	11	11	11	10	9	9	8	8	10	10

PHILADELPHIA CALENDAR OF EVENTS

For more details and up-to-the-minute information, contact the **Independence Visitor Center,** 6th and Market streets, Philadelphia, PA 19107 (& 800/537-7676), or see the calendar at www.gophila.com.

January

Mummer's Parade. Starting at 8am and lasting most of the day, this parade of 30,000 spangled strutters march with feathers and banjos in a celebration that must have been pagan in origin. (The word "mummer" comes from the French *momer,* meaning "to go masked.") Since 1999, the parade has been on Market Street west of City Hall rather than on the traditional Broad Street (north-south) route, and it's gotten slower and more confusing every year. If they keep this route, let's hope for improved flow! If you have visited the Mummer's Museum beforehand, the gaudiness and elaborateness of the costumes won't amaze you quite so much, but the music (everyone ends up humming "Oh, Dem Golden Slippers") and festivity will have you entranced. Call © 215/336-3050 for details. January 1 (or the following Sat in case of bad weather).

Benjamin Franklin's Birthday. The Franklin Institute Science Museum (p. 120) celebrates its namesake's birthday with scientific demonstrations and a big birthday cake. Call © 215/448-1200 for details. Second or third Sunday of the month.

February

Black History Month. The African-American Museum in Philadelphia, 7th and Arch streets, offers a full complement of exhibitions, lectures, and music. Call © 215/574-0380 for details. All month long.

Chinese New Year. You can enjoy dragons and fireworks at 11th and Arch streets, traditional 10-course banquets at Chinese restaurants, or a visit to the Chinese Cultural Center at 125 N. 10th St. Call © 215/923-6767 for details on the festivities. Mid- to late February.

March

Philadelphia Flower Show. Now held in the Convention Center, this is the largest indoor flower show in the world, with acres of gardens and rustic settings. With the citywide institution of Flower Show Week, the show and surrounding festivities are even bigger and better than before. You can usually get tickets at the door, but the Pennsylvania Horticultural Society at 325 Walnut St. sells them in advance. Call © 800/611-5960 or 215/988-8800 for information or for tour packages. Late February to early March.

The Book and the Cook Festival. For the past decade, Philadelphia has combined its love for reading and eating into this festival. For five days, eminent food critics, cookbook authors, and restaurateurs are invited to plan dream meals with participating city restaurants. If you're a foodie, you know that the chance to stroll through Reading Terminal Market with Alice Waters, or to dine on what she cooks up, is an experience you'll remember for a long time. The festival has recently expanded into food samplings and wine and beer tastings all over town. The list of participating restaurants is published in January, and many get booked quickly. Call ☎ **215/686-3662** for a schedule and to make a reservation. Usually the third week of the month.

St. Patrick's Day Parade. The parade starts at noon on 20th Street and the Parkway, turns on 17th Street to Chestnut Street, then goes down Chestnut Street to Independence Mall. The Parkway is the most spacious vantage point, and the Irish Pub at 2007 Walnut St. will be packed. Call the Independence Visitor Center for details (☎ **215/636-1666**). Sunday closest to March 17.

April

Philadelphia Antiques Show. Started in 1961, this antiques show is probably the finest in the nation, with 50-odd major English and American exhibitors. It's held at the 103rd Engineers Armory, 33rd and Market streets. Call ☎ **215/387-3500** for information. First weekend of the month.

American Music Theater Festival. Begun in 1983, this festival offers premieres of musical theater works by major American artists, ranging from traditional Broadway-bound musicals to avant-garde works. Now it has a permanent home at a renovated grand old movie palace at 1412 Chestnut St. Call ☎ **215/893-1570** for information. Runs through June.

Easter Sunday. This day brings fashion shows and music to Rittenhouse Square. The Easter Bunny usually makes an appearance at Lord & Taylor's and the Gallery. Call ☎ **215/686-2876** for details.

Spring Tour of Fairmount Park. The dogwood and cherry trees along both sides of the Schuylkill are in blossom. Trolley buses make a special run along Wissahickon Creek, a lovely woodland minutes away from Center City. Call ☎ **215/636-1666** for details. Last Sunday of the month (or first Sun in May).

May

Philadelphia Open House. These tours give you a rare chance to see Germantown, Society Hill, and University City mansions. Call ☎ **215/928-1188** for information. Late April to early May.

PrideFest America. This diverse set of panels, programs, and parties for the world's GLBT communities is held throughout the city. Call (☎ **215/735-7356**) for information. First week in May.

Dad Vail Regatta. This is one of the largest collegiate rowing events in the country. You can picnic on East River Drive near Strawberry Mansion. Call ☎ **215/248-2600** for details. Second week of the month.

Israel Independence Day. This holiday brings a Center City parade and daylong Israeli bazaar to the Parkway. Call ☎ **215/922-7222** for details. Second or third Sunday of the month.

Rittenhouse Square Flower Market. This market has been an annual event since 1914. Plants, flowers, and baked goods are some of the irresistibles for sale. The more than 2,000 azaleas and rhododendrons in bloom behind the Museum of Art literally stop traffic with their brilliance. Call ☎ **215/525-7182** for details. Third Thursday of the month.

Philadelphia International Children's Festival. This festival, featuring excellent kid-oriented performances, plus craft-making and food, takes place on or near the University of Pennsylvania campus, based at 3680 Walnut St. Call

© **215/898-3900** for programs and prices. First week of the month.

Jam on the River. This event was cooked up as Philadelphia's homage to New Orleans and has expanded to include blues as well as jazz. It's based at the expanded Festival Pier, now with a video wall, at Penn's Landing. In recent years, Little Feat and the Preservation Hall Jazz Band have been in attendance. Call *©* **215/636-1666** for particulars. Late May.

Devon Horse Show, Route 30, Devon. This event, held outside of Philadelphia, includes jumping competitions, carriage races, and a great country fair with plenty of food stalls — burgers as well as watercress sandwiches — under cheerful awnings. Call *©* **610/964-0550** for details. End of the month.

June

Head House Square. Local craftspeople, food vendors, and street artists set up shop on Saturday from noon to midnight and Sunday from noon to 6pm. Throughout the summer.

Elfreth's Alley Days. Row-house dwellers, many in colonial costumes, open up their homes for inspection and admiration. There are demonstrations of colonial crafts. Call *©* **215/574-0560** for details. First weekend of the month.

First Union Pro Cycling Championships. The 156-mile course of this country's premier 1-day cycling event starts and finishes on the Parkway, following the incredible climb up the cliffs at Manayunk. First weekend of the month.

Rittenhouse Square Fine Arts Annual. Philadelphia moves outdoors with this event, in which hundreds of professional and student works of art go on sale. Call *©* **215/634-5060** for details. First 2 weeks of June.

Betsy Ross House. Flag Day festivities, invented here in 1891, are held at 12:30pm, usually with a national guard band and a speech. Call *©* **215/627-5343** for details. June 14.

Bloomsday. The Rosenbach Museum and the Irish Pub at 2007 Walnut St. both celebrate the 24-hour time span of James Joyce's novel *Ulysses.* Call *©* **215/732-1600** for details. June 16.

Mellon Jazz Festival. A top-drawer collection of jazz artists is featured at the Mann Music Center, jazz clubs like Zanzibar Blue, and the Academy of Music. Call the Visitors Bureau for details. Second or third week of the month.

July

Sunoco Welcome America! The whole town turns out for this week-long festival to celebrate America's birthday with theater, free entertainment, and assorted pageantry. The Fourth of July brings special ceremonies to Independence Square, including a reading of the Declaration of Independence, a presentation of the prestigious Liberty Medal, and an evening parade up the Parkway. Principal locations are the terrace by the Philadelphia Museum of Art, City Hall (where the world's largest hoagie is assembled), and Penn's Landing. Call *©* **215/636-1666** or log onto **www.americasbirthday.com** for information. The week before July 4th, with fireworks on the Delaware River July 3.

Mann Music Center Summer Concerts. This outdoor venue in Fairmount Park offers selected free concerts through August, and cheap lawn seats for pop performers and the Philadelphia Orchestra. See chapter 10 for more information about the concerts, or call *©* **215/567-0707** for a schedule.

August

Pennsylvania Dutch Festival. Reading Terminal Market is the venue for this weeklong festival featuring quilts, music, food, crafts, and the like. Call ✆ **215/922-2317** for more information. First week of August.

Philadelphia Folk Festival. Suburban Poole Farm, Schwenksville. This festival offers bluegrass, Irish, Cajun, Klezmer, and cowboy music, as well as dancing, juggling, puppetry, and crafts. It has a national reputation and draws major crowds. Call ✆ **215/247-1300** for details. Usually late in the month.

September

Philadelphia Fringe Festival. Inaugurated in 1997, this festival brings up to 500 cutting-edge performances, experimental films, and art installations to the nooks and crannies of the Old City. Call ✆ **215/413-9006** for details. Throughout the first half of the month.

Fairmount Park Festival. This festival, which runs through November, includes the Harvest Show at Memorial Hall and parades of varying themes down the Parkway. Call ✆ **215/685-0052** for details. Most weekends in September, October, and November.

Philadelphia Distance Run. One of the nation's premier races, this is a half marathon through Center City and Fairmount Park. In town, it's bigger than the November marathon and gets plenty of national running figures. Call ✆ **215/665-8500** if you wish to join the ranks of 7,500 runners. Usually the third Sunday of the month.

October

Columbus Day Parade. There's a parade along the Parkway; also look for South Philadelphia fairs. Call 215/686-2085 for details. Second Monday of the month at noon.

Super Sunday. Think of it as a block party for an entire city — that's Super Sunday, held on the Benjamin Franklin Parkway from Logan Circle to the Museum of Art. There are clowns, jugglers, mimes, rides, craft vendors, and a flea market. The museums and academies along the Parkway have sponsored this event since 1970, rain or shine, and most have reduced admissions and special programs. This is one day when parking on the grass won't get you a ticket. Call ✆ **215/665-1050** for information. Third Sunday of the month.

November

Philadelphia Marathon. The marathon starts and finishes at the Art Museum, looping through Center City and then Fairmount Park. Call ✆ **215/683-2070** for more information. Usually the Sunday before Thanksgiving.

Philadelphia Museum of Art Craft Show. This preeminent exhibition and retail sale of the finest American contemporary crafts involves works in clay, glass, fiber, jewelry, metal, wearables, and wool. Tickets are $12 (2 days for $18). At the Convention Center. Call ✆ **215/684-7930.** Usually the second weekend of the month.

Thanksgiving Day Parade. This parade features cartoon characters, bands, floats, and Santa Claus. Thanksgiving Day.

December

Holiday Activities Around Town. Christmas sees many activities in Center City, beginning with the tree lighting in City Hall courtyard. The Gallery at Market East, "A Christmas Carol" at Strawbridge and Clothier, a Colonial Christmas Village at Market Place East and

Hecht's all host elaborate extravaganzas, with organs and choruses. The Society Hill and Germantown Christmas walking tours are lovely, with the same leafy decorations as Fairmount Park. Throughout the month. Ask about specific events at the Independence Visitor Center (see p. 13).

Nutcracker Ballet. The Pennsylvania Ballet performs Tchaikovsky's classic at the Academy of Music, Broad and Locust streets. Call © **215/551-7014** for details. Throughout the month.

Private Lights. For an unusual Christmas experience, visit the 2700 block of South Colorado Street, south of Oregon Avenue, between 17th and 18th streets. The sight of some 40 houses bathed in interconnected strands of holiday lights is spectacular. The lights usually go up right after Thanksgiving.

Lucia Fest. American Swedish Historical Museum, 1900 Pattison Ave. in South Philadelphia. It sounds Italian, but the Lucia Fest is a Swedish pageant held by candlelight. Call © **215/389-1776** for information. First weekend of the month.

Christmas Tours of Fairmount Park and Germantown. Colonial mansions sparkle with wreaths, holly, and fruit arrangements donated by local garden clubs. Call © **215/787-5449** or 215/848-1777 for details. Tours begin mid-month.

New Year's Eve. Fireworks are held at the Great Plaza of Penn's Landing on December 31.

4 Insurance, Health & Safety

TRAVEL INSURANCE AT A GLANCE

Check your existing insurance policies before you buy travel insurance to cover trip cancellation, lost luggage, medical expenses, or car-rental insurance. You're likely to have partial or complete coverage. But if you need insurance, ask your travel agent about a comprehensive package. The cost of travel insurance varies widely, depending on the cost and length of your trip, your age and overall health, and the type of trip you're taking.

And keep in mind that in the aftermath of the September 11, 2001, terrorist attacks, a number of airlines, cruise lines, and tour operators are no longer covered by insurers. *The bottom line:* Always, always check the fine print before you sign on; more and more policies have built-in exclusions and restrictions that may leave you out in the cold if something does go awry.

For information, contact one of the following popular insurers:

- **Access America** (© **800/284-8300**); www.accessamerica.com)
- **Travel Guard International** (© **800/826-1300**; www.travelguard.com)
- **Travel Insured International** (© **800/243-3174**; www.travelinsured.com)
- **Travelex Insurance Services** (© **800/228-9792**; www.travelexinsurance.com)

TRIP-CANCELLATION INSURANCE (TCI)

There are three major types of trip-cancellation insurance — one, in the event that you pre-pay a cruise or tour that gets canceled, and you can't get your money back; a second if you or someone in your family gets sick or dies, and you can't travel (but beware that you may not be covered for a pre-existing condition); and a third, if bad weather makes travel impossible. Some insurers provide coverage for events like jury duty; natural disasters close to home, like floods or fire; even the loss of a job. A few have added provisions for cancellations due to terrorist activities. Always check the fine print before signing on, and don't buy trip-cancellation insurance from the tour operator that may be responsible for the cancellation; buy it only from a reputable travel insurance agency. Don't overbuy. You won't be reimbursed for more than the cost of your trip.

MEDICAL INSURANCE

Most health insurance policies cover you if you get sick away from home — but check, particularly if you're insured by an HMO. Members of **Blue Cross/Blue Shield** can now use their cards at select hospitals in most major cities worldwide (𝒞 **800/810-BLUE** or www.bluecares.com for a list of hospitals). Also, check to see if your medical insurance covers you for emergency medical evacuation: If you have to buy a one-way same-day ticket home and forfeit your nonrefundable round-trip ticket, you may be out big bucks.

Some credit cards (American Express and certain gold and platinum Visa and MasterCards, for example) offer automatic flight insurance against death or dismemberment in case of an airplane crash if you charged the cost of your ticket.

If you require additional insurance, try one of the following companies:

- **MEDEX International,** 9515 Deereco Rd., Timonium, MD 21093-5375 (𝒞 **888/MEDEX-00** or 410/453-6300; fax 410/453-6301;www.medexassist.com).
- **Travel Assistance International,** 9200 Keystone Crossing, Suite 300, Indianapolis, IN 46240 (𝒞 **800/821-2828;** www.travel assistance.com). For general information on services, call the company's Worldwide Assistance Services, Inc., at 𝒞 **800/777-8710.**

LOST-LUGGAGE INSURANCE

On domestic flights, checked baggage is covered up to $2,500 per ticketed

passenger. On international flights (including U.S. portions of international trips), baggage is limited to approximately $9.07 per pound, up to approximately $635 per checked bag. If you plan to check items more valuable than the standard liability, you may purchase "excess valuation" coverage from the airline, up to $5,000. Be sure to take any valuables or irreplaceable items with you in your carry-on luggage. If you file a lost luggage claim, be prepared to answer detailed questions about the contents of your baggage, and be sure to file a claim immediately, as most airlines enforce a 21-day deadline. Before you leave home, compile an inventory of all packed items and a rough estimate of the total value to ensure that you're properly compensated if your luggage is lost. Once you've filed a complaint, persist in securing your reimbursement; there are no laws governing the length of time it takes for a carrier to reimburse you. If you arrive at a destination without your bags, ask the airline to forward them to your hotel or to your next destination; they will usually comply. If your bag is delayed or lost, the airline may reimburse you for reasonable expenses, such as a toothbrush or a set of clothes, but the airline is under no legal obligation to do so.

Lost luggage may also be covered by your homeowner's or renter's policy. Many platinum and gold credit cards cover you as well. If you choose to purchase additional lost-luggage insurance, be sure not to buy more than you need. Buy in advance from the insurer or a trusted agent (prices will be much higher at the airport).

CAR-RENTAL INSURANCE (LOSS/DAMAGE WAIVER OR COLLISION DAMAGE WAIVER)

If you hold a private auto insurance policy you probably are covered in the U.S. for loss or damage to the car, and liability in case a passenger is injured. The credit card you used to rent the card also may provide some coverage.

Car-rental insurance probably does not cover liability if you caused the accident. Check your own auto insurance policy, the rental company policy, and your credit card coverage for the extent of coverage: Is your destination covered? Are other drivers covered? How much liability is covered if a passenger is injured? (If you rely on your credit card for coverage, you may want to bring a second credit card with you, as damages may be charged to your card and you may find yourself stranded with no money.)

Car-rental insurance costs about $20 a day.

THE HEALTHY TRAVELER

Philadelphia can be hot and is always humid in summer. Limit your exposure to the sun, especially during the period between 11am and 2pm. Use a sunscreen with a high protection factor and apply it liberally. Remember that children need more protection than adults do.

WHAT TO DO IF YOU GET SICK AWAY FROM HOME

If you worry about getting sick away from home, consider purchasing **medical travel insurance** and carrying your ID card in your purse or wallet. In most cases, your existing health plan will provide the coverage you need. See the section on medical insurance earlier in this chapter for more information.

If you suffer from a chronic illness, consult your doctor before your departure. For conditions like epilepsy, diabetes, or heart problems, wear a **Medic Alert Identification Tag** (© 800/825-3785; www.medicalert.org), which will immediately alert doctors to your condition and give them access to your records through Medic Alert's 24-hour hot line.

Pack **prescription medications** in your carry-on luggage, and carry prescription medications in their original containers. Also bring along copies of your prescriptions in case you lose your pills or run out. And don't forget sunglasses and an extra pair of contact lenses or prescription glasses.

If you get sick, consider asking your hotel concierge to recommend a local doctor — even his or her own. You can also try the emergency room at a local hospital (see chapter 4 for names and numbers under "Fast Facts"); many have walk-in clinics for emergency cases that are not life-threatening. You may not get immediate attention, but you won't pay the high price of an emergency room visit (usually a minimum of $300 just for signing your name).

THE SAFE TRAVELER

Philadelphia's Center City is quite safe. If you are planning to explore in off-the-beaten-path neighborhoods, around the college campuses in West Philadelphia, or at unusual hours, be careful.

5 Tips for Travelers with Special Needs

TRAVELERS WITH DISABILITIES

Most disabilities shouldn't stop anyone from traveling. There are more options and resources out there than ever before.

For basic Philadelphia information, contact the **Mayor's Commission on People with Disabilities,** Municipal Services Building, Room 900, 1401 JFK Boulevard, Philadelphia, PA 19107 (© 215/686-2798), or see the excellent website at **www.phila.gov/aco/index.html**. SEPTA (the local transit authority) publishes a special "Transit Guide for the Disabled"; you can request it from **SEPTA Special Services,** 1234 Market St., 4th Floor, Philadelphia, PA 19107 (℃ **215/580-7145**). All SEPTA buses will be lift-equipped by 2004. Market East and University City subway stations are wheelchair accessible, but most other stops are not. Artreach publishes "Access the Arts: A Guide for People with Disabilities," providing information for more than 75 area facilities; the brochure is $5 and can be ordered at (℃ **215/951-0316**). The Philadelphia airport has a variety of services including 15 TDD telephones, elevators and escalators, Braille ATMs, and curb cuts.

Travelers with disabilities will find the tourist areas of Philadelphia accessible. All Center City curbs are cut at intersections, even though some streets in Society Hill and those bordering Independence National Historical Park have uneven brick sidewalks, and Dock Street itself is paved with rough cobblestones.

Parking is tough, however, as ISA-designated spots are rare. The same is true for Chestnut Street, the Parkway, and the University of Pennsylvania campus. The Independence Visitor Center has a level entrance and publishes "Accessibilities," a brochure detailing all park sites.

Virtually all theaters and stadiums accommodate wheelchairs. Call ahead to plan routes. To aid people with hearing impairments, the Kimmel Center and Academy of Music provide free infrared headsets for concerts; the Annenberg Center rents them for $2.

The Free Library of Philadelphia runs a **Library for the Blind and Physically Handicapped,** very conveniently located at 919 Walnut St. (℃ **215/683-3213**); it's open Monday through Friday from 9am to 5pm. It adjoins the **Associated Services for the Blind,** which offers transcriptions into Braille for a fee.

If you are handicapped and travel with Amtrak or Greyhound/Trailways, be aware that on the former you can receive a 25% discount and a special seat with advance notification (℃ **800/523-6590**), and on the latter a free seat for a companion (℃ **800/345-3109**).

Many of the major car-rental companies now offer hand-controlled cars for disabled drivers. Avis can provide such a vehicle at any of its locations in the United States with 48-hour advance notice; Hertz requires between 24 and 72 hours advance reservation at most of its locations.

AGENCIES/OPERATORS
- **Flying Wheels Travel** (℃ **507/451-5005;** www.flyingwheels travel.com) offers escorted tours and cruises that emphasize sports, and private tours in minivans with lifts.
- **Access Adventures** (℃ **716/889-9096**), a Rochester, New York–based agency, offers customized itineraries for a variety of travelers with disabilities.
- **Accessible Journeys** (℃ **800/TINGLES** or 610/521-0339; www.disabilitytravel.com) caters specifically to slow walkers and wheelchair travelers and their families and friends.

ORGANIZATIONS
- **The Moss Rehab Hospital** (℃ **215/456-9603;** www.moss resourcenet.org) provides friendly, helpful phone assistance through its **Travel Information Service.**
- **The Society for Accessible Travel and Hospitality** (℃ **212/447-7284;** fax 212/725-8253; www.sath.org) offers a wealth of travel resources for travelers with all different types of disabilities, and informed recommendations on destinations, access guides, travel agents, tour operators, vehicle

rentals, and companion services. Annual membership costs $45 for adults; $30 for seniors and students.

- **The American Foundation for the Blind** (© 800/232-5463; www.afb.org) provides information on traveling with Seeing Eye dogs.

PUBLICATIONS

- **Mobility International USA** (© 541/343-1284; www.miusa. org) publishes *A World of Options,* a 658-page book of resources, covering everything from biking trips to scuba outfitters, and a biannual newsletter, *Over the Rainbow.* Annual membership is $35.
- **Twin Peaks Press** (© 360/694-2462) publishes travel-related books for travelers with special needs.
- *Open World for Disability and Mature Travel* magazine, published by the Society for Accessible Travel and Hospitality (see above), is full of good resources and information. A year's subscription is $13 ($21 outside the U.S.).

GAY & LESBIAN TRAVELERS

Center City is tolerant of gays and lesbians, and the rectangle bordered by 9th and Juniper streets and Walnut and South streets is filled with gay social services, restaurants, bookstores, and clubs. See chapter 10 for specific clubs and bars. You might also check the weekly *Philadelphia Gay News* (www.epgn.com), which is widely available. The lesbian-oriented *Labyrinth* is available free at Giovanni's Room (see below), which is the hot spot for media figures at 12th and Pine streets. Outside the city, New Hope (see chapter 11) is a popular destination for gay and lesbian travelers.

For meetings, classes, gallery exhibitions, and social events, consult **William Way Community Center,**

1315 Spruce St. (© 215/732-2220; www.waygay.org), or drop by **Millennium Coffee,** 212 S. 12th St. (© 215/731-9798), a sleek scene open until midnight. The **Blackwell Center for Women,** 1124 Walnut St. (© 215/923-7577), can direct you to health clinics. The **Women's Switchboard** is at © 215/829-1976.

The bookstore **Giovanni's Room,** 345 S. 12th St., Philadelphia, PA 19107 (© 215/923-2960), is a 28-year-old national resource for publications produced by and for gays and lesbians as well as for feminist and progressive literature.

The local **Gay Switchboard** (open daily 7–10pm) is at © 215/546-7100; the **Lesbian Hotline** is at © 215/222-5110.

To report antigay violence or discrimination, call the **Philadelphia Lesbian and Gay Task Force Hotline** at © 215/563-4581. **ACT UP/ Philadelphia** meets on Monday; call © 215/731-1844.

The **International Gay & Lesbian Travel Association (IGLTA)** (© 800/ 448-8550 or 954/776-2626; fax 954/ 776-3303; www.iglta.org) links travelers up with gay-friendly hoteliers, tour operators, and airline and cruise-line representatives. It offers monthly newsletters, marketing mailings, and a membership directory that's updated once a year. Membership is $200 yearly, plus a $100 administration fee for new members.

AGENCIES/OPERATORS

- **Above and Beyond Tours** (© 800/397-2681; www.above beyondtours.com) offers gay and lesbian tours worldwide and is the exclusive gay and lesbian tour operator for United Airlines.
- **Now, Voyager** (© 800/255-6951; www.nowvoyager.com) is a San Francisco–based gay-owned and operated travel service.

PUBLICATIONS

- *Out and About* (✆ **800/ 929-2268** or 415/644-8044; www.outandabout.com) offers guidebooks and a newsletter 10 times a year packed with solid information on the global gay and lesbian scene.
- *Spartacus International Gay Guide* and *Odysseus* are good, annual English-language guidebooks focused on gay men, with some information for lesbians. You can get them from most gay and lesbian bookstores, or order them from **Giovanni's Room** bookstore, 345 S. 12th St., Philadelphia, PA 19107 (✆ **215/ 923-2960;** www.giovannisroom. com).
- *Gay Travel A to Z: The World of Gay & Lesbian Travel Options at Your Fingertips,* by Marianne Ferrari (Ferrari Publications; Box 35575, Phoenix, AZ 85069) is a very good gay and lesbian guidebook series.

SENIOR TRAVEL

Mention the fact that you're a senior when you first make your travel reservations. All major airlines and many hotels offer discounts for seniors. Major airlines also offer coupons for domestic travel for seniors over sixty. Typically, a book of four coupons costs less than $700, which means you can fly anywhere in the continental U.S. for under $350 round-trip. In most cities, people over the age of 60 qualify for reduced admission to theaters, museums, and other attractions, as well as discounted fares on public transportation.

Most Philadelphia attractions grant special discounts to seniors, especially during weekdays. Some hotels, too, will lower their rates, particularly on weekends. The Convention and Visitors Bureau publishes "Seniors on the Go," which lists dozens of specific senior benefits around town — from flat taxi fares to reduced museum admissions; write ahead or pick the brochure up at the Independence Visitor Center. Seniors should bring photo ID.

Members of **AARP** (formerly known as the American Association of Retired Persons), 601 E St. NW, Washington, DC 20049 (✆ **800/ 424-3410** or 202/434-2277; www. aarp.org), get discounts on hotels, airfares, and car rentals. AARP offers members a wide range of benefits, including *AARP Modern Maturity* magazine and a monthly newsletter. Anyone over 50 can join.

The Alliance for Retired Americans, 8403 Colesville Rd., Suite 1200, Silver Spring, MD 20910 (✆ **301/ 578-8422;** www.retiredamericans. org), offers a newsletter six times a year and discounts on hotel and auto rentals. Annual dues are $13 per person or couple. *Note:* Members of the former National Council of Senior Citizens receive automatic membership in the Alliance.

AGENCIES/OPERATORS

- **Grand Circle Travel** (✆ **800/ 221-2610** or 617/350-7500; www.gct.com) offers package deals for the 50-plus market, mostly of the tour-bus variety, with free trips thrown in for those who organize groups of 10 or more.
- **Elderhostel** (✆ **877/426-8056;** www.elderhostel.org) arranges study programs for those aged 55 and over (and a spouse or companion of any age) in the U.S. and in more than 80 countries around the world. Most courses last five to seven days in the U.S. (2–4 weeks abroad), and many include airfare, accommodations in university dormitories or modest inns, meals, and tuition.
- **Interhostel** (✆ **800/733-9753;** www.learn.unh.edu/interhostel), organized by the University of New

Hampshire, offers educational travel for seniors. On these escorted tours, the days are packed with seminars, lectures, and field trips, with sightseeing led by academic experts. **Interhostel** takes travelers 50 and over (with companions over 40), and offers one- and two-week trips, mostly international.

PUBLICATIONS

- *The Book of Deals* is a collection of more than 1,000 senior discounts on airlines, lodging, tours, and attractions around the country; it's available for $9.90 by calling (✆ **800/460-6676.**
- *101 Tips for the Mature Traveler* is available from Grand Circle Travel (✆ **800/221-2610** or 617/350-7500; fax 617/346-6700).
- *The 50+ Traveler's Guidebook* (St. Martin's Press).
- *Unbelievably Good Deals and Great Adventures That You Absolutely Can't Get Unless You're Over 50* (Contemporary Publishing Co.).

FAMILY TRAVEL

Philadelphia is just great for families; the layout is accessible, the sights are meaningful to all age levels, and the city is more of a collection of warm neighborhoods than a faceless metropolis. See "Especially for Kids" in chapter 7, featuring the best kid-friendly sights to explore in Philadelphia. Children under 12 (and in many cases under 18) can stay free in the same room as their parents in virtually all Philadelphia hotels. Be sure to reserve cribs and playpens if needed in advance. We've sprinkled the chapters on where to stay and dine with "Family-Friendly" features (see p. 99 for "Family-Friendly Restaurants" and p. 74 for "Family-Friendly Hotels.")

The best resource for family travel in Philadelphia is *Metrokids,* a bimonthly newspaper. It lists all cultural attractions geared toward families, along with special newspaper issues devoted to factory tours, the Camden aquarium, and the like. Call (✆ **888/890-4668** toll-free with specific questions.

I cannot recommend this enough: a family trip to Amish Country or, a bit farther, to Hershey and Gettysburg is a great idea. You'll encounter different ways of life, and basic American themes such as sacrifices for freedom, in ways that will trigger everyone's imaginations. See chapter 12 for specific recommendations.

AGENCIES/OPERATORS

Familyhostel (✆ 800/733-9753; www.learn.unh.edu/familyhostel) takes the whole family on moderately priced domestic and international learning vacations. All trip details are handled by the program staff, and lectures, fields trips, and sightseeing are guided by a team of academics. For kids ages 8 to 15 accompanied by their parents and/or grandparents.

PUBLICATIONS

The Frommer's publication line has great resources for you. If you're in the Philadelphia area, try *The Unofficial Guide to the Mid-Atlantic with Kids; Frommer's New York City with Kids;* and *Frommer's Washington, D.C. with Kids.*

- *How to Take Great Trips with Your Kids* (The Harvard Common Press) is full of good general advice that can apply to travel anywhere.

STUDENT TRAVEL

There are more colleges and universities in and around Philadelphia than there are in any other city in the country — so students will find a warm reception from area vendors and sights. A valid student ID will get you special discounts on cultural sights, accommodations, car rentals, and more. While in Philadelphia, head for the **University of Pennsylvania,** 34th and Walnut streets (© **215/898-5000**); **Temple University,** Broad Street and Montgomery Avenue (© **215/787-8561**); or **International House,** 3701 Chestnut St. (© **215/387-5125**). All of the above publish free papers listing lectures, performances, films, and social events.

TRAVELING WITH PETS

We have made a special note in the accommodations listings if pets are allowed at that particular lodging.

6 Getting There

BY PLANE

THE MAJOR AIRLINES   By air, Philadelphia is 2½ hours from Miami or Chicago, and 6 hours from the West Coast. Some two dozen carriers fly from more than 100 cities in the U.S. and 16 destinations abroad. Since **US Airways** uses Philadelphia International Airport (PIA) as a hub, this airline has terrific schedules and frequent low fares into town, so I would contact **US Airways** (© 800/428-4322; www.usairways.com) first. You can also check flight schedules and make reservations on all of the following other domestic airlines:

American Airlines and **American Eagle** (© 800/433-7300 or 215/365-4000; www.americanair.com); **America West** (© 800/235-9292; www.americawest.com); **Continental Airlines** and **Continental Express** (© 800/525-0280; www.flycontinental.com); **Delta Air Lines** (© 800/221-1212 or 215/667-7720; www.delta.com); **Midwest Express** (© 800/452-2022; www.midwestexpress.com); **National Airlines** (© 888/757-5387; www.nationalairlines.com); **Northwest Airlines** (© 800/225-2525 domestic, or 800/447-4747 international; www.nwa.com); and **United Airlines** (© 800/241-6522 or 215/568-2800; www.ual.com).

For international carriers with direct flights, see chapter 3.

GETTING INTO TOWN FROM THE AIRPORT

For information, see "Getting Into Town from the Airport" under "Orientation" in chapter 4.

AIR TRAVEL SECURITY MEASURES

In the wake of the terrorist attacks of September 11, 2001, the airline industry implemented sweeping security measures in airports. Expect a lengthier check-in process and possible delays. Although regulations vary from airline to airline, you can expedite the process by arriving at the airport at least 2 hours before your scheduled flight, trying not to drive your car to the airport (since some parking lots are closed for security reasons), not counting on curbside check-in due to security measures, carrying plenty of documentation with you (you must have a government-issued photo ID), and checking with the Transportation Security Administration (www.tsa.gov) to find out what you can carry on and what you can't.

FLYING FOR LESS: TIPS FOR GETTING THE BEST AIRFARE

Passengers who can book their ticket long in advance, who can stay over Saturday night, or who are willing to travel on a Tuesday, Wednesday, or Thursday after 7pm, will pay a fraction of the full fare. Here are a few other easy ways to save:

- Check the travel section of your Sunday newspaper for advertised discounts or call the airlines directly and ask if any **promotional rates** or special fares are available. In periods of low-volume travel, you should pay no more than $400 for a domestic cross-country flight. If your

---

(**Tips** **Canceled Plans**

If your flight is canceled, don't book a new fare at the ticket counter. Find the nearest phone and call the airline directly to reschedule. You'll be relaxing while other passengers are still standing in line.

---

schedule is flexible, say so, and ask if you can secure a cheaper fare by staying an extra day, by flying midweek, or by flying at less-trafficked hours. If you already hold a ticket when a sale breaks, it may even pay to exchange your ticket, which usually incurs a $100 to $150 charge. *Note:* The lowest-priced fares are often nonrefundable, require advance purchase of 1 to 3 weeks and a certain length of stay, and carry penalties for changing dates of travel.

- **Consolidators,** also known as bucket shops, are a good place to find low fares. Consolidators buy seats in bulk from the airlines and then sell them back to the public at prices usually below even the airlines' discounted rates. Their small ads usually run in Sunday newspaper travel sections. Before you pay, request a confirmation number from the consolidator and then call the airline to confirm your seat. Be aware that bucket shop tickets are usually nonrefundable or rigged with stiff cancellation penalties, often as high as 50% to 75% of the ticket price. Protect yourself by paying with a credit card rather than cash. Also check out the name of the airline; you may not want to fly on some obscure Third World airline, even if you're saving $10. And check whether you're flying on a charter or a scheduled airline; the latter is more expensive but much reliable. **Council Travel** (© 800/ 226-8624; www.counciltravel. com) and **STA Travel** (© 800/ 781-4040; www.sta-travel.com)

cater especially to young travelers, but their bargain-basement prices are available to people of all ages. **The TravelHub** (© 888/AIR-FARE; www.travelhub.com) represents nearly 1,000 travel agencies, many of whom offer consolidator and discount fares. Other reliable consolidators include **1-800-FLY-CHEAP** (www. 1800flycheap.com); **TFI Tours International** (© 800/745-8000 or 212/736-1140; www. lowestairprice.com), which serves as a clearinghouse for unused seats; or "rebators" such as **Travel Avenue** (© 800/333-3335; www. travelavenue.com) and the **Smart Traveller** (© 800/448-3338 in the U.S. or 305/448-3338), which rebate part of their commissions to you.

- Search the **Internet** for cheap fares. Great last-minute deals are available through free weekly e-mail services provided directly by the airlines. See "Planning Your Trip Online," below, for more information.

- Join a travel club such as **Moment's Notice** (© 718/234-6295; www.moments-notice.com) or **Sears Discount Travel Club** (© 800/433-9383 or 800/ 255-1487 to join; www.travelers advantage.com), which supply unsold tickets at discounted prices. You pay an annual membership fee to get the club's hot line number. Of course, you're limited to what's available, so you have to be flexible.

- Join **frequent-flier clubs.** It makes sense to open as many accounts as possible, no matter how seldom you fly a particular airline. It's free, and you'll get the best choice of seats, faster response to phone inquiries, and prompter service if your luggage is stolen, your flight is canceled or delayed, or if you want to change your seat.

BY CAR

It's no wonder that 67% of all visitors arrive by car — Philadelphia is some 300 miles (6 or so hr.) from Boston, 100 miles (2 hr.) from New York City, 135 miles (3 hr.) from Washington, D.C., and 450 miles (9 hr.) from Montreal. Tolls between Philadelphia and either New York City or Washington come to about $12.

Philadelphia is easy accessible via a series of interstate highways that circle or pass through the city. Think of Center City as a rectangle. I-95 whizzes by its bottom and right sides. The Pennsylvania Turnpike (I-276) is the top edge, just widened to six lanes with the same E-ZPass electronic toll system that the New Jersey Turnpike and New York City use. I-76 splits off and snakes along the Schuylkill River along the left side into town. I-676 traverses Center City under Vine Street, connecting I-76 to adjacent Camden, New Jersey, via the Ben Franklin Bridge over the Delaware. The "Blue Route" of I-476 forms a left edge for the suburbs, about 15 miles west of town, connecting I-276 and I-76 at its northern end with I-95 to the south.

Here are routes to City Hall, in the very center of town, from various directions:

NEW JERSEY TURNPIKE SOUTHBOUND EXIT 6   Take the Pennsylvania Turnpike westbound to exit 29 and change to U.S. 13 southbound. Follow the signs a short distance to I-95 southbound and enter at exit 22, heading south. Exit for Center City at I-676 (Vine St. Expressway)

westbound to 15th Street, then turn left and travel southbound 2 blocks.

NEW JERSEY TURNPIKE EXIT 4 Take N.J. 73 northbound to N.J. 38 westbound, then change to U.S. 30 westbound (the signage is abominable) and follow it over the Ben Franklin Bridge ($3 this way, but free eastbound; E-ZPass is accepted) to I-676. Go south on 6th Street to Walnut Street (historic district will be on the left), turn right, and travel westbound to 15th Street.

FROM I-95 NORTHBOUND Just past Philadelphia International Airport, take Pa. 291 toward Center City, Philadelphia. Cross the George C. Platt Memorial Bridge and turn left onto 26th Street, then follow 26th Street directly onto I-76 (Schuylkill Expressway) westbound to exit 39 (30th St. Station). Go 1 block to Market Street and turn right. Go east on Market Street to City Hall, which will be in front of you.

FROM THE PENNSYLVANIA TURNPIKE (I-76)   Take exit 24 to I-76 (Schuylkill Expressway) eastbound to I-676 (Vine St. Expressway). Take I-676 eastbound to 15th Street, turn right, and proceed southbound 2 blocks.

BY TRAIN

Philadelphia is a major Amtrak stop (© **800/USA-RAIL;** www.amtrak. com). It's on the Boston–Washington, D.C., northeast corridor, which has extensions south to Florida, west to Pittsburgh and Chicago, and east to Atlantic City. The Amtrak terminal is Penn Station (30th St.), about 15 blocks from City Hall. Regular service, called Northeast Direct, takes 85 minutes from New York City; Metroliner service is 70 minutes for the same trip, or 5 hours from Boston and 100 minutes from Washington. The new Acela, implemented in 2001, should trim the Boston trip to 4 hours once they get the kinks worked out.

Tips   **Major Money-Saving Travel Tip**

Keep in mind that a trip to Philadelphia can be much cheaper if you take **New Jersey Transit** (© 800/582-5946, 215/569-3752, or 973/762-5100) commuter trains out of Penn Station in New York City or Newark to Trenton, then switch across the platform to the R7 Philadelphia-bound SEPTA commuter train that makes several convenient Center City stops before heading out to Chestnut Hill. The New Jersey Transit train from New York to Trenton travels every 20 minutes from 6am to 1:45am, takes 80 minutes, and costs $10.40 one-way or $15.75 round-trip. The SEPTA portion costs another $7 each way, $9.50 round-trip and takes about 30 minutes. Rates and times are, of course, subject to change.

SEPTA commuter trains (© 215/580-7800; www.septa.com) also connect 30th Street Station and several Center City stations to Trenton, New Jersey, to the northeast; to Harrisburg to the west; and directly to airport terminals to the south.

Sample round-trip fares on Amtrak as of press time were: New York City to Philadelphia, $96 peak, $88 excursion; Washington to Philadelphia, $90 peak, $78 excursion; one train daily to or from Chicago, around $220. Peak hours are Friday and Sunday, and days surrounding major holidays, from 11am to 11pm.

7 Escorted Tours & Package Deals

Before you start your search for the lowest airfare, you may want to consider booking your flight as part of a travel package such as an escorted tour or a package tour. You're not the only one with an interest in Philadelphia's history and culture, or in the Amish Country's unique community. What you lose in adventure, you'll gain in time and money saved when you book accommodations, and maybe even food and entertainment, along with your flight.

PACKAGE TOURS FOR INDEPENDENT TRAVELERS

Package tours are not the same thing as escorted tours. Package tours are simply a way to buy the airfare, accommodations, and other elements of your trip (such as car rentals, airport transfers, and sometimes even activities) at the same time and often at discounted prices — kind of like one-stop shopping. Packages are sold

in bulk to tour operators — who resell them to the public at a cost that drastically undercuts standard rates.

RECOMMENDED PACKAGE TOUR OPERATORS

One good source of package deals is the airlines themselves. Most major airlines offer air/land packages, including **American Airlines Vacations** (© 800/321-2121; http://aav1.aavacations.com), **Delta Vacations** (© 800/221-6666; www.deltavacations.com), and **US Airways Vacations** (© 800/455-0123 or 800/422-3861;www.usairwaysvacations.com), **Continental Airlines Vacations** (© 800/301-3800; www.coolvacations.com), and **United Vacations** (© 888/854-3899; www.unitedvacations.com).

Online Vacation Mall (© 800/839-9851; www.vacationtogether.com) allows you to search for and book packages offered by a number of tour operators and airlines. The **United States Tour Operators Association's** website (www.ustoa.com) has a search engine that allows you to look for operators that offer packages to a specific destination. Travel packages are also listed in the travel section of your local Sunday newspaper. **Liberty Travel** (© **888/271-1584;** www.libertytravel.com), one of the biggest packagers in the Northeast, often runs full-page ads in Sunday papers. Or check ads in the national travel magazines such as *Arthur Frommer's Budget Travel Magazine, Travel & Leisure, National Geographic Traveler,* and *Condé Nast Traveler.*

THE PROS & CONS OF PACKAGE TOURS

Packages can save you money because they are sold in bulk to tour operators, who sell them to the public. They offer group prices but allow for independent travel. The disadvantages are that you're usually required to make a large payment up front; you may end up on a charter flight; and you have to deal with your own luggage and with transfers between your hotel and the airport, if transfers are not included in the package price. Packages often don't allow for a wide range of choices (the hotels may be unremarkable and are usually located more for the packager's convenience than for yours), or have a fixed itinerary that doesn't allow for an extra day of shopping. In some packages, your choices of travel days may be limited. Some packages let you choose between escorted vacations and independent vacations; others

allow you to add on a few guided excursions or escorted day trips (also at prices lower than if you booked them yourself) without booking an entirely escorted tour. Your choice of travel days may be limited as well.

ESCORTED TOURS (TRIPS WITH GUIDES)

Escorted Tours are structured group tours, with a group leader. The price usually includes everything from airfare to hotels, meals, tours, admission costs, and local transportation.

THE PROS & CONS OF ESCORTED TOURS

If you book an escorted tour, most everything is paid for up front, so you deal with fewer money issues. They allow you to enjoy the maximum number of sights in the shortest time, with the least amount of hassle, as others arrange all the details. Escorted tours give you the security of traveling in a group and are convenient for people with limited mobility. Many escorted tours are theme tours, putting people who share the same interest or activity (such as cooking or sailing) together.

On the downside, if you book an escorted tour you often have to pay a lot of money up front, and your lodging and dining choices are predetermined. Escorted tours can be jam-packed with activities, leaving little room for individual sightseeing, whim, or adventure. They also often focus only on the heavily touristed sites, so you miss out on the lesser-known gems. Plus, you may not always be happy rubbing suitcases with strangers.

8 Planning Your Trip Online

Researching and booking your trip online can save time and money. Then again, it may not. It is simply not true that you always get the best deal online. Most booking engines do not include

schedules and prices for budget airlines, and from time to time you'll get a better last-minute price by calling the airline directly, so it's best to call the airline to see if you can do better before

---

Frommers.com: The Complete Travel Resource

For an excellent travel-planning resource, we highly recommend **Frommers.com** (www.frommers.com). We're a little biased, of course, but we guarantee that you'll find the travel tips, reviews, monthly vacation giveaways, and online-booking capabilities thoroughly indispensable.

---

booking online. Also, although online booking sites offer tips and hard data to help you bargain shop, they cannot endow you with the hard-earned experience that makes a seasoned, reliable travel agent an invaluable resource, even in the Internet age. And for consumers with a complex itinerary, a trusty travel agent is still the best way to arrange the most direct flights to and from the best airports.

On the plus side, Internet users today can tap into the same travel-planning databases that were once accessible only to travel agents — and do it at the same speed. Sites such as **Frommers.com**, **Travelocity.com**, **Expedia.com**, and **Orbitz.com** allow consumers to comparison shop for airfares, access special bargains, book flights, and reserve hotel rooms and rental cars. The benefits of researching your trip online can be well worth the effort.

Last-minute specials, such as weekend deals or Internet-only fares, are offered by airlines to fill empty seats. Most of these are announced on Tuesday or Wednesday and must be purchased online. They are only valid for travel that weekend, but some can be booked weeks or months in advance. Sign up for weekly e-mail alerts at airline websites or check mega-sites that compile comprehensive lists of last-minute specials, such as **Smarter Living** (smarterliving.com) or **WebFlyer** (www.webflyer.com).

Some sites, such as Expedia.com, will send you **e-mail notification** when a cheap fare becomes available to your favorite destination. Some will also tell you when fares to a particular destination are lowest.

TRAVEL PLANNING & BOOKING SITES

Keep in mind that because several airlines are no longer willing to pay commissions on tickets sold by online travel agencies, these agencies may either add a $10 surcharge to your bill if you book on that carrier — or neglect to offer those carriers' schedules.

The list of sites below is selective, not comprehensive. Some sites will have evolved or disappeared by the time you read this.

- **Travelocity** (www.travelocity.com or http://frommers.travelocity.com) and **Expedia** (www.expedia.com) are among the most popular sites, each offering an excellent range of options. Travelers search by destination, dates, and cost.
- **Orbitz** (www.orbitz.com) is a popular site launched by United, Delta, Northwest, American, and Continental Airlines. With this site, you're granted access to the largest data bank of low rates, airline tickets, rental cars, hotels, vacation packages, and other travel products. You get, among other offerings, available fares from more than 450 airlines.
- **Qixo** (www.qixo.com) is another powerful search engine that allows you to search for flights and accommodations from some 20 airline and travel-planning sites (such as Travelocity) at once. Qixo sorts results by price.

Tips Easy Internet Access Away from Home

There are a number of ways to get your e-mail on the Web, using any computer.

- Your **Internet Service Provider (ISP)** may have a Web-based interface that lets you access your e-mail on computers other than your own. Just find out how it works before you leave home. The major ISPs maintain local access numbers around the world so that you can go online by placing a local call. Check your ISP's Website or call its toll-free number and ask how you can use your current account away from home, and how much it will cost. If you're traveling outside the reach of your ISP, you may have to check the Yellow Pages in your destination to find a local ISP; Philadelphia has dozens.

- You can open an account on a free, Web-based **e-mail provider** before you leave home, such as Microsoft's **Hotmail** (hotmail.com) or **Yahoo! Mail** (mail.yahoo.com). Your home ISP may be able to forward your home e-mail to the Web-based account automatically.

- Check out **www.mail2web.com**. This amazing free service allows you to type in your regular e-mail address and password and retrieve your e-mail from any Web browser, anywhere, so long as your home ISP hasn't blocked it with a firewall.

- **Priceline** (www.priceline.com) lets you "name your price" for airline tickets, hotel rooms, and rental cars. For airline tickets, you can't say what time you want to fly — you have to accept any flight between 6am and 10pm on the dates you've selected, and you may have to make one or more stopovers. Tickets are nonrefundable, and no frequent-flyer miles are awarded.

ONLINE TRAVELER'S TOOLBOX

Veteran travelers usually carry some essential items to make their trips easier. Following is a selection of online tools to bookmark and use.

- **Visa ATM Locator** (www.visa.com), for locations of PLUS ATMs worldwide, or **MasterCard ATM Locator** (www.mastercard.com), for locations of Cirrus ATMs worldwide.

- **Intellicast** (www.intellicast.com) and **Weather.com** (www.weather.com). Gives weather forecasts for all 50 states and for cities around the world.

- **Mapquest** (www.mapquest.com). This best of the mapping sites lets you choose a specific address or destination, and in seconds, it will return a map and detailed directions.

- **Cybercafes.com** (www.cybercafes.com) or **Net Café Guide** (www.netcafeguide.com/mapindex.htm). Locate Internet cafes at hundreds of locations. There's a **Euro Cyber Café** in Terminal D at Philadelphia International Airport.

- **Universal Currency Converter** (www.xe.net/currency). See what your dollar or pound is worth in more than 100 other countries.

9 Tips on Accommodations

TIPS FOR SAVING ON YOUR HOTEL ROOM

The **rack rate** is the maximum rate that a hotel charges for a room. It's the rate you'd get if you walked in off the street and asked for a room for the night. Hardly anybody pays these prices, and there are many ways around them: Don't be afraid to bargain, rely on a qualified professional (certain hotels give travel agents discounts in exchange for steering business their way), dial the hotel directly for the best rate, and look into group or long-stay discounts. You should also investigate reservations services. These outfits usually work as consolidators, buying up or reserving rooms in bulk, and then dealing them out to customers at a profit. You may get a decent rate, but always call the hotel as well to see if you can do better.

Among the more reputable reservations services, offering both telephone and online bookings, are: **Accommodations Express** (© 800/950-4685; www.accommodationsexpress.com); **Hotel Reservations Network** (© 800/715-7666; www.hoteldiscounts.com or www.180096HOTEL.com); and **Quikbook** (© 800/789-9887, includes fax on demand service; www.quikbook.com). Online, try booking your hotel through **Frommers.com** (www.frommers.com). **Microsoft Expedia** (www.expedia.com) features a "Travel Agent" that will direct you to affordable lodgings.

10 Recommended Reading & Viewing

BOOKS

ART & ARCHITECTURE Try *Philadelphia's Architecture* (MIT Press, 1984), which goes into environmental issues as well, or the more coffee-table *An Architectural Guidebook to Philadelphia* (Gibbs Smith, 1999) by Frances Morrone and James Iska. Roslyn Brenner's *Philadelphia's Outdoor Art: A Walking Tour* (Camino Books, 1987) has a makeshift text but contains good photography.

Old Philadelphia in Early Photographs, 1839–1914 (Dover, 1976) by Robert F. Looney is a superb photographic history. Robert Llewellyn has also assembled a sensitive book of more recent photographs in *Philadelphia* (Thomasson-Grant, 1986).

BIOGRAPHY John Lukacs's *Philadelphia: Patricians & Philistines 1900–1950* (Farrar, Straus & Giroux, 1981) is a charming, slightly offbeat collection of profiles of seven colorful figures who flourished during this period and have faded into obscurity since.

The Kelly family — John, Jack, and Grace — receives a hagiographic and slightly dated treatment in John McCallum's *That Kelly Family* (A.S. Barnes, 1957). Another "immigrant made good" story, although more measured, is the biography of former Mayor Frank Rizzo, Joseph Daughen's *The Cop Who Would Be King* (Little, Brown, 1977).

FICTION Try Pete Dexter's *God's Pocket* (Warner Books, 1990) for a gritty contemporary look at the city by a former newspaper reporter turned big-league novelist and script-writer. Donald Zochert's *Murder in the Hellfire Club* (Holt, Rinehart & Winston, 1978) is an amusing historical mystery, with Colonists framed for murder in 1770s London and Ben Franklin on hand to solve the case.

HISTORY It is impossible to read about the transformation of the Colonies to the United States, and the first 50 years of independence, without learning about Philadelphia.

⌒Tips Using a Cellphone on Your Trip

Cellphone rental at the Philadelphia International Airport can be done at **Cingular Wireless,** in the corner of the "Philadelphia Marketplace" area between Terminals B and C, and at **Airport Wireless,** on the eastern edge of Concourse E. Renting a cellphone is much like renting a car: It comes fully equipped and ready to use; you just pick it up and go.

A highly recommended wireless rental company is **InTouch USA** (𝒞 **800/872-7626;** www.intouchusa.com). Give them your itinerary and they will tell you which wireless products and services you need. For this free evaluation, call 𝒞 **703/222-7161** between 9am and 4pm.

Christopher and James Collier, two brothers — one a writer on jazz, the other a history professor — have an intensely novelistic and readable summary of the 1787 Constitutional Convention with *Decision in Philadelphia* (Ballantine, reissued 1987). Carl Bridenbaugh's *Rebels and Gentlemen* (Oxford University Press, 1965) is a good summary of events leading up to independence. Catherine Drinker Bowen's *Miracle at Philadelphia* (Atlantic-Little, Brown, 1960) is a vivid retelling of the 1787 Constitutional Convention.

E. Digby Baltzell's *Puritan Boston and Quaker Philadelphia* (Free Press, 1960) is a thoughtful and amusing comparison between these two preeminent colonial cities, explaining why their histories turned out so differently. Baltzell's first classic effort here was *Philadelphia Gentlemen: The Making of a National Upper Class* (Free Press, 1958).

The transformation from ideal seaport to ideal manufacturing city is covered in *Civil War Issues in Philadelphia 1956–1965* by William Dusinberre (University of Pennsylvania Press, 1965).

W.E.B. Du Bois's *The Philadelphia Negro* (University of Pennsylvania Press, 1899) is a classic analysis of racism and its social effects in the North since the Civil War. Jean Seder has edited *Voices of Another Time: 3 Memories* (Institute for the Study of Human Issues, 1985), three oral histories of Afro-American women who were born in the South but who spent their lives in Philadelphia, complete with recipes, cures, and proverbs.

Edwin Wolf II's *Philadelphia: Portrait of an American City* (Stackpole Books, 1975) is one of the more engaging histories, with beautiful and appropriate illustrations. The building of the Benjamin Franklin Parkway, a Champs Elysées in the midst of the colonial grid, is covered in David Bruce Brownlee's *Building the City Beautiful* (Philadelphia Museum of Art catalog, 1989).

From the moment that the superb 1990s mayor Ed Rendell took office, he allowed Buzz Bissinger complete behind-the-scenes access to his ideas and meetings. Bissinger's written the best recent history of the city in *A Prayer for the City: The True Story of a Mayor and Five Heroes in a Race Against Time* (Random House, 1998).

3

For International Visitors

Whether it's your first visit or your tenth, a trip to the United States may require an additional degree of planning. This chapter will provide you with essential information, helpful tips, and advice for the more common problems that some visitors encounter.

The **International Visitors Council** at 1 Parkway, 1515 Arch St., 12th Floor, Philadelphia, PA 19102 (☎ **215/683-0999**) offers special services to international visitors, as does the **Independence Visitor Center,** 6th and Market streets, Philadelphia, PA 19106 (☎ **800/537-7676**).

1 Preparing for Your Trip

ENTRY REQUIREMENTS

Check at any U.S. embassy or consulate for current information and requirements. You can also obtain a visa application and other information online at the **U.S. State Department's** website, at **www.travel.state.gov.**

VISAS The U.S. State Department has a **Visa Waiver Program** allowing citizens of certain countries to enter the United States without a visa for stays of up to 90 days. At press time these included Andorra, Australia, Austria, Belgium, Brunei, Denmark, Finland, France, Germany, Iceland, Ireland, Italy, Japan, Liechtenstein, Luxembourg, Monaco, the Netherlands, New Zealand, Norway, Portugal, San Marino, Singapore, Slovenia, Spain, Sweden, Switzerland, the United Kingdom, and Uruguay. Citizens of these countries need only a valid passport and a round-trip air or cruise ticket in their possession upon arrival. If they first enter the United States, they may also visit Mexico, Canada, Bermuda, and/or the Caribbean islands and return to the United States without a visa. Further information is available from any U.S. embassy or consulate. Canadian citizens may enter the United States without visas; they need only proof of residence.

Citizens of all other countries must have (1) a valid passport that expires at least 6 months later than the scheduled end of their visit to the United States, and (2) a tourist visa, which may be obtained without charge from any U.S. consulate.

To obtain a visa, the traveler must submit a completed application form (either in person or by mail) with a 1½-inch-square photo, and must demonstrate binding ties to a residence abroad. Usually you can obtain a visa at once or within 24 hours, but it may take longer during the summer rush from June through August. If you cannot go in person, contact the nearest U.S. embassy or consulate for directions on applying by mail. Your travel agent or airline office may also be able to provide you with visa applications and instructions. The U.S. consulate or embassy that issues your visa will determine whether you will be issued a multiple- or single-entry visa and any restrictions regarding the length of your stay.

British subjects can obtain up-to-date passport and visa information by calling the **U.S. Embassy Visa Information Line** (✆ **0891/200-290**) or the **London Passport Office** (✆ **0990/210-410** for recorded information) or they can find the visa information on the U.S. Embassy Great Britain website at www.ukpa. gov.uk.

Irish citizens can obtain up-to-date passport and visa information through the **Embassy of USA Dublin,** 42 Elgin Rd., Dublin 4, Ireland (✆ **353/1-668-8777**) or by checking the visa page on the website at www.irigov.ie/iveagh.

Australian citizens can obtain up-to-date passport and visa information by calling the **U.S. Embassy Canberra,** Moonah Place, Yarralumla, ACT 2600 (✆ **02/6214-5600**) or check the website's visa page at www. usis-australia.gov/consular/niv.html.

Citizens of **New Zealand** can obtain up-to-date passport and visa information by calling the **U.S. Embassy New Zealand,** 29 Fitzherbert Terr., Thorndon, Wellington, New Zealand (✆ **644/472-2068**) or get the information directly from the website at http://usembassy.org.nz.

MEDICAL REQUIREMENTS Unless you're arriving from an area known to be suffering from an epidemic (particularly cholera or yellow fever), inoculations or vaccinations are not required for entry into the United States. If you have a medical condition that requires **syringe-administered medications,** carry a valid signed prescription from your physician — the Federal Aviation Administration (FAA) no longer allows airline passengers to pack syringes in their carry-on baggage without documented proof of medical need. If you have a disease that requires treatment with **narcotics,** you should also carry documented proof with you — smuggling narcotics aboard a plane is a serious offense that carries severe penalties in the U.S.

For **HIV-positive visitors,** requirements for entering the United States are somewhat vague and change frequently. According to the latest publication of *HIV and Immigrants: A Manual for AIDS Service Providers,* the Immigration and Naturalization Service (INS) doesn't require a medical exam for entry into the United States, but INS officials may stop individuals because they look sick or because they are carrying AIDS/HIV medicine.

If an HIV-positive noncitizen applies for a non-immigrant visa, the question on the application regarding communicable diseases is tricky no matter which way it's answered. If the applicant checks "no," INS may deny the visa on the grounds that the applicant committed fraud. If the applicant checks "yes" or if INS suspects the person is HIV-positive, it will deny the visa unless the applicant asks for a special waiver for visitors. This waiver is for people visiting the United States for a short time, to attend a conference, for instance, to visit close relatives, or to receive medical treatment. It can be a confusing situation. For further up-to-the-minute information, contact the Centers for Disease Control's **National Center for HIV** (✆ **404/332-4559;** www.hivatis.org) or the **Gay Men's Health Crisis** (✆ **212/367-1000;** www.gmhc.org).

DRIVER'S LICENSES Foreign driver's licenses are mostly recognized in the U.S., although you may want to get an international driver's license if your home license is not written in English.

PASSPORT INFORMATION

Safeguard your passport in an inconspicuous, inaccessible place like a money belt. Make a copy of the critical pages, including the passport number, and store it in a safe place, separate from the passport itself. If you lose your passport, visit the nearest consulate of your native country as soon as possible for a replacement. Passport applications are downloadable from the Internet sites listed below.

Note that the International Civil Aviation Organization (ICAO) has recommended a policy requiring that *every* individual who travels by air have his or her own passport. In response, many countries are now requiring that children must be issued their own passport to travel internationally, where before those under 16 or so may have been allowed to travel on a parent or guardian's passport.

FOR RESIDENTS OF CANADA

You can pick up a passport application at one of 28 regional passport offices or most travel agencies. As of December 11, 2001, Canadian children who travel must have their own passport. However, if you hold a valid Canadian passport issued before December 11, 2001, that bears the name of your child, the passport remains valid for you and your child until it expires. Passports cost C$85 for those 16 years and older (valid 5 yr.), C$35 children 3 to 15 (valid 5 yr.), and C$20, children under 3 (valid for 3 yr.). Applications, which must be accompanied by two identical passport-sized photographs and proof of Canadian citizenship, are available at travel agencies throughout Canada or from the central **Passport Office,** Department of Foreign Affairs and International Trade, Ottawa, ON K1A 0G3 (© **800/ 567-6868;** www.ppt.gc.ca). Processing takes 5 to 10 days if you apply in person, or about 3 weeks by mail.

FOR RESIDENTS OF THE UNITED KINGDOM

To pick up an application for a standard 10-year passport (5-yr. passport for children under 16), visit your nearest passport office, major post office, or travel agency. You can also contact the **United Kingdom**

Passport Service at © **0870/521- 0410** or search its website at www. ukpa.gov.uk. Passports are £30 for adults and £16 for children under 16. Processing takes about 2 weeks.

FOR RESIDENTS OF IRELAND

You can apply for a 10-year passport, costing €57, at the **Passport Office,** Setanta Centre, Molesworth Street, Dublin 2 (© **01/671-1633;** www.irl gov.ie/iveagh). Those under age 18 and over 65 must apply for a €12 3-year passport. You can also apply at 1A South Mall, Cork (© **021/272-525**) or over the counter at most main post offices.

FOR RESIDENTS OF AUSTRALIA

You can pick up an application from your local post office or any branch of Passports Australia, but you must schedule an interview at the passport office to present your application materials. Call the **Australian Passport Information Service** at © **131- 232,** or visit the government website at www.passports.gov.au. Passports for adults are A$144 and for those under 18 are A$72.

FOR RESIDENTS OF NEW ZEALAND

You can pick up a passport application at any New Zealand Passports Office or download it from their website. Contact the **Passports Office** at © **0800/225-050** in New Zealand or 04/474-8100, or log on to www. passports.govt.nz. Passports for adults are NZ$80 and for children under 16 NZ$40.

CUSTOMS
WHAT YOU CAN BRING IN

Every visitor more than 21 years of age may bring in, free of duty, the following: (1) 1 liter of wine or hard liquor; (2) 200 cigarettes, 100 cigars (but not from Cuba), or 3 pounds of smoking tobacco; and (3) $100 worth of gifts. These exemptions are offered to travelers who spend at least 72 hours in the United States and who have not claimed them within the preceding 6 months. It is altogether forbidden to bring into the country foodstuffs (particularly fruit, cooked meats, and canned goods) and plants (vegetables, seeds, tropical plants, and the like). Foreign tourists may bring in or take out up to $10,000 in U.S. or foreign currency with no formalities; larger sums must be declared to U.S. Customs on entering or leaving, which includes filing form CM 4790. For more specific information regarding U.S. Customs, contact your nearest U.S. embassy or consulate, or the **U.S. Customs** office (© **202/927-1770** or www.customs.ustreas.gov).

WHAT YOU CAN TAKE HOME

U.K. citizens returning from a non-EU country have a customs allowance of: 200 cigarettes; 50 cigars; 250 grams of smoking tobacco; 2 liters of still table wine; 1 liter of spirits or strong liqueurs (over 22% volume); 2 liters of fortified wine, sparkling wine or other liqueurs; 60cc (ml) perfume; 250cc (ml) of toilet water; and £145 worth of all other goods, including gifts and souvenirs. People under 17 cannot have the tobacco or alcohol allowance. For more information, contact HM Customs & Excise at © **0845/010-9000** (from outside the U.K., 020/8929-0152), or consult their website at www.hmce.gov.uk.

For a clear summary of **Canadian** rules, request the booklet *I Declare,* issued by the **Canada Customs and Revenue Agency** (© **800/461-9999** in Canada, or 204/983-3500; www.ccra-adrc.gc.ca). Canada allows its citizens a C$750 exemption, and you're allowed to bring back duty-free one carton of cigarettes, 1 can of tobacco, 40 imperial ounces of liquor, and 50

cigars. In addition, you're allowed to mail gifts to Canada valued at less than C$60 a day, provided they're unsolicited and don't contain alcohol or tobacco (write on the package "Unsolicited gift, under $60 value"). All valuables should be declared on the Y-38 form before departure from Canada, including serial numbers of valuables you already own, such as expensive foreign cameras. *Note:* The $750 exemption can only be used once a year and only after an absence of 7 days.

The duty-free allowance in **Australia** is A$400 or, for those under 18, A$200. Citizens can bring in 250 cigarettes or 250 grams of loose tobacco, and 1,125 milliliters of alcohol. If you're returning with valuables you already own, such as foreign-made cameras, you should file form B263. A helpful brochure available from Australian consulates or Customs offices is *Know Before You Go.* For more information, call the **Australian Customs Service** at © **1300/363-263,** or log on to www.customs.gov.au.

The duty-free allowance for **New Zealand** is NZ$700. Citizens over 17 can bring in 200 cigarettes, 50 cigars, or 250 grams of tobacco (or a mixture of all 3 if their combined weight doesn't exceed 250g); plus 4.5 liters of wine and beer, or 1.125 liters of liquor. New Zealand currency does not carry import or export restrictions. Fill out a certificate of export, listing the valuables you are taking out of the country; that way, you can bring them back without paying duty. Most questions are answered in a free pamphlet available at New Zealand consulates and Customs offices: *New Zealand Customs Guide for Travelers, Notice no. 4.* For more information, contact **New Zealand Customs,** The Customhouse, 17–21 Whitmore St., Box 2218, Wellington (© **04/473-6099** or 0800/428-786; www.customs.govt.nz).

HEALTH INSURANCE

Although it's not required of travelers, health insurance is highly recommended. Unlike many European countries, the United States does not usually offer free or low-cost medical care to its citizens or visitors. Doctors and hospitals are expensive, and in most cases will require advance payment or proof of coverage before they render their services. Policies can cover everything from the loss or theft of your baggage and trip cancellation to the guarantee of bail in case you're arrested. Good policies will also cover the costs of an accident, repatriation, or death. See section 4, "Insurance, Health & Safety," in chapter 2 for more information. Packages such as **Europ Assistance's "Worldwide Healthcare Plan"** are sold by European automobile clubs and travel agencies at attractive rates. **Worldwide Assistance Services,** Inc. (© **800/ 821-2828;** www.worldwideassistance. com) is the agent for Europ Assistance in the United States.

Though lack of health insurance may prevent you from being admitted to a hospital in nonemergencies, don't worry about being left on a street corner to die: the American way is to fix you now and bill the living daylights out of you later.

INSURANCE FOR BRITISH TRAVELERS Most big travel agents offer their own insurance and will probably try to sell you their package when you book a holiday. Think before you sign. **Britain's Consumers' Association** recommends that you insist on seeing the policy and reading the fine print before buying travel insurance. **The Association of British Insurers** (© **020/ 7600-3333;** www.abi.org.uk) gives advice by phone and publishes *Holiday Insurance,* a free guide to policy provisions and prices. You might also shop around for better deals: Try **Columbus Direct** (© **020/7375- 0011;** www.columbusdirect.net).

INSURANCE FOR CANADIAN TRAVELERS Canadians should check with their provincial health plan offices or call **Health Canada** (© **613/957-2991;** www.hc-sc.gc.ca) to find out the extent of their coverage and what documentation and receipts they must take home in case they are treated in the United States.

MONEY

CURRENCY The U.S. monetary system is very simple: The most common **bills** are the $1 (colloquially, a "buck"), $5, $10, and $20 denominations. There are also $2 bills (seldom encountered), $50 bills, and $100 bills (the last two are usually not welcome as payment for small purchases). All the paper money was recently redesigned, making the famous faces adorning them disproportionately large. The old-style bills are still legal tender.

There are seven denominations of coins: 1¢ (1 cent, or a penny); 5¢ (5 cents, or a nickel); 10¢ (10 cents, or a dime); 25¢ (25 cents, or a quarter); 50¢ (50 cents, or a half dollar); the new gold "Sacagawea" coin worth $1; and, prized by collectors, the rare, older silver dollar.

Note: The "foreign-exchange bureaus" so common in Europe are rare even at airports in the United States, and nonexistent outside major cities. It's best not to change foreign money (or traveler's checks denominated in a currency other than U.S. dollars) at a small-town bank, or even a branch in a big city; in fact, leave any currency other than U.S. dollars at home — it may prove a greater nuisance to you than it's worth.

TRAVELER'S CHECKS Though traveler's checks are widely accepted, make sure that they're denominated in U.S. dollars, as foreign-currency

---

> **Tips** **Travel Tip**
>
> Be sure to keep a copy of all your travel papers separate from your wallet or purse, and leave a copy with someone at home should you need it faxed in an emergency.

---

checks are often difficult to exchange. The three traveler's checks that are most widely recognized — and least likely to be denied — are **Visa, American Express,** and **Thomas Cook.** Be sure to record the numbers of the checks, and keep that information in a separate place in case they get lost or stolen. Most businesses are pretty good about taking traveler's checks, but you're better off cashing them in at a bank (in small amounts, of course) and paying in cash. *Remember:* you'll need identification, such as a driver's license or passport, to change a traveler's check.

CREDIT CARDS & ATMS   Credit cards are the most widely used form of payment in the United States: **Visa** (Barclaycard in Britain), **MasterCard** (EuroCard in Europe, Access in Britain, Chargex in Canada), **American Express, Diners Club, Discover,** and **Carte Blanche.** There are, however, a handful of stores and restaurants that do not take credit cards, so be sure to ask in advance. Most businesses display a sticker near their entrance to let you know which cards they accept. (*Note:* Businesses may require a minimum purchase, usually around $10, to use a credit card.)

It is strongly recommended that you bring at least one major credit card. You must have a credit or charge card to rent a car. Hotels and airlines usually require a credit-card imprint as a deposit against expenses, and in an emergency a credit card can be priceless.

You'll find **automated teller machines (ATMs)** on just about every block — at least in almost every

town — across the country. Some ATMs will allow you to draw U.S. currency against your bank and credit cards. Check with your bank before leaving home, and remember that you will need your personal identification number (PIN) to do so. Most accept Visa, MasterCard, and American Express, as well as ATM cards from other U.S. banks. Expect to be charged up to $3 per transaction, however, if you're not using your own bank's ATM.

One way around these fees is to ask for cash back at grocery stores that accept ATM cards and don't charge usage fees. Of course, you'll have to purchase something first.

ATM cards with major credit card backing, known as "debit cards," are now a commonly acceptable form of payment in most stores and restaurants. Debit cards draw money directly from your checking account. Some stores enable you to receive "cash back" on your debit-card purchases as well.

SAFETY
GENERAL SUGGESTIONS   Although tourist areas are generally safe, U.S. urban areas tend to be less safe than those in Europe or Japan. You should always stay alert. This is particularly true of large American cities. If you're in doubt about which neighborhoods are safe, don't hesitate to make inquiries with the hotel front desk staff or the local tourist office.

Avoid deserted areas, especially at night, and don't go into public parks after dark unless there's a concert or similar occasion that will attract a crowd.

Avoid carrying valuables with you on the street, and keep expensive cameras or electronic equipment bagged up or covered when not in use. If you're using a map, try to consult it inconspicuously — or better yet, study it before you leave your room. Hold onto your pocketbook, and place your billfold in an inside pocket. In theaters, restaurants, and other public places, keep your possessions in sight.

Always lock your room door — don't assume that once you're inside the hotel you are automatically safe and no longer need to be aware of your surroundings. Hotels are open to the public, and in a large hotel, security may not be able to screen every one who enters.

DRIVING SAFETY Driving safety is important too, and carjacking is not unprecedented. Question your rental agency about personal safety and ask for a traveler-safety brochure when you pick up your car. Obtain written directions — or a map with the route clearly marked — from the agency showing how to get to your destination. (Many agencies now offer the option of renting a cellular phone for the duration of your car rental; check with the rental agent when you pick

up the car.) And, if possible, arrive and depart during daylight hours.

If you drive off a highway and end up in a dodgy-looking neighborhood, leave the area as quickly as possible. If you have an accident, even on the highway, stay in your car with the doors locked until you assess the situation or until the police arrive. If you're bumped from behind on the street or are involved in a minor accident with no injuries, and the situation appears to be suspicious, motion to the other driver to follow you. Never get out of your car in such situations. Go directly to the nearest police precinct, well-lit service station, or 24-hour store. You may want to look into renting a cellphone on a short-term basis. One recommended wireless rental company is **InTouch USA** (© **800/872-7626;** www.in touchusa.com).

Park in well-lit and well-traveled areas whenever possible. Always keep your car doors locked, whether the vehicle is attended or unattended. Never leave any packages or valuables in sight. If someone attempts to rob you or steal your car, don't try to resist the thief/carjacker. Report the incident to the police department immediately by calling © **911.**

2 Getting to the U.S.

International carriers that fly into **Philadelphia International Airport** (© 215/937-6800) include **Air Canada** (© 800/268-7240 in Canada), **Air Jamaica** (© 800/523-5585); **British Airways** (© 0345/222-111 in London); and **Lufthansa** (© 800/645-3880). From Ireland, **Aer Lingus** (© 01/844-4747 in Dublin, or 061/415-556 in Shannon) can fly you into New York and arrange an add-on flight to Philadelphia. From New Zealand and Australia, there are flights to Los Angeles on **Qantas** (© 008/177-767 in Australia) and on **Air New**

Zealand (© 0800/737-000 in Auckland, or 3/379-5200 in Christchurch); both airlines can book you through to Philadelphia. You can get to Philadelphia by train from Montreal using Amtrak (www.Amtrak.com).

AIRLINE DISCOUNTS The smart traveler can find numerable ways to reduce the price of a plane ticket simply by taking time to shop around. For example, overseas visitors can take advantage of the APEX (Advance Purchase Excursion) reductions offered by all major U.S. and

European carriers. For more money-saving airline advice, see "Getting There" in chapter 2. For the best rates, compare fares and be flexible with the dates and times of travel.

IMMIGRATION & CUSTOMS CLEARANCE Visitors arriving by air, no matter what the port of entry, should cultivate patience and resignation before setting foot on U.S. soil. Getting through immigration control can take as long as 2 hours on some days, especially on summer weekends, so be sure to carry this guidebook or something else to read. This is especially true in the aftermath of the September 11, 2001, terrorist attacks, when security clearances have been considerably beefed up at U.S. airports.

People traveling by air from Canada, Bermuda, and certain countries in the Caribbean can sometimes clear Customs and Immigration at the point of departure, which is much quicker.

3 Getting Around the U.S.

BY PLANE Some large airlines (for example, Northwest and Delta) offer travelers on their transatlantic or transpacific flights special discount tickets under the name Visit USA, allowing mostly one-way travel from one U.S. destination to another at very low prices. These discount tickets are not on sale in the United States and must be purchased abroad in conjunction with your international ticket. This system is the best, easiest, and fastest way to see the United States at low cost. You should obtain information well in advance from your travel agent or the office of the airline concerned, since the conditions attached to these discount tickets can be changed without advance notice.

BY TRAIN International visitors (excluding Canada) can also buy a **USA Railpass,** good for 15 or 30 days of unlimited travel on Amtrak (© **800/USA-RAIL;** www.amtrak. com). The pass is available through many foreign travel agents. Prices in 2002 for a 15-day pass were $295 off-peak, $440 peak; a 30-day pass costs $385 off-peak, $550 peak. With a foreign passport, you can also buy passes at some Amtrak offices in the United States, including locations in San Francisco, Los Angeles, Chicago, New York, Miami, Boston, and Washington, D.C. Reservations are generally required and should be made for each part of your trip as early as possible. Regional rail passes are also available.

BY BUS Although bus travel is often the most economical form of public transit for short hops between U.S. cities, it can also be slow and uncomfortable — certainly not an option for everyone (particularly when Amtrak, which is far more luxurious, offers similar rates). **Greyhound/Trailways** (© **800/231-2222;** www.greyhound.com), the sole nationwide bus line, offers an **International Ameripass** that must be purchased before coming to the United States, or by phone through the Greyhound International Office at the Port Authority Bus Terminal in New York City (© **212/971-0492**). The pass can be obtained from foreign travel agents or through Greyhound's website (order at least 21 days before your departure to the U.S.) and costs less than the domestic version. 2003 passes cost as follows: 4 days ($155), 7 days ($204), 10 days ($254), 15 days ($314), 21 days ($364), 30 days ($424), 45 days ($464), or 60 days ($574). You can get more info on the pass at the website, or by calling © **402/330-8552.** In addition, special rates are available for seniors and students.

BY CAR Philadelphia (like New York City, Boston, or New Orleans) is a city where walking is the best and easiest way to get around. But unless you plan to spend the bulk of your vacation time in Philadelphia, the most cost-effective, convenient, and comfortable way to travel around the rest of the United States is by car. The interstate highway system connects cities and towns all over the country; in addition to these high-speed, limited-access roadways, there's an extensive network of federal, state, and local highways and roads. Some of the national car-rental companies include **Alamo** (© 800/327-9633; www.goalamo.com), **Avis** (© 800/331-1212; www.avis.com), **Budget** (© 800/527-0700; www.budget.com), **Dollar** (© 800/800-4000; www.dollar.com), **Hertz** (© 800/654-3131; www.hertz.com), **National** (© 800/227-7368; www.nationalcar.com), and **Thrifty** (© 800/367-2277; www.thrifty.com).

If you plan to rent a car in the United States, you probably won't need the services of an additional automobile organization. If you're planning to buy or borrow a car, automobile-association membership is recommended. **AAA, the American Automobile Association** (© 800/222-4357), is the country's largest auto club and supplies its members with maps, insurance, and, most important, emergency road service. The cost of joining runs from $63 for singles to $87 for two members, but if you're a member of a foreign auto club with reciprocal arrangements, you can enjoy free AAA service in America. See section 6, "Getting There," in chapter 2 for more information.

✐ FAST FACTS: For the International Traveler

Automobile Organizations Auto clubs will supply maps, suggested routes, guidebooks, accident and bail-bond insurance, and emergency road service. The **American Automobile Association (AAA)** is the major auto club in the United States. If you belong to an auto club in your home country, inquire about AAA reciprocity before you leave. You may be able to join AAA even if you're not a member of a reciprocal club; to inquire, call AAA (© **800/222-4357**). Locally, **Keystone AAA** is at 2040 Market St. (© **215/864-5000**). For local emergency road service, call © **215/569-4411**.

Business Hours Offices are usually open weekdays from 9am to 5pm. Banks are open weekdays from 9am to 3pm or later and sometimes Saturday mornings. Stores typically open between 9 and 10am and close between 5 and 6pm Monday through Saturday, and in Philadelphia often stay open until 8pm on Wednesdays. Stores in shopping complexes or malls tend to stay open late: until about 9pm on weekdays and weekends, and many malls and larger department stores are open on Sundays.

Currency & Currency Exchange See "Entry Requirements" and "Money" under "Preparing for Your Trip," above; while exchange desks are dwindling and less urgent, you can exchange money at the following places in Center City: American Express Travel Service, 2 Penn Center Plaza (© **215/587-2342** or 215/587-2343); Thomas Cook Currency Services, 1800 John F. Kennedy Blvd. (© **800/287-7362**); First Union, 15th and Market streets (© **215/973-6812**); and Dickens Inn, Head House Square at 2nd Street (© **215/928-9307**).

Drinking Laws The legal age for purchase and consumption of alcoholic beverages is 21; proof of age is required and often requested at bars, nightclubs, and restaurants, so it's always a good idea to bring ID when you go out. Beer and wine often can be purchased in supermarkets, but liquor laws vary from state to state.

Do not carry open containers of alcohol in your car or any public area that isn't zoned for alcohol consumption. The police can fine you on the spot. And nothing will ruin your trip faster than getting a citation for DUI ("driving under the influence"), so don't even think about driving while intoxicated.

Electricity Like Canada, the United States uses 110 to 120 volts AC (60 cycles), compared to 220 to 240 volts AC (50 cycles) in most of Europe, Australia, and New Zealand. If your small appliances use 220 to 240 volts, you'll need a 110-volt transformer and a plug adapter with two flat parallel pins to operate them here. Downward converters that change 220–240 volts to 110–120 volts are difficult to find in the United States, so bring one with you.

Embassies & Consulates All embassies are located in the nation's capital, Washington, D.C. Some consulates are located in major U.S. cities, and most nations have a mission to the United Nations in New York City. If your country isn't listed below, call for directory information in Washington, D.C. (© **202/555-1212**) or log on to **www.embassy.org/embassies**.

The embassy of **Australia** is at 1601 Massachusetts Ave. NW, Washington, DC 20036 (© **202/797-3000**; www.austemb.org). There are consulates in New York, Honolulu, Houston, Los Angeles, and San Francisco.

The embassy of **Canada** is at 501 Pennsylvania Ave. NW, Washington, DC 20001 (© **202/682-1740**; www.canadianembassy.org). Other Canadian consulates are in Buffalo (N.Y.), Detroit, Los Angeles, New York, and Seattle.

The embassy of **Ireland** is at 2234 Massachusetts Ave. NW, Washington, DC 20008 (© **202/462-3939**; www.irelandemb.org). Irish consulates are in Boston, Chicago, New York, and San Francisco.

The embassy of **Japan** is at 2520 Massachusetts Ave. NW, Washington, DC 20008 (© **202/238-6700**; www.embjapan.org). Japanese consulates are located in Atlanta, Kansas City, San Francisco, and Washington, D.C.

The embassy of **New Zealand** is at 37 Observatory Circle NW, Washington, DC 20008 (© **202/328-4800**; www.nzembassy.com). New Zealand consulates are in Los Angeles, Salt Lake City, San Francisco, and Seattle.

The embassy of the **United Kingdom** is at 3100 Massachusetts Ave. NW, Washington, DC 20008 (© **202/462-1340**; www.britainusa.com). The British Honorary Consulate in Philadelphia is at 1818 Market St., 33rd floor (© **215/557-7665**).

Many European countries have consulates in Philadelphia; call information at © **215/555-1212** for the telephone number for your consulate.

Emergencies Call © **911** to report a fire, call the police, or get an ambulance anywhere in the United States. This is a toll-free call. (No coins are required at public telephones.)

If you encounter serious problems, contact the **Traveler's Aid Society International** (© 202/546-1127; www.travelersaid.org) to help direct you to a local branch. This nationwide, nonprofit, social-service organization geared to helping travelers in difficult straits offers services that might include reuniting families separated while traveling, providing food and/or shelter to people stranded without cash, or even emotional counseling. If you're in trouble, seek them out. The local chapter is at ✆ **215/ 546-0571.**

Gasoline (Petrol) Petrol is known as gasoline (or simply "gas") in the United States, and petrol stations are known as both gas stations and service stations. Gasoline costs about half as much here as it does in Europe (about $1.65 per gal. at press time), and taxes are included in the printed price. One U.S. gallon equals 3.8 liters or .85 Imperial gallons.

Holidays Banks, government offices, post offices, and many stores, restaurants, and museums are closed on the following legal national holidays: January 1 (New Year's Day), the third Monday in January (Martin Luther King Jr. Day), the third Monday in February (Presidents' Day, Washington's Birthday), the last Monday in May (Memorial Day), July 4 (Independence Day), the first Monday in September (Labor Day), the second Monday in October (Columbus Day), November 11 (Veterans' Day/Armistice Day), the fourth Thursday in November (Thanksgiving Day), and December 25 (Christmas). Also, the Tuesday following the first Monday in November is Election Day and is a federal government holiday in presidential-election years (held every 4 yr., and next in 2004).

Legal Aid If you are "pulled over" for a minor infraction (such as speeding), never attempt to pay the fine directly to a police officer; this could be construed as attempted bribery, a much more serious crime. Pay fines by mail, or directly into the hands of the clerk of the court. If accused of a more serious offense, say and do nothing before consulting a lawyer. Here the burden is on the state to prove a person's guilt beyond a reasonable doubt, and everyone has the right to remain silent, whether he or she is suspected of a crime or actually arrested. Once arrested, a person can make one telephone call to a party of his or her choice. Call your embassy or consulate (see "Embassies & Consulates," above).

Mail If you aren't sure what your address will be in the United States, mail can be sent to you, in your name, c/o General Delivery at the main post office of the city or region where you expect to be. (Call ✆ **800/ 275-8777** for information on the nearest post office.) Philadelphia's main post offices are located at 9th and Market streets and across from Penn Station at 30th Street. The addressee must pick up mail in person and must produce proof of identity (driver's license, passport, and so forth). Most post offices will hold your mail for up to one month, and are open Monday through Friday from 8am to 6pm, and Saturday from 9am to 3pm.

Generally found at intersections, mailboxes are blue with a red-and-white stripe and carry the inscription U.S. MAIL.

At press time, domestic postage rates were 23¢ for a postcard and 37¢ for a letter. For international mail, a first-class letter of up to one-half ounce costs 80¢ (60¢ to Canada and Mexico); a first-class postcard costs 70¢ (50¢ to Canada and Mexico); and a preprinted postal aerogramme costs 70¢.

Measurements See the chart on the inside front cover of this book for details on converting metric measurements to U.S. equivalents.

Taxes The United States has no value-added tax (VAT). Philadelphia's sales tax is 7% except on clothing, which has no tax, making visits to outlet malls such as Franklin Mills very popular with international tourists. For hotels, Philadelphia tax surcharges are a total of 13%.

Telephone & Fax The telephone system in the United States is run by private corporations, so rates, especially for long-distance service and operator-assisted calls, can vary widely. Generally, hotel surcharges on long-distance and local calls are astronomical, so you're usually better off using a **public pay telephone,** which you'll find clearly marked in most public buildings and private establishments as well as on the street. Convenience stores and gas stations always have them. Many convenience groceries and packaging services sell **prepaid calling cards** in denominations up to $50; these can be the least expensive way to call home. Many public phones at airports now accept American Express, MasterCard, and Visa credit cards. **Local calls** made from public pay phones in most locales cost either 25¢ or 35¢. Pay phones do not accept pennies, and few will take anything larger than a quarter.

You may want to look into leasing a cellphone for your trip.

Most long-distance and international calls can be dialed directly from any phone. **For calls within the United States and to Canada,** dial 1 followed by the area code and the seven-digit number. **For other international calls,** dial 011 followed by the country code, city code, and the telephone number of the person you are calling.

Calls to area codes **800, 888,** and **877** are toll-free. However, calls to numbers in area codes **700** and **900** (chat lines, bulletin boards, "dating" services, and so on) can be very expensive — usually a charge of 95¢ to $3 or more per minute, and they sometimes have minimum charges that can run as high as $15 or more.

For **reversed-charge or collect calls,** and for person-to-person calls, dial 0 (zero, not the letter O) followed by the area code and number you want; an operator will then come on the line, and you should specify that you are calling collect, or person-to-person, or both. If your operator-assisted call is international, ask for the overseas operator.

For **local directory assistance** ("information"), dial 411; for long-distance information, dial 1, then the appropriate area code and ✆ **555-1212.**

Most hotels have **fax machines** available for guest use (be sure to ask about the charge to use one). Many hotel rooms are even wired for guests' fax machines. A less expensive way to send and receive faxes may be at stores such as Mail Boxes Etc., a national chain of packing service shops. (Look in the Yellow Pages directory under "Packing Services.")

There are two kinds of telephone directories in the United States. The so-called **White Pages** list private households and business subscribers in alphabetical order. The inside front cover lists emergency numbers for police, fire, ambulance, the Coast Guard, poison-control center, crime-victims hot line, and so on. The first few pages will tell you how to make long-distance and international calls, complete with country codes and area codes. Government numbers are usually printed on blue paper within the White Pages. Printed on yellow paper, the so-called **Yellow Pages** list all local services, businesses, industries, and houses of worship according to activity with an index at the front or back.

Time The continental United States is divided into **four time zones:** Eastern Standard Time (EST), Central Standard Time (CST), Mountain Standard Time (MST), and Pacific Standard Time (PST). Alaska and Hawaii have their own zones. For example, noon in New York City (EST) is 11am in Chicago (CST), 10am in Denver (MST), 9am in Los Angeles (PST), 8am in Anchorage (AST), and 7am in Honolulu (HST). Philadelphia is in the Eastern Standard Time zone.

Daylight saving time is in effect from 1am on the first Sunday in April to 1am on the last Sunday in October, except in Arizona, Hawaii, part of Indiana, and Puerto Rico. Daylight saving time moves the clock 1 hour ahead of standard time.

Tipping Tips are a very important part of certain workers' salaries, so it's necessary to leave appropriate gratuities. In hotels, tip **bellhops** at least $1 per bag ($2–$3 if you have a lot of luggage) and tip the **chamber staff** $1 to $2 per day (more if you've left a disaster area for him or her to clean up). Tip the **doorman** or **concierge** only if he or she has provided you with some specific service (for example, calling a cab for you or obtaining difficult-to-get theater tickets). Tip the **valet-parking attendant** $1 every time you get your car.

In restaurants, bars, and nightclubs, tip **service staff** 15% to 20% of the check, tip **bartenders** 10% to 15%, tip **checkroom attendants** $1 per garment, and tip **valet-parking attendants** $1 per vehicle. Tip the **doorman** only if he has provided you with some specific service (such as calling a cab for you). Tip **cab drivers** 15% of the fare.

As for other service personnel, tip **cab drivers** 15% of the fare; tip **skycaps** at airports at least $1 per bag ($2–$3 if you have a lot of luggage); and tip **hairdressers** and **barbers** 15% to 20%.

Toilets You won't find public toilets or "restrooms" on the streets in most U.S. cities, but they can be found in hotel lobbies, bars, restaurants, museums, department stores, railway and bus stations, and service stations. In Philadelphia, Independence National Historical Park sights have clean, free restrooms. Within Center City, most hotel lobbies and fast-food restaurants have public restrooms. Outside of town, if possible, avoid the toilets at parks and beaches, which tend to be dirty; some may be unsafe. Restaurants and bars in resorts or heavily visited areas may reserve their restrooms for patrons. Some establishments display a notice indicating this. You can ignore this sign or, better yet, avoid arguments by paying for a drink.

4

Getting to Know Philadelphia

This chapter sets out to answer all your travel questions, furnishing you with the practical information that you'll need to handle any and every experience during your stay in Philadelphia — from figuring out the city layout and transportation to knowing business hours.

1 Orientation

ARRIVING

BY PLANE All flights into and from Philadelphia use **Philadelphia International Airport** (© 215/937-6800; www.phl.org), at the southwest corner of the city. For up-to-the-minute information on airline arrival and departure times and gate assignments, call © **800/PHL-GATE.** With 24 million passengers in 2001, it's one of the country's fastest growing airports. There are flights to more than 100 cities in the United States and more than 1,000 arrivals and departures daily.

The airport is laid out with a central corridor connecting the five basic depots. US Airways, the 'hub' tenant, has already collaborated on a new Terminal F for commuters, and the airport is doubling Terminal A to the west, for international service. Terminal B is the place to catch taxis, buses, and hotel limousines. The areas with the most amenities are between Terminals B and C and Terminals D and E.

Since security concerns increased in 2001, short-term parking is not allowed, so your parking options are garage or economy (long term). Economy parking is available for $7 per day at more distant lots, while garage parking opposite the terminals is $2 for the first 30 minutes, $12 for up to 3 hours, and $16 for 4 to 24 hours.

For medical emergencies at the airport, call © **215/937-3111.**

Getting into Town from the Airport A high-speed rail link with direct service between the airport and Center City runs daily every 30 minutes from 5:30am to 11:25pm. Trains leave the airport at 10 and 40 minutes past the hour; they follow the loop of a raised pedestrian bridge, stop in front of every terminal and are easy to find. Trains to the airport depart from Market East (a Convention Center connection), Suburban Station at 16th Street, and 30th Street Station. The 30-minute trip costs $5.50 for adults; children's fares are $1.50 weekdays and $1 weekends; and the family fare is $16.

A taxi from the airport to Center City takes about 25 minutes and costs a flat rate of $20 plus tip.

If you're interested in airport limousines or shuttles to garages, hotels, or area destinations, fares range from $10 to $16. Try **Deluxe Limo** (© **215/463-8787**) from 6am to 11pm, **Lady Liberty** (© **215/724-8888**) from 5am to midnight, or **Philadelphia Airport Shuttle** (© **215/333-1441**) from 5am to 10pm. **BostonCoach** (© **800/342-7121**) quotes sedan rates of $43 from the airport to a Center City address; $83 to Valley Forge; and $122 to Atlantic City;

the others listed above are $30 to $50 cheaper. Taxi dispatch is available 24 hours a day at the airport (there is a flat rate of $20 to Center City).

All major car-rental operations have desks at the airport and Zone 2 pick-up (a section of the parking area). These include **Alamo** (© 800/327-9633); **Avis** (© 800/331-1212); **Budget** (© 800/527-0700); **Dollar** (© 800/800-4000); **Hertz** (© 215/654-3131); and **National** (© 800/227-7368).

BY TRAIN   Trains arrive at Penn (30th St.) Station in West Philadelphia, just on the other side of the Schuylkill River from Center City, and about 15 blocks from City Hall. Take a taxi or SEPTA (see below) from the station to your hotel.

VISITOR INFORMATION

The newly constructed **Independence Visitor Center,** 6th and Market streets, Philadelphia, PA 19106 (© **800/537-7676,** 215/965-7676, or 215/636-1666; **www.independencevisitorcenter.com**), is one of the very best visitor centers in America. It's extremely convenient, with underground parking just off I-95, and it has rejuvenated Independence Mall one block north of the Liberty Bell. The $38 million facility has a great offering of customer services through volunteers and automated kiosks; five exhibition nooks, a film theater; a cafe; and a gift shop and bookstore. The second floor balconies are great for photo ops of Independence National Park highlights.

The center parcels out free tickets to the major landmarks of Independence National Historical Park such as Independence Hall and the Liberty Bell Pavilion. This service is vital since security concerns have clamped down on who gets in and when. They sell other tickets such as the SEPTA (an extensive network of trolleys, buses, commuter trains, and subways) DayPass ($5.50) and "A Gift of Gardens" pass for 14 regional sites. Plus, you can make any kind of reservations — hotel, restaurant, event — here. Many bus tours, trolley rides, and walking tours conveniently begin at the visitor center.

The center is open daily from 8:30am to 5pm, and until 6pm during the summer. If you're planning in advance, call © **800/537-7676** to get material on all the special seasonal promotions.

CITY LAYOUT

MAIN ARTERIES & STREETS   Unlike Boston, Philadelphia has no colonial cow paths that were turned into streets. If you can count and remember the names of trees (many of the east-west streets sport tree names), you'll know exactly where you are in the Center City grid. For the overview, go to (or pretend you're at) the top of **City Hall,** that over-iced wedding cake in the very center of things, at the intersection of Broad and Market streets. **Broad Street** runs 4 miles south, where the Delaware and Schuylkill flow together, and 8 miles north — all perfectly straight. (Broad has been renamed Avenue of the Arts for 8 blocks just south of City Hall, to highlight the concentration of performing halls.) The other major north-south streets are numbered. Except for a few two-way exceptions, traffic on even-numbered streets heads south and on odd-numbered streets, north. **Front Street** (which would be 1st St.), near the Delaware's edge off to the right, and neighboring **2nd Street** were the major thoroughfares in colonial times. Smaller streets between the numbered streets are named. The major east-west streets in Philadelphia's Center City run from Spring Garden Street in the north down to South Street. You'll spend much of your time between Arch and Pine streets, especially south of Chestnut Street, both for the historical attractions and for the current restaurant and nightlife vibrancy.

The colonial city, now **Independence National Historical Park,** with its reconstructed row houses, grew up along the Delaware River north and south of **Market Street,** extending west to 6th Street by 1776. The 19th century saw the development of the western quadrants of the city (including most museums and cultural centers) and the growth of the suburbs in every direction. The city blocks planned by Pennsylvania founder William Penn included five parks spaced between the two rivers. Four parks have been named for local notables (including George Washington, who headed the federal government here in the 1790s). The fifth supports City Hall. The broad northwest boulevard of Benjamin Franklin Parkway divides the grid, ending in the majestic arms of the Philadelphia Museum of Art in the west. The entire quadrant west and north of City Hall has been the site of intensive development and redevelopment of hotels, office buildings, and apartment houses.

To the west of this, the winding Schuylkill separates Philadelphia from West Philadelphia — if you're looking for an address between 24th Street and about 30th Street in this area, ask which side it's on. **Fairmount Park** lines both sides of the Schuylkill for miles north of the Philadelphia Museum of Art.

Helpful directional signs were posted at every Center City corner in 2000, displaying the name and a color-coded ID of the district you're in as well as listings of nearby destinations.

FINDING AN ADDRESS   Addresses on these streets add 100 for every block away from the axis of Market Street (north-south) or Front Street (east-west): 1534 Chestnut St. is between 15th and 16th streets, and 610 S. 5th St. is between 6 and 7 blocks south of Market.

STREET MAPS   The **Independence Visitor Center,** 6th and Market streets (© **800/537-7676** or 215/636-1666), has a very good street map in its "Official Visitors Guide." You can pick it up at the center and at all hotels.

THE NEIGHBORHOODS IN BRIEF

Philadelphia is more of a collection of neighborhoods than a unified metropolis. Here are short descriptions of those that you're likely to find yourself in.

Chestnut Hill This enclave of suburban gentility, with its "Main Street" flavor, is centered around upper Germantown Avenue, and is the highest point within city limits. It's filled with galleries and boutiques, tearooms, and comfortable restaurants.

Chinatown Nowadays it's largely commercial rather than residential, but there are lots of good restaurants, a growing number of hotels, and cheaper parking only 5 minutes from the Convention Center. And it stays awake forever.

Germantown One of Philadelphia's most ancient settlements, this area was founded by German émigrés, attracted by Penn's religious

tolerance. Outside of its wonderful historic mansions, however, it is not especially attractive now.

Manayunk This neighborhood, 4 miles up the Schuylkill River from Center City, has rocketed to gentility in the last 15 years, with many of the city's hottest boutiques, galleries, and cafe/restaurants on Main Street, overlooking a 19th-century canal adjoining the river. It's a picturesque and vital place for an afternoon stroll, and there's a great farmer's market. Visit it virtually at www.manayunk.com.

Old City In the shadow of the Benjamin Franklin Bridge just north of Independence National Historical Park lies an eclectic blend

Philadelphia Neighborhoods

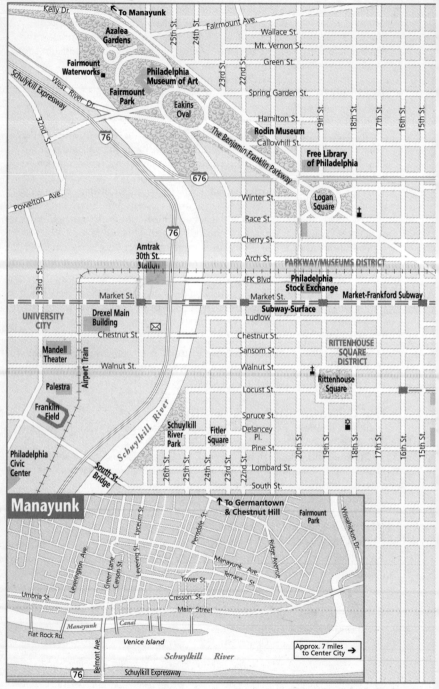

To Manayunk

Kelly Dr.

Azalea Gardens

Fairmount Waterworks

Philadelphia Museum of Art

Fairmount Park

Eakins Oval

Fairmount Ave.

Wallace St.
Mt. Vernon St.
Green St.
Spring Garden St.
Hamilton St.

Rodin Museum

Callowhill St.

Free Library of Philadelphia

The Benjamin Franklin Parkway

Schuylkill Expressway

West River Dr.

32nd St.

Powelton Ave.

33rd St.

Winter St.
Race St.
Cherry St.
Arch St.

Logan Square

PARKWAY/MUSEUMS DISTRICT

Amtrak 30th St. Station

JFK Blvd.

Philadelphia Stock Exchange

Market St.

UNIVERSITY CITY

Drexel Main Building

Chestnut St.

Market St.

Subway-Surface

Market-Frankford Subway

Ludlow

Chestnut St.
Sansom St.
Walnut St.

RITTENHOUSE SQUARE DISTRICT

Mandell Theater

Walnut St.

Palestra

Franklin Field

Locust St.

Rittenhouse Square

Airport Train

Schuylkill River

Schuylkill River Park

Fitler Square

Spruce St.
Delancey Pl.
Pine St.

Philadelphia Civic Center

South St. Bridge

Lombard St.
South St.

19th St., 18th St., 17th St., 16th St., 15th St.

20th St., 19th St., 18th St., 17th St., 16th St., 15th St.

26th St., 25th St., 24th St., 23rd St., 22nd St.

Manayunk

To Germantown & Chestnut Hill

Fairmount Park

Wissahickon Dr.

Levering St.

Lyceum St.

Pensdale St.

Ridge Avenue

Leverington Ave.

Green Lane

Carson St.

Manayunk Ave.

Terrace St.

Tower St.

Cresson St.

Umbria St.

Main Street

Manayunk Canal

Flat Rock Rd.

Belmont Ave.

Venice Island

Schuylkill River

Approx. 7 miles to Center City

Schuylkill Expressway

52

Edgar Allan Poe Nat'l Hist. Site

German Society of Philadelphia

Spring Garden St.

† Church
⊠ Post Office
☼ Synagogue
▬ Subway stop

I-95

Pier 24

13th St.
12th St.

Broad Street Subway

11th St.
10th St.
9th St.
8th St.
7th St.

Broad St.

Hamilton St.
Noble St.

Callowhill St.

To New Jersey →

Vine St.
Vine St.
Vine St.

Painted Bride Art Center

(Delaware Ave.)

676

Benjamin Franklin Bridge

CONVENTION CENTER DISTRICT

Franklin Square

Race St.

Christopher Columbus Blvd.

Pennsylvania Convention Center

CHINATOWN

Cherry St.

Chinese Cultural Center

Franklin St.

U.S. Mint

Cherry St.

Elfreth's Alley

Betsy Ross House

Pier 5

Pier 3

Reading Terminal Market

Chinese Friendship Gate

Arch St.

U.S. Federal Building

OLD CITY CULTURAL DISTRICT

☼

Arden Theater

City Hall

Juniper St.
13th St.
12th St.
11th St.
10th St.

Market St.

St. Stephen's Alley Theater

⊠

The Liberty Bell

The Bourse

2nd St.

Front St.

Penn's Landing

Delaware River

Chestnut St.

Sansom St.
Walnut St.

Thomas Jefferson University

Forrest Theater

WASHINGTON SQUARE DISTRICT

Locust St.

Independence National Park

Washington Square

Tomb of the Unknown Soldier

†

3rd St.

Dock St.

95

Merriam Theater

Spruce St.

Kimmel Performing Arts Center

University of the Arts

Pennsylvania Hospital

SOCIETY HILL

Delancey St.

☼

Pine St.

"Antique Row"

9th St.
8th St.
7th St.
6th St.
5th St.
4th St.

†

Lombard St.

Head House Square

Walkway

Pier 34

Broad Street Subway

SOUTH STREET

South St.

Bainbridge St.

Fleischer Art Memorial

Fitzwater St.

"Fabric Row"

Catharine St.

SOUTH PHILADELPHIA

Passyunk Ave.

Queen St.

Christian St.

QUEEN VILLAGE

Swanson St.

Italian Market

Carpenter St.

Washington Ave.

To Airport ↓

of row houses dating from William Penn's time, 19th-century commercial warehouses, and 20th-century rehabs à la SoHo in New York City. If you're interested in either the very old or the very new, this is the place to spend a few hours. The odd alleyways between the city grid streets here provide nooks for quaint and quiet cafes and shops. The first Friday night of every month is like a giant block party, with all the galleries and stores open until 9pm.

Queen Village On a pleasant day you'll want to walk south from Society Hill along the Delaware or 2nd Street (known as "Two Street" among old Philadelphians). There are lots of small, reasonably priced cafes and bistros here, and pedestrian bridges constructed over I-95 have recently reconnected the area to the waterfront.

Rittenhouse Square This urban park illustrates the elegance, wealth, and culture of pre-skyscraper Philadelphia. From the Rittenhouse Hotel on a sunny day, walk through the square to Walnut Street, which can rival any district in Paris or London for charm and sophistication.

Society Hill This heart of reclaimed 18th-century Philadelphia is loosely defined by Walnut and Lombard streets and Front and 7th streets. Today, it's a fashionable section of the old city, just south of Independence National Historical Park, where you can stroll among restored Federal, colonial, and Georgian homes — even the more contemporary architecture is interesting and immaculately maintained.

South Philadelphia It's Rocky Balboa and more. Three hundred years of immigration have made South Philadelphia the city's most colorful and ethnically diverse neighborhood, although the overwhelming feel is distinctly Italian (think 1910s Calabria). I love strolling the Italian Market at 9th and Christian and heading south, snacking all along the way until dinner.

South Street Located below Society Hill and above Queen Village, South Street was the city limit in William Penn's day. The 1960s saw bohemian artists reclaiming this street in the name of peace and love; newer spirits, just as young and somewhat cockier, have replaced the previous hipsters, and the place is undeniably hopping day or night. Look for good restaurants and bars, bookstores, hoagie shops, contemporary handcrafted furniture stores, natural-food stores, European-style cafes, and art galleries. The neighborhood has an appropriately retro website at www.south-street.com.

University City West Philadelphia was farmland until the University of Pennsylvania moved here from 9th and Chestnut streets in the 1870s. Wander through the main campus for the architecture and the cultural attractions. The original college quadrangle, built in 1895, was modeled on Oxford and Cambridge, with the added touch of Dutch gables. Penn is pumping in development and enticing major cinemas, retail, and bookstores to gentrify the area, following a long slump.

2 Getting Around

BY PUBLIC TRANSPORTATION

SEPTA (Southeastern Pennsylvania Transportation Authority) operates a complicated and extensive network of trolleys, buses, commuter trains, and subways. Ridership has increased since Center City has encouraged less auto traffic on

---

(*Tips* **Ride Cheap**

A $5.50 DayPass is good for all buses, subways, and one ride on the Airport loop. A weekly TransPass, good from Monday to the next Sunday, is $18.75.

---

historic streets, so it's crowded but safe. Busy Suburban Station, in the heart of Center City at 16th Street and JKF Boulevard, is streamlining through the end of 2004 but remains open.

Fares for any SEPTA route are $2 cash or $1.30 for tokens purchased before you ride (at stations, Rite Aid stores, and machines in various city concourses). Transfers are 60¢, and exact change is required. Seniors pay only during rush hours, and passengers with disabilities pay half-fare during off-peak hours. Certain buses and trolleys run 24 hours a day.

If you have questions about how to reach a specific destination, call SEPTA at ℃ **215/580-7800** between 6am and midnight — but expect to wait — or hit the website www.septa.org.

BY SUBWAY-SURFACE LINE   This "local" connects City Hall and 30th Street Station, stopping at 19th and 22nd streets along the way. West of the Amtrak station it branches out, moving aboveground beyond U. Penn to the north and south.

BY RAPID TRANSIT   In Center City, these fast cars speed under Broad Street and Market Street, intersecting under City Hall. The Broad Street line now connects directly to Pattison Avenue and Philadelphia sporting events to the south. The Market Street line stops at the 2nd, 5th, 8th, 11th, 13th (Convention Center), 15th, and 30th Street stations and stretches to the west and northeast. Both lines run all night, but exercise caution during late-hour use.

BY PATCO   This commuter rail line (℃ **215/922-4600**) begins at Walnut and Locust streets around Broad Street, connects with rapid transit at 8th and Market, and crosses the Ben Franklin Bridge to Camden. To get to the aquarium, transfer at Broadway in Camden to the New Jersey Transit's Aqualink Shuttle. Transfers connect to the Jersey shore from Lindenwold.

BY BUS   Those purple vans with the turquoise wings go pretty much everywhere tourists want to go. Every 10 minutes between 10am and midnight in summer (until 6pm Sept–May) the **PHLASH Bus** service (℃ **215/474-5274**) links Independence Park sites, the Delaware waterfront, the Convention Center, Rittenhouse Square shopping, and the cultural institution at Logan Circle. The total loop takes 50 minutes and makes 30 stops. A one-time pass is $2, but get the all-day unlimited ride-pass for $4 per person or $10 per family. Passes are not transferable to SEPTA. Children under 6 ride free, as do seniors outside of 4:30 to 5:30pm.

Route 76, the **Ben FrankLine,** connects Society Hill at 3rd and Chestnut streets to the Parkway all the way to the Museum of Art and the zoo. It operates every 10 minutes weekdays, every 20 minutes weekends. The first trip from 3rd Street is at 9am, and the last pickup at the Museum of Art is at 6:11pm.

For a straight crosstown route, you'll often find yourself on Chestnut Street, and bus no. 42 swoops along Chestnut from West Philadelphia to 2nd at all hours. Several bus routes serve Market Street; the **SPREE** route connects Penn's Landing and 18th Street, going up Market and down Walnut streets. Route 32 goes up Broad Street and the Parkway and through Fairmount Park to Andorra; the full trip is 15 miles.

BY TROLLEY There are no more "true" city trolleys such as you would find in Boston or San Francisco. A privately operated **Penn's Landing Trolley** chugs along Christopher Columbus Boulevard (formerly Delaware Ave.) between the Benjamin Franklin Bridge and Fitzwater Street; you can board at Dock Street or Spruce Street. The fare is $1.50 for adults, 75¢ for children, and the trolley runs Thursday through Sunday from 11am to dusk in the summer.

Buses that are replicas of 1930s open-air trolleys are operated by **American Trolley Tours** (© 215/333-2119). Guides point out all the highlights along the way. Tour prices range from $7.50 to $16, depending on tour length and family size. Pickup spots include Liberty Bell Pavilion, Independence Visitor Center, and the Franklin Institute. This is a single ride, without any hopping on or off.

BY TRAIN The Philadelphia area is served by one of the best commuter-rail networks in America. Chestnut Hill, a wealthy enclave of fine shops and restaurants, can be reached from both Penn Center (Suburban) Station at 16th Street and John F. Kennedy Boulevard and Reading Terminal at 12th and Market streets; the two are now connected by the new rail link. What in the suburbs would interest you? Merion is home to the great Barnes Foundation art collection and the Buten Museum of Wedgwood. Bryn Mawr, Haverford, Swarthmore, and Villanova are sites of noted colleges. Devon hosts a great horse and country fair. One-way fares for all destinations are less than $7, and you can buy tickets at station counters or vending machines.

BY CAR

Be forewarned that *all streets are one way* — except for lower Market Street, the Parkway, Vine Street, and Broad Street. The Convention and Visitors Bureau at the foot of the Parkway offers a Center City traffic map. Traffic around City Hall runs counterclockwise, but traffic lights seem to follow a logic of their own.

Since Philadelphia is so walkable, it's easier to leave your car while you explore. Many hotels offer free or reduced-rate parking to registered guests.

If you need emergency car repair, try **Center City Sunoco,** 1135 Vine St. (© 215/928-9574), or **Mina Motors,** Broad and Fitzwater streets (© 215/735-2749), for same-day service. **Keystone AAA** is at 2040 Market St. (© 215/864-5000).

RENTALS Philadelphia has no shortage of rental cars and very good rates as a consequence. For example, you can pick up a weekend sedan from **Avis** (© 800/331-1212) for $45 per day, with unlimited mileage, at one of their lots: 2000 Arch St. (© 215/563-8976), 30th Street Station (© 215/386-6426), or near Independence Hall at 37 S. 2nd St. (© 215/928-1082). Avis and all other major renters maintain offices at the airport. These include **Alamo** (© 800/327-9633); **Budget** (© 800/527-0700, 215/492-9447 at the airport, or 215/492-9400 at 21st and Market); **Dollar** (© 800/800-4000, or 215/365-2700 at the airport); and **Hertz** (© 800/654-3131 for all locations). Also check smaller local companies and car dealers like **Chapman Ford** (© 215/698-7000).

On top of the standard rental prices, other optional charges apply to most car rentals, including liability insurance (if you harm others in an accident), personal accident insurance (if you harm yourself or your passengers), and personal effects insurance (if your luggage is stolen from your car). If your own insurance doesn't cover you for rentals, you should consider the additional coverages. But weigh the likelihood of getting into an accident or losing your luggage against the cost of these coverages (as much as $20 per day combined), which can significantly add to the price of your rental.

PARKING   Call the **Philadelphia Parking Authority** (© 215/683-9600) for current information. It's the expected mix of metered, free limited on-street, and garage parking. Parking tickets are $15 and up.

Garage rates are fairly uniform: Outside of hotels, no place exceeds $25 per day, with typical charges of $5 per hour and $12 for an evening out.

Parking can be found for **Independence Mall and Park** underneath the new Visitor Center between 5th and 6th streets and Market and Arch streets; 125 S. 2nd St. (Sansom St. is the cross street); Spruce Street between 5th and 6th streets (private lot); and Head House Square, 2nd and Lombard streets (city meters). **Convention Center Area** parking includes Kinney Chinatown at 11th and Race streets (private garage); Kinney underneath the Gallery II mall at 11th and Arch streets; the Autopark beside the Gallery mall at 10th and Filbert streets; or the garage underneath the adjoining Marriott at Arch and 13th streets. **City Hall Area** parking is underneath Lord & Taylor (formerly Wanamaker's), between Market and Chestnut streets at 13th Street; a private garage adjoining the Doubletree Hotel at Broad and Spruce streets; and Kennedy Plaza, 15th Street and John F. Kennedy Boulevard (underground city garage; enter on Arch, 1 block north of the plaza).

BY TAXI

Fares are currently $1.80 for the first ½ mile and 30¢ for each additional ½ mile or minute of the motor running. Tips are expected, usually 15% of the fare.

If you need to call for a cab while in the city, the three largest outfits are **Olde City Taxi** (© 215/338-0838), **United Cab** (© 215/291-0203), and **Quaker City** (© 215/728-8000).

ⓔ *FAST FACTS:* Philadelphia

American Express There are Amex offices at 16th Street and John F. Kennedy Boulevard (© 215/587-2342) and at the airport (© 215/492-4200).

Area Code Philadelphia's telephone area code is **215.** Bucks County and half of Montgomery County also use **215,** but the Brandywine Valley area of Delaware, Chester, and half of Montgomery have switched to **610.** Lancaster County and the Pennsylvania Dutch region use area code **717.**

Babysitters Check with your hotel, or contact Rocking Horse Child Care Center at the Curtis Center, Walnut and 6th streets (© 215/592-8257); rates are $9 per hour for children under 2, $8 per hour for ages 3 to 6. Call-A-Granni, 1133 E. Barringer St. (© 215/924-8723), is comparable.

Business Hours Banks are generally open Monday through Thursday from 10am to 3pm, Friday until 6pm, with some also open on Saturday from 9am to noon. Most bars and restaurants serve food until 10 or 10:30pm (some Chinatown places stay open until 3am), and social bars are open Friday and Saturday until 1 or 2am. Offices are open Monday through Friday from 9am to 5pm. Stores are open daily from 9am to 5pm, and most Center City locations keep the doors open later on Wednesday evening. Old City, South Street, the Delaware waterfront, and Head House Square are the most active late-night districts. Some SEPTA routes run all night, but the frequency of buses and trolleys drops dramatically after 6pm.

Business Services Most hotels have onsite business facilities, but for quick professional production of materials, try Printers Place near the Convention Center at 1310 Walnut St. (℃ **215/546-6562**), or the various 24-hour Kinko's, whose downtown locations include 1201 Market St. (℃ **215/923-2520**) at the Marriott Convention Center, and 2001 Market St. (℃ **215/561-5170**). For shipping, the local UPS is at ℃ **215/895-8984.**

Car Rentals See "Getting Around," earlier in this chapter.

Dentist Call the **Philadelphia County Dental Society** ℃ **215/925-6050** in a dental emergency.

Doctor Call the Philadelphia County Medical Society (℃ **215/563-5343**). You can always dial ℃ **911** in an emergency. Every hospital in town has an emergency room.

Embassies & Consulates See chapter 3.

Emergencies In an extreme emergency, dial ℃ **911.** In case of accidental poisoning, call ℃ **215/386-2100.** For police, call ℃ **215/231-3131;** for fire and rescue, call ℃ **215/922-6000.** Ambulance and emergency transportation can be summoned through Care & Emergency (℃ **215/877-6300**), or SEPTA Paratransit (℃ **215/574-2780**). For 24-hour pet emergencies, call the referral office of the University of Pennsylvania Veterinary Hospital at ℃ **215/898-4685.**

Hospitals Medical care in Philadelphia is excellent. Major hospitals include Children's Hospital, 34th Street and Civic Center Boulevard (℃ **215/590-1000**); Graduate Hospital, 1800 Lombard St. (℃ **215/893-2000**); Hahnemann University Hospital, Broad and Vine streets (℃ **215/762-7000**); University of Pennsylvania Hospital, 3400 Spruce St. (℃ **215/662-4000**); Pennsylvania Hospital, 8th and Spruce streets (℃ **215/829-3000**); and Thomas Jefferson, 11th and Walnut streets (℃ **215/955-6000**).

Information See "Visitor Information," earlier in this chapter.

Liquor Laws The legal drinking age is 21, and closing time for bars (as opposed to private clubs) is 2am, 7 days a week. You can buy wine and spirits only in state stores, which are usually open Monday through Wednesday from 9am to 5pm and Thursday through Saturday from 9am to 9pm. Beer, champagne, and wine coolers are available at most supermarkets and delis. See chapter 9 for the best state store locations.

Lost Property If you lose something on a SEPTA train or subway, try the stationmaster's office in Suburban Station (℃ **215/580-7800**).

Newspapers & Magazines Philadelphia has two main print journals, both now owned by the same firm. You'll want to check out the Friday "Weekend" supplement of the *Inquirer* for listings and prices of entertainment as well as special events and tours. The *Daily News* has more local news. Free tabloid weeklies with surprisingly good articles and listings include *City Paper* and *Philadelphia Weekly;* you'll find them at record and bookstores and in street-corner boxes. For the most complete selection of journals and newspapers, try **Avril 50**, 3406 Sansom St. (✆ **215/222-6108**), in University City. Center City equivalents are the archrivals **Barnes & Noble** at 1805 Walnut St. (✆ **215/656-0716**), and **Borders** at 1727 Walnut St. (✆ **215/568-7400**), both near Rittenhouse Square.

Pharmacies There's a 24-hour **CVS** at 1826 Chestnut St., corner of 19th St. (✆ **215/972-0909**), and at 10th and Reed streets (✆ **215/465-2130**) in South Philadelphia. For northeast locations, try the 24-hour **Pathmark** at City Line and Monument avenues (✆ **215/879-1322**). The **Medical Tower Pharmacy,** 255 S. 17th St. (✆ **215/545-3525**), is open until 9pm Monday through Friday and until 6pm on Saturday. During regular hours near Independence Hall, try **Green Drugs,** 5th and South streets (✆ **215/922-7441**).

Police The emergency telephone number is ✆ **911.**

Post Office The main post office at 2970 Market St. (✆ **215/596-5577**), just across the Schuylkill and next to 30th Street station, is always open; you can reach its 24-hour window at ✆ **215/895-8989.** The post office on the subway concourse at 2 Penn Center, 15th Street and John F. Kennedy Boulevard, is open Monday through Friday from 7am to 6pm, Saturday from 9am to noon. You can also go to the post office Ben Franklin used, at 316 Market St.

Radio All news, WKYW (1060 AM); album-oriented rock, WMMR (93.3 FM); classic rock, WYSP (94.1 FM) and WMGK (102.9 FM); oldies, WOGL (98.1 FM); soft rock, WIOQ (102.1 FM); country, WCZN (1590 AM) and WXTU (92.5 FM); ethnic urban orientation, WUSL (98.9 FM); R&B and classic soul, WDAS (1480 AM); jazz, WJJZ (106.1 FM); and National Public Radio, WHYY (91.0 FM) and WXPN (88.5 FM).

Restrooms Public restrooms can be found at 30th Street Station; the Independence National Historical Park Visitors Center; and at major shopping complexes such as Liberty Place, the Bourse, the Gallery, and Downstairs at the Bellevue. You can usually use hotel lobby and restaurant facilities.

Safety See "The Safe Traveler" on p. 22.

Taxes Lodging charges add 13% onto room rates, 7% for state tax and 6% city surcharge. There is a 7% tax on restaurant meals and on general sales. Clothing is tax-free.

Taxis See "Getting Around," earlier in this chapter.

Time Zone Philadelphia is in the Eastern Time zone — Eastern Standard Time (EST) or eastern daylight time, depending on the time of year, making it the same as New York and 3 hours ahead of the West Coast.

Transit Information To find out how to reach a specific destination, call SEPTA headquarters at ✆ **215/574-7800** — but expect to wait — or visit www.septa.org.

Weather Call ✆ **215/936-1212** for weather information.

5

Where to Stay

A century ago, Philadelphia was full of inns, hostelries, and European-style hotels for all pocketbooks and tastes. Today, after decades of frankly disappointing choices, Philadelphia is again paying serious attention to the comfort of its guests, and this renewed interest shows.

Philadelphia geared up for the Republican National Convention in 2000, increasing Center City hotel rooms from 6,000 to 11,000 and airport rooms to 4,000 in order to accommodate the 55,000 delegates and press.

But since 2000, demand hasn't kept pace — and that's good news for you. Occupancy rates in 2001 were 60%, and the average double rate was $131, down from $142 in 2000. At press time, 2002 faces another 10% decline. So discounts and promotions, especially at luxury and near luxury hotels, abound. Despite the new enhancements to Independence National Historical Park, the abundance of empty beds is likely to continue in 2003 and 2004, as the current recession limits convention business.

So how to approach the choices? Concentrate on the great weekend packages around town, particularly near the airport, land of $90 to $120 specials. Find several hotels that look appealing, call their toll-free numbers, check out their websites, or use the websites of the many travel discounters to find out about package deals. Many hotels also advertise in the travel sections of major newspapers. Ask about senior discounts, or holiday, family, or all-inclusive packages with meals or sightseeing tours. No matter where you decide to stay, *always ask for the lowest-priced package available.* Remember that reservation agents won't necessarily volunteer the cheapest rates — you might have to insist. And check out the increased bed-and-breakfast and smaller inn listings for a cheaper, unique alternative. Ask about hotel and special admissions packages offered through coordinated city tourism (☎ **800/537-7676**).

Geographically, look to hotels in the Rittenhouse Square area for larger, more individualized pre-World War II spaces. Other large hotels in town serve corporate headquarters in the northwest quadrant between City Hall and the Philadelphia Museum of Art. Medium-size hotels are popping up in historic Society Hill, in Chinatown, and on residential blocks. Business amenities such as Internet access ports, voice mail, and functional desks have become standard in all accommodations.

There are an additional 9,000 hotel beds within a 20-mile circumference outside of town. These offerings include a full complement of increasingly good airport hotels, only 20 minutes away. Two fine hotels sit atop a bluff near I-76 that overlooks the downtown skyline. Roosevelt Boulevard hides some smaller properties, about 20 minutes out of town.

Outside the city, you can find plenty of lovely old inns, such as Evermay-on-the-Delaware in Bucks County — see chapter 11 for listings of inns in the surrounding areas. The **Independence**

Visitor Center, 6th and Market streets, Philadelphia, PA 19106 (② **800/ 537-7676**), can help with any accommodations questions.

RATES Unless otherwise specified, all prices quoted are for double occupancy and all rooms have private bathrooms and phones. You can count on a state tax of 7%, plus a city surcharge of 6%. Remember that the prices listed here are "rack rates" — the room rate charged without any discount — and you can usually do better. Be sure to ask about parking and/or arrangements for children.

B&B AGENCIES The region has more than 250 bed-and-breakfasts, each as charming and/or eccentric as its owner. One good agency to contact is **A Bed & Breakfast Connection/ Bed & Breakfast of Philadelphia,** Box 21, Devon, PA 19333 (② **800/ 448-3619** or 610/687-3565; fax 610/ 995-9524; www.bnbphiladelphia. com). This reservation service represents more than 100 personally inspected accommodations in Philadelphia, Valley Forge, the Brandywine Valley, and in Lancaster, Montgomery, and Bucks counties. The agency has assembled a group of interesting, warm hosts, including linguists, gourmet cooks, and therapists. Philadelphia B&B accommodations include a contemporary loft with a spectacular view of the Delaware River, a mid-18th-century inn, a Victorian home with a magnificent 3-story open staircase, and a town house tucked in an alley seconds from Rittenhouse Square. In greener pastures, you can

pick from the second oldest house in Pennsylvania, a former stagecoach stop, or a converted carriage house complete with pool.

Prices range from $50 to $225 for a couple. Many accommodations at lower prices have shared bathrooms. Children are a point to discuss when booking since they are sometimes not welcome under a certain age and sometimes are especially welcome. The B&B agency listed above will select a compatible lodging for you or send you its free brochure. American Express, Visa, and MasterCard are accepted; phone reservations can be made Monday through Friday from 9am to 6pm, and Saturday from 9am to 1pm.

Janice Archbold at **Guesthouses,** Box 2137, West Chester, PA 19380 (② **610/692-4575;** fax 610/692-4451), has more than 200 host situations lined up, not only in Philadelphia but also throughout the mid-Atlantic region. Most buildings are architecturally or historically significant, and rates average $80 and up. Monthly rentals are also available.

The **Association of Bed and Breakfasts in Philadelphia, Valley Forge, and Brandywine,** P.O. Box 562, Valley Forge, PA 19481 (② **800/ 344-0123,** or 215/783-7838 for reservations 9am–9pm daily; fax 610/783-7783), is a no-fee reservation service with 600 rooms in more than 130 town-and-country choices, from Main Line to Bucks County, Lancaster County, and West Chester. Singles start at $40 per night, and doubles at $45.

1 Historic Area

VERY EXPENSIVE

Hyatt Regency Philadelphia at Penn's Landing ✦ The newest (Dec 2000) major hotel in town stands alone on the Delaware River waterfront, easily accessible from I-95. With its solid Deco-style angles and boxes, it's impossible to miss. It seems to be waiting for more Penn's Landing neighbors to be built. Walkways over the highway at Walnut and Dock streets mean 5 easy colonial

Philadelphia Accommodations

Alexander Inn **19**
Bank Street Hotel **24**
Best Western
   Independence Park Inn **23**
Buttonwood Square Hotel **1**
Comfort Inn
   Downtown/Historic Area **27**
Courtyard by Marriott **6**
Crowne Plaza
   Philadelphia Center City **11**

Doubletree Hotel Philadelphia **17**
Embassy Suites Center City **5**
Four Seasons Hotel **4**
Hawthorn Suites Philadelphia
   at the Convention Center **2**
Holiday Inn—Independence Mall **26**
Hyatt Regency Philadelphia
   at Penn's Landing **28**
The Latham **13**

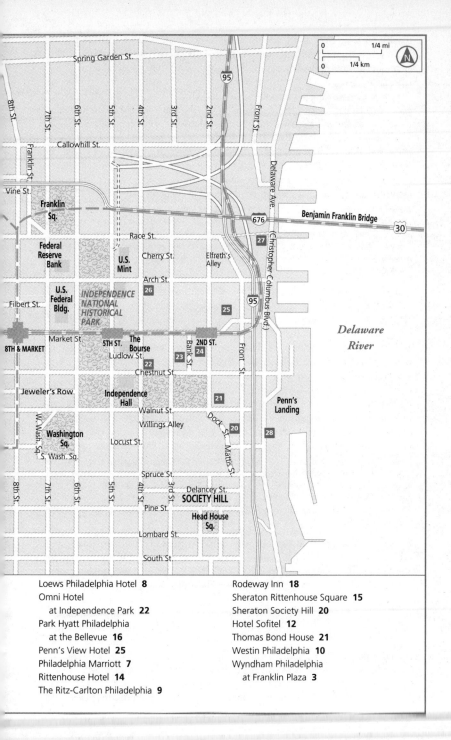

Loews Philadelphia Hotel **8**
Omni Hotel
   at Independence Park **22**
Park Hyatt Philadelphia
   at the Bellevue **16**
Penn's View Hotel **25**
Philadelphia Marriott **7**
Rittenhouse Hotel **14**
The Ritz-Carlton Philadelphia **9**

Rodeway Inn **18**
Sheraton Rittenhouse Square **15**
Sheraton Society Hill **20**
Hotel Sofitel **12**
Thomas Bond House **21**
Westin Philadelphia **10**
Wyndham Philadelphia
   at Franklin Plaza **3**

blocks separate you from the historic sights. The well-lit, marble-floored lobby — not your expected, run-of-the-mill Hyatt atrium — features a sofa encircling an enormous flower urn, flanked by warm cherry walls and swoops of fabrics; check-in is tucked near the elevator banks. The guest rooms continue the Art Deco theme, with patterns in browns and cherry furniture. Rooms have stupendous views of the riverfront or city. I've heard comments that the room maintenance is shaky, and also that the I-95 noise does percolate up, so choose a river view room if quiet is important to you. Bathrooms are marbled and swanky. Self-parking can be tedious here, with a small garage elevator and long waits for it, so go with the valets. Keating's River Grill (Dan Keating owns the site, which Hyatt's manages) can seat 200 guests indoors and 75 outdoors on an elegant plaza featuring artist-commissioned wrought iron rails and overlooking the Delaware River.

201 S. Columbus Blvd., Philadelphia, PA 19106. © **800/228-3360** or 215/928-1234. Fax 215/521-6543. www.hyatt.com. 350 units. $185 double. Weekend rates available. Children 18 and under stay free in parent's room. AE, DC, MC, V. Valet parking $19 per day, self-parking $15 per day. Bus: 21, 76. **Amenities:** Restaurant; 2 lounges; glass-enclosed indoor lap pool (no lifeguard); large health club; sauna; concierge; great meeting facilities; 24-hr. room service; laundry service. *In room:* A/C, TV w/pay movies, dataport, minibar, coffeemaker, hair dryer, iron.

Omni Hotel at Independence Park This small, polished hotel, opened in 1990, has a terrific location in the middle of Independence National Historical Park. All rooms have Independence Park views and are newly renovated, and horse-drawn carriages clip-clop past the valet parking drop-off and elegant glass-and-steel canopy. The lobby is classic, with current newspapers, huge vases of flowers, and a bar featuring a piano or jazz trio and dancing nightly. Every room is cheery, with plants and original pastels of city views. The staff here is noteworthy for its quality and its knowledge of the park. The hotel's Azalea is a fine restaurant where Adam Sturm continues his imaginative treatments of American regional dishes, with tasting menus as an option. The restaurant is open for breakfast, lunch, brunch, and dinner. Hearty (not English) afternoon tea is served in the lobby lounge. A Ritz five-movie theater is tucked into the back corner.

4th and Chestnut sts., Philadelphia, PA 19106 (3 blocks south of Ben Franklin Bridge [Chestnut St. runs one way east, so approach from 6th St.]). © **800/843-6664** or 215/925-0000. Fax 215/931-1263. www.omni hotels.com. 150 units. $179–$209 double; $575–$675 suite. Weekend rates available. Children stay free in parent's room. AE, DC, DISC, MC, V. Self-parking $19, valet parking $23. Bus: PHLASH, 21, 42, 76. **Amenities:** Restaurant; lounge; indoor lap pool; exercise area with Stairmasters; Jacuzzi; sauna; concierge; 24-hr. room service. *In room:* A/C, TV/VCR, 2 dataports, voice mail, minibar, hair dryer, iron.

Sheraton Society Hill (Kids) Located 3 blocks from Head House Square and 4 blocks from Independence Hall, the 1986 Sheraton Society Hill sits among the tree-lined cobblestone streets of this historic district. Set on a triangular 2½-acre site between Dock and South Front streets, the building was designed in keeping with the area's Georgian architecture and Flemish Bond brickwork. Its skylit, four-story atrium is entered via a circular courtyard with a splashing fountain.

The guest rooms are on the long low second, third, and fourth floors (the only Delaware River views are from the fourth floor). Rooms are a bit smaller than you'd expect (as are the bathrooms); half have one king-size bed, and the others have two double beds. All rooms were renovated in winter 1998–99 with top-quality Drexel Heritage mahogany; they have four lamps, two-post headboards, an upholstered love seat and chair, and glass-and-brass coffee tables. In each bathroom, dark marble tops the vanity, and Martex bathrobes are provided. The decor is rich and patterned, with American art prints on the walls.

> ### ⸤*Tips*⸣ Smoke Gets in Your Eyes
>
> Accommodations reserved for nonsmokers — often in blocks as large as several floors — are so common that we no longer single out hotels that offer them. However, nonsmokers should not assume that they'll get a smoke-free room without specifically requesting one, except at the totally smoke-free Sheraton Rittenhouse Square. As smokers are squeezed into fewer and fewer rooms, the ones they are allowed to use become saturated with the smell of smoke, even in hotels that are otherwise antiseptic. Be sure to stress your need for a smoke-free room to avoid this disagreeable situation.

On Dock St. at 2nd and Walnut sts., Philadelphia, PA 19106. ℰ **800/325-3535** or 215/238-6000. Fax 215/238-6652. www.sheraton.com/societyhill. 365 units. $209–$310 double, depending on view; $350–$650 suite. Weekend rates available. Children 17 and under stay free in parent's room. AE, DC, MC, V. Valet parking $23 per day, self-parking $19 per day. Bus: PHLASH, 21, 42, 76. **Amenities:** Restaurant; lounge; indoor pool (daily 6am–10pm); small health club with trainers; Jacuzzi; sauna; concierge; free weekday shuttle van to Center City; superior meeting facilities; 24-hr. room service; laundry service. *In room:* A/C, TV, dataport, minibar.

EXPENSIVE

Holiday Inn Independence Mall This eight-floor Holiday Inn, set back from the street, is absolutely the closest you can sleep to the Liberty Bell — just turn the corner and you're at the pavilion that houses it. The continued renovation of the bedrooms and public spaces and the addition of dataports, voice mail, and a concierge have given it a "superior" rating within the Holiday Inn organization. Rooms are standard size and decor.

4th and Arch sts., Philadelphia, PA 19106. ℰ **800/843-2355** or 215/923-8660. Fax 215/829-1796. 364 units. $160 standard with double or king bed. Excellent weekend rates available. Extra person $10 (up to 5 in a room). Children 18 and under stay free in parent's room; children 12 and under eat free. AE, DC, MC, V. Parking $10 per day. Bus: PHLASH, 76. **Amenities:** 2 restaurants; rooftop outdoor pool; children's programs in the summer; game room; concierge and room service 6am–midnight; laundry room. *In room:* A/C, TV, dataport, voice mail, coffeemaker.

Penn's View Hotel ★★ ⸤*Finds*⸣ Tucked behind the Market Street ramp to I-95 in a renovated 1856 hardware store, this small, exquisite inn exudes European flair — when you enter you'll feel like you're in a private club. It was developed by the Sena family, which started La Famiglia restaurant 150 yards south (see chapter 6 for details), and has grown a small neighborhood empire. The decor is floral and rich. The main concern is traffic noise, but the rooms are well insulated and contain large framed mirrors, armoires, and efficient bathroom fixtures. The ceilings have been dropped for modern heat and air-conditioning, and you'll find Jacuzzis and fireplaces in 12 of the rooms. A third bed can be wheeled into your room for $15. Ristorante Panorama offers excellent contemporary Italian cuisine at moderate prices. Next to the restaurant is Il Bar, a world-class wine bar that offers 120 different wines by the glass.

Front and Market sts., Philadelphia, PA 19106. ℰ **800/331-7634** or 215/922-7600. Fax 215/922-7642. www.pennsviewhotel.com. 52 units. $165 double. Weekend rates available; $275 package includes 2 nights, champagne upon arrival, and $70 Panorama restaurant voucher. Rates include deluxe continental breakfast. Guarantee requested on reservation. AE, MC, V. Bus: PHLASH, 21, 76. Parking $16 at adjacent lot. **Amenities:** Restaurant; wine bar. *In room:* A/C, TV, no phone.

MODERATE

Best Western Independence Park Inn ✦ This top choice for bed-and-breakfast-style lodging has a great location, 2 blocks from Independence Hall. Now a Best Western franchise, the inn is housed in a handsome 1856 former dry-goods store with renovated rooms and a renovated exterior.

The guest rooms, on eight floors, are normal size, but the ceilings are nice and high. The bathrooms have big beveled mirrors, dropped ceilings, and hair dryers. Although all the windows are triple casement and double-glazed, specify an interior room if you're sensitive to noise, since some rooms face the traffic on Chestnut Street. A third bed can be wheeled into your room for a child at no additional charge. The hotel serves a very passable continental breakfast with Belgian waffles in a glass-enclosed garden courtyard, with a complimentary afternoon tea.

235 Chestnut St., Philadelphia, PA 19106. © **800/624-2988** or 215/922-4443. Fax 215/922-4487. www.independenceparkhotel.com. 36 units. $169 double. Rates include breakfast and afternoon tea. Children 12 and under stay free in parent's room; 15% AAA discount. AE, DC, DISC, MC, V. Parking $10.50 at nearby enclosed garage. Bus: PHLASH, 21, 42. Pets accepted. **Amenities:** Special discount coupons to nearby restaurants and a nearby health club ($10) are available. *In room:* A/C, TV, hair dryer.

Comfort Inn Downtown/Historic Area Comfort Inn at Penn's Landing is the area's only moderately-priced waterfront hotel (often offering specials from $69–$79), in a corner of the Old City between I-95 and the Delaware River. It tends to attract a lot of student or senior groups. The rooms are past their prime and service staff is not tops, so be forewarned that you might receive sketchy treatment. A courtesy shuttle van to Center City stops here, and the crosstown subway line is 2 blocks away. Comfort Inn has been built to airport-area noise specifications, with insulated windows and other features to lessen the din of traffic. The eastern views of the river from the upper floors are stupendous. A complimentary continental breakfast is served in the cocktail lounge. There's a coin laundry on the second floor, and half the rooms are designated for non-smokers. The fitness room stocks weights and has cardio-fitness machines.

100 N. Columbus Blvd., Philadelphia, PA 19106 (3 blocks from the northbound ramp off the expressway). © **800/228-5150** or 215/627-7900. Fax 215/238-0809. www.comfortinnphila.com. 185 units. $109–$119 double. Rates include continental breakfast. Children 18 and under stay free in parent's room. Ask about discounts for AAA members. AE, DC, DISC, MC, V. Parking $14 (unlimited in-and-out) in adjacent lot. SEPTA: 2nd Street. Bus: PHLASH, 42, 76. **Amenities:** Golf course nearby; exercise room. *In room:* A/C, TV.

Thomas Bond House *Finds* This 1769 Georgian row house sits almost directly across from the back of Independence Park and is owned by the federal government, which kept the shell and gutted the interior. The proprietors, who hail from North Carolina, have turned the guest rooms into cheerful, comfortable, colonial-style accommodations, renovated completely in 2002. The entrance is decorated with map illustrations and secretary desks. The charming parlor has pink sofas and a replica Chippendale double chair, while the breakfast room has four tables for four. All rooms are individually decorated and feature private bathrooms and period furnishings. Fresh-baked cookies are put out each evening for bedtime snacking. The hotel is named for its first occupant, the doctor who co-founded Pennsylvania Hospital with Benjamin Franklin.

129 S. 2nd St., Philadelphia, PA 19106. © **800/845-2663** or 215/923-8523. Fax 215/923-8504. 12 units. $105–$175 double; $175 suite. Rates include breakfast and afternoon wine and cheese. AE, MC, V. Parking $15 at adjacent lot. Bus: PHLASH, 21, 42. Children over 10 welcome. **Amenities:** Exercise room; limited business services and conference room. *In room:* A/C, TV, hair dryer.

2 Center City

VERY EXPENSIVE

Four Seasons Hotel ★★★ *Kids* Five diamonds from AAA, one of the top 20 U.S. hotels in *Condé Nast Traveler,* Best Hotel in Zagat's Philadelphia 2001 . . . the Four Seasons has no shortage of excellence awards. Its luxury is refined and understated. Built in 1983, the Four Seasons is an eight-story curlicue on Logan Square. The complex also contains two corporate skyscrapers, separated by a fountain and landscaped courtyard that opens as a cafe in summer. The hotel has landscaped the garden of the Parkway's Logan Circle to the north as well.

As you're waved into the porte-cochere on 18th Street, your first view is of enormous masses of flowers, with stepped-stone levels, water, and honeyed woods stretching far into the distance. The lounge and promenade serve as foyers to the dining and meeting facilities and are paneled in a rare white mahogany. The guest rooms mix Federal period furniture with richer, more Victorian color schemes. There is a very direct American elegance in each room: The desk, settee, armoire, and wing chair/ottoman combinations are top-quality Henredon and in-room business and tech capabilities are tops. All the rooms have windows or private verandas boasting marvelous views of Logan Circle or the interior courtyard.

The Four Seasons restaurants regularly collect raves from local reviewers. The Fountain Restaurant, under newly promoted Martin Hamann, is neck-and-neck with Le Bec-Fin as the city's top classic restaurant, usually getting the nod for unstuffy service and a fabulous Sunday brunch. Natural light streams over 150 wide armchair seats and tapestries, fresh flowers, and walnut paneling. The Swann Lounge, closer to the lobby corridor, has marble-top tables and a colorful, civilized look like something out of a Maurice Prendergast sketch. It's open for an extensive lunch, afternoon tea, early evening cocktails, and dessert and drinks until midnight. The Courtyard Café offers light refreshments in summer.

1 Logan Sq., Philadelphia, PA 19103. ℂ 800/332-3442 or 215/963-1500. Fax 215/963-9506. www.four seasons.com. 365 units. Doubles from $310; suites from $400. Weekend rates available from $220. AE, DC, MC, V. Valet parking $25, self-parking $20. SEPTA: Suburban Station. Bus: PHLASH, 76. **Amenities:** 3 restaurants; cafe; indoor heated pool; health club with Universal machines, Exercycles, and exercise mats; spa; Jacuzzi; concierge; town-car service within Center City; salon; 24-hr. room service; massage, babysitting, laundry service and dry cleaning available. *In room:* A/C, TV w/pay movies, fax available, hi-speed dataport, minibar/fridge, iron, safe, in-room exercise equipment available.

Hotel Sofitel ★★ Sofitel is the premier French luxury chain, and this urbane, sleek sanctuary of limestone and glass feels very much connected to both French and Philadelphian hospitality. The location is wonderful for business or adult travelers, located between Rittenhouse Square and the Avenue of the Arts. Unfortunately, the long, low floors don't make for much in the way of views. Rooms are more contemporary than the norm — think Ian Schrager watered down — with a glass-and-chrome coffee table, two armchairs, and an opulent bed with four wall-mounted bedside lights squeezed into walls of handsome checkerboard cherry wood. The bathrooms are truly sumptuous. Business travelers will find high-speed Internet jacks on the desk with easy tabletop plug-ins. The porte-cochere is small, so give yourself some time to reclaim your car.

Chez Colette is a traditional French brasserie open for breakfast as well. I love the bar — a cool, New York–style lounge with a blue Brazilian granite bar, torch-style singing, and French appetisers.

17th and Sansom sts. Philadelphia PA 19103 ℂ 800/SOFITEL or 215/569 0300. Fax 215/569 1492. www.sofitel.com. 306 units. $159–$289 double, $269 suites. Weekend packages available. AE, DC, DISC, MC,

---

Finds   Historic Bed & Breakfasts

Many B&Bs are listed through A Bed & Breakfast Connection/Bed & Breakfast of Philadelphia (see contact info under "B&B Agencies" earlier in this chapter). However, some B&Bs list themselves independently. My favorite among the latter is **Shippen Way Inn** ⭐, 418 Bainbridge St. (℅ **800/245-4873** or 215/627-7266), a tiny row house in Queen Village built around 1750 and lovingly maintained. During summer, you can wake up in a four-poster bed and have breakfast in the back herb garden for $90 to $110 per night. You might also try **Ten Eleven Clinton,** 1011 Clinton St. (℅ **215/923-8144**), an elegant 1836 Federal town house (that means high ceilings!) on a beautiful tree-lined residential street near Pine and 11th. Rates run $145 to $200.

V. Valet parking $24 per day in underground garage. SEPTA: Suburban Station. Bus: PHLASH, 21, 42. Pets allowed. **Amenities:** Brasserie; lounge; fully equipped fitness center; 24-hr. room service. *In room:* A/C, TV w/pay movies, dataport, hair dryer, iron.

Park Hyatt Philadelphia at the Bellevue ⭐⭐   The "grande dame of Broad Street" was the most opulent hotel in the country when it first opened in 1904. It was fully renovated in 1989 and is now a notch below the Four Seasons, the Rittenhouse, or the Ritz-Carlton. It's still a grand experience in a great location, and the value on weekends is substantial.

The ground floor houses internationally renowned retailers like Tiffany & Co. and Polo/Ralph Lauren, while the below-ground level features quick and easy gourmet fare and takeout from a food court. A separate elevator lifts you to the 19th-floor registration area and foyer for the hotel restaurants. The rooms, occupying floors 12 to 17, are as large as ever and all slightly different, with a green-and-white decor and wall moldings reproduced from the 1904 designs. Each room boasts extra large goose-down pillows, three two-line phones with dataports, a VCR, a large bed, a writing desk, a round table, and four upholstered chairs. Closets have built-in tie racks and automatic lighting. The bathrooms are dated but have amenities like hair dryers, TVs, and illuminated close-up mirrors.

Founders (see chapter 6), voted one of the top 50 restaurants in the nation by *Condé Nast Traveler,* has two spectacular semicircular windows draped with dramatic swags of brown and cream, and offers dancing to a swing trio on weekends. The Library Lounge is quiet and a bit precious, with a copy of a Gilbert Stuart full-length portrait and a collection of books by and about Philadelphians.

Staying at the Hyatt Bellevue is also about the only way you, as a tourist, can get a crack at The Sporting Club, Philadelphia's top health club facility. A fourth-floor skywalk from the hotel leads directly to the Sporting Club, a Michael Graves–designed facility that boggles the eye with 93,000 square feet of health club space, including a half-mile jogging track; a four-lane, 25-meter junior Olympic pool; and corridors of squash and racquetball courts. The walkway also goes to the garage on the other side of Chancellor Court.

Broad and Walnut sts., or 1415 Chancellor Court (between Walnut and Locust sts.), Philadelphia, PA 19102. ℅ **800/223-1234** or 215/893-1234. Fax 215/732-8518. www.parkphiladelphia.hyatt.com. 172 units. $209 double; $254 suites. Weekend packages often available. AE, DC, DISC, MC, V. Self-parking $16 at connected garage, valet parking $25. SEPTA: Walnut-Locust. Bus: PHLASH, 21, 42. **Amenities:** Restaurant; lounge; indoor pool at health club; use of the excellent health club facilities at The Sporting Club; full-day child-care facility at the Sporting Club; concierge; 24-hr. room service; laundry service and dry cleaning. *In room:* A/C, TV/VCR w/pay movies, dataport, minibar, hair dryer, iron.

Rittenhouse Hotel ★★★ *Kids*   Among Philadelphia's luxury hotels, the Rittenhouse has the fewest and largest rooms, the most satisfying views, and the most pride in service and setting. Built in 1989, it's a jagged concrete-and-glass high-rise off the western edge of Philadelphia's most distinguished public square. The lobby is truly magnificent, with inlaid marble floors and a series of frosted-glass chandeliers and sconces. Along with the Four Seasons and the Ritz-Carlton, it's the only AAA Five-Diamond Award holder in the state.

Every room at the Rittenhouse is actually a suite with a full living room area, bay windows, reinforced walls between rooms, and solid-wood doors. All have great views: The park is wonderfully green most of the year, but the western view of the Schuylkill River and the Parkway is even more dramatic. Spirited renderings of city scenes by local artists decorate the walls.

Jean-Marie Lacroix, a superb chef formerly at the Four Seasons, has re-emerged to open Lacroix at the Rittenhouse, a handsome and elegant second-floor balcony restaurant overlooking the park, offering classic French cuisine. Smith & Wollensky, the New York steakhouse, has an outpost on the second floor, and the more casual Boathouse Row Bar & Grill has a late night bar with separate entrance on the Square. Completing the picture is the ground floor's Cassatt Tea Room and Lounge, which serves traditional afternoon tea and cocktails daily. The site was the original town house of painter Mary Cassatt's brother, and the charming trellised private garden is adorned with three drypoints by Cassatt.

210 W. Rittenhouse Sq., Philadelphia, PA 19103. (*C*) **800/635-1042** or 215/546-9000. Fax 215/732-3364. www.rittenhousehotel.com. 98 units. Doubles from $310. Weekend rates and packages including health club, dinners, and other amenities usually available. AE, DC, MC, V. Valet parking $24. Bus: 21, 42. **Amenities:** 2 restaurants; bar; lounge; 5-lane indoor pool; Adolf Biecker fitness club with sun deck, Cybex weight machines, and aerobic equipment; spa; sauna; steam room; cooking classes and/or lunch events for children; concierge; executive business center; 24-hr. room service; massage; laundry service and dry cleaning. *In room:* A/C, TV/VCR w/pay movies, fax, dataport, minibar, hair dryer, iron.

The Ritz-Carlton Philadelphia ★★★   The Ritz-Carlton, spanking new in fall 2000, electrified the city for the painstaking and glorious resuscitation of the corner between City Hall and the Avenue of the Arts. The Ritz-Carlton has incorporated a 120-foot neoclassical domed structure designed by McKim, Mead, and White, dating from 1908, and its 30-story marble-clad neighbor. The tower has been converted into the hotel, with a meeting and ballroom space and a fitness facility. The Rotunda Dome houses an eye-popping atrium and three restaurants (full-service, power grill, and grill/bar) and a downstairs ballroom. Many architectural details have been preserved, including marble flooring and a bank teller desk.

The hotel rooms occupy floors 4 to 29; the top three are reserved for Club members, with a spectacular concierge/club area on the 30th floor. In guest rooms, you'll find more space than normal allotted to generous bathrooms with an opulent marble tub/shower alcove, and less to the snug bedrooms, decorated with stippled paper in peach and warm ochres. The furnishings and amenities are exquisite, from the old Philadelphia prints and engravings to plush terry robes to the high-speed Internet access for laptops. Lighting is excellent.

Pantheon, with its magnificent marble Ionic columns on the side facing the Rotunda and 18-foot high windows on the opposite side, serves breakfast daily, weekend brunch, and light dining with jazz Wednesdays through Saturdays. The Paris Bar and Grille ★, a clubby space on the City Hall side, features an open kitchen, with Craig Hopson supervising light sauces and fresh ingredients for wonderfully prepared dishes. The downstairs Vault is a snug, tobacco-heavy lounge with warm woods and tapestries.

10 Avenue of the Arts (corner of South Broad and Chestnut sts.), Philadelphia, PA 19102. ℂ **800/241-3333** or 215/735-7700. Fax 215/568-0942. www.ritzcarlton.com. 331 units. $269–$299 double. Weekend rates available from $230. AE, DC, DISC, MC, V. Valet parking $32, no self-parking. SEPTA: 15th Street/City Hall. Bus: PHLASH, 21, 42. **Amenities:** 2 restaurants; lounge; fitness center; spa; sauna; steam room; concierge; 24-hr. room service; massage; laundry service and dry cleaning. In room: A/C, TV w/pay movies, 2 dataports, mini-bar, hair dryer, iron, safe.

Westin Philadelphia ★★ (Value) The Westin opened with great fanfare as a Ritz-Carlton in 1990. Although it's been fumbled with a bit by its owner, Starwood Hotels, this wonderful place seems to have emerged intact, with a blend of luxury amenities and service. And the location can't be beat — steps away from the best in urban life. While it's a bit higher priced than other Westins, it's a value compared to its luxury peers.

A small porte-cochere and a ground-floor lobby on 17th Street lead to a series of smaller, almost residential rooms that contain the front lobby and concierge desks, the dining areas, and the elevators on the second floor. The guest rooms feature bedside walnut tables, desks, firm beds with spindle-top headboards (and a luxurious four pillows), and Wedgwood or Sandwich glass lamps. Large walnut armoires house TVs, clothing drawers, and minibars. All rooms are provided with two phone lines and dataports. The modern bathrooms, improved by Westin, are outfitted with black-and-white marble, silver plate fixtures, magnifying mirrors, and lots of toiletries. The hotel runs frequent packages in tandem with museum exhibitions or other events.

17th and Chestnut sts. (at Liberty Place), Philadelphia, PA 19103. ℂ **800/228-3000** or 215/563-1600. Fax 215/564-9559. www.westin.com. 290 units. $199 and up double. Weekend rates available. AE, DISC, MC, V. Self-parking $21, valet parking $25. SEPTA: Suburban Station. Bus: PHLASH, 21, 42, 76. **Amenities:** Restaurant; lounge; small exercise facility; sauna; 24-hr. concierge; transport to and from airport; fully equipped business center and meeting rooms; internal connection to the 70 Shops at Liberty Place (see chapter 9); 24-hr. room service; laundry service and dry cleaning. In room: A/C, TV w/pay movies, fax, dataport, minibar, coffeemaker, hair dryer, iron, safe.

EXPENSIVE

Buttonwood Square Hotel ★★ (Value) The amenities, the location and the great views make this hotel an excellent value even at rack rates; the weekend packages make it an outstanding bargain. You'll recognize it by the bright neon scribble near its roof. Located north of Logan Circle, it's visible from anywhere south. A marble-and-mahogany lobby leads to the 28-story tower, and a glass-enclosed corridor connects to the restaurant and lush Japanese sculpture garden and pool.

The standard rooms are unbelievably spacious, with a microwave, minibar, and coffeemaker. The suites add full kitchens with dishwashers, stoves, coffeemakers, and telephones. Each living area has a full dining table for four, TV, full couch, and three double closets. Each bedroom features a queen-size bed and another TV (in suites, with built-in VCR), and the adjoining bathroom has a stacked washer/dryer. The views are great: to the north, highlights of 19th century manufacturing and churches; to the south, 20th-century Center City.

2001 Hamilton St. (just off the Parkway), Philadelphia, PA 19130. ℂ **888/456-7626** or 215/569-7000. Fax 215/569-0584. www.korman1.com. 170 units. $179 efficiency; $199 2-bedroom plus kitchen; $239 1-bedroom suite with connecting den. Other options available for stays of 2 weeks or more. Children stay free in parent's room. Rates include continental breakfast 6–10am. AE, DC, MC, V. Free covered parking. Bus: PHLASH, 76. **Amenities:** Restaurant; outdoor pool; 2 tennis courts; fitness center; high-tech spa; Jacuzzi; concierge; complimentary shuttle van running hourly through Center City to Independence Park; salon. In room: A/C, TV w/pay movies, dataport, kitchen, fridge, coffeemaker, hair dryer, iron.

Doubletree Hotel Philadelphia ⭐   The Avenue of the Arts location of this hotel couldn't be better for culture-seekers and families. The garage entrances ingeniously keep traffic flows separate for three floors of meeting facilities. The decor features rich paisleys and Degas-style murals alluding to the orchestral and ballet life at the Academy of Music across the street. Thanks to the saw-toothed design of the building, the guest rooms, all completely renovated in the last 8 years, each have two views of town. Obviously, the higher floors afford the better views. The views of the Delaware River (eastern corner) or City Hall (northeastern corner) are the most popular. The bathrooms are clean and bland, and the Doubletree signature is a box of great chocolate chip cookies delivered to your room upon arrival.

Broad St. at Locust St., Philadelphia, PA 19107. ☎ **800/222-8733** or 215/893-1600. Fax 215/893-1664. www.doubletreehotels.com. 427 units. $109–$263 double. Weekend packages available. AE, DC, DISC, MC, V. Self-parking $15 in adjoining garage, valet parking $19. SEPTA: Walnut-Locust. Bus: PHLASH, 21, 42. **Amenities:** Restaurant; lounge; health and racquet club with Cybex exercise machines, Lifesteps, Schwinn Airdynes, and a small jogging track circling a huge rooftop deck; indoor pool; Jacuzzi; steam room; activities desk; car-rental desk; laundry service and dry cleaning. *In room:* A/C, TV w/pay movies, 2 dataports, minibar, coffeemaker, hair dryer, iron.

Embassy Suites Center City ⭐ *Value*   The big 28-story cylinder of marble and glass on the Parkway at 18th Street has had its ups and downs. It's a bit shabby at the moment, but the all-suite structure coupled with the location and the price makes this a fine choice. In 1993, $10 million was put into a refurbishment.

The hotel has an interesting set of strengths and weaknesses. It was designed in the 1960s as luxury apartments radiating out from a central core, but the quality of views varies widely, and the basic shape is weirdly disorienting. It's evident that the elevators and lobby weren't equipped to handle this volume. On the other hand, amenities such as the full breakfast at TGI Friday's (the connected restaurant), the fitness room, and the nightly manager's reception exceed expectations. The suites themselves have a sleek severity, with black matte and putty surfaces for TV stands and a spare walnut armoire. The kitchenette includes microwave, under-the-counter refrigerator, and coffeemaker (no oven or dishwasher); dishes and silverware are provided upon request. An especially nice 48-inch round table with four chairs overlooks the small balcony terrace, which is accessible through sliding door. Bathrooms have large Italian marble tiles, plush white towels, and hair dryers. With two double beds, the bedrooms don't have a lot of extra room.

TGI Friday's, connected on two levels, is open until 1am daily and is used for the complimentary hotel breakfast. When the hotel is full, service at the restaurant backs up quite a bit. The lobby lounge hosts happy hour.

1776 Benjamin Franklin Pkwy. (at Logan Sq.), Philadelphia, PA 19103. ☎ **800/362-2779** or 215/561-1776. Fax 215/963-0122. www.embassysuites.com. 288 units. $174 suite. Excellent weekend packages available. Rates include full breakfast. AE, DC, DISC, MC, V. Valet parking $24, self-parking $20 underground. SEPTA: Suburban Station. Bus: PHLASH, 76, 21, 42. **Amenities:** Restaurant; fitness center with Nordic Track, Stairmasters, and rowing machines; sauna; children's play room for ages 2–7; laundry service and dry cleaning. *In room:* A/C, 2 TVs w/pay movies, dataport, minibar, coffeemaker, microwave, hair dryer, iron.

The Latham ⭐   A landmark apartment house from 1915 to 1970, the Latham's charm, congeniality, and small attentions brings to mind a small, superbly run Swiss hostelry. On weekday mornings, the lobby — a high-ceilinged salon with terrazzo highlights — is filled with refreshed executives, though the hotel does no convention business. Weekend packages are great bargains. Dealings with the reception area are quick and professional. The guest rooms, redone in Victorian motif in 1998, are not huge or lavish but perfectly proportioned and decorated with cheerful striped silk. Full-wall and lighted facial mirrors, large marblelike basins, and oversize towels highlight the white-toned bathroom interiors.

135 S. 17th St. at Walnut St., Philadelphia, PA 19103. ℂ 877/528-4261 or 215/563-7474. Fax 215/568-0110. www.lathamhotel.com. 139 units. $159 double. Weekend packages from $119. 1 or 2 children stay free in parent's room. Rates include breakfast and parking. AE, DC, DISC, MC, V. Valet parking $20. SEPTA: Walnut-Locust. Bus: PHLASH, 21, 42. **Amenities:** Restaurant; small fitness room and free access to a nearby fitness club with an indoor pool; concierge; laundry service and dry cleaning. *In room:* A/C, TV, dataport, mini-bar, coffeemaker, hair dryer, iron.

Loews Philadelphia Hotel 🌟🌟   The Loews, opened in spring 2000, is the product of a great marriage of an architectural landmark and a prestigious hotel chain. The tower, located across from the Reading Terminal Headhouse and the Convention Center, was the nation's first skyscraper of modern design and construction, with gleaming polished stone and Art Deco clocks by Cartier. Loews Hotels turned the 1932 granite and glass tower into a first-class property. The three-story entrance hall has been preserved, and rooms feature 10-foot ceilings, Art Deco interiors, and miles of spectacular views. Business aids are extensive, but watch out for the surcharges levied on phone use.

The Restaurant at PSFS is chic and trendy, with a bit of retro style thrown in; a hook is the 50+ styles of grilled cheese sandwiches, but the real star is the excellent American regional cuisine with Caribbean flavors.

1200 Market St., Philadelphia, PA 19107. ℂ 800/235-6397 or 215/627-1200. www.loewshotels.com. 585 units. $199–$250 double. Weekend packages available from $169. AE, DC, DISC, MC, V. Parking $24. SEPTA: 11th St. Station. Bus: PHLASH, 76. **Amenities:** Restaurant; bar; library lounge; 15,000-sq.-ft. fitness facility with 2-lane lap pool available for $10/day; concierge service; laundry service and dry cleaning. *In room:* A/C, TV w/pay movies, fax, high-speed dataport, minibar, hair dryer, iron.

Philadelphia Marriott and **Courtyard by Marriott** 🌟🌟 *Value*   After more than a decade of planning and construction, the Marriott chain opened the biggest hotel in Pennsylvania in January 1995, linked by an elevated covered walkway to the Reading Terminal Shed of the Convention Center. And it's gotten bigger. In late 1999 Marriott converted the historic City Hall Annex across 13th Street at Filbert into a 500-room Courtyard by Marriott, the largest in the Courtyard division. So all together, you have your choice of 1,910 rooms, two fitness centers, and 10 restaurants and lounges — all linked with one another and with the Convention Center.

The hotel's major auto entrance is on Filbert Street (two-way between Market and Arch sts.), with an equally grand pedestrian entrance adjoining Champions Sports Bar and retail on Market Street. The lobby is sliced up into a five-story atrium, enlivened by a 10,000-square-foot water sculpture, a lobby bar, and a Starbucks. Setbacks and terraces provide plenty of natural light and views from the rooms on floors 6 to 23. Rooms are tastefully outfitted with dark woods, maroon and green drapes and bedspreads, a TV armoire, a desk, a club chair and ottoman, and a round table, but, overall, rooms are slightly less elegant than those of the top hotels. Comfortably sized bathrooms have heavy chrome fixtures and tuck sinks and counters in the corners for more dressing room space. Closets are spacious. Concierge-level rooms feature private key access and use of a special lounge. Service is impeccable, thanks to the well-trained, knowledgeable staff.

Philadelphia Marriott: 12th and Market sts., Philadelphia, PA 19107. ℂ 800/228-9290 or 215/625-2900. Fax 215/625-6000. www.marriott.com/marriott/phldt. 1,410 units. $240 double; $255–$275 concierge-level rooms. Weekend rates available. **Courtyard by Marriott:** 13th and Filbert sts., Philadelphia, PA 19107. ℂ **215/496-3200**. 498 units. $155 standard; $250 suite. AE, DC, DISC, MC, V. Valet parking $23. Bus: PHLASH, 76. SEPTA: Direct internal connection to 13th St. Station and airport train. **Amenities:** *Philadelphia Marriott:* 2 restaurants; bar; 3 lounges; coffee bar; indoor lap pool; health club; Jacuzzi; saunas. Concierge-floor rooms have special amenities. *Courtyard by Marriott:* Restaurant; indoor pool, fitness center. *In room for both hotels:* A/C, TV w/pay movies, dataport, minibar, coffeemaker, hair dryer, iron.

Sheraton Rittenhouse Square ⭐
This renovated apartment building has brought some competition to its neighborhood, with a wonderful location and a very smart cafe right on urbane Rittenhouse Square. This Sheraton is being marketed as the first "environmentally smart" hotel in the continental United States, with fresh filtered air, organic cotton bedding, bamboo plants and recycled granite in the lobby, energy efficient lighting, and no smoking anywhere. (You agree to pay $50 as a sanitizing fee if you smoke in the rooms.) Rooms are modern but unpretentious; a spacious 400 square feet on average, with 9½-foot ceilings and state-of-the-art technology. The same standards of care and cleanliness apply to the large, marbled bathrooms. Many have separate sitting areas and balconies, and kitchenettes are available. I'd avoid the interior rooms, facing all-night airshaft lighting instead of Rittenhouse Square.

Bleu is an urbane, romantic cafe with outdoor seating, while **Potcheen Restaurant,** just off the square, has one of the best happy hours around and cozy American fare.

227 S. 18th St. (at Rittenhouse Sq.), Philadelphia, PA 19103. ℂ **800/325-3535** or 800/854-8002. Fax 215/875-9457. www.sheraton.com. 192 units. $199 double. Excellent weekend packages and discounts available. Children under 18 stay free in parent's room. AE, DC, DISC, MC, V. Off-site valet parking $20. SEPTA: 15th–16th St. Station. Bus: PHLASH, 21, 42. **Amenities:** 2 restaurants (1 with outdoor seating on Rittenhouse Sq.); fitness facility; room service 6am–midnight. *In room:* A/C, TV w/pay movies, dataport, voice mail, coffeemaker, hair dryer, iron.

Wyndham Philadelphia at Franklin Plaza *(Value)*
The Wyndham has been functioning as a convenient meeting center and urban resort since 1980, and now the convention center, only 4 blocks away, fills this hotel sporadically. The complex uses a full city block, and the lobby, lounge, and two restaurants are beautifully integrated under a dramatic 70-foot glass roof. In terms of service and maintenance, the Wyndham has definite signs of fatigue, but a major 1998 renovation of rooms should last for several years. Request a west view above the 19th floor for an unobstructed peek at the Parkway, but be forewarned that the cathedral bells below ring at 7am, noon, and 6pm daily. Bathrooms are clean and bland.

17th and Race sts., Philadelphia, PA 19103. ℂ **800/996-3426** or 215/448-2000. Fax 215/448-2864. www.wyndham.com. 758 units. $209 double. Excellent weekend rates available. Children 18 and under stay free in parent's room. AE, DC, MC, V. Self-parking $17, valet parking $24. SEPTA: Race-Vine. Bus: PHLASH, 76. **Amenities:** 2 restaurants; room service 6am–midnight. Clark's Uptown health club includes free use of indoor pool (21 ft. × 45 ft.), sauna, sun deck around ⅛ mile track, whirlpool, Nautilus machines, jogging track; all-day fee of $10 adds racquetball (3 courts), squash (3 courts), outdoor handball (3 courts), and tennis (2 courts). *In room:* A/C, TV w/pay movies, dataport (but $10/day fee), minibar, hair dryer, iron.

MODERATE

Alexander Inn ⭐ *(Value)*
The Alexander Inn bills itself as a four-star hotel at reasonable rates. The *Newsweek* crew that took over all 48 rooms during the Republican National Convention had nothing but praise for its amenities and top-notch staff. It's got all the comfort and friendliness of a bed-and-breakfast, with a classy 1930s Art Deco/cruise boat feel to the furnishings. Rooms feature DirecTV with on all movie channels, direct dial phones, and individual artwork, and bathrooms sparkle with cleanliness. Room rates include a breakfast buffet — until noon on weekends (though there's no restaurant) — and use of the fully-equipped 24-hour

---

Kids   Family-Friendly Hotels

Family-Friendly Philadelphia (© 800/770-5889) offers special packages that include 2 nights at a number of hotels, free parking and breakfast, and free admission to attractions such as Sesame Place, the Franklin Institute, the Zoo, the Academy of Natural Sciences, the Please Touch Museum, and "The Liberty Tale Tour" run by the Historic Philadelphia guides near Independence Hall. Call for details.

Four Seasons Hotel (p. 67)   The Saturday Lunch Club is a three-course meal designed for kids; it's featured on the first Saturday of the month.

The Inn at Penn (p. 75)   The comfortable and safe public areas, including the "Living Room" with its fireplace and thousands of books, give your kids a chance to let off steam indoors. Plus, it's across the street from the green lawns of the U. Penn campus. Frisbee, anyone?

Rittenhouse Hotel (p. 69)   This hotel intermittently offers children's cooking classes taught by Rena Coyle and also features Saturday theme lunches for kids and their parents.

Sheraton Society Hill (p. 64)   There's a special children's check-in, free snacks, the use of the game room, and so on.

---

fitness center. Note that the Alexander Inn is in the heart of the gay/lesbian district of Center City, and its clientele is both straight and gay.

12th and Spruce sts., Philadelphia, PA 19107. © 877/253-9466 or 215/923-3535. Fax 215/923-1004. www.alexanderinn.com. 48 units. From $99–$109; $10 per additional person. Complimentary breakfast buffet. AE, DC, DISC, MC, V. Garage parking $10 nearby. SEPTA: Market East. **Amenities:** Fitness center. *In room:* A/C, TV w/pay movies, dataport, hair dryer and iron available.

Crowne Plaza Philadelphia Center City *Value*

The Crowne Plaza offers solid, generic, primarily business-traveler-oriented accommodations. It's very popular with conventioneers and relocating executives, but hotel policy is to leave at least 40% of the 515 rooms free for non-business travelers. The hotel prices are very competitive in an effort to maintain occupancy. The lobby, which dispenses coffee and apples all day, has entrances from both 18th Street and the garage. A parking garage and meeting halls occupy the next 6 floors, and rooms and several suites fill the next 17 floors. By Philadelphia standards, the rooms are large. Furnishings include coffeemakers, telephones with dataports, and plush carpeting. Bathrooms are slightly shabby. Two floors are devoted to Executive Level suites, offering upgraded decor and complimentary breakfast.

18th and Market sts., Philadelphia, PA 19103. © 800/227-6963 or 215/561-7500. Fax 215/561-4484. 515 units. $139 double; B&B packages available. Children 19 and under stay free in parent's room; children 12 and under eat free with parents. AE, DC, MC, V. Parking $24. SEPTA: 19th St. Bus: 76. **Amenities:** Restaurant; outdoor pool; fitness room with rowing and Nautilus machines. *In room:* A/C, TV w/pay movies, dataport, hair dryer, iron.

Hawthorn Suites Philadelphia at the Convention Center *Value*

Opened in summer 1998, the Hawthorn Suites is directly adjacent to the Convention Center, and weekend packages make it an excellent family choice. The second floor houses a large fitness center and dining area, while the 14 floors above comprise studio and one-bedroom suites, each with efficiency or full kitchens, microwaves, refrigerators, and coffeemakers. The decor and bathrooms are bland and blond.

1100 Vine St., Philadelphia, PA 19107. ℭ **800/527-1133** or 215/829-8300. Fax 215/829-8104. www.hawthornphila.com. 294 units. $89 double; $179 suite. Rates include full hot buffet breakfast and complimentary social hour, Mon–Thurs. AE, DC, DISC, MC, V. Valet parking $19 nearby. SEPTA: 11th St. Station. Bus: PHLASH. **Amenities:** 24-hr. fitness center; guest laundry. *In room:* A/C, TV, dataport, voice mail.

Rodeway Inn   Robert and Thomas Manning bought this late 1800s shell in 1992 and it is now part of the Rodeway franchise chain. They've constructed seven floors of comfortable, bigger-than-average rooms with solid-core doors, four-poster beds and private bathrooms. Six rooms boast Jacuzzis. The front desk is attended 24 hours a day. All suites have gas fireplaces. A state-of-the-art gym is available around the corner for $8.

1208 Walnut St., Philadelphia, PA 19107. ℭ **800/887-1776** or 215/546-7000. Fax 215/546-7573. www.rodeway.com/hotel/pa271. 32 units. $99 double. Rates include continental breakfast and local calls. AE, DC, DISC, MC, V. Bus: 21, 42. **Amenities:** Free local calls. *In room:* A/C, TV, dataport, hair dryer, iron.

3 University City (West Philadelphia)

EXPENSIVE

The Inn at Penn ★★ *Kids*   When U. Penn decides to take on a project, it doesn't skimp. The handsome and elegantly appointed Inn at Penn has jumped to become *the* favorite place to stay in city limits when west of the Schuylkill River. The Inn, managed by Hilton Hotels, is the keystone of the block-long Sansom Commons, an attractive 6-story brick area that includes the outstanding University Bookstore, collegiate trendy stores such as Steve Madden, Ma Jolie, and Urban Outfitters, and an XandO coffee bar. While the front door faces the Penn campus across Walnut Street, you'll enter through a porte-cochere off the north side of Sansom Street. Expansive stairways and corridors connect entrances to registration and to The Living Room, a fully-stocked library where complimentary tea and coffee are dispensed until 4pm, and wine and spirits are sold thereafter. Artwork and bas-reliefs of U. Penn's athletic triumphs from decades past adorn the Mission-style walls. The rooms are done in warm olive and beige tones, with top-quality furnishings, firm beds, and individual temperature controls. The academic flavor translates into efficient lighting and amenities such as dual-line phones, voice mail, and coffeemakers.

The **Ivy Grille** serves all meals in an American bistro atmosphere. The futuristic Asian-themed **Pod,** with a highly creative menu trundling by diners on a conveyor belt, and exciting color-shifting decor, is within the Sansom Commons complex. And don't forget that University City is rich in ethnic restaurants, many within a block of the inn.

3600 Sansom St., Philadelphia, PA 19104. ℭ **800/445-8667** or 215/222-0200. Fax 215/222-4600. www.theinnatpenn.com. 238 units. $179–$199 double. Children 18 and under stay free in parent's room. Weekend packages from $100 available. AE, DC, DISC, MC, V. Valet parking $24. SEPTA: 34th St. Station. Bus: 21. **Amenities:** 2 restaurants; library lounge; exercise room; concierge. *In room:* A/C, TV w/pay movies, dataport, voice mail, coffeemaker, hair dryer, iron.

Penn Tower Hotel   Penn Tower is a very convenient, if less than stellar, version of a former Hilton, built with a direct skywalk to University Hospital and within steps of the University of Pennsylvania, 30th Street Station, the Civic Center, Drexel University, and a direct train to the airport. The hotel part of the tower comprises floors 17 to 19, as well as an enclosed garage and ground-floor restaurants and shops. U. Penn takes over more floors every year for medical offices. You'll have to get used to spirited displays of red and blue, Penn's colors, and a long lobby corridor of rough-textured concrete that leads to the reception desk. The rooms and bathrooms are nothing extraordinary, but clean.

Civic Center Blvd. at 34th St., Philadelphia, PA 19104. (C) **800/356-7366** or 215/387-8333. Fax 215/386-8306. www.upenn.edu/penntower. 74 units. $165 double; $115 for relatives of patients in University and Children's Hospitals. Packages available. AE, DC, MC, V. Parking $9. Bus: 42. **Amenities:** Access for U. Penn indoor tennis court reservations; complimentary guest passes to Penn's nearby Hutchinson Health Complex for track and rowing machines; dry cleaning. *In room:* A/C, TV, dataport.

MODERATE

Sheraton University City This concrete block of a Sheraton, midway between Drexel University and the University of Pennsylvania, has finally spruced up by reducing the number of guest rooms and providing new light wood Art Deco furniture, luxurious plush beds, oversize business desks with ergonomic chairs, and all new amenities. It still remains popular with visiting parents and conference attendees, and it's one block from the subway, and four from the Amtrak station and the three University City hospitals. The Sheraton offers a heated outdoor pool and sun deck on the Chestnut Street side of the building. Shula's Steak 2 restaurant is very popular with sports fans.

3549 Chestnut St., Philadelphia, PA 19104. (C) **800/325-3535** or 215/387-8000. Fax 215/307-7920. www.sheraton.com/universitycity. 374 units. $99–$159 double. Children 18 years or under stay free in parent's room. Packages available. AE, DC, MC, V. Enclosed self-parking $15. SEPTA: 34th St. Station. Bus: 42. **Amenities:** Restaurant; lounge; heated outdoor pool; fitness center; Enterprise car-rental desk; room service 6am–midnight; laundry service and dry cleaning. *In room:* A/C, TV w/pay movies, dataport, 2-line phones, coffeemaker, hair dryer, iron.

INEXPENSIVE

Gables *(Value* This 1889 Victorian, a boardinghouse until a few years ago, was one of West Philadelphia's first and finest mansions. The location is about 8 blocks west of the University of Pennsylvania's main campus. It's right at the SEPTA trolley line stop into Center City, 5 minutes from 30th Street Station and 15 minutes from the airport. It's an excellent choice for visiting academics, parents of students, prospective applicants, and relaxed tourists.

Eight formal areas are filled with antiques. There are sitting rooms, a breakfast room, and a wraparound porch; five bedrooms with private bathrooms and four bedrooms with shared bathrooms are on the top two floors. All rooms have gorgeous inlaid wood floors, and three have charming corner turrets, and most rooms have recently-added private bathrooms. Closets, armoires, lamps, and desks fit in with the Victorian decor. Home-baked muffins, breads, fresh fruit, and casseroles make up the breakfasts.

4520 Chester Ave. (at S. 46th St.), Philadelphia, PA 19143. (C) **215/662-1918.** Fax 215/662-1918. www.gablesbb.com. 10 units, 8 with bathroom. $80–$125 double. Rates include full breakfast. AE, DISC, MC, V. Free off-street parking. SEPTA: #13 Green Line trolley stop. *In room:* A/C, TV, private phone with answering machine, dataport, wireless DSL; plus fax, fridge, microwave, hair dryer, and iron available.

University City Guest Houses *(Value* This is basically a neighborhood collection of bed-and-breakfasts, most within walking distance of the University of Pennsylvania and University Hospital. Most hosts are academically affiliated. Parking is provided at most places, and most have in-room telephones.

P.O. Box 28612, 2933 Morris Rd., Philadelphia, PA 19151. (C) **215/387-3731.** $60–$100 double. Children allowed in some situations. No credit cards; traveler's checks accepted. Amenities vary depending on B&B, so ask when you call.

4 Near the Airport

Hotel chain options are very well represented at the moderate to inexpensive level in this area. Your choices include: **Holiday Inn Philadelphia Stadium,** 10th Street and Packer Avenue, Philadelphia, PA 19148 (✆ **800/424-0291** or 215/755-9500), which charges $110 for a double; **Airport Ramada Inn,** 76 Industrial Hwy., Essington, PA 19029 (✆ **800/277-3900** or 610/521-9600), with rates of $89 for a double, $69 weekends; **Four Points by Sheraton Philadelphia Airport,** 4101a Island Ave. (between I-95 and Pa. 291), Philadelphia, PA 19153 (✆ **800/325-3535** or 215/492-0400), a slimmed-down version of the Sheraton suites across the way, but quite a value at $99; **Comfort Inn Airport,** 53 Industrial Hwy., Essington, PA 19029 (✆ **800/228-5150** or 610/521-9800), with rates of $99 for a double; and **Red Roof Inn,** 49 Industrial Hwy., Essington, PA 19029 (✆ **800/843-7663** or 610/521-5090), at $85 for a double.

EXPENSIVE

Philadelphia Airport Marriott Hotel ⭐ ⟨Value⟩   Opened in 1995, this is the only hotel linked by skywalk to Philadelphia International Airport. The facility caters to business travelers with voice mail, speakerphone, free incoming faxes, and two dataport jacks. However, it's not a bad choice for families, since the soundproof rooms are mostly angled away from the runways, and it's very convenient to I-95. When you throw in the very complete fitness center and pool, a reasonable restaurant, easy train or bus shuttle into Center City, and frequent weekend packages, it's well worth considering.

Arrivals Rd., Philadelphia, PA 19153. ✆ 800/628-4087 or 215/492-9000. Fax 215/492-7464. www.marriott. com. 419 units. $185 double; $199 concierge-level room for up to 5 people. Excellent weekend rates. AE, DC, DISC, MC, V. Parking free to guests in Level 2 of the airport garage at Terminal B. SEPTA: Airport Shuttle. **Amenities:** Restaurant; lounge; indoor pool, exercise room; Jacuzzi; laundry service and dry cleaning. *In room:* A/C, TV w/pay movies, dataport, minibar, coffeemaker, hair dryer, iron.

Sheraton Suites Philadelphia Hotel ⟨Value⟩   The occupancy rates at the Sheraton are among the highest in town. For just a bit more dough than the Four Points across the street requires, you get deluxe suites with beautifully furnished bedrooms and living rooms that encircle a dramatic eight-story atrium. A 1998 rehab redecorated suites in taupe and olive, with cherrywood furniture. The outer room contains a business desk and chair, convertible sofa bed, and armoire with TV. The bedroom, with the choice of a king or two twin beds, has another TV and phone, and bathrooms are similarly handsome and beautifully maintained. There is a wet bar with coffeemaker and small refrigerator in the kitchenette, and the bathroom has a marble-topped vanity. Airport noise is minimal.

4101b Island Ave., Philadelphia, PA 19153. ✆ 800/325-3535 or 215/365-6600. Fax 215/492-9858. www.sheraton.com. 251 units. $119 double. Weekend and seasonal specials available. Children 18 and under stay free in parent's room. Rates include full buffet breakfast. AE, DC, DISC, MC, V. Free parking. SEPTA: Airport shuttle and courtesy bus. **Amenities:** Restaurant/lounge; indoor pool; sauna; steam room; Jacuzzi; car-rental desk; complimentary shuttle to and from airport; same-day laundry service and dry cleaning. *In room:* A/C, 2 TVs w/pay movies, dataport, 2 dual-line phones, multi-port speakerphone, fridge, coffeemaker, hair dryer, iron.

MODERATE

Philadelphia Airport Hilton   The Philadelphia Airport Hilton is out of the way of flight patterns and features a lobby and cocktail lounge built around a lushly planted indoor pool. Like all airport hotels, business travelers predominate during the week, and reservations are recommended. The guest rooms, with whirlpool-equipped bathrooms redone in 2000, are classically American — spacious, comfortable, and anonymously elegant.

4509 Island Ave., Philadelphia, PA 19153. © **800/HILTONS** or 215/365-4150. Fax 215/937-6382. www.hilton.com. 331 units. $139 double. Children 18 and under stay free in parent's room. Weekend packages available. AE, DC, DISC, MC, V. Free parking, with courtesy transport to and from the airport. SEPTA: Airport shuttle and courtesy bus. **Amenities:** Restaurant; lounge; indoor pool; health club; Jacuzzi; sauna; laundry service and dry cleaning. *In room:* A/C, TV w/pay movies, dataport, minibar, coffeemaker, hair dryer, iron.

5 City Line & Northeast

City Line Avenue (U.S. 1), just off the Schuylkill Expressway, is a good jumping-off point for West Philadelphia, Bucks County, or Lancaster County. Its retail outlets are struggling with the emergence of the huge King of Prussia mall, so nearby Saks Fifth Avenue and Lord & Taylor have frequent sales.

Thoroughly comfortable national chains dot this area, including **Holiday Inn City Line,** 4100 Presidential Blvd. (City Line Ave. at I-76), Philadelphia, PA 19131 (© **800/465-4329** or 215/477-0200) and the **Best Western Philadelphia Northeast,** 11580 Roosevelt Blvd., Philadelphia, PA 19116 (© 800/528-1234 or 215/464-9500).

MODERATE

Adam's Mark Philadelphia *Value* The Adam's Mark looks like an airport control tower, but you'll find an extensive brick complex of connected restaurants and function rooms. Eighty percent of the hotel's business is conventioneers, and the lower levels contain 50,000 square feet of meeting space. Friendly service, good value, and individual touches such as customized safe keys make up for the hotel's somewhat ungainly size and its slow elevators. Rooms are on the large side.

The Adam's Mark's food and beverage operation really shines. The gardenlike Appleby's is several notches above your average coffee shop, with all-you-can-eat meals, 30-foot ziggurat skylights, and local antiques. Lines start forming early at the Marker, an improbable re-creation (and improbable combination) of French château, paneled English library, and Western ranch that's somehow relaxing. It seats 150 on three levels, and evenings bring American regional cuisine. Quincy's, with some of the city's best hors d'oeuvres (complimentary until 7pm), offers nightly backgammon, big-band dancing, or jazz. There's no cover from Monday to Thursday, $10 Friday and Saturday (8pm–2am).

City Ave. and Monument Rd., Philadelphia, PA 19131. © **800/444-2326** or 215/581-5000. Fax 215/581-5069. www.adamsmark.com. 515 units. $119 double; $154 executive room. Weekend packages and promotions available. AE, DC, DISC, MC, V. Free parking in front lots or rear-connected garage, valet parking $12. SEPTA: R6 Bala Cynwyd stop ½ mile away. Bus: 1, 44, 65. **Amenities:** 2 restaurants; lounge; bar; indoor pool and outdoor pool; 2 racquetball courts ($10/session); fitness facility with Stairmaster, Nautilus and Life-cycle equipment; Jacuzzi; sauna; car-rental desk; salon; same-day laundry service and dry cleaning. *In room:* A/C, TV w/pay movies, dataport, voice mail.

6 Hostels

A $25 annual membership with **American Youth Hostels,** 733 15th St. NW, No. 840, Washington, DC 20005 (© **202/783-6161**), will give you discounts on already-low hostel rates.

Bank Street Hostel This 140-year-old former factory and its two neighbors, located in a very convenient part of town, offer spartan (although newly repainted) accommodations for travelers on a budget. The dormitory-style rooms are spread over four floors of the complex. Extras include free coffee and tea, a pool table, and a lounge with a large-screen TV. Kitchen facilities and washer/dryer are available for use. Clean, dorm-style bathrooms are shared. Discounts on food and other items at area merchants are available.

32 S. Bank St. (between 2nd and 3rd sts. and Market and Chestnut sts.), Philadelphia, PA 19106. ℂ 800/ 392-4678 or 215/922-0222. Fax 215/922-4082. 70 beds (shared bathroom). $18 for AYH members; $21 for nonmembers; $2 sheet charge. No credit cards. Check in before 10am or after 4:30pm; curfew at 12:30am Sun–Thurs, 1am Fri–Sat. Parking $14 at nearby garages. SEPTA: 2nd St. Station. Bus: PHLASH, 21, 42, 76.

Chamounix Hostel Mansion   The oldest building offering accommodations in town, this renovated 1802 Quaker farmhouse is also the cheapest. Chamounix Mansion is a Federal-style edifice constructed as a country retreat at what is now the upper end of Fairmount Park. It has 6 dormitory rooms for 44 people, with limited family arrangements, and another 37 spots in a fully renovated adjoining carriage house. Guests have use of the renovated self-serve kitchen, free videos, and bicycles. Write or call ahead for reservations, since the hostel is often 90% booked in summer by groups of boat crews or foreign students. You can check in daily between 4:30pm and midnight and show an American Youth Hostel card or IYHF card for member rates. Checkout is from 8 to 11am. Call **AYH** directly at ℂ **215/925-6004** for information on hostel trips in the area.

W. Fairmount Park, Philadelphia, PA 19131. ℂ **800/379-0017** or 215/878-3676. Fax 215/871-4313. www.philahostel.org. $15 AYH members; $18 nonmembers; $2 sheet charge. MC, V. Closed Dec 15–Jan 15. By car: Take I-76 (Schuylkill Expressway) to Exit 33, City Line Ave., turn right (south) on City Ave. to Belmont Ave., left on Belmont to first traffic light at Ford Rd., left on Ford, through stone tunnel to stop sign, then a left onto Chamounix Dr. and follow to the end. Bus: Take SEPTA route 38 from John F. Kennedy Blvd. near City Hall to Ford and Cranston sts. (a 30-min. ride), then walk under the overpass and left onto Chamounix Dr. to the end. **Amenities:** TV/VCR lounge; Internet kiosk; free bike loan; game room with Ping-Pong and piano; access to kitchen; coin-op washer and dryer. *In room:* A/C.

6

Where to Dine

Like so many things in Philadelphia, the city's restaurants are a reflection of its 300-year history — from rediscovered colonial favorites, to early 1900s Italian cuisine served in restaurants that have barely changed since they were opened, to the new, contemporary cuisine spots that are constantly popping up. In a recent *Condé Nast Traveler* readers' poll, seven Philadelphia restaurants were ranked among America's top 50, including Le Bec-Fin, and Fountain Restaurant at the Four Seasons Hotel. Dozens of young culinary entrepreneurs have chosen Philadelphia as their home, reinventing the dining scene and blurring the line between traditional "special-occasion" restaurants and more casual, moderately priced bistros. With the drop in tourism and the local economy, only those restaurants that concentrate on good value, at whatever price level, are going to survive and thrive, and I've tried to pinpoint these restaurants in this chapter. Compared to New York, Philadelphia restaurants set a higher standard for quality and attention, at prices that are up to one-third less (particularly at the high end).

Don't neglect the rich "local favorites" culture in town: cheesesteaks, pizza, "hoagies" (large deli-meat-based sandwiches on Italian rolls), and pretzels all claim fervent local connoisseurship.

This chapter unfortunately cannot include many renowned Main Line and other suburban restaurants. If you're heading out that way, many of the volunteers who staff the desk at the **Independence Visitor Center,** 6th and Market streets, Philadelphia, PA 19107 (© **215/965-7676**), hail from those parts and have crackerjack knowledge of the dining options there. For Web surfers, the best site I've seen for metro Philadelphia is **www.digital city.com/philadelphia**, which combines its own breezy synopses about 1500 restaurants with uncensored comments from the public.

Two persistent irritants: first, all those new hotels and restaurants make good service from experienced waitstaff a rare thing. Second, the economics of the restaurant business are causing many quality places to restrict service to dinners, since lunch prices don't allow for much of a profit.

This chapter will categorize **very expensive** restaurants as those charging $55 or more per person for dinner without wine; **expensive** as $40 to $55 per person; **moderate** as $20 to $40; and **inexpensive** as under $20. Meal tax is 7%, and standard tipping is 15% (the latter is occasionally included on the tab).

The service of wine and liquor is fraught with politics. Some restaurants are BYOB due to high fees to get a license, and restaurants with licenses may charge as much as 300% what they paid for a bottle of wine. The state Liquor Control Board does allow restaurants with licenses to permit customers to bring their own bottles, but don't look for quick acceptance of this policy.

Note: For most restaurants I have given only summer hours; you can expect 9pm (as opposed to 10pm) closings in other seasons.

1 Historic Area

VERY EXPENSIVE

Morimoto ★★★ FUSION/JAPANESE   The restaurant world buzzed when Masaharu Morimoto, one of the world's great sushi chefs, was lured to open his own place right here in Philadelphia. Stephen Starr built him a glowing, cool-but-friendly bamboo-clad $1 million destination, and you should expect to pay those design fees back at $100+ per person for dinner. The decor is a softly undulating series of translucent booths, with pastel lights that subtly change colors every few minutes; downstairs and throughout the meal, the utensils and pots are coordinated with the smooth Japanese stones that appear in the interior decoration. The menu is a series of tastings meant for sharing. You could go with the $80 to $120 *omakase* (chef's choice) menu of dishes — there are 40 to 50 dishes, and most are spectacular. A warm whitefish carpaccio melts in the mouth, and chilled green tea noodles are a revelation. Desserts range from white chocolate mousse to a tofu cheesecake to fig cake. Note that Mr. Morimoto is almost certainly going to expand back to New York by 2005, so catch him before his attention is divided.

723 Chestnut St. (Ⓒ) **215/413-9070.** www.morimotorestaurant.com. Reservations recommended. Sushi $3–$5.50 per piece; main courses $17–$35. AE, DC, MC, V. Mon–Fri 11:30am–2pm; Mon–Thurs 5–11pm; Fri–Sat 5pm–midnight; Sun 4–10pm.

EXPENSIVE

Buddakan ★★ (Moments) FUSION   There's one Philadelphian identified with the "theme restaurant": His name is Stephen Starr, and his Buddakan has captured the prize in the theme restaurant genre since it opened in August 1998, followed by Blue Angel a few blocks away, Pod in West Philadelphia, and Alma de Cuba in 2001. You'll find a shimmering waterfall; Japanese river stones; luminescent walls; and a gold-coated, candle-bedecked, 10-foot Buddha who dominates the main room and the 22-seat onyx-topped community table directly under its bellybutton. It's a noisy scene, but the fare is so fine and inventive that you won't care. Try the Indonesian jumbo shrimp, wasabi-crusted filet mignon, and sesame-crusted tuna. The energy level and the chance to spot celebrities are consistently high, and the bar scene is cool and trendy until 2am nightly. The staff takes all the rave reviews personally, which can be off-putting.

325 Chestnut St. (Ⓒ) **215/574-9440.** Reservations required. AE, DC, MC, V. Main courses $15–$28. Lunch $12–$18. Mon–Thurs 11:30am–2pm and 5–11pm; Fri 11:30am–2pm and 5pm–midnight; Sat 5pm–midnight; Sun 5–11pm.

Chart House ★ STEAKHOUSE/SEAFOOD   The busiest restaurant in all of Philadelphia has to be the Chart House, a veritable three-story convention center right on the Delaware River with spectacular views and a tableside waterfall to boot. It's part of a chain, of course, but many prefer this outpost for its views, spaciousness, huge portions, and quality. Expect a spirited crowd and frequent birthday celebrations. Stick with the New England clam chowder; prime rib, or a steak of halibut or tuna; and one of their signature desserts, such as mud pie, Key lime pie, cheesecake, or ice cream. Try to get a window seat if you call in advance.

555 S. Columbus Blvd. (formerly Delaware Ave.) at Penn's Landing. (Ⓒ) **215/625-8383.** Reservations recommended. Main courses $18–$40. Sun fixed-price brunch $24. Children's menu available. AE, DC, MC, V. Mon–Thurs 5–10pm; Fri 5–11pm; Sat 4pm–midnight; Sun 4–11pm, brunch 11am–2:30pm. Free valet parking.

La Famiglia ★★ ITALIAN   The name La Famiglia refers to both the proprietors and the clientele of this refined Italian restaurant, chosen some time ago as

Philadelphia Dining

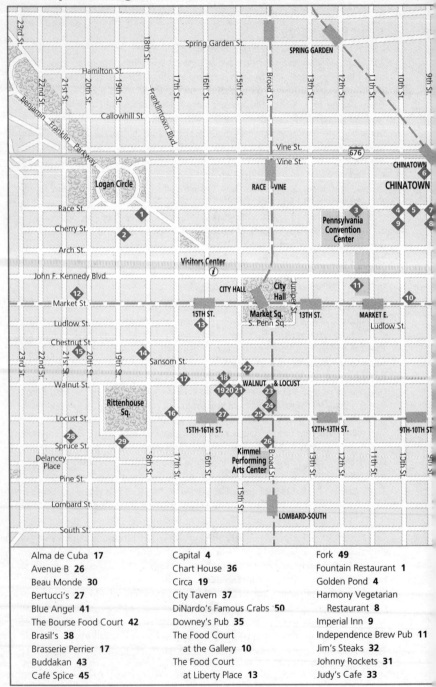

one of the 25 best Italian restaurants in the country by *Bon Appétit* magazine and with many awards since. The Neapolitan Sena family aims for elegant dining, service, and presentation; their success here has spawned Penn's View Inn and its Ristorante Panorama (see below).

The restaurant seats 60 in a private, warm setting of hand-hammered Venetian chandeliers, majolica tiles, and fresh flowers. The chefs at La Famiglia make most of their own pasta, and you might concentrate on such dishes as *gnocchi al basilico,* which adds basil and sweet red pepper sauce to potato dumplings. There's a choice of five or six vegetables with meals; the marinated string beans and zucchini with pepper have never failed to please. The wine cellar is legendary. For dessert, try a *mille foglie,* the Italian version of the napoleon, or the profiteroles in chocolate sauce, accompanied by one of the grappas over the fireplace. People often remain here well after the closing hour, lingering over sambuca while arias play in the background. The $21.99 full lunch special has garnered many repeat patrons.

8 S. Front St. ⓒ **215/922-2803.** Reservations required. Main courses $23–$45; lunch $22 menu. AE, DC, MC, V. Tues–Fri noon–2pm and 5:30–9:30pm; Sat 5:30–10pm; Sun 5–9pm.

Tangerine ★★ MEDITERRANEAN The theme of this Stephen Starr–designed extravaganza is Morocco, or the Morocco of Western dreams. After a super-trendy 2000 opening, Tangerine still racks up "chic-est restaurant" awards while maintaining a solid and inventive menu that riffs off Moroccan classics. In design terms, it's a brilliant division of a long, narrow space into chambers punctuated by curtains, extensive and eclectic lighting, and wild, exotic decor. A corridor festooned with hundreds of inset votive lights connects the various rooms. The restaurant is run by a cheerful and knowledgeable staff.

To do it right, start with one of the specialty cocktails; the signature drink combines tangerine puree with vodka and club soda — an alcoholic Creamsicle. The lower end of the menu offers couscous and wonderful tagine stews; the lamb and honey version is almost black with caramelizing. A pan-seared red snapper comes with spinach dumplings and toasted pepper sauce. The sharing-size portions and big tables make this an ideal choice for large groups out to have some fun. The austere, black-lighted bar area in front gets packed and noisy late at night.

232 Market St. ⓒ **215/627-5116.** Reservations strongly recommended. Main courses $24–$29. AE, MC, V. Sun–Wed 5–11pm; Thurs–Sat 5pm–midnight.

MODERATE

Azalea ★ *Value* AMERICAN For imaginative interpretations of American cuisine, including local dishes, this is one of the best spots in town, with a treetop view of Independence National Historical Park. The French Provincial faux zebra skin armchairs, arched windows, and multi-lighted chandeliers and wall sconces don't seem American — but they are.

Chef Gary Flora's selections include such traditional (and updated) Pennsylvania Dutch specialties as chicken-corn soup with saffron and apple fritters, shad in sorrel sauce (what saved the troops at Valley Forge), and pheasant potpie. The menus change seasonally, with surprise appearances by various dishes, such as the Chilean sea bass with lobster Bolognese sauce. Kennett Square mushrooms, Lancaster County persimmons and quinces, and elderberry preserves all show up on the menu. Given the way prices can add up, I'd recommend the fixed-price dinner. For dessert, choose between the five freshly made sorbets or an old-fashioned apple-and-sour-cherry pie.

Omni Hotel, 4th and Chestnut sts. ✆ **215/931-4260**. Reservations recommended. Main courses $15–$30; breakfast $7–$14; lunch $10.50–$17. Fixed-price 5-course dinner $34. AE, DC, MC, V. Mon–Fri 6:30–10:30am, 11am–2pm, and 5:30–10pm (Fri until 11pm); Sat–Sun 7am–1pm and 5:30–10pm (Sat until 11pm); Sun 5:30–9pm. Sat dancing to 3-piece group.

The Blue Angel ★★★ *Value* FRENCH BISTRO This 1999 "Best New Restaurant" winner is a comfortable, first-class French bistro that revitalized a block that for many years was known for its 99-cent stores. The 1920s home of an automat, Blue Angel has kept the hexagonal tile floors and milk glass ceiling, adding comfortable scalloped leather booths and a center corridor of free tables. The glowing wall and ceiling tiles foster a feeling of chortling self-satisfaction that the warm French bread, the rich cuisine, and the fairly moderate prices quickly help along. A typical appetizer is the terrine of cooked yellow beets, layered with goat cheese and roasted peppers and drizzled with sweet vinegar. A pan-roasted salmon is simultaneously sweet and spicy with the addition of Dijon and turmeric. Desserts are splendid, from the warm apple tart with cinnamon ice cream to the chocolate pot de crème. The staff is unfailingly courteous.

706 Chestnut St. ✆ **215/925-6889**. Reservations recommended. Main courses $16–$24; lunch $10–$17. AE, DC, MC, V. Mon–Thurs 11:30am–3pm and 5–11pm; Fri 11:30am–3pm and 5pm–midnight; Sat 5pm–midnight; Sun 5–10pm.

Café Spice INDIAN Café Spice, opened in April 2000 by Sushil Malhotra (owner of Dawat in New York), is a contemporary Indian restaurant with a menu that tours the subcontinent in a fairly standard way. The interior features textured beige walls with recessed display boxes for spice jars, hanging lanterns and cut-out windows — very dramatic and soothing all at once. All main courses include fragrant basmati rice, nan bread, and several vegetable dishes; I find the vegetarian entrees most satisfying for their size and complex textures. The restaurant looks more expensive than it is; most entrees are priced at $16 or less, and portions are large. And don't worry about the hours; the doors stay open until 2am most nights.

35 S. 2nd St. ✆ **215/627-6273**. Main courses $15–$24. AE, DC, DISC, MC, V. Mon–Thurs 11:30am–3pm and 5–10:30pm; Fri 11:30am–3pm and 4–11:30pm; Sat 11:30am–4pm and 4–11:30pm; Sun 11:30am–4pm and 5–10:30pm.

City Tavern ★ *Finds* AMERICAN If the hunger to relive those good old 1780s overcomes you in Independence Park, there's at least one authentic restaurant that will let you use that newfangled credit card to pay for colonial fare. City Tavern is the same tavern that members of the Constitutional Convention used as a coffee shop, ballroom, and club some 200 years ago. The U.S. government now owns the building, which is operated by a concessionaire, Walter Staib. He's pumped in $500,000 to completely renovate and open up 10 dining areas plus a garden and veranda, all serviced by a discreet state-of-the-art kitchen (well, almost — true to its roots, the only freezer space is for the ice cream!). Chef Craig Peck puts out menus tending toward the meaty — roast duckling, tenderloin tips, and turkey potpie. The taproom features microbrewed and custom beers and ales. The "shrub" (a kind of punch) packs a wallop. Service can be inattentive and slow-moving.

138 S. 2nd St., near Walnut St. ✆ **215/413-1443**. Reservations recommended. Main courses $18–$26; lunch $11–$17. AE, DC, DISC, MC, V. Daily 11:30am–9pm.

The Dark Horse ★ ENGLISH/CONTINENTAL This three-story Federal town house on Head House Square has proven to have real staying power. It's taken on a new name but not much else has changed — good news for the English expats and pub lovers who adore this casual slice of the homeland.

The atmosphere is all paneling, wooden tables, exposed beams, and frosted-glass lamps. They've added buffalo wings and Caesar salad to traditional offerings such as beef Wellington and prime rib with Yorkshire pudding. The seafood choices, displayed raw on a cart, include bay scallops poached with basil, tomatoes, and Muscadet. To finish, select a dessert from the restaurant's own bakery or sample the English Stilton cheese with fresh fruit. Lunch is a less ambitious affair, with Cornish pasty (traditional pastry filled with lamb, carrots, and potatoes and flavored with fresh herbs), shepherd's pie, trout filet, and a wild-mushroom-and-vegetable crepe. There are four bars, with 14 English imported beers.

421 S. 2nd St. ℂ **215/928-9307**. Reservations recommended. Main courses $14–$25; lunch $5–$10. AE, DC, DISC, MC, V. Tues–Sat 11:30am–3pm and 5:30–10pm; Sun 4:30–9pm; brunch Sun 11am–2:30pm. Pub only Mon 4–10pm, bar until 2am nightly.

DiNardo's Famous Crabs ★★ *Value* SEAFOOD DiNardo's, now 27 years old, springs to mind as the best moderately priced spot in the area around the Betsy Ross House and Elfreth's Alley. The door nearest 3rd Street is the real entrance. DiNardo's is notable for three things: its site, its reasonable prices, and its staggering collection of fish lures. The building was an inn for Tory soldiers in 1776 and later served as an Underground Railroad stop and Prohibition-era brothel.

Prime catches from the Gulf of Mexico are flown up daily to the restaurant, where experienced hands season the crabs with the house blend of 24 spices and steam them to perfection. Only the DiNardo family mixes the secret crab seasonings. If you're not in a crabby mood, there are at least 30 other succulent items on the menu, from raw-bar oysters to seafood platters. Monday is all-you-can-eat crab night, now at $30. Service is especially patient with families with small kids.

312 Race St. ℂ **215/925-5115**. Reservations required for 5 or more. Crabs $3–$5 each; other main courses $15–$30; lunch $7–$11. Wed 3-course prix-fixe dinner $34. AE, DC, MC, V. Mon–Thurs 11am–10pm; Fri–Sat 11am–11pm; Sun 3–9pm.

Downey's Pub IRISH/AMERICAN Two hundred and fifty years ago, Front Street from Race to Fitzwater streets was a jumble of docks, shops, and public houses that reminded English and Irish seamen of home. Downey's Pub has succumbed to such modern features as electricity, quiche, and a new island bar with cocktail seating, but it's still a place that any Irish person would be proud to frequent. Much of the ground floor was lifted from a Dublin bank built in 1903, and the upstairs is from a pub in Cork City. Don't expect spotlessness.

In summer, cafe tables grace both the South Street and the river patios. Upstairs, with a wraparound deck, is a tonier venue. Lunch and dinner menus offer some Irish dishes with American embellishments, along with Italian and lighter fare. The soups are strong; roast beef and turkey are carved on your order; and the fish of the day, done any way you like, is served with a fresh vegetable. But most popular are the crab cakes.

Live music is a staple of Downey's, both at the weekend brunches and in the upstairs Piano Bar on Friday and Saturday from 8pm.

Northwest corner of Front and South sts. ℂ **215/625-9500**. Reservations recommended. Main courses $7–$20; lunch $8–$13. AE, DC, DISC, MC, V. Mon–Fri 11:30am–4pm and 4:30–10:45pm; Sat 11:30am–4pm and 4:30pm–12:30am; Sun 10:30am–4pm and 4:30–9:45pm. Pub fare until 2am.

Fork ★★★ CONTINENTAL Fork is the best example in Old City of an affordable, stylish bistro that's fairly priced and centrally located. Since it seats only 68 and has caught a second wave of rave reviews, make sure you call beforehand to get a table. The restaurant features a hip circular bar, open rear kitchen, supersize banquette walls, and glorious lighting. Most of the ingredients come from organic farms and Amish purveyors; the menu is changed and reprinted daily. Executive chef Dave Ballentine, with experience at Odeon and La Terrasse, incorporates classic French techniques into the service of American bistro cuisine — look for grilled coriander-crusted ahi tuna with a basil coulis and white bean salad with portobello mushroom, for example.

306 Market St. ☎ 215/625-9425. Reservations recommended. Main courses $15–$24; lunch $7–$11. AE, DC, DISC, MC, V. Mon–Fri 11:30am–2:30pm and 5:30–10:30pm; Fri–Sat 2:30–4:30pm and 5–11:30pm; Sun 11am–2:30pm.

Judy's Café ✦ AMERICAN An agreeable bistro that's long outgrown its countercultural beginnings, Judy's is one of the finest examples of the South Street renaissance. Judy herself is gone, but owner Eileen Plato maintains a neighborhood feeling, though it's not really a family place. The regulars banter with the waiters, who dine here on their nights off, and the well-stocked bar gets an assortment of gay and straight folks settling into a relaxing ambience.

The main courses are eclectic. A Monday-to-Thursday special includes your choice of stir-fried duck, lamb stew, or the catch of the day, with soup and coffee. Whatever seafood is on the menu will undoubtedly be fresh. The very, very chocolate cake is almost fudgelike; the mocha or amaretto cheesecakes are likewise superb.

3rd and Bainbridge sts. ☎ 215/928-1968. Reservations recommended for parties of 4 or more. Main courses $12–$21. Local papers often advertise 2-for-1 weeknight specials. AE, DC, MC, V. Mon–Thurs 5:30–11pm; Fri–Sat 5:30pm–midnight; Sun 10:30am–3pm and 5:30–10pm.

Meiji-en on the Waterfront ✦✦ *Moments* JAPANESE/AMERICAN Meiji-en is an indoor theme park, with separate areas for sushi, tempura, teppanyaki (stove top cooking at the table), and regular table seating (the latter two feature river views to the east), as well as a bar with live jazz Friday and Saturday and a lavish jazz brunch Sunday. There's something for everyone here, from romantic couples to large families. The decor features lots of hanging rice-paper globes, blond-wood screens and seats, and comfortable black-and-red cushions. Try to get one of those spectacular views of the river and the Ben Franklin Bridge as it twinkles at night.

Many of Meiji-en's dishes have the same basic ingredients — filets of fish and chicken — prepared in different ways, from boiled to quick-grilled to diced in gyoza dumplings. Many dishes are marked as especially health conscious. The teppanyaki dishes are the cheapest and most fun; your group will sit around horseshoe-shaped tables with granite-and-steel stovetops while you're served seared meat and greens. If you're ordering regular service, expect beautifully presented fish steaks or marbled beef. At brunch, French toast and omelets to order occupy the hibachi grills. Valet parking nearby is $6.

Upstairs at Pier 19, on the Delaware River at Callowhill St., 4 blocks north of the Benjamin Franklin Bridge. ☎ 215/592-7100. Reservations recommended. Main courses $18–$30. AE, DC, DISC, MC, V. Tues–Thurs 5–9:30pm; Fri–Sat 5–10:30pm; Sun 10:30am–3pm and 4–9:30pm. Valet parking nearby $6.

Painted Parrot Café ✦ *Value* AMERICAN There's something delectable about a restaurant where the dessert choices outnumber the entrees. Beyond its signature desserts, this cafe, steps away from Independence Historical National Park, offers innovative and reasonable American-based meals. Under new manager Ian Hall, the slow, bad service and sometimes mediocre dinner dishes have improved. The restaurant is pretty but not precious, with a bright parrot mural. Most Philadelphians associate this spot with the amazing $14.95 fixed-price dinner on Tuesday night and the delightful $5 desserts — showcased in an all-you-can-savor $7.50 dessert buffet on Wednesday starting at 5pm. Fudge torte, mousse torte, old-fashioned apple pie — the list goes up to 17 most nights, including a token low-fat choice. The La Colombe roast coffee is excellent day and night. BYOB.

211 Chestnut St. ℂ 215/922-5971. Reservations recommended. Main courses $13.50–$18.50; lunch $5–$8. AE, DC, DISC, MC, V. Tues–Thurs 5:30–11:30pm; Fri–Sat 5:30pm–1am; Sun 4–10pm.

Philadelphia Fish & Company ★★ 🄥alue SEAFOOD/AMERICAN   It's inevitable that you'll pass Philadelphia Fish & Company, given its location next to Independence National Historical Park. So it's great that owner Kevin Meeker and chef Amy Coben work so hard to deliver a reasonable, high-quality, exciting selection of fresh fish that's served with warmth and flair. The main courses run to towers of crab cakes or halibut on mashed potatoes or nests of bok choy or rice. The $10 executive lunch is a great deal: a cup of soup, the fish special, vegetable, green salad, and beverage. And the 3-choice $6 dinner special at the bar (often seared perch or a burger) has been rated the best tavern deal in the city by *Philadelphia* magazine. The wine list, skewed toward whites, is of a good quality and very reasonable for Philadelphia. There's outdoor dining when seasonable.

207 Chestnut St. ℂ 215/625-8605. Reservations recommended. Main courses $17–$21; lunch $8–$12. AE, DC, MC, V. Mon–Thurs 11:30am–10:30pm; Fri 11:30am–4pm and 5pm–midnight; Sat noon–3pm and 4:30pm–midnight; Sun 4–10:30pm.

Ristorante Panorama 🄖 ITALIAN   Although the Ristorante Panorama is on the waterfront, its "view" is a colorful mural of the Italian countryside, and the vast majority of the staff is from the Naples area. The principal reason to visit is that Panorama is a legendary wine bar, with 120 wines (not just Italian) served to a sophisticated, lively crowd. It's a lot of fun to order "flights," or a series of 3.5-ounce glasses of wines chosen to complement the food you order. The food doesn't stack up to this exalted level either in value or sheer class, but it's very good by any standard. Pasta, salads, and fish predominate, with a few veal and beef dishes. The bread is served not with butter, but with a tiny bowl of pesto. Fish courses are usually grilled and lightly seasoned with garlic and tomatoes. The tiramisu, with its triple-cream mascarpone cheese drizzled with chocolate, needs either an espresso or a dessert wine as an accompaniment.

Front and Market sts. ℂ 215/922-7800. Reservations recommended. Main courses $18–$26. AE, DC, MC, V. Daily noon–midnight, with dinner service Mon–Thurs noon–2pm and 5:30–10pm; Fri noon–2pm and 5:30–11pm; Sat 5:30–11pm; and Sun 5–9pm.

INEXPENSIVE

Beau Monde 🄖 🄥alue FRENCH   Americans love calzones, pita sandwiches, and dough wraps of all kinds — so it makes sense that they would love crepes. This pretty (but noisy) 65-seat restaurant is usually filled with Gen-Xers and their parents. The restaurant prepares two types of crepes: a savory, made with buckwheat flour and filled with anything from herbs to roasted chicken or shrimp; and a sweet wheat flour dessert crepe, filled with sliced fruits or berries. Appetizers and salads are also offered, but they don't hit the spot as nicely. Thursday nights bring a French accordionist.

624 S. 6th St. (at the corner of Bainbridge, 1 block south of South St.). ℂ 215/592-0656. Reservations accepted for 6 or more. Crepe main courses $2.75–$10. AE, DC, DISC, MC, V. Tues–Fri noon–11pm; Sat 10am–11pm; Sun 10am–10pm.

Brasil's ★★ *Value* BRAZILIAN   This warm, welcoming bistro in the heart of the historic district has gotten positive press for all-you-can-eat feijoada (the Brazilian national stew of black beans, sausage, seafood, and orange garnish) for $16, offered on Friday, Saturday and Sunday, and the $20 spicy grilled rodizio (meat and sausages served on sword-like skewers) feast on Tuesday and Thursday. There are plenty of standard meat and poultry offerings. There is live jazz on Sunday and I can't say enough about the spirited salsa dancing upstairs on weekends — great crowd, great music.

112 Chestnut St. ℂ 215/413-1700. Reservations recommended. Main courses $9–$20. AE, DC, MC, V. Tues–Thurs 5–10pm; Fri–Sat 5–11pm; Sun 5–9pm.

Johnny Rockets *Kids* AMERICAN   Johnny Rockets, a national chain, is a harmless enough place — retro for the kids and comforting for their parents. Clean red-and-white booths surround an open grill. Burgers and sandwiches predominate, along with fries, onion rings, excellent malts and milkshakes, gooey desserts and pies — it's all here. Every so often, the staff bursts into song.

443 South St. ℂ 215/829-9222. Sandwiches and burgers $3.50–$6. AE, DC, DISC, MC, V. Sun–Wed 11am–11pm; Thurs 11am–midnight; Fri–Sat 11am–1am.

Thai Palace THAI   Thai Palace boasts all the sweet and hot pastes and spices you'd expect. It isn't much to look at, so start right in on the satay, a highly spiced and marinated meat kebab. For something hot that doesn't sear the taste buds, try the chicken ka prow (chicken with fried hot pepper) cooked in an unusual basil-and–lemon grass sauce. The desserts here are not a strong point. BYOB.

117 South St. ℂ 215/925-2764. Reservations recommended. Main courses $9–$16. AE, DC, MC, V. Daily 5:30–10pm.

2 Center City

VERY EXPENSIVE

Founders ★ CONTINENTAL   Founders is on the top (19th) floor of the Park Hyatt at the Bellevue, and its location under the massive 45-foot dome of this French Renaissance landmark makes it attractive for fans of views, as well as for anyone who is looking for romantic dinner and dancing on the weekends. The elegant dining room features arched windows, flourishes and swags of draperies, and plush armchairs. The "founders" are the statues of Philadelphia luminaries that surround you. At these prices, you will get fine European traditional preparations, particularly French, from David Wolf, the executive chef: look for filet of beef with marrow, chateaubriand for two, and baked chicken breast with berries. The award-winning wine list includes over 400 selections, and there's dancing every Friday and Saturday from 8 to 11pm with the Eileen Duffy Trio. Jimmy Rudolph holds sway on piano most weeknights.

Broad and Walnut sts. ℂ 215/790-2814. Reservations recommended. Main courses $25–$39. 3-course $38 pretheater dinner. AE, DISC, MC, V. Mon–Sat 7–10am, 11:30am–2:30pm, and 5:30–10pm (Sat until 10:30pm); Sun 11:30am–2:30pm and 5:30–9pm.

Fountain Restaurant ★★★ *Moments* INTERNATIONAL   Fountain Restaurant and Le Bec-Fin (see below) are Philadelphia's two most nationally acclaimed restaurants. *Food & Wine* magazine chose Fountain as one of America's top 25 restaurants. The views partially explain why, with a view of the plumes of water from the Swann Fountain in Logan Circle on one side, and the hotel's own courtyard cascade on the other. The cuisine, first under legend Jean Marie

Lacroix and now under protégé Martin Hamann, is expertly prepared and quietly served in expansive surroundings. If you're pulling out all the stops, it's $250 a couple without wine — but worth every penny.

The menu is complicated and understated, and the easy dinner route is the $110 set menu of four savory and two sweet courses. A la carte choices include a sautéed wild bass filet with roasted figs and swiss chard, or a melt-in-your-mouth rosemary filet mignon. The Sunday brunch, which is also very pricey, induces a top of the world feeling. Brunch is based on incredible dishes like chicken breast marinated in bourbon and caramelized onions. A chocolate soufflé or selections from the cheese cart are perfect ends to your meal. Service is basically tops in the city.

The Four Seasons Hotel, 1 Logan Sq. (between 18th St. and the Franklin Pkwy.). © **215/963-1500.** Reservations required. Main courses $38–$46; fixed-price "Spontaneous Taste" 6-course dinner menu $110; lunch $21–$29; set 3-course lunch menu $39.50. AE, DC, MC, V. Mon–Fri 6:30am–10:30am and 11:30–2pm; Sat–Sun 7–10:30am; Sat–Thurs 5:45–10:30pm; Fri–Sat 5:45–10pm. Brunch served Sun 11am–2:15pm. Fri–Sat from 8pm until everyone goes home: dessert and dancing in Swann Lounge.

Le Bec-Fin ★★★ *Moments* FRENCH   Le Bec-Fin — can it really be 32 years old? — is unquestionably the best restaurant in Philadelphia and certainly one of the top 10 restaurants in the country. Owner/chef Georges Perrier hails from Lyon, France's gastronomic capital, and commands the respect of restaurateurs on two continents for his culinary accomplishments.

A new generation has taken hold at Le Bec-Fin, with a new look and staffing. Daniel Stern, 31 years old and self-taught, is the chef with the chance of a lifetime here, and Gregory Castells is building a new wine list and including more wines by the glass. Perrier spent a fortune in summer 2002 transforming the interior from a Louis XVI homage to an elegant turn-of-the-century Parisian salon setting, with a marble fireplace, 14 pilasters containing silk inlays, and sconces on floral fabric panels amid antiqued mirrors. The table settings include bountiful bouquets, Christofle silver, and the same 18th-century Limoges pattern that Paul Bocuse uses in his Lyon restaurant. It is virtually impossible not to enjoy yourself here, even before your meal begins.

With leisurely timing, an evening at Le Bec-Fin waltzes through hors d'oeuvres, a fish course, a main course, a salad, cheese, a dessert, and coffee with petits fours. Since most of the menu changes seasonally — and your special orders are welcome as well — dishes listed here are illustrative. A roast lobster in a butter sauce infused with black truffles is unbelievably flavorful. The terrine of three fish contains a layer of turbot mousse, then a layer of salmon mousse, then one of sole mousse, each with its own dressing; the total effect, with shallots, couldn't be more subtle and delicious. The escargots in champagne are renowned as a first course — the garlic butter in this dish includes inspired touches of Chartreuse and hazelnuts.

The main dishes give you the opportunity to try some culinary rarities — pheasant, venison, and pigeon. The last (stuffed with goose liver, leeks, and mushrooms) comes in a truffle sauce. The mouth-watering dish of four filets of venison comes covered in a thick milk-mustard sauce. The serving of desserts becomes a grand opera, with trays, tables, and ice cream and sherbets (in the little aluminum canisters that they were churned in) zooming from guest to guest. With the addition of pastry chef Bobby Bennett, the treats on the dessert tray look and tastes like Dante's Paradiso, especially the 18-inch-high Mont Blanc with sides of sheet chocolate. And now there's a separate dessert menu! The finest coffee in the city, served in Villeroy & Boch flowered china, washes those petits fours down perfectly. Cigars, cordials, liqueurs, and marcs and other fortified spirits gild the lily. And did I mention that lunch at $40 is actually a great, great deal?

The lower-level **Le Bar Lyonnais** offers more affordable snacking and champagne toasts. Open until midnight, it has only four tables and bar stools, but trompe l'oeil pilasters and paisley wallpaper give it a bigger feel. Expect to spend about $10 a nibble and $7 for a glass of house wine. The later it gets, the more likely dishes from upstairs are to arrive — and M. Perrier himself, for that matter. In 1997, Perrier opened the more relaxed **Brasserie Perrier** down the street (see below), and in late 2000 brought the spirit of Provence to the Main Line with **Le Mas Perrier** (© **610/964-2588**), at 503 W. Lancaster Ave. in Wayne, quickly recognized by *Esquire* as one of the country's best new restaurants.

1523 Walnut St. © 215/567-1000. Reservations required a week ahead for weeknights, months ahead for Fri–Sat. 3-course fixed-price lunch $40; fixed-price dinner $120; $155 for 11-course marathon of riches. AE, DC, MC, V. Lunch seatings Mon–Fri at 11:30am–1:30pm; dinner seatings Mon–Thurs at 6 and 9pm, Fri–Sat at 6 and 9:30pm. Bar Lyonnais downstairs serves food and drink Mon–Fri 11:30am–midnight, Sat 6pm–1am. Valet parking $16.

EXPENSIVE

Alma de Cuba ★★★ LATIN AMERICAN   Douglas Rodriguez, already one of the country's most highly respected chefs (with Pipa and Chicama in Manhattan to his credit), was intrigued by two things: a Walnut Street town house with pre-Castro details located in the epicenter of fine dining, and the imagination and pocketbook of restaurateur Stephen Starr. Their vision has animated Alma de Cuba, the "soul of Cuba," with new interpretations of Cuban classics, from daiquiris to dishes like slow roasted pork shank and crispy fried whole snapper. The atmosphere is evocative, with glass walls shimmering with tobacco leaf images, slow fans in pinpointed light amid deep red fabrics, and mambo dancing. Unlike Pasion! (see below), where flavors are exquisitely blended and balanced, Alma de Cuba's dishes are rushes of strong flavors, ingredients and heat; delicate stomachs should choose with care, and wait for soothing deserts like tapioca, served in a fresh coconut half. It's not perfect — quite loud, and service is rushed — but it is an original. The first floor is one of the city's great bars, with Cuban metal-work sculptures and luscious mojitos.

1623 Walnut St. © 215/988-1799. Reservations recommended. Main courses $22–$29. AE, DC, DISC, MC, V. Mon–Thurs 5–11pm; Fri–Sat 5pm–midnight; Sun 5pm–10pm.

Avenue B ★★ AMERICAN   The prime real estate at the corner of 260 South Broad St. across from the Kimmel Center was claimed early by veteran star restaurateurs Neil Stein and Gabe Marabella, whose dedication to quality and flair is complete. Everything else has been a continuing journey, as the restaurant nearly died waiting for the Kimmel Center to open, and is now on its third chef in less than two years. Architecturally, it's a stunner, with two glamorous rooms where Tuscan-inspired meals arrive on the tables like clockwork in time for patrons to get to the theater. A lively hubbub pervades the place until late in the evening. The decor is angular with little McIntosh or Deco touches in the booths and sepia pictures of '30s film stars; there are lots of high pinlights focused on tables, and the WCs have unbelievably elegant stone sinks. Linen and china are understated and monogrammed, and the menu features handcut pappardalle, fried calamari with a spicy twist, and big platters of roasted veal chops and tuna loins. The *Frangelico semifreddo* (a sort of frozen mousse) is a must for dessert.

260 Avenue of the Arts (S. Broad St.). © 215/790-0705. Reservations recommended, especially for pretheater. Main courses $22–$34; lunch $8–$16. AE, DC, DISC, MC, V. Mon–Thurs 11:30am–11pm; Fri 11:30am–1am; Sat 5pm–1am; Sun 5–11pm.

Brasserie Perrier ★★ FRENCH Proprietor Georges Perrier rules the food scene in Philadelphia, so it was big news when he opened this brasserie in 1997. Now with chef Chris Scarduzio at the helm, it's more a French restaurant with international influence than a bistro, although there's a brasserie dining menu throughout the day alongside scheduled lunch and dinner menus. If you like a place that aims to make a serious stir, and you don't mind high prices, this is a good choice. The Art Deco–style venue is decorated with plush banquettes, silver leaf ceilings, light cherrywood, and dramatic lighting. It's built around a retro-cubist version of Marcel Duchamp's *Nude Descending a Staircase*. Don't expect the hearty or casual here — we're talking exquisite yellowfin sashimi with wasabi-spiced greens; or a crispy black bass with Asian sticky rice, Chinese eggplant, and ginger sauce. 2002 brought a fondue bar: not just the Swiss choices of cheese or chocolate, but spicy seafood and fresh fruit options as well. The wine list features small, quality-oriented French, Italian, and U.S. varietals in the $26 to $65 range, with specially priced gems from southern France.

1619 Walnut St. © **215/568-3000.** Reservations usually required. Main courses $22–$35; lunch prix-fixe 3-course $26. AE, DC, MC, V. Mon–Sat 11:30am–3pm and 5:30–11pm; Fri–Sat 5:30–11:30pm; Sun 5–9pm.

Friday Saturday Sunday AMERICAN/CONTINENTAL There's a lot to be said for a restaurant that installed a window on Rittenhouse Street for the kitchen staff. A romantic survivor of Philadelphia's early restaurant renaissance, Friday Saturday Sunday has adapted to the times by offering informality, a renovated bar upstairs, and relaxed, confident cuisine. You'll enjoy it if you have a taste or bemused affection for the funky. It's a bargain for its location, and the markup for the wine list is $10, the lowest in town.

Recently renovated, Friday Saturday Sunday is classy but not ostentatious: The cutlery and china don't match, flowers are rare, and the menu is a wall-mounted slate board. Pin lights frame a row of rectangular mirrors set in wood paneling. An aquarium bubbles behind the upstairs Tank Bar. Dress is everything from jeans to suits, and the service is vigilant but hands-off.

Try the fairly spicy Thai green salad with chicken breast, served with a soy, honey, and sesame sauce; or a colorful Szechuan salad with sweet red peppers and wok-fried beef slivers. The double-baked and mildly curried half duck is excellent. Portions of fish, such as grilled salmon with a creamy side of minced artichokes and red peppers, are enormous. You're advised to split an appetizer and even a dessert between two. The wine card lists about 30 vintages. The desserts change often.

261 S. 21st St. (between Locust and Spruce sts.). © **215/546-4232.** Reservations accepted. Main courses $15.50–$24.50. AE, DC, MC, V. Tues–Fri 11:30am–2:30pm; Mon–Sat 5:30–10:30pm; Sun 5–10pm.

Morton's of Chicago ★★ STEAK Looking for sirloin? Morton's of Chicago has become a staple for both business lunches and celebratory evenings. The quality of the specialties is amazing — they bring those carts of aged, well-marbled tender masses of double-cut filets, sirloins, and T-bones, along with live lobster and fresh veggies, right to your table for your own selection, and then prepare them in the open kitchen. The house porterhouse weighs in at 24 ounces. The cauliflower soup is highly touted, and the Sicilian veal chop with garlic breadcrumbs is a "hometown" hit. If you must stray further, sample the crab cocktail or the smoked salmon served on dark bread with horseradish cream, capers, and onions.

Morton's looks as clubby and sedate as you'd expect, with glass panels between the tables and booths and dim lighting that makes the brass glow. There's a cigar lounge for postprandial puffing. I have a beef (no pun intended) about the wine list, which features quality American reds like cabernets, but at a markup of at least 300%.

1411 Walnut St., 2nd floor. ℂ 215/557-0724. Reservations recommended. Jacket and tie required for men. Main courses $20–$40. AE, DC, MC, V. Mon–Sat 11:30am–2:30pm and 5:30–11pm; Sun 5–10pm.

Pasion! ★★ LATIN AMERICAN/FUSION   Pasion!, which opened at the end of 1998, has a reason for its hot status. Chef Guillermo Pernot is a young star, named as one of *Food and Wine's* ten best new American chefs. The restaurant is the first and foremost of Philadelphia's Nuevo Latino spots, with cuisine that's an exciting blend of authentic Latin ingredients, exotic presentation, and various preparation styles (though you might check out the swanky Alma de Cuba or moderate tapas-based Cibucan in this arena). It's a no-miss hit for a $100 dinner date, and recently doubled its dining space with Moorish tiles and a heavenly cathedral ceiling.

Pasion! has taken pedestrian sun-baked rooms seating 10 and given them warmth and mystery, with stone walls, louvered windows and candlelit sconces. Floral prints and stripes, sea grass cloth, and bamboo details evoke a tented tropical courtyard. The twelve stools at the granite and weathered wood bar in the rear — my favorite dining spot — perch near the unhurried and spotless open kitchen. Cuisine itself is intense. Many people start and end with one of five ceviche courses (marinated fresh, raw fish) offered daily (three for $28), and move on to cumin-crusted roasted salmon, Argentinean sirloin, or unusual grilled or baked root vegetables. Desserts feature sweet pastries and custards, and wines are the expected California and South American vintages, with bottles averaging $45 and glasses at about $8.50.

211 S. 15th St. ℂ 215/875-9895. Reservations recommended. Main courses $18–$32. AE, DC, MC, V. Mon–Thurs 5–10pm; Fri–Sat 5–11pm; Sun 5–9pm. Closed Sun in summer.

The Prime Rib ★★ STEAK   The Prime Rib, a small chain from Washington, D.C., and Baltimore, claimed the restaurant spot at the Warwick Hotel in 1998, and has captured the reputation of "best steakhouse in town," as opined by Zagat's and *Philadelphia* Magazine. Basically, the quest to become a top steakhouse becomes a question of serving quality cuts — which most chains do — prepared consistently, without dulling the kitchen's style and inspiration. This latter point is where The Prime Rib pulls ahead. It's got that classic 1930s look and feel, with sleek leopard-print carpeting, black leather furniture and black walls trimmed in gold. The array of appetizers and sides includes wonderful potato skins. Nightly jazz piano and bass duets play cocktail and dining background music.

1701 Locust St. ℂ 215/772-1701. Reservations recommended. Jackets required for men. Main courses $22–$38. AE, DC, MC, V. Sun–Mon 4:30–9pm; Tues–Thurs 4:30–10pm; Fri–Sat 4:30–11pm.

Striped Bass ★★★ SEAFOOD   *Bon Appétit, Town & Country, Esquire,* and *Gourmet* have called this one of the hottest seafood restaurants in the country. The setting and ambience are absolutely spectacular: A 16-foot steel sculpture of a leaping bass poised over the exhibition kitchen sets the tone. With rows of plateaued banquettes, warm lighting, and carpeted floors to soak up the din bouncing off the marble walls, you'll experience a rare and exotic sense of theater here. No one doubts that it can set you, or your expense account, back by $100 per person for dinner, but most people find the quality and value well worth it.

The kitchen delivers simple, creative preparations of seafood, with an emphasis on fresh herbs and clean flavors. Appetizers include a potato mousseline cake with Sevruga caviar and dill egg salad. The signature entree — wild striped bass with garlic mash, spring onions, and vegetables — is firm and flavorful. But take chances — this is the type of restaurant where you can feel comfortable asking the waitstaff for advice. The restaurant has recently added a nightly meat special. Rising star Patrick Feury, late of New York's Le Bernardin, was nominated "Best Mid-Atlantic Chef" by the James Beard Foundation in 2002 and has instituted an opulent tasting menu of seven courses. An extensive raw bar features oysters from the East and West coasts, clams, shrimp, and caviars. Desserts and ice creams are extravagant. A mostly domestic wine list starts at $22.

1500 Walnut St. ⓒ **215/732-4444.** Reservations almost always necessary. Main courses $17–32; lunch $13.50–$20. Chef tasting menu $90. AE, DC, MC, V. Mon–Thurs 11:30am–2:30pm and 5–11pm; Fri 11:30am–2:30pm and 5–11:30pm; Sat 5–11:30pm; Sun 5–10pm; brunch Sat–Sun 11am–2:30pm.

Toto ★★ ITALIAN   This wonderful Italian restaurant, close to the Academy of Music and the city's theaters, has undergone a change of management and style, morphing from a bastion of opulent grandeur to a lighter Italian bistro. A huge copper antipasto cart, enlarged copies of Impressionist and Expressionist art, and a brighter new look in the series of booths separated by etched glass and ebonied wood, define the space.

You can opt for the *cheese*, or samplings of delightful tapas-sized plates available at the bar for about $8 per platter. Otherwise, begin a meal with an antipasto such as sautéed buffalo-milk mozzarella slices; marinated pepperoni; sun-dried tomatoes; or a seafood terrine or mousse. Italian meals of this quality demand a small first course of pasta followed by a second course of fish, meat, or poultry with vegetables; and finally optional fruit, sweets, and coffee. If you feel like splurging, try the fazzoletti de mare, pasta triangles filled with savory shrimp and scallops. Main courses include thin-sliced fresh monkfish in lemon sauce, and marinated sautéed veal loin. If you order a grilled dish, be aware that many Americans perceive the Italian style as underdone. You'll want to finish with an espresso and some dessert (especially the house-made gelato).

1407 Locust St. ⓒ **215/546-2000.** Reservations recommended. Main courses $21–$31. AE, DISC, DC, MC, V. Mon–Sat 5–10pm; Sun 4–9pm; Fri noon–3pm.

MODERATE

Circa ★★ *Value* AMERICAN/ECLECTIC   This is one of Philadelphia's hottest spots. It serves great food on a great restaurant block, combining dinner with a sophisticated club. It's impressive yet comfortable, and it's cheaper than you might think, though new chef Tom Harkin has upped the ante since his 2000 arrival.

A former bank building provides Circa with great beaux arts columns and windows along the east wall's long bar, opening up to a square, pleasant room upstairs, and original steel-and-brass vault fittings downstairs. Chef Harkin likes strong, congenial, flavorful food. You'll find such choices as duck ravioli with goat cheese and sun-dried cherries, or roast salmon prepared *osso buco* style. The wines are well chosen, starting at $18.

At 11pm on Friday and Saturday (except in summer) the ground floor and mezzanine turn into a jammed dance floor, and the line to get in extends around the block.

1518 Walnut St. ⓒ **215/545-6800.** Reservations recommended. Main courses $16–$29; lunch $7–$15. Prix-fixe 4-course dinner $29–$32. AE, DC, MC, V. Mon 5–10pm; Tues–Wed 11:30am–2:30pm and 5–10pm; Thurs–Sat 11:30am–2:30pm and 5–11pm; Sun 4:30–9pm. Dancing schedule changes, so phone for details.

Ruth's Chris Steak House ★ STEAK   Perfectly situated for the Kimmel Center or any performance on the Avenue of the Arts, Ruth's Chris has gotten rave reviews since 1989 for food, although the service-bashing is unfortunately justified. Ruth's Chris only serves U.S. prime beef that's custom aged, never frozen, and rushed to Philadelphia by the New Orleans distributor for the chain. Their steak is more charred on the outside than the steak at most other steak-houses, but the charring does lock in the flavors. The rib-eye steak in particular is presented lovingly, almost ritually, in a quiet and respectful setting, and with almost no garnishes. The portions are so large that you might want to skip the side dishes, although Ruth's Chris boasts nine ways of cooking potatoes. Several fish and chicken choices are also available. The desserts, mostly Southern recipes with lots of sugar and nuts, average $6. Several tables are partially in the hallway, so make sure you request to avoid these.

260 S. Broad St. ⓒ 215/790-1515. Reservations recommended. Main courses $17–$39. AE, DC, DISC, MC, V. Mon–Sat 5–11:30pm; Sun 5–10:30pm.

Sansom Street Oyster House ✸ SEAFOOD   Sansom Street knows every-thing there is to know about oysters — where they come from, how their flavors differ, and how to prepare them. The space was altered in 1999 from a tradi-tional seafood parlor with a tile floor to a colorful, light-filled space. Blackboards listing the daily specials perch beside a large collection of antique oyster plates and nautical lithographs. Some of the regulars resent this change in decor. Nobody, however, resents the arrival of inventive Cary Neff, who has added Asian and contemporary notes to the traditional fresh seafood menu.

The oysters are air-freighted several times a week here, and you'll probably want an appetizer of several types: metallic belons; cooler, meatier Long Island half-shells; the new, fruity hybrids like Trevenen and Westcott from the Northwest; and larger, fishier box oysters. All are opened right at the raw bar. For dinner, most people choose from the daily selections of 8 to 10 fresh fish, often including local shad or tilefish. The homemade bread pudding is the most reliable dessert. The liquor prices are moderate and draft beer starts at $3.75. The brewpub upstairs, with its mahogany bar, exposed hardwood floors and (of course) copper brewing tanks, was the first brewpub in town. The pub is no longer theirs, but it's hitting new heights as the Nodding Head Brewery and Restaurant. Free parking after 5pm at 15th and Sansom with a $20 meal minimum.

1516 Sansom St. ⓒ 215/567-7683. Reservations accepted for 5 or more. Main courses $13.50–$20; lunch $6–$12.50. 4-course fixed-price dinner $19. AE, DC, DISC, MC, V. Mon–Sat 11am–10pm; Sun 3–9pm.

Susanna Foo ✸✸✸ Finds CHINESE   Susanna Foo has been touted in *Gourmet, Bon Appétit, Esquire* and just about everywhere else for serving one of the best blends of Asian and Western cuisines in the country. After 15 years, the restaurant has gotten a second wind with the addition of chef Terence Feury (brother of Striped Bass' chef Patrick!) and the excitement is back. The refined cuisine is enhanced by the space, which comprises a crisp, clean, fragrant garden of stone, glass, and silks, and a collection of Chinese art and textiles. The new second floor dining room renovation is also a hit.

The cuisine is the main thing, but be forewarned: If you're the type that finds exquisite but small portions at high prices off-putting, choose something heartier. Dim sum (entrees at lunch, appetizers at dinner) features such delicacies as curried chicken ravioli with grilled eggplant, slightly crispy but not oily. Noodle dishes, salads, and main courses combine East and West: water chestnuts and radicchio, savory quail with fresh litchi nuts, smoked duck and endive, grilled chicken with Thai lemon grass sauce, and spicy shrimp and pear curry. The Asian technique is to sear small amounts of ingredients, combining

⟨*C*⟩ A Taste of Ethnic Philly: Reading Terminal Market

The **Reading Terminal Market**, at 12th and Arch streets (*C* 215/ 922-2317), has been a greengrocer, snack shop, butcher, fish market, and sundries store for Philadelphians since the late 1900s. The idea was to use the space underneath the terminal's tracks for food vendors so that commuters and businesspeople could stock up easily and cheaply. Half of the stalls make up an English-style covered market with cool brick floors and the scent of fresh food and baked bread; the other half is a gourmet grocer/charcuterie.

Scrapple, mangoes, clam chowder, pretzels — you name it, if it's fresh and unpackaged, you can find it here. The northwest corner (12th and Arch sts.) is where most of the "retail" (as opposed to restaurant or institutional) Amish farm products come to market. You can still see the Amish in the city on their market days (Wed and Sat), and you can buy sticky buns at **Beiler's Pies,** soft pretzels made before your eyes at **Fisher's,** and individual egg custards ($1) and chicken potpies ($6) at **The Dutch Eating Place.** If you're in the market for meat, **Harry Ochs** and **Halteman Family** have the most extensive selections, with great country hams and local honey as well. **Reading Terminal Cheese Shop and Salumeria** offers gourmet cheeses and tinned goods, while **Margerum's,** now in its fourth generation, sells flours, spices, and coffee beans from barrels and kegs. The best coffee is sold at **Old City Coffee.**

If your stomach is rumbling uncontrollably by now, **Termini Brothers Bakery** will satisfy it with terrific bagels (50¢) or **Braverman's** will fill it with an egg challah ($3.75), Danish, or other pastry. For more protein,

---

them just before service. Ms. Foo does caramelize some dishes in French style, but her menu contains no butter-based sauces or roux. The wine list, designed to complement these dishes, specializes in French and California white wines. Desserts such as ginger créme with strawberries and hazelnut meringue are light and delicate. My only complaint is the service, which runs the gamut from the brusque to the smooth.

1512 Walnut St. *C* 215/545-2666. Reservations recommended for dinner. Main courses $18–$35; lunch $14–$25, with 3-course prix-fixe for $24.95. AE, MC, V. Mon–Fri 11:30am–2:30pm and 5–10pm (Fri until 11pm); Sat 5–11pm; Sun 5–9pm.

Twenty21 ⟨*⟩ *Kids* AMERICAN   This is what you'd expect from a restaurant in a big, impressive skyscraper, with modern, cool lighting, and a huge bar (120 seats) for singles. In August 2002, the place underwent a hurried change in ownership from the hands of Seattle absentees to those of three locals. The new owners took a corporate banquet hall and created a quieter, more intimate setup, with softened earth tones and a curtained facade. Twenty21 remains an impeccable, convenient, 180-seat restaurant that's surprisingly warm and romantic.

The 20-foot bar is noted for its huge selection and garnered the 2002 *Wine Spectator* Award of Excellence. The bottles are stacked vertically, forcing bartenders to scamper up and down ladders like gymnasts. Look for highly polished wood and stone surfaces and handblown glass chandeliers. Fortunately, high ceilings soak up much of the din.

Pearl's Oyster Bar practically gives away six cherrystone clams for $4.50, and a shrimp platter with french fries, bread, and coleslaw goes for $7.95. Or try **Coastal Cave Trading Co.,** which has great clam chowder ($3.50), oyster crackers, and smoked fish. Just inside 12th Street, **Bassett's** ⭐ (see "Best Restaurant Bets," in chapter 1) purveys Philadelphia's entry in the best American ice-cream contest at $2 a cone. The shakes ($3.75) are no less enticing, and the turkey sandwiches ($5.95) are simply the best anywhere. **Old Post Road Farm** makes a delicious cherry pie.

The 1990s renovation of the market has left it with more seating. The **Down Home Diner** ⭐ (see "Best Restaurant Bets," in chapter 1) is an excellent choice for breakfast or lunch. **Jill's Vorspeise** has a great selection of hearty soups. A lunch such as linguine with clam sauce will cost $5.50 at **By George Pasta & Pizza. Spataro's,** an old-time favorite, vends buttermilk, cottage cheese, and huge slabs of fresh pie. The **12th Street Cantina** sells not only tasty enchiladas and burritos, but also authentic ingredients, like blue cornmeal. Some consider **Rick's Philly Steaks** — a third generation of Pat's down in South Philly — the best purveyor of this distinctly Philadelphian dish. The **Beer Garden** draws pints of Yuengling Porter and Dock Street Beer, among other more mass-market brews.

The market is open Monday through Saturday from 9am to 6pm, but many vendors close at 5pm. Prices vary by vendor, and about half accept cash only. There are public restrooms here.

Twenty21 showcases American edibles, from Nebraska beef to various pastas, and its Seattle roots show through in the popular filet of salmon (flown in fresh from the West coast daily) grilled over mesquite wood. Chef Martin Doyle has upgraded the fare, making more pastas from scratch and including surprises, such as grouper roasted in an Indian tandoori pot, on the menu. The desserts are as good as you'd expect, with lots of chocolate and a wonderful Jameson-flavored crème brulée.

Commerce Square building, 2005 Market St. (between 20th and 21sts). 📞 215/851-6262. Reservations recommended. Main courses $20–$32; lunch $15–$22, with 3-course prix-fixe for $20.21. AE, DC, DISC, MC, V. Mon–Fri 11:30am–3:30pm and 5–10pm; Sat 5–10pm. Validated garage parking is complimentary after 5pm.

Zanzibar Blue ⭐⭐ CONTINENTAL   Philadelphia's premier venue for live jazz is also a great place to have dinner — witness the many happy pretheater and symphony diners who take the Bellevue's escalator downstairs for Zanzibar Blue's glamorous surroundings and mixed, sophisticated group of patrons. The menu changes quarterly, but you can expect some Creole and Latin spices and seafood, along with basic steaks and fish. How about Southern fried catfish, stuffed with crab and lobster and accompanied by impeccable hush puppies and collard greens with Asian spices? Many people make a meal of the appetizers while listening to a jazz set.

200 S. Broad St. 📞 215/732-5200. Reservations not required. Main courses $19–$39; Sun brunch $24. Fixed-price 3-course pretheater dinner $24. AE, DC, DISC, MC, V. Daily 5:30pm–2am; Sun jazz brunch 11am–2pm.

> ⸤Tips⸥ **Simple Pretheater Choices**
>
> Not every performance on the Avenue of the Arts requires a prethe-
> ater extravaganza. Since the December 2001 opening of the Kimmel
> Center, simple restaurants serving mostly no-frills Italian pastas and
> quickly-done main courses have sprung up in the neighborhood, to get
> you in and out before your show. You could always dine superbly at
> the bar at **Pasion!, Toto,** or **Avenue B,** or take your chances with the
> Kimmel Center's own pre-concert fare, but if you want something less
> exalted, try the soups, salads, sandwiches and simple platters at yuppie
> coffee shop **Cosi,** 235 S. 15th St. (✆ **215/893-9696**); the affordable
> wines and strip steak, squash-stuffed ravioli and grilled salmon with
> basil at **Ernesto's 1521 Café,** 1521 Spruce St. (✆ **215/546-1521**); the
> homemade pasta and pizza (cooked in a wood-burning oven) at **Gira-
> sole Ristorante,** 1305 Locust St. (✆ **215/985-4659**); the modestly priced
> gnocchi, risotto, and osso buco (which is truly wonderful), at **La Viola,**
> 253 S. 16th St. (✆ **215/735-8630**); or the rustic antipasti and marinara
> at charming **Trattoria Primadonna,** 1506 Spruce St. (✆ **215/790-0171**),
> where the owner chooses a "prima donna" nightly to receive a free
> meal and sit in a throne seat.

INEXPENSIVE

Bertucci's ⸤Kids⸥ ITALIAN   I grew up with the original Bertucci's and its bocce
lanes in Cambridge, Massachusetts — since then, they've gone national. What
remains from those days is a delicious thin-crust pizza baked in a brick oven. Be
open to experimenting here. Locals love the barbecued chicken pizza, for example. Recently, Bertucci's has added antipasti of meats and vegetables, pasta, and
now panini. The ambience is busy and noisy, but completely smoke-free and
quite convenient to concerts and theaters.

1515 Locust St. ✆ **215/731-1400.** Main courses $9–$15; average large pizza $14. AE, DC, MC, V.
Mon–Thurs 11am–10pm; Fri 11am–11pm; Sat 11am–11:30pm; Sun noon–9pm.

Independence Brew Pub ✦ AMERICAN   May 2000 brought this three-
story brewpub and playground to Reading Terminal Headhouse inside the Convention Center complex. The main bar and dining room is on the first floor,
with games and a second bar upstairs, all winding around enormous brewpub
tanks. The all-day menu specializes in European thin-crust pizzas, grilled items
in the $13 to $18 range, spectacular sundaes, and, of course, six or more fresh
types of beer on tap, listed on a chalkboard. The atmosphere is woody and comfortable, with photos of the good old days of 1920s Center City and a very varied crowd of conventioneers and regulars. Happy hour is from 5 to 7pm, when
draft beer is $2 a pint.

1150 Filbert St. (between Market and Arch sts. at 12th St.). ✆ **215/922-4292.** Main courses $13–$18; lunch
$9–$15, with $8.95 Express lunch menu. Fresh-brewed tap beer $4.75 per 12-oz. glass. AE, DC, DISC, MC, V.
Mon–Fri 11:30am–3pm and 5–10pm (Fri until 11pm); Sat 5–11pm; Sun 5–10pm. Bar menu until midnight.

Marathon Grill ✦ AMERICAN   Since 1984, the Borish family has run laps
around the competition. They now have six bland but comfortable Marathon

Grills, each with gigantic menus boasting an enormous selection of comfort foods, from seven versions of grilled chicken breast sandwiches, to filet mignon under $10 to award-winning soups. The new location at 2 Commerce Square (2001 Market St.) is the first with a liquor license, and a wood-burning oven for thin-crust gourmet pizzas. The 19th and Spruce street locations seats 60, and the service until 2am and flexible menu make this a focal point for posttheater meals on the way back to Rittenhouse Square. You can take out from any of these branches.

Locations: 121 S. 16th St. ✆ **215/569-3278**; 1613 John F. Kennedy Blvd ✆ **215/564-4745**; 1818 Market St. ✆ **215/561-1818**; 1339 Chestnut St. ✆ **215/561-4460**; 1839 Spruce St. ✆ **215/731-0800**; 2 Commerce Square, 2001 Market St. ✆ **215/568-7766**. Reservations not accepted. Main courses $6–$14. AE, DC, MC, V. Daily 8:30am–2am, depending on location.

Sawan's Mediterranean Bistro ✪ MEDITERRANEAN   I like to sit close to the front of this narrow, softly-lit room and plunge into a selection of dips such as baba ghanouj and tzadziki, a yogurt laced with dill and a bit of garlic; three or four dips with pita bread makes a great light meal in itself. Though they do have some European choices on the menu (and some swear by the seafood paella), I say stick to the ethnic entrees such as kebabs. Service is on the relaxed side.

114–116 S. 18th St. (near Sansom St.). ✆ **215/568-3050**. Reservations recommended. Main courses $10–$15. AE, MC, V. Mon–Thurs 11am–10pm; Fri 11am–11pm; Sat noon–11:30pm; Sun 5–10pm.

⟮Kids⟯ Family-Friendly Restaurants

Ben's Garden Cafe (p. 121)   In the Franklin Institute at Logan Circle, Ben's is well set up for kids, serving cafeteria food, hamburgers, and hot dogs. You can enter without museum admission.

Bertucci's (p. 98)   Excellent thin-crust pizza and more, served within steps of the Avenue of the Arts.

Chinatown   You'll find loads of family-oriented places between 9th and 11th streets and Race and Vine streets.

Dave & Buster's (p. 194)   Children will love eating at this playground for all ages (carnival and arcade games are featured) on the Delaware Waterfront.

Food Court at Liberty Place (p. 109)   Kids have their choice of cuisines from among 25 stalls.

Johnny Rockets (p. 89)   The location at 5th and South is convenient to South Street or the pedestrian walk from Penn's Landing, and the cheerful 1950s diner theme (red-and-white vinyl, indestructible booths) goes well with the very reasonable prices. The milkshakes are a favorite.

More Than Just Ice Cream   This spot at 1119 Locust St. sets kids up in a cool cafe with 20-foot ceilings, serving healthy wraps and sandwiches before the finale of dozens of ice cream flavors and toppings.

Twenty21 (p. 96)   Lunch and dinner menus for children feature a $4.50 peanut butter and jelly sandwich, $6 fettuccine Alfredo, grilled cheese sandwiches, and fish and chips. Try for a window banquette.

3 South Philadelphia

South Philly is the best place on earth to find south and central Italian dishes adapted to American palates. You can always tell by the decor, menu, and music what decade a particular restaurant is frozen in. That said, there's a decided decline of these classic "red gravy" places, as a younger generation of chefs shies away from the heavily sauced cuisine and moves to a more nuanced style of cooking.

EXPENSIVE

The Saloon ★★ ITALIAN/CONTINENTAL   The Santore family has been serving fresh, quality cuisine here since 1965. The restaurant is probably better known for its huge herbed and marinated steaks than for its classic Italian dishes, but new chef Clark Gilbert is someone to watch. The decor is solid wood paneling, sconces, antiques, and Tiffany lamps. The Saloon has a long menu and many daily specials to consider as you savor the pesto tapenade, Parmesan, and olive oil delivered automatically with your bread. The Santores favor standards such as clams casino and crabmeat salads but also serve sautéed radicchio with shiitake mushrooms and superb salads. Heavy artillery includes the 12-ounce prime sirloin, the 26-ounce porterhouse with greens and roasted potatoes, or the lightly breaded veal slices with sweet and hot peppers. The wines are expensive. Desserts are exquisite.

750 S. 7th St. ℂ 215/627-1811. Reservations required. Main courses $19–$34. AE, MC, V. Mon 5–11pm; Tues–Fri 11:30am–2pm and 5–11pm (Fri until midnight); Sat 5pm–midnight.

MODERATE

Victor Cafe ★ (Finds) ITALIAN   Victor's is a South Philly shrine to opera, with servers who deliver arias along with hearty Italian classics. Opened in the 1930s by John Di Stefano, who covered the walls with photos of Toscanini, local Mario Lanza, and the like, the restaurant still has more than 45,000 classical recordings from which to choose and hires the best voices it can find. The food has received some quizzical comments recently, though; it's best to stick to basics like the cannelloni Don Carlos, with its two enormous shells filled with beef and veal and covered in marinara sauce, or the cutlet Baron Scarpia, a chop with wild mushrooms and marsala served over roasted garlic mashed potatoes.

1303 Dickinson St. ℂ 215/468-3040. Reservations recommended. Main courses $13–$20. AE, MC, V. Mon–Thurs 5–10pm; Fri–Sat 4:30pm–12am; Sun 4:30–9:30pm. SEPTA: Board & Tasker sts.; 1 block north of Tasker; make a right onto Dickinson. By car: Follow Broad Street 15 blocks south of City Hall, then 2 blocks east on Dickinson.

INEXPENSIVE

Marra's ★★ (Value) ITALIAN   Marra's wins the South Philly "Best Pizza" award hands down. It's in the heart of South Philadelphia (supposedly the oldest surviving restaurant here, in fact), and the brick ovens give these thin-crust versions (and the walls, and the cozy booths) a real Italian smokiness. Marra's has a large, comprehensive Italian menu and is noted for its homemade lasagna, its tomato sauce, and its squid on Friday.

1734 E. Passyunk Ave. (between Morris and Moore sts.). ℂ 215/463-9249. Reservations not necessary. Main courses $5–$12. Basic pizza $5.75 small, $7 large. No credit cards. Tues–Thurs 11:30am–10pm; Fri 11:30am–midnight; Sat 11am–midnight; Sun 2–10pm.

Ralph's Italian Restaurant ITALIAN   This two-story restaurant a few blocks north of the Italian Market is the epitome of the "red gravy" Italian style: unpretentious, comfortable, reasonable, and owned by the same family for decades. The baked lasagna, spaghetti with sausage, and chicken Sorrento have fans all over the city, and the extensive menu is long on veal and chicken dishes. The service is friendly and attentive. To park, try the Rite Aid lot nearby, but don't get caught without buying something.

760 S. 9th St. ℭ **215/627-6011.** Reservations recommended. Main courses $9–$16; pasta $8.25. No credit cards. Sun–Thurs noon–9:45pm; Fri–Sat noon–10:45pm.

4 University City (West Philadelphia)

MODERATE

La Terrasse ⭐⭐ CONTINENTAL/FRENCH   After years of closure, David Grear brought La Terrasse back to life (to general applause) in 1997. The look is slightly more sleek and sophisticated, but it still has the interior clubby spaces and wraparound covered terrace, one with a tree (not the old fat one, but a black-olive sapling) growing right through it. You can choose between the first floor bar and atrium, or on the floor above, a formal yellow "chateau room" or a more intimate and romantically-decorated "kissing room" across the hallway. La Terrasse is one of the area's pioneers in great dining and atmosphere; its cuisine is an imaginative mix of Southern French standards and ingredients like polenta and mahimahi. The $45 full dinner is an excellent value. Salads are spectacular in their variety and crispness, and wines are reasonable finds from smaller vineyards. Weekdays between 4:30 and 6:30pm bring half-price drinks and $6 wines by the glass, with complimentary hors d'oeuvres at the popular bar. Live piano music is offered most evenings. The waitstaff? Generally U. Penn students who'd rather be elsewhere.

3432 Sansom St. ℭ **215/386-5000.** Reservations recommended. Main courses $19–$26; lunch $7.50–$14; fixed-price dinner $45. AE, DC, MC, V. Mon–Fri 11:30am–2:30pm and 5:30–9:30pm (Fri until 10pm); Sat 5:30–10pm; Sun 5:30–9pm; late suppers to 1am daily. Bus: 21, 42.

Palladium ⭐ CONTINENTAL   In the heart of the University of Pennsylvania campus (Wharton, specifically) is Palladium, an elegantly appointed full-service restaurant and bar. It's reminiscent of an old-time faculty club — chesterfields and wing chairs with footstools face an old stone fireplace, while leaded-glass windows, oak wainscoting, and an ornate ceiling are nice touches. Prices here are a little high to make the Palladium a student hangout, but they're reasonable for this quality, with a la carte dishes, a fixed-price menu, and a pretheater special. Menus change completely four times a year, with items ranging from Tunisian grilled shrimp to French classic lamb chops. Potatoes au gratin (good enough to be a meal in themselves) and a mélange of fresh vegetables accompany most main dishes. Watch the (largely student) service, which is at best uneven, and sometimes downright slow. Also, drop-off by car is at least a half-block away, on Walnut at 36th Street.

3601 Locust Walk. ℭ **215/387-3463.** Reservations recommended. Main courses $11.50–$17.50; lunch $6.50–$11.50. AE, DC, DISC, MC, V. Mon–Fri 11:30am–2:30pm and 5–9pm; Sat 5–9pm; late suppers daily. Closed Sat and Sun June–Aug. Bus: 21.

Pod ⭐⭐ *Finds* JAPANESE   Definitely the coolest, swankiest, most retro-futuristic decor in all Philadelphia, with two gimmicks underlying the sushi and cuisine that falls just short of excellent. One gimmick is the three pods or curved semi-private seating areas, where you can self-select color of your pod from nine possible pastels, depending on your mood. The other is the conveyor belt that carries sushi or small, delectable Japanese dishes like sesame-crusted scallops, miso-glazed sea bass, and crepes around an oval seating area with

---

Fun Fact **Food to Cure What Ails You**

The name "White Dog Café" is indebted to the theosophist and mystic Madame Blavatsky, who resided here a century ago. Blavatsky was about to have an infected leg amputated when a white dog in the house slept on her leg and cured it.

---

sit-down-light-up stools. (Dishes revolve unclaimed only 20 min. before they're disappeared.) But the decor scene is really the thing, with molded rubber, sculpted plastic, and video displays punctuated by a glass exterior curtain wall and bold lighting. Specialty drinks $8.

3636 Sansom St. ℂ 215/387-1803. Reservations recommended. Main courses $20–$30; small plates $7.50–$14. AE, DC, MC, V. Mon–Thurs 11:30am–11pm; Fri 11:30am–midnight; Sat 4pm–midnight; Sun 4–10pm. Bus: 21.

White Dog Café ★★★ *(Finds)* AMERICAN   Judy Wicks is one of Philadelphia's great citizens: She led the fight against the University of Pennsylvania to save this block of Sansom Street and has evolved into a smart, tough, and fun-loving entrepreneur. She and her partner/chef Kevin von Klause have even written a cookbook.

You'll enter two row houses with the dividing wall knocked out and with sophisticated kitchen equipment and electronics concealed behind an eclectic mix of checkered tablecloths, antique furniture, lights, and white dogs galore. The friendly pups are everywhere — on the menu, holding matchbooks, pouring milk, and in family photographs.

Off Sansom Street, the three-counter bar specializes in such all-American beers as McSorley's Ale, New Amsterdam, and Anchor Steam, as well as inexpensive American wines by the glass or bottle. Several dining areas lie to the rear and right, and there's a new glassed-in porch across the rear.

The staff offers frequently changing menus as well as "theme" dinners based on the season or a particular American region. They buy produce locally, which eliminates the middleman and results in dishes that underprice the market by $3 to $5. Starters include a lemon pepper grilled calamari salad and black olive crostini, or freshly made ravioli with European mushrooms braised with white truffle oil and herbs. The grilled yellowtail filet with sweet-and-sour eggplant relish is delicious, and pastry chef Heather Carb turns out signature rolls and cakes.

The White Dog attracts everyone from Penn students to the mayor. Just next door at 3424 Sansom St., **The Black Cat** (ℂ 215/386-6664) offers more of Judy's antiques and crafts. It's open Tuesday through Thursday from 11am to 11pm, Friday and Saturday from 11am to midnight, and Sunday and Monday from 11am to 9pm.

3420 Sansom St. ℂ 215/386-9224. Reservations recommended. Main courses $16–$24; lunch $8–$16. AE, DC, DISC, MC, V. Mon–Fri 11:30am–2:30pm and 5:30–10pm (Fri until 11pm); Sat 5:30–11pm; Sun 5–10pm; brunch Sat–Sun 11am–2:30pm. Grill open until midnight. Frequent theme dinners and parties. SEPTA: 34th St. station (Market-Frankfort line). Bus: 21, 42.

INEXPENSIVE

New Deck Tavern IRISH/AMERICAN   Virtually next door to the White Dog (see above), Mike Doyle's New Deck Tavern is less of a restaurant than a relaxed watering hole, with real Irish beers and bartenders and a 37-foot solid cherrywood bar. The Tavern specializes in crab cakes, homemade soups, and

Irish fare such as shepherd's pie. Specials abound during the 5-to-7pm happy hour. Try to catch Dottie Ford, a secretary in Penn's physics department, at the piano nightly between 7 and 9pm; she knows thousands of show and other tunes, an amazing range built up over the past 50 years.

3408 Sansom St. © **215/386-4600**. Main courses $7–$13. AE, DISC, MC, V. Daily 11am–2am. Bus: 21, 42.

New Delhi INDIAN   New Delhi is a fairly good Indian restaurant near the U. Penn campus, with a 26-item all-you-can-eat buffet, including desserts like pistachio ice cream and sweet rice pudding. It boasts quality ingredients, a tandoor clay oven, and friendly service. Given these prices, it's often crowded with students and teachers from the university. Look for discount coupons in student newspapers.

4004 Chestnut St. © **215/386-1941**. Reservations not required. Main courses $4.95–$10; all-you-can-eat lunch buffet $5.95; dinner buffet $8.95. AE, DISC, MC, V. Mon–Thurs noon–3pm and 4:30–10pm; Fri noon–3pm and 4:30–11pm; Sat noon–11pm; Sun noon–10pm. SEPTA: 40th St. Station.

The Restaurant School at Walnut Hill College 👉 *Value* ECLECTIC Housed in an elegant Victorian complex with a courtyard and several mansion-like wings, the Restaurant School is a respected and major institution among Philadelphia restaurateurs. After 8 months of instruction, teams of students plan a menu and kitchen protocol, then take over the ground floor for eight weeks at a time; a whopping 96% of them find relevant jobs immediately upon graduation.

You have three dining choices; each has a room of its own, but mingle in the connecting courtyard if the weather permits. Since the students are paying for the right to cook your meal, the prices are extremely low. The formal restaurant, Great Chefs of Philadelphia, is housed in a totally renovated parlor dining room, and the city's premier chefs, who serve as mentors to student staffers, designed its $35 fixed-price menu for two courses. Two casual restaurants — one American, one Italian trattoria — also have students in the kitchen, and you'd be hard-pressed to spend more than $25 for appetizer and entree without wine. The restaurant has acquired a liquor license and offers a fine selection of aperitifs, wines, and cocktails.

4207 Walnut St. © **215/222-4200**. Reservations required on weekends, accepted after 3pm. $35 fixed price for formal restaurant; $5–$20 at more casual student-run rooms. AE, DC, MC, V. Tues–Sat 5:30–10pm. Bus: 21.

Zocalo 👉 MEXICAN   This restaurant, 4 blocks from the U. Penn campus, offers contemporary Mexican cuisine from all the provinces. Chef Jackie Pestha has returned to the

---

Value **Good to Go**

Dozens of vendors have permits to operate on the streets around the University of Pennsylvania campus. I like **Bento Box** and **Quaker Shaker** at 37th and Walnut streets, or **Aladdin** at 34th and Spruce near University Museum.

---

kitchen she founded 14 years ago, to everyone's benefit. It's grown to sprawl through four or five separate dining areas, so it's quiet and civilized. It's undoubtedly the best Mexican place around, and the prices reflect the quality (some say the restaurant is overpriced). You'll find everything from such traditional dishes as *carne asada* to such modern classics as fresh shrimp in chile sauce. They pat out the tortillas by hand before your eyes using fresh-flown or -grown ingredients. There's lively Latin music on most nights, with a pleasant deck in back for use in summer.

36th St. and Lancaster Ave. (1 long block north of Market St.). ☎ **215/895-0139.** Reservations recommended. Main courses $14–$21. AE, DC, DISC, MC, V. Mon–Fri noon–10pm (Fri until 11pm); Sat 5:30–11pm; Sun 4:30–9pm. SEPTA: 34th St. Station.

5 Chinatown

MODERATE

Golden Pond ★★ CHINESE   This very stylish Hong Kong–style restaurant, occupying three floors, costs a bit more than others in the neighborhood, but the impeccable service and the obviously fresh preparation are worth it. The cuisine features potato dishes, chicken, duck, and seafood, but no pork or beef. It's one of the few places that serves brown rice.

1006 Race St. ☎ **215/923-0303.** Reservations recommended. Main courses $10–$17; lunch special $6. AE, DC, MC, V. Mon–Fri 11:30am–10pm; Sat–Sun noon–11pm.

Sang Kee Peking Duck House ★ CHINESE   A stalwart since 1980, Sang Kee still churns out Chinatown's best Peking duck (crispy on the outside, juicy inside, and delectable in a wrap with scallions and hoisin sauce), Szechuan duck, and barbecued pork. Its fans are many, fervent, and varied, and service is quick and bilingual. Other menu highlights are the spare ribs, fried dumplings, and the wonton noodle soup, and just about every fish dish; if there's a weakness, it's probably the vegetarian choices. Portions are enormous. There's another Sang Kee at the Reading Terminal Market; it's newer and owned by relatives, but the quality is a notch lower there.

238 N. 9th St. ☎ **215/922-3277.** Reservations recommended. Main courses $21–$30. No credit cards. Sun–Thurs 11am–11pm; Fri–Sat 11am–midnight.

INEXPENSIVE

Capital ★ VIETNAMESE   The positive restaurant reviews placed at every table are well deserved: Capital is one of the best spots in town for Vietnamese cuisine. Look for ground pork, sweet or pungent herbs and greens, and slight French touches. *Bun thit nuong* is a small, savory serving of pork with garlic flavor over rice noodles. No alcohol is served, but you may bring your own.

1008 Race St. ☎ **215/925-2477.** Reservations recommended. Main courses $5–$10. AE, DC, DISC, MC, V. Daily 11am–11pm.

Harmony Vegetarian Restaurant ★ VEGETARIAN/CHINESE   Despite the menu listings for "meat" and "fish," absolutely everything here is made with vegetables (no eggs or dairy either). George Tang makes his own gluten by washing the starch out of flour. This miracle fiber is then deep-fried and marinated to simulate beef, chicken, even fish. The decor is intimate and candlelit, and there's no smoking. Raves go to the hot-and-sour soup and the various mushroom dishes. BYOB.

135 N. 9th St. ☎ **215/627-4520.** Reservations recommended. Main courses $7.50–$13. AE, MC, V. Sun–Thurs 11am–10:30pm; Fri–Sat 11am–midnight.

Imperial Inn CHINESE   This longtime citizen of Chinatown (I find the decor outdated) serves an enormous variety of Szechuan, Mandarin, and Cantonese dishes. Lunch here features dim sum: appetizer-size dishes trundled around on carts that you can take or leave as you like; each dish is $2.50 or so. It's a great form of instant gratification. For dinner, the lemon chicken features a sautéed boneless breast in egg batter, laced with a mild lemon sauce. You can order a full-course dinner, which includes a choice of soup, rice, a main course, and a dessert for about $3 more than the main course alone. Service is efficient. If your party is eight or more, you can order a 10-course feast in advance for the bargain price of $19 per person.

142–6 N. 10th St. ℭ 215/627-5588. Reservations recommended. Main courses $9–$17. AE, DC, MC, V. Mon–Thurs 11am–midnight; Fri–Sat 10:30am–2am; Sun 10am–11:30pm.

Ray's Coffee Shop ✿ CHINESE/COFFEE BAR   This unlikely precursor to the city's penchant for coffee bars, with 30 seats in a pleasant room located near the Convention Center, features an unusual combination of subtle Taiwanese cuisine (the dumplings are especially recommended) and dozens of exotic coffees, each smartly priced and brewed to order in little glass siphons. The iced coffee and house special noodle soup here are great.

141 N. 9th St. ℭ 215/922-5122. Main courses $9–$19; coffee $3.50–$8. AE, MC, V. Mon–Thurs noon–9pm, Fri–Sat 10am–10pm.

Shiao Lan Kung ✿ CHINESE   This modest Cantonese-oriented place close to the Convention Center unassumingly turns out fresh and adventuresome dishes like jellyfish, along with most Chinese standards. The Pa-chen tofu in hot pot throws together ham, barbecued pork, fish balls, and several vegetables with unusual subtlety, and the mashed beef egg drop soup is a real restorative. You won't find many other restaurants in town open this late.

930 Race St. ℭ 215/928-0282. Main courses $8–$14. AE, DC, MC, V. Sun–Thurs 4pm–3am; Fri–Sat 4pm–4am.

6 Manayunk

This neighborhood, 8 miles up the Schuylkill from the Art Museum and Center City, soared in popularity over the mid-1990s, with some of Philadelphia's hippest restaurants and shops (see chapter 9 for the latter). It cooled somewhat as the district put a moratorium on new restaurants over the period of 1997 to 2002, to counteract overwhelming traffic; now the challenge will be to start the crowds going again. Manayunk has lots of long, thin, energetic bistros, as well as off-the-street venues for snacks and appetizer-size dishes. Getting there is simple: From the Belmont Avenue exit (north, crossing the Schuylkill River and its adjoining canal) off I-76 or 1 block south of the Green Lane SEPTA stop on the R6 line, just follow Main Street east alongside the river from the 4400 to the 3900 addresses. A cohesive local development group runs a continuous series of weekend festivals and events to attract business. Parking is plentiful, and store hours tend to run late to match dinner reservations.

EXPENSIVE

Kansas City Prime ✿✿ STEAK/SEAFOOD   Derek Davis is the entrepreneur most associated with Manayunk as a restaurant destination, and this (along with his Sonoma and Arroyo Grille, which operate on the banks of the canal) was a real surprise — I mean, a 140-seat steakhouse for yuppies? Well, it's a steakhouse with a difference, and not just because it's the lone non-chain left in the city. The original room is creamy, curving, and unclubby; a 2001 $1 million expansion next door brought blond wood paneling, leather banquettes, and a pianist, as well as a 20-person wine cellar room. The kitchen turns out all the classic entrees (rib-eye steak, at least five choices of fish/lobsters) with exceptional quality; the side dishes, desserts, and presentation aren't quite as awe-inspiring. If you're up for a splurge, try the Kobe beef from Japan — at $125 per order.

4417 Main St. ℂ **215/482-3700.** Reservations recommended. Main courses $20–$32; $64 porterhouse for 2. AE, DC, DISC, MC, V. Mon–Thurs 5:30–11pm; Fri–Sat 5:30pm–midnight; Sun 5–10pm. SEPTA: R6 to Manayunk from Center City.

MODERATE

Hikaru ☆ JAPANESE This restaurant has added top-notch Japanese cuisine to Manayunk, with its high, elegant greenhouse and more traditional tatami room. With other branches in Queen Village and Rittenhouse Square, Hikaru is known for its sushi selection, but the teppan grill is great fun for tabletop drama, with a server searing meat, fish, or vegetables before your eyes.

4348 Main St. ℂ **215/487-3500.** Reservations recommended. Main courses $13.75–$18.50. AE, DC, DISC, MC, V. Mon–Thurs noon–2:15pm and 5–10:30pm; Fri–Sat noon–2:15pm and 5pm–midnight; Sun 5–10:30pm.

Le Bus Main Street AMERICAN/ECLECTIC   Le Bus got its name dishing out funky homespun food from a van on the University of Pennsylvania campus, and still dishes out fresh, affordable, home-style cuisine featuring American classics. Homemade breads and pastries are baked fresh daily, and the weekend brunch features omelets, frittatas, and pancakes. The menu, featuring everything from meatloaf to great pasta, and the wholesomeness of the place make it especially attractive to families. There's outdoor seating, weather permitting. Watch out for lines at peak hours.

4266 Main St. ℂ **215/487-2663.** Reservations accepted only for 6 or more. Main courses $10–$18; lunch $6–$9. AE, MC, V. Mon–Thurs 11am–3pm and 5–10pm; Fri 11am–3pm and 5–10:30pm; Sat 9:30am–3pm and 5–10:30pm; Sun 9:30am–3pm and 5–10pm.

Sonoma ☆☆ AMERICAN/ITALIAN   In 1992, Sonoma was the original hot Manayunk restaurant, and its Italian/California cuisine and service have only gotten stronger. A renovation of the dining room and bar took place in 1999. Set in a double storefront with 35-foot windows, three levels of seating, and a decor of black-and-brushed steel as a backdrop, this restaurant is always crowded, with a hectic exposed kitchen and thin waitstaff. The second-floor bar serves 87 varieties of vodka. The food is wonderful, with Italian specialties like risotto and American standards such as roasted chicken. With this noise level, kids won't be noticed.

4411 Main St. ℂ **215/483-9400.** Reservations recommended. Main courses $12–$19. AE, DC, DISC, MC, V. Mon–Sat 11:30am–4:30pm and 5:30–10:30pm; Sun 11am–4pm and 5:30–10:30pm; late bar.

Zesty's GREEK/ITALIAN   Tom and Shelley Konidaris have transformed a small Roxborough diner to this agreeable upgraded cafe (one person called it the "anti-Sonoma"), featuring gourmet grilled fish and meat along with Italian and Greek dishes such as pastas and moussaka. Don't rule out the meatier stuff like grilled lamb chops and giant, delicious portobello mushrooms. The enormous espresso and cappuccino machine in the center of the room turns out coffee drinks that complement sweet desserts as well.

4382 Main St. ℂ **215/483-6226.** Reservations not necessary. Main courses $14–$28; lunch $7–$12. AE, DC, DISC, MC, V. Tues–Sat 11am–11pm; Sun 3–11pm. Closed Mon Nov 15–Apr 15.

7 Local Favorites: Cheesesteaks, Hoagies & More

CHEESESTEAKS & HOAGIES

Philadelphia cheesesteaks are nationally known. Preparing a cheesesteak is an art here — ribbons of thinly sliced steak are cooked quickly ('wid' or 'widout' onions) and then slapped onto a roll on top of overlapping slices of provolone or a thick smear of Cheez Wiz. The perfect cheesesteak achieves a flavorful but not soggy balance between the cheese, onion, meat, and roll. Hoagies are the local name for the sandwiches known variously throughout the Northeast as submarines, grinders, or torpedoes.

Jim's Steaks 🖈 *Value* AMERICAN   The best practitioner of the fine art of "hoagistry" in this area is Jim's Steaks in Queen Village, which also offers the mightiest steak sandwiches in town. Jim's has a certain Art Deco charm, with a black-and-white enamel exterior, tile interior, and omnipresent chrome. Containers and ovens take up most of the ground floor, but there is a counter with bar stools along the opposite wall. Takeout is highly recommended in pleasant weather.

Proper hoagie construction can be debated endlessly, but Jim's treatment of the Italian hoagie with prosciutto is a benchmark. A fresh Italian roll is slit before your eyes and layers of sliced salami, provolone, and prosciutto are laid over the open faces. You choose your condiment: mayonnaise or oil and vinegar. Salad fixings — lettuce, tomatoes, and green peppers, with options of onion and hot peppers — come next, with more seasoning at the end. The result may not be subtle, but it's pungent, filling, and delicious. The steak sandwiches aren't as succulent as they used to be, but they're cheaper, at $4.25 (melted cheese or Cheez Wiz additional). Beer and soft drinks are sold in cans and bottles.

400 South St. ℭ **215/928-1911.** Reservations not accepted. Lunch and main courses $5–$6. No credit cards. Mon–Thurs 10am–1am; Fri–Sat 10am–3am; Sun noon–10pm. SEPTA: 5th and Market sts.

Pat's King of the Steaks and Geno's 🖈 AMERICAN   It's the quintessential American competition, two South Philadelphia neighborhood joints on the same corner duking it out for the hearts of hoagie lovers. Pat's, so its adherents claim, invented the steak sandwich, without the cheese, in the 1930s, and still serves the best one this side of the equator. Geno's, to my palate, serves a more succulent and memorable version these days. The location and 24-hour competition make for an interesting mix at the takeout counters.

Pat's: 1237 E. Passyunk Ave. (between 9th and Wharton sts.). ℭ **215/468-1546.** $4.25–$10. Geno's: 1219 S. 9th St. ℭ **215/389-0659.** $5.50–$6.50. Both: always open, no credit cards.

Primo Hoagies 🖈 AMERICAN   Primo has the right pedigree. It's from South Philadelphia and the Jersey shore, and bustles during the weekday with office orders. Size-wise they carry a small, medium, and giant; the regular is basically an elongated spicy cold-cuts sandwich measuring 7 inches long, the giant about twice as long. Various lauded combinations are the spicy tuna; a Sicilian made with capicola ham and sharp provolone; and an Abruzzi of roast pork, topped with provolone and broccoli rabe. The menu also includes plenty of low-fat, low-sodium healthy choices.

2043 Chestnut St. ℭ **215/564-1264.** Sandwiches $3.50–$14. Credit cards for orders over $25. Mon–Fri 9am–3pm.

PRETZELS

Soft, salted pretzels served warm with a dollop of mustard are an authentic local tradition, dating from the German settlers of the early 1700s. The best in town continue to be made by the Amish farmers who bring them to Reading Terminal Market. If you're outdoors, check out the vendor stand in front of the Franklin Institute.

PIZZA

I think **Marra's** (see "South Philadelphia," above) is the best of Philadelphia's hundreds of pizza parlors and restaurants, and **Bertucci's** (see "Center City" above) is also a good bet for pizza and more. The following is a good bet as well.

Tacconelli's ★★ (Finds) ITALIAN   A real insider recommendation for pizza is Tacconelli's — not, as you'd think, in South Philly, but north of the new discos along Christopher Columbus Boulevard (formerly Delaware Ave.). The greatly expanded Tacconelli's is open until whenever the crusts run out (about 9pm). It's imperative to call ahead to reserve the type of pizza you want, which is prepared in a brick oven. The white pizza with garlic oil, and the spinach and tomato pies are particularly recommended.

2604 E. Somerset St. at Aramingo Ave. ℭ 215/425-4983. Reservations required; place pizza orders in advance. Pizzas $10.50–$18. No credit cards. BYO wine (and glasses, too). Wed–Sat 4:30–9pm; Sun 4–8pm. SEPTA: Frankfort subway line from Market St. to Somerset St., then walk 8 blocks east. Driving directions: from Society Hill, take Front St. north, make a right onto Kensington Ave., then another right onto Somerset.

COFFEE BARS

In the last few years, Center City has been transformed with the addition of dozens of coffee bars serving everything from inky espresso to mocha (chocolate milk for grown-ups). Depending on where you are, you can blow in for a 2-minute respite at a stand-up counter, or linger for an hour at a window seat.

My wife, who is a true addict (and to whom this section is dedicated), adores **Torreo Coffee & Tea Company,** 130 S. 17th St., near Liberty Place (ℭ 215/988-0061), open daily, which roasts all its own coffees from light to full-bodied and has a selection of premium loose teas. It also has a full espresso bar and excellent muffins, scones ($1.75), and biscotti. The top restaurateurs in town all love **La Colombe,** both as a supplier of beans for New York's best, such as Daniele, and as its own shop at 130 S. 19th St. **Old City Coffee,** at 221 Church St., behind Christ Church (ℭ 215/629-9292), and at Reading Terminal Market (ℭ 215/592-1897; see the box "A Taste of Ethnic Philly: Reading Terminal Market," on p. 96), is relaxed to the point of somnolence and somewhat expensive, but the coffee selection is rich, varied, and strong. The Church Street location has eclectic acoustic acts during Old City's "First Friday" festivals. **XandO** (as in "hugs and kisses") has become the local cafe of choice with a chatty, *Friends*-like ambience during the day at seven locations, including 235 S. 15th St. at Locust Street (ℭ 215/893-9696); 1720 Walnut St. near Rittenhouse Square; near Independence Hall at 4th and Chestnut streets (ℭ 215/399-0214); and by U. Penn at Sansom Commons. All XandOs add cocktails (see chapter 10) to the mix after 4pm and have recently teamed up with the equally hip sandwich chain Cosi, so I refer to the 235 S. 15th St. venue as a simple but quality pretheater choice.

In a more corporate vein, **ING Direct,** the Dutch financial giant, has opened a bright orange and glass cafe at the corner of Walnut and 17th streets; you can get a very decent cup of coffee, and then surf the Internet for free on one of 8 flat-screen computers. Everyone has heard of Seattle-based **Starbucks,** which has set up outposts at 1528 Walnut St. (ℭ 215/732-0708) and in the Convention Center Marriott at Market and 11th streets (ℭ 215/569-4223). Don't forget about the cafes inside the bookstores of **Borders** at 1 S. Broad St. (ℭ 215/568-7400) and **Barnes & Noble** at 1805 Walnut St. (ℭ 215/665-0716); the former is lauded for its café au lait. In Manayunk, try **Péché** at 4436 Main St. (ℭ 215/925-2855), with a sinful selection of desserts along with the standard blends.

FOOD COURTS & MARKETS

The **Reading Terminal Market,** 12th and Arch streets (ℭ 215/922-2317), in the space underneath the train terminal, has served Philadelphians since the turn of the 20th century. For a full description, see the box "A Taste of Ethnic Philly: Reading Terminal Market," on p. 96.

The Bourse Food Court   This location has 11 snack/restaurant operations, all moderately priced and designed for takeout to be eaten at the tables that fill this cool and stunning restoration of the 1895 merchant exchange. The entire operation was recently upgraded, and representative stalls include **Sbarro's** for pizza and pasta, **Bain's Delicatessen** for turkey sandwiches, and **Grand Old Cheesesteak** for sandwiches.

111 S. Independence Mall E. (just east of the Liberty Bell). Mon–Sat 10am–6pm; Sun 11am–5pm summers only.

Downstairs at the Bellevue   This is a sparkling 1993 effort to attract a clientele less willing to pay upscale prices. It's usually very quiet, with bright tiles, great lighting, and public restrooms. Quiet center tables surround food-court vendors such as **Montesini Pizza, Saladworks,** and **Rocco's Italian Hoagies** ($5 and up).

The Hyatt Regency at the Bellevue Hotel, S. Broad and Walnut sts. Mon–Fri 10am–6pm; Sat 10am–5pm.

The Food Court at Liberty Place ⭐ *Kids*   This court, in a gleaming urban mall in the heart of Center City, hosts branches Reading Terminal favorites like Bain's Deli, Bassett's Original Turkey, and Original Philly Steaks, along with Mandarin Express, Montesini Pizza and Pasta Gourmet, Sbarro, and Chick-Fil-A. The prepared sandwiches at New World Coffee are outstanding. It's spotless, large, and reasonably priced, with full lunches from $3.75. You'll find it easy to keep your eyes on the kids as they wander.

Second level (accessible by escalator or elevator) of Liberty Place between Chestnut and Market sts. and 16th and 17th sts. Mon–Sat 9:30am–7pm; Sun noon–6pm.

The Food Court at The Gallery   Throngs of people parade up and down four floors of shops under a massive glass roof at The Gallery. The lowest level near Gimbels houses an enclave of oyster bars, ice cream stands, and stalls with baked potatoes, Greek snacks, and egg rolls.

The Gallery, Market St. at 9th St. Mon, Tues, Thurs, and Sat 10am–7pm; Wed and Fri 10am–8pm; Sun noon–5pm.

Italian Market ⭐ *Value*   While touring South Street or South Philadelphia, be sure to visit the Italian Market for fresh produce, pasta, seafood, and other culinary delights. It's vibrant, if often crowded to near immobility. Purists (not I) bemoan the $2.5 million project to repave the streets and add new building facades, new awnings, and night lighting. It's most interesting to head for the market from South Street, which has been gentrified from Front to Ninth streets. Fast-talking vendors, opera-singing butchers, and try-it-before-you-buy-it cheese merchants hawk their wares here. The Market is also a great place to pick up ultracheap clothing, if you're willing to wade through racks of items. **Fante's Cookware** is famous nationally, and **DiBruno Bros. House of Cheese** combines a great selection with upscale savvy.

9th St. between Christian and Federal sts. Daily, dawn to dusk. Bus: 47, 64.

7

Exploring Philadelphia

Consider Philadelphia's sightseeing possibilities — the most historic square mile in America; more than 90 museums; innumerable colonial churches, row houses, and mansions; an Ivy League campus; more Impressionist art than you'll find in any place outside of Paris; and leafy, distinguished parks, including the largest one within city limits in the United States. Philadelphia has come a long way since 1876, when a guidebook recommended seeing the new Public Buildings at Broad and Market streets, the Naval Yards, the old YMCA, and the fortresslike prison (which is still a tourist site as the Eastern State Penitentiary!).

Most of what you'll want to see within the city falls inside a rectangle on a map between the Delaware and Schuylkill rivers in width, and between South and Vine streets in height. It's easy to organize your days into walking tours of various parts of the city — see chapter 8 for suggestions. Nothing is that far away. A stroll from City Hall to the Philadelphia Museum of Art takes about 25 minutes, although the flags and flowers along the Parkway will undoubtedly sidetrack you. A walk down Market or one of the "tree" streets (Chestnut, Spruce, Pine, Locust) to Independence National Historical Park and Society Hill should take a little less time — but it probably won't, since there's so much to entice you on the way. If you'd rather ride, the spiffy PHLASH buses loop past most major attractions about every 10 minutes, and the all-day fare is $4. SEPTA also has an all-day $5.50 fare for city buses, but the two systems do *not* accept each other's passes.

The city is trying to wrap some of its attractions together in various packages. The Independence Visitor Center and other locations have two "package priced" offers. The first is the **combined RiverPass ticket** for Independence Seaport Museum, Camden attractions such as the Battleship New Jersey and the Aquarium, and the ferry between them; prices vary, but the deluxe version is $22 adults, $15 seniors, and $16 children 3 to 11. The second is **Philadelphia Citypass,** which offers admission to six major attractions, including the Philadelphia Museum of Art, the Franklin Institute, the Zoo, and the Seaport Museum; prices are $30 adults, $25 seniors, and $18 children 3 to 11, and they may be purchased in advance on http://citypass.net/cgi-bin/citypass (click on "Philadelphia") or at any one of the attractions. Tickets are good up to 9 days from first use, and they represent about a 50% discount from full admissions to all of the attractions.

SUGGESTED ITINERARIES

If You Have 1 Day

Start at the Independence Visitor Center and the adjacent Liberty Bell Pavilion in Independence National Historical Park, then move south through Independence Hall and on to residential Society Hill, which is steeped in U.S. history. In the evening, if you've still got the history bug, stay for the multimedia "Lights of Liberty" show that uses the Park as backdrop. If not, see what's on at the Academy of Music, the Kimmel Center, the Annenberg Center at the University of Pennsylvania, or the CoreStates Spectrum for sports.

If You Have 2 Days

Follow the itinerary above for Day 1. On **Day 2,** starting at City Hall, walk up the Benjamin Franklin Parkway to Logan Circle and spend the afternoon at Franklin Institute or the Philadelphia Museum of Art. Try to circle back to Rittenhouse Square and the Liberty Place complex before it closes (7pm most nights, Wed to 8pm).

If You Have 3 Days

On Days 1 and 2, follow the itinerary given above. On **Day 3,** spend the morning in Old City viewing its Christ Church and Elfreth's Alley, then explore the expanding Delaware River waterfront attractions and the Independence Seaport Museum at Penn's Landing. Finally, either visit the New Jersey State Aquarium and the newly docked Battleship *New Jersey* (take the ferry to Camden for these attractions) or on shore to eclectic South Street.

If You Have 4 Days or More

Days 1 through 3, follow the itinerary given above. On **Day 4,** explore the Rittenhouse Square/South Broad Street area, with a visit to the Pennsylvania Academy of Fine Arts, winding up with a stroll through Reading Terminal Market (it closes at 5pm) and Chinatown. On **Day 5,** hit Fairmount Park's Zoo and the many restored colonial mansions. Farther out, Franklin Mills and King of Prussia Court and Plaza have become magnets for millions of tourists who want to save on clothing from America's finest stores, retail and discounted, with no state sales tax.

1 Independence National Historical Park: America's Most Historic Square Mile

Is there anyone who doesn't know about the Liberty Bell in Independence Hall? It may not be there anymore, but you get the point: The United States was conceived on this ground in 1776, and the future of the young nation was assured by the Constitutional Convention held here in 1787. The choice of Philadelphia as a site was natural because of its centrality, wealth, and gentility. The delegates argued at Independence Hall (then known as the State House) and boarded and dined at City Tavern. Philadelphia was the nation's capital during Washington's second term, so the U.S. Congress and Supreme Court met here for 10 years while awaiting the construction of the new capital in Washington, D.C. From the first penny to the First Amendment, Philadelphia led the nation.

The **Independence National Historical Park** 🎯 comprises 40 buildings on 45 acres of Center City real estate (see the map on the inside back cover of this guide, as well as Walking Tour 1 in chapter 8). Independence Hall and the Liberty Bell, in its glass pavilion, lie between 5th and 6th streets. The Independence Visitor Center one block north is well equipped to illustrate the early history of this country, and will be joined on the Mall on July 4, 2003, by the even more explanatory National Constitution Center.

This neighborhood is a superb example of successful revitalization. Fifty years ago, this area had become glutted with warehouses, office buildings, and rooming houses. The National Park Service stepped in, soon followed by the Washington Square East urban renewal project now known as Society Hill, after the

Philadelphia Attractions

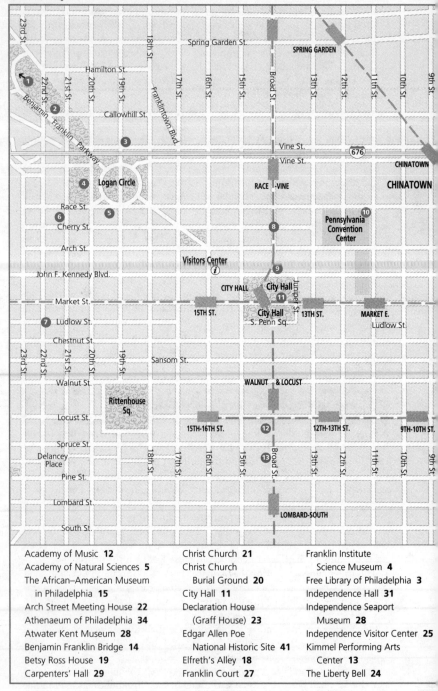

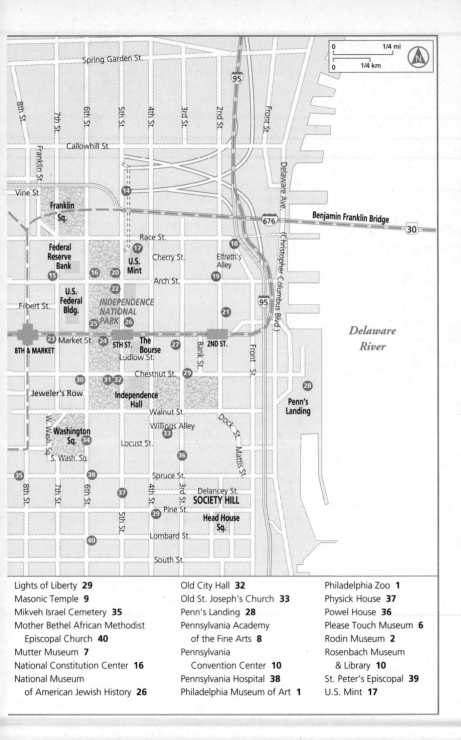

historic neighborhood it's in. To the east, gardens replaced buildings as far as the Dock Street food market, which was replaced by Society Hill Towers in 1959. Graff House, City Tavern, Pemberton House, and Library Hall were reconstructed on their original sites. Liberty Bell Pavilion and Franklin Court are contemporary structures erected for the Bicentennial of the Declaration of Independence celebrations. The most questionable project was the condemnation and destruction of 3 blocks' worth of commercial buildings to create Independence Mall, a wide swath of greenery opposite Independence Hall. After many years, the new Visitor Center, the new Constitution Center, and improved landscaping promise to fill this empty space by the end of 2003.

September 11, 2001, had a negative impact on the spontaneous excitement of stepping into the birthplace of American independence, as well as on the physical appearances of the buildings. The most visited sights have been blocked by an ugly assortment of concrete barriers, chain-link fences, and crime-scene tape, and the block of Chestnut Street in front of Independence Hall closed to all traffic. Let's hope that as redevelopment is completed, these symbols of freedom become easily accessible once again.

Between March and October, and during Thanksgiving and end-of-year holidays, everyone in your group will need a ticket to visit Independence Hall. They're free, but it's preferable to pay the $1.50 handling charge by calling ✆ **800/967-2283** or visiting http://reservations.nps.gov and reserving up to 12 months ahead, than to count on same-day walkup service. If you do take the latter course, go to the Visitor Center as early as possible (it opens at 8:30am), to claim up to 6 tickets for a time slot. The line for $2 tickets to take one of the frequent interior tours of the Second Bank of the United States, Bishop White House, and the Todd House is less intense.

The place to get tickets and most everything else is the **Independence Visitor Center,** 6th and Market streets (✆ **800/537-7676** voice, or 215/597-1785 TDD; www.independencevisitorcenter.com). The Visitor Center should be your first stop in the park, since it's the official visitors service for the Park, and also provides general tourism services and trip planning information. There's a cafe and a gift shop selling mementoes and park publications, and every 30 minutes the center shows a John Huston feature, *Independence,* free of charge.

To get here, you can take the SEPTA Market-Frankford Line to 5th and Market streets or 2nd and Market streets. By bus, take the PHLASH, 76, or any Chestnut Street Transitway bus from Center City.

If you're driving, from I-76, take I-676 east to 6th Street (last exit before the Ben Franklin Bridge), then turn south (right) along Independence Mall. From the Ben Franklin Bridge, make a left onto 6th Street and it's right there after the National Constitution Center. From I-95 southbound, take the Center City exit to 2nd Street. From I-95 northbound, use the exit marked "Historic Area." Turn left on Columbus Boulevard (formerly Delaware Ave.) and follow it to the exit for Market Street (on the right). There's metered parking along most streets, as well as parking facilities (all $12 per day) under the Visitor Center, at 2nd and Sansom streets, and at the corner of Dock and 2nd streets.

Independence Hall ✮✮✮ Even if you knew nothing about Independence Hall, you could guess that noble and important events took place here. Although these buildings are best known for their national role, they also functioned as the seat of government for the city of Philadelphia and the state of Pennsylvania both before and after Philadelphia was the capital of the U.S. From an architectural standpoint, the edifice is graceful and functional; from the standpoint of history and American myth, it's unforgettable. Independence Square sets you thinking about the bold idea of forming an entirely sovereign state from a set of disparate colonies and about the strength and intelligence of the representatives who gathered here to do it. For some historical context, try the wonderful website of the **Independence Hall Association** at www.us history.org.

When the French and Indian War (1754–63) required troops, which required money, King George III believed the colonists should pay for their own defense through taxes. The colonists disagreed, and the idea that the king harbored tyrannical thoughts swept through the colonies. Philadelphia, as the wealthiest and most cultured of the seacoast cities, was leery of radical proposals of independence. Even Franklin himself, an American agent in London at the time, was wary of this scheme. But the news that British troops had fired on citizens defending their own property in Concord pushed even the most moderate citizens to reconsider what they owed to England and what they deserved as free people endowed with natural rights.

The Second Continental Congress convened in May 1775, in the Pennsylvania Assembly Room, to the left of the entrance to Independence Hall. Each colony had its own green baize-covered table, but not much of the original room's furnishings escaped use as firewood when British troops occupied the city in December 1777. The Congress acted quickly, appointing a tall Virginia delegate named George Washington as commander of the Continental Army. After the failure of a last "olive branch" petition, the Congress, through John Adams, instructed each colony's government to reorganize itself as a state. Thomas Jefferson worked on a summary of why the colonists felt that independence was necessary. The resulting Declaration of Independence, wrote noted historian Richard Morris, "lifted the struggle from self-interested arguments over taxation to the exalted plane of human rights." Most of the signatories of the Declaration of Independence used Philip Syng's silver inkstand, which is still in the room. The country first heard the news of the Declaration on July 8 in Independence Square.

Before and after the British occupied the city, Independence Hall was the seat of the U.S. national government. Here, the Congress approved ambassadors, pored over budgets, and adopted the Articles of Confederation, a loose and problematic structure for a country composed of states. Congress moved to New York after the war's end, and it grudgingly allowed delegates to recommend changes to the Articles.

The delegates who met in the Assembly Room in Philadelphia in 1787 created a new Constitution that has guided the country for more than 200 years. Jefferson's cane rests here, as does a book belonging to Franklin. Washington, as president of the convention, kept order from his famous "Rising Sun Chair." Delegates were mature, urbane (24 of the 42 had lived or worked abroad), and trained to reason, and many had experience drafting state constitutions and laws. They decided on approaches to governance that are familiar today: a bicameral Congress, a single executive, an independent judiciary, and a philosophical belief in government by the people and for the people. No wonder John Adams called the convention "the greatest single effort of national deliberation that the world has ever seen."

Across the entrance hall from the Assembly Room, the courtroom served as Pennsylvania's Supreme Court chamber. Like the court at Williamsburg, Virginia, this room exemplifies pre Bill of Rights justice. For example, your ranger guide will probably point out the tipstaff, a wooden pole with a brass tip that was used to keep onlookers subdued. Other period details include little coal-burning boxes to keep feet warm on chilly days. This was one of the first court-rooms in America to hear the argument that disagreement with a political leader isn't sedition, one of the great concepts in modern Anglo-American law.

The stairwell of Independence Hall held the Liberty Bell until 1976. The ranger will conduct you upstairs to the Long Gallery. Now it's set up as a ban-quet hall with a harpsichord (some of the guides even play) and a rare set of maps of the individual 13 colonies. Its view of Independence Mall is superb.

Two smaller rooms adjoin the Long Gallery. To the southwest, the royal governors of Pennsylvania met in council in a setting of opulent blue curtains, silver candlesticks, and a grandfather clock. Beneath a portrait of William Penn, governors met with foreign and Native American delegations, and conducted their everyday business. On the southeast side, the Committee Room fit the whole Pennsylvania Assembly while the Second Continental Congress was meet-ing downstairs. When it wasn't being used to house the Assembly, it stored the Assembly's reference library or arms for the city militia.

As you descend the stairs, look at leafy, calm **Independence Square,** with its statue of Commodore John Barry. The clerk of the Second Congress, John Nixon, first read the Declaration of Independence here, to a mostly radical and plebeian crowd. (Philadelphia merchants didn't much like the news at first, since it meant a disruption of trade, to say the least.)

Chestnut St. between 5th and 6th St., flanked by Old City Hall to the left and Congress Hall to the right. © 215/597-8787. Free admission. Daily 9am–5pm, later in summer. Free tours are led by park rangers every 15 min. 9am–4:45pm. You must take a tour in order to see the interior of the building. As noted above, if you haven't reserved a time slot in advance, go to the Visitor Center at 6th and Market sts., at or around 8:30am, to pick up time-reserved tickets so that you won't have to wait all day to get inside. Bus: PHLASH, 76.

The Liberty Bell ✮✮✮   You can't leave Philadelphia without seeing the Lib-erty Bell. As of March 2003, the Bell is housed in a brand-new $12.4 million glass pavilion, angled so you can see it against the backdrop of Independence Hall, but avoiding the brutal modern Penn Mutual skyscraper flanking the Hall.

The Liberty Bell, America's symbol of freedom and independence, was com-missioned in 1751 to mark the 50th anniversary of a notable event: William Penn, who governed Pennsylvania alone under Crown charter terms, decided that free colonials had a right to govern themselves, so he established the Philadelphia Assembly under a new Charter of Privileges. The 2000-pound bell, cast in Eng-land, cracked while it was being tested, and the Philadelphia firm of Pass and Stow recast it by 1753. It hung in Independence Hall to "proclaim liberty throughout the land" as the Declaration of Independence was read aloud to the citizens. In 1777, it survived a trip to an Allentown church so the British wouldn't melt it down for ammunition. The last time it tolled was to celebrate Washington's birth-day in 1846. The term *Liberty Bell* was coined by the abolitionist movement, which recognized the relevance of its inscription: "Proclaim Liberty throughout all the land unto all the inhabitants thereof," in the fight against slavery.

You can no longer touch the bell, but you can still photograph it. The sur-rounding pavilion features interpretive areas — outside information panels on abolitionism and slavery, and a historic collection inside — as well. You can also see the bell through the glass walls at night.

Chestnut St. between 5th and 6th sts. © 215/597-8974. Free with ticket from the Visitor Center (see p. 114). The pavilion is open daily 9am–8pm during the summer, and daily 9am–5pm during the rest of the year. You can see the bell at all times.

National Constitution Center ★★   Opening July 4, 2003, on Philadelphia's redesigned Independence mall, the National Constitution Center is the first museum in the world devoted to the United States Constitution — its history and its relevance in the daily lives of Americans. The 160,000-square-foot, state-of-the-art facility has departments of history, education, and outreach, all using a blend of the most exciting and attention-grabbing technological tools to offer something for everyone, from scholars to casual visitors.

As you stroll north from Independence Visitor Center, you'll cross Arch Street and a broad walk to the gleaming white stone entrance to the Constitution Center, emblazoned with those three magic words, "We The People . . ." A 12-minute show with a live actor, multi-media activity and a 360-degree movie screen explains the Constitution's early history. From there, visitors learn how the Constitution affects the functioning of government — you can take your own Presidential Oath of Office, explore a national family tree, try on a Supreme Court robe, and check out the Bill of Rights. Signers Hall has bronze life-sized figures of the 39 men who signed the Constitution, and the 3 who dissented. There will be plenty of daily events, talks and programs, as well as a 225-seat, glass-enclosed restaurant and store.

525 Arch St. ✆ **215/923-0004.** Planned admission to the NCC is $5 for adults, $4 for seniors and children 3–12. Daily 9am–5pm. SEPTA: 5th St. Station. Bus: PHLASH, 76.

Franklin Court ★★ *Kids*   Franklin Court is an imaginative, informative, and downright fun (and free) museum run by the National Park Service. Designed by noted architect Robert Venturi, it was very much a sleeper when it opened in April 1976, because Market and Chestnut streets' arched passages give little hint of the court and exhibit within.

Franklin Court was once the home of Benjamin Franklin, who had resided with his family in smaller row houses in the neighborhood prior to living here. Like Jefferson at Monticello, Franklin planned much of the interior design of the house, though he spent the actual building period first as colonial emissary to England, and then to France. His wife, Deborah, oversaw the construction, as the flagstones engraved with some of her correspondence show, while Ben sent back continental goods and a constant stream of advice. Sadly, they were reunited in the family plot at Christ Church Burial Ground, since Deborah died weeks before the end of Ben's 10-year absence. Under the stewardship of his daughter Sarah and her husband, Richard Bache, Franklin Court provided a comfortable home for Ben until his death in 1790.

Since archaeologists have no exact plans of the original house, a simple frame in girders indicates its dimensions and those of the smaller print shop. Excavations have uncovered wall foundations, bits of walls, and outdoor privy wells, and these have been left as protected cutaway pits. It is all very interesting, but enter the exhibition for the really fun part. After a portrait and furniture gallery, a mirrored room reveals Franklin's far-ranging interests as a scientist, an inventor, a statesman, a printer, and so on. At the Franklin Exchange, dial various American and European luminaries to hear what they thought of Franklin.

The middle part of the same hall has a 15-minute series of three climactic scenes in Franklin's career as a diplomat. On a sunken stage, costumed doll figures brief you, and each other, on the English Parliament in 1765, the Stamp Act, the Court at Versailles (when its members were wondering whether to aid America in its bid for independence), and the debates of the Constitution's framers in 1787, which occurred right around the corner at Independence Hall. Needless to say, Ben's pithy sagacity wins every time.

On your way in or out on the Market Street side, stop in the 1786 houses that Ben rented out. One is the Printing Office and Bindery, where you can see colonial methods of printing and bookmaking in action. The house at 322 Market St. is the restored office of *The Aurora and General Advertiser,* the newspaper published by Franklin's grandson. Next door, get a letter postmarked at the Benjamin Franklin Post Office (remember, Ben was Postmaster General, too!). Employees still stamp the marks by hand. Upstairs, a postal museum is open in summer.

Chestnut St. between 3rd and 4th sts., with another entrance at 316–322 Market St. ✆ **215/965-2305.** Free admission. Daily 9am–5pm, including the post office and postal museum. SEPTA: Market East. Bus: PHLASH, 21, 42.

Lights of Liberty ★ *Kids*   Since the summer of 1999, the most important park sights have been the backdrop for the world's first interactive sound-and-light show, providing visitors with a high-tech immersion into the drama of the American Revolution as it happened and where it happened. Five-story projections on historic buildings and wireless headsets equipped with movie-style "surround" sound make it the closest "virtual" colonial experience money can buy.

The ground floor of the PECO Energy Center, next to Independence and Congress Halls on Chestnut Street, has been transformed into a group ticketing and holding area. Try to arrive at dusk, especially with kids, since there's a maximum of 50 per tour and it's first-come, first-served. You'll pick up headsets automatically tuned to a script read by such actors as Ossie Davis and Charlton Heston, and which is triggered automatically as your group arrives at the planned Park destinations. Younger children might prefer the alternative kids' headsets, with their own Whoopi Goldberg–narrated script (mine, 8 and 10, found it too juvenile).

Led by a guide, you'll walk across the moonlit cobblestone streets to Park sites, where the Revolutionary story is compressed into five acts. Rifles crackle, cannons boom, and the founders of America argue with actual quotes interwoven into the script. They're backed with choral music and a soundtrack performed by members of the Philadelphia Orchestra. The visuals are somewhere between shadow-box projections and animation, with superb color and resolution. The finale of 1776 takes place right in back of Independence Hall, and it's irresistibly thrilling.

1-hr. tour shows depart from PECO Energy Center, 6th and Chestnut sts., ✆ **877/462-1776** or 215/LIBERTY. www.lightsofliberty.org. Admission $17.76 adults, $16 seniors, $12 children 6–12. Family pack (2 adults, 2 children) $50. AAA discount of 10%. Up to 6 shows per hour. Tues–Sat dusk–11:15pm Apr–Oct. Shows available in Chinese, French, German, Italian, Japanese, and Spanish, as well as English; Hebrew and Russian available in print versions. SEPTA: Market East. Bus: PHLASH, 21, 42.

2 The Top Museums

Barnes Foundation ★★★ *Finds*   If you're interested in art, the magnificent Barnes Foundation will stun you. Albert Barnes crammed his French provincial mansion with more than 1,000 masterpieces — 180 Renoirs, 69 Cézannes, innumerable Impressionists and post-Impressionists, and a generous sampling of European art from the Italian primitives onward. The Barnes reopened in November 1995 after a world tour of more than 80 masterworks from the collection and a $12 million renovation of the galleries.

Barnes believed that art has a quality that can be explained objectively — for example, one curve will be beautiful and hence art, and another that's slightly different will not be art. That's why the galleries display antique door latches, keyholes, keys, and household tools with strong geometric lines right next to the paintings. Connections beg to be drawn between neighboring objects — an unusual van Gogh nude, an Amish chest, New Mexico rural icons. Virtually every first-rank European artist is included: Degas, Seurat, Bosch, Tintoretto, Lorrain, Chardin, Daumier, Delacroix, Corot, and more. Not a bad use of a fortune made from patent medicine!

The bad news is the foundation administration. They've apparently mishandled the finances of the foundation, and (with an assist from "not in my backyard" neighbors) have established restricted visiting hours, Tuesday, Wednesday, and Thursday only, during the peak summer months of July and August. In fall 2002, the Trustees filed court papers to move the museum to a new downtown home on Benjamin Franklin Parkway — Barnes himself would've hated this and the collection looks great where it is, but money may be a sweetener. Stay tuned, and call well ahead of your anticipated visit for reservations.

300 N. Latch's Lane, Merion Station. © 610/667-0290. Fax 610/667-8315 for reservations, or e-mail reserve@barnesfoundation.org. www.barnesfoundation.org. Admission $5 per person, but reservations at least a month in advance are essential. Sept–June Fri–Sun 9:30–5pm; July–Aug Wed–Fri 9:30am–5pm. On-site parking $10. SEPTA: Take Paoli local train R5 to Merion Station; walk up Merion Rd. and turn left onto Latch's Lane. Bus: 44 to Old Lancaster Rd. and Latches Lane. Car: I-76 (Schuylkill Expressway) west to City Line Ave. (Rte. 1), then south on City Line 1½ miles to Old Lancaster Rd. Turn right onto Old Lancaster, continue 4 blocks, and turn left onto Latch's Lane.

Philadelphia Museum of Art ★★★

Even on a hazy day you can see America's third-largest art museum from City Hall — a resplendent, huge, beautifully proportioned Greco-Roman temple on a hill. Because the museum, established in the 1870s, has relied on donors of great wealth and idiosyncratic taste, the collection does not aim to present a comprehensive picture of Western or Eastern art. But its strengths are dazzling: It houses undoubtedly one of the finest groupings of art objects in America, and no visit to Philadelphia would be complete without at least a walk-through; allow 2 hours minimum. Late hours on Wednesday and Friday have become a city favorite.

The museum is designed simply, with L-shaped wings off the central court on two stories. A major rearrangement of the collections was recently completed, and paintings, sculptures, and decorative arts are grouped within set periods. The front entrance (facing City Hall) admits you to the first floor. Special exhibition galleries and American art are to the left; the collection emphasizes that Americans came from diverse cultures, which combined to create a new, distinctly national esthetic. French- and English-inspired domestic objects, such as silver, predominate in the Colonial and Federal galleries, but don't neglect the fine rooms of Amish and sturdy Shaker crafts. The 19th-century gallery has many works by Philadelphia's Thomas Eakins, which evoke the spirit of the city in watercolors and oils.

Originally controversial 19th and 20th-century European and contemporary art galleries highlight Cézanne's monumental *Bathers* and Marcel Duchamp's *Nude Descending a Staircase,* which doesn't seem nearly as revolutionary as it did in 1913. The recent gift of the McIlhenny $300 million collection of paintings is one of the great donations of this type and adds strength in the French Impressionist area.

Upstairs, spread over 83 galleries, is a chronological sweep of European arts from medieval times through about 1850. The John G. Johnson Collection, a Renaissance treasure trove, has been added to the museum's holdings. Roger van der Weyden's diptych *Virgin and Saint John* and *Christ on the Cross,* one of the

Johnson Collection, is renowned for its exquisite sorrow and beauty. Another, Van Eyck's *Saint Francis Receiving the Stigmata* is unbelievably precise (borrow the guard's magnifying glass). Other masterpieces include Poussin's frothy *Birth of Venus* (the USSR sold this and numerous other canvases in the early 1930s, and many were snapped up by American collectors) and Rubens's sprawling *Prometheus Bound.* The remainder of the floor takes you far away — to medieval Europe, 17th-century battlefields, Enlightenment salons, and Eastern temples.

The museum has excellent dining facilities. A cafeteria, open Tuesday through Sunday from 10am to 4:30pm, dispenses simple hot lunches and salad plates for about $4. The museum restaurant down the hall is open Tuesday through Saturday from 11:45am to 2:30pm, Sunday from 11am to 3:30pm, and Wednesday and Friday from 5pm to closing. All main courses are under $20.

The PMA has recently mounted shows of contemporary artists Barnett Newman and Anselm Kiefer, and has brought millions into the economy with blockbuster exhibits of Picasso still lifes, Cézanne, Delacroix's late works, and van Gogh's portraits. The Museum recently acquired the massive Art Deco former insurance headquarters across the way, though they are not sure what they will feature here.

26th St. and Ben Franklin Pkwy. ℂ **215/763-8100** or 215/684-7500 for 24 hr. information. www.philamuseum.org. Admission $10 adults; $7 students, seniors, and children 12–18; free for children under 12. Pay-what-you-wish Sun. Tues–Sun 10am–5pm; Wed and Fri evening hours to 8:45pm with music, talks, movies, and socializing. Bus: 7, 32, 38, 43, 48, 76; the last is door-to-door, but runs only until 6pm. Car: From the Parkway headed west (away from City Hall), follow signs to Kelly Dr. and turn left at the first light at 25th St. to the lots at the rear entrance. Plentiful parking, free Tues–Fri and $5 Sat–Sun.

Pennsylvania Academy of the Fine Arts ★★
Located 2 blocks north of City Hall is the Pennsylvania Academy of the Fine Arts (PAFA), the first art school in the country (1805) and at one time the unquestioned leader of American beaux arts. The museum got a healthy dose of Cinderella treatment in 1976, when its headquarters celebrated its centennial. At the end of all the scrubbing, repainting, and stuccoing, Philadelphians were once again amazed by the imagination of the Frank Furness masterpiece, built in 1876. Following 6 months of further renovation in late 1994, the academy unveiled a major reinstallation of 300 works from the past 200 years.

The ground floor houses an excellent bookstore, a cafe, and the academy's offices. A splendid staircase, designed by Furness, shines with red, gold, and blue. Each May the annual academy school exhibition takes over the museum. The school itself moved to 1301 Cherry Street years ago, but has acquired and is renovating the factory building to its north by 2004, to re-centralize operations.

As is evident from the PAFA galleries, such early American painters as Gilbert Stuart, the Peale family, and Washington Allston congregated in Philadelphia, America's capital and wealthiest city. The main galleries feature works from the museum's collection of more than 6,000 canvases. The rotunda has been the scene of cultural events ever since Walt Whitman listened spellbound to concerts here. The adjoining rooms display works from the illustrious mid-19th-century years, when PAFA enjoyed its most innovative period.

118 N. Broad St. at Cherry St. ℂ **215/972-7600**. www.pafa.org. Admission $5 adults, $4 seniors and students with ID, $3 children 5–18. Tues–Sat 10am–5pm; Sun 11am–5pm. Special exhibition rates may apply. Bus: C, 48.

Franklin Institute Science Museum ★★★ *Kids*
The Franklin Institute Science Museum isn't just kid stuff. All ages love it because it's a thoroughly

Book your air, hotel, and transportation all in one place.

Hotel or hostel? Cruise or canoe? Car? Plane? Camel? Wherever you're going, visit Yahoo! Travel and get total control over your arrangements. Even choose your seat assignment. So. One hump or two? travel.yahoo.com

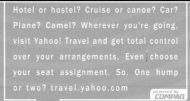

powered by
COMPAQ

YAHOO!
Travel

imaginative trip through the worlds of science that demonstrates the influence of science in our lives. The complex has four parts. The first is the home of the Franklin National Memorial, with a 30-ton statue of its namesake and a collection of authentic Franklin artifacts and possessions.

The second part is a collection of science- and technology-oriented exhibition areas, with innovative hands-on displays, from a gigantic walk-through heart to the Train Factory, an interactive setting where you can play engineer for a 350-ton locomotive. For a hair-raising experience, plug into a Van de Graaff generator at the lightning gallery. On the third floor, an energy hall bursts with Rube Goldberg contraptions, noisemakers, and light shows. The nearby Discovery Theater gives afternoon shows featuring liquid air and other oddities. The fourth floor specializes in astronomy and mathematical puzzles. The basement **Fels Planetarium** (✆ 215/563-1363), just renovated and accompanied by the new "space station" on the first floor, rounds out the offering here.

The third part of the Franklin Institute is the result of an ambitious 1991 campaign, funded by $22 million from the city and state, and $36 million from private donors, to construct the **Mandell Futures Center** addition. Just past the Franklin National Memorial on the second floor, you'll enter an atrium with cafes, ticket counters, and ramps and stairs leading to the new exhibits. Just beyond is a separate-admission IMAX arena, showing films ranging from undersea explorations to the Rolling Stones in spectacular 70mm format. Eight permanent interactive exhibits, including space, earth, computers, chemistry, and health, take you into the 21st century with Disney World–style pizzazz. My personal favorites are "The Sports Challenge," a full body exploration of the science behind popular sports like surfing and rock climbing, a video driving exercise in "Future Vision," "The Jamming Room" of musical synthesizers, and the "See Yourself Age" computer program in "Future and You." The texts throughout are witty and disarming. Quite thrilling is the new **Skybike,** which you can ride along a 1" cable three stories above the Bartol Atrium floor and its huge new sci-store.

The fourth section is the 1995 **CoreStates Science Park,** a collaboration with the Please Touch Museum. It uses the 38,000-square-foot lawn between the two museums — it's free with admission to museum. The imaginative urban garden is filled with high-tech play structures, including a high-wire tandem bicycle, 12-foot tire, step-on organ, maze, and optical illusions.

Of course, you'll eventually get hungry — with a family, the institute is a full afternoon. Your choices are excellent: a vending-machine space in the **Wawa Lunchroom** on the first floor, open only to museum-goers; the new all-American-with-a-nutritional-twist **Ben's Garden Cafe** on the second floor, accessible without museum admission, and open Monday through Friday from 8:30am to 2:30pm and Saturday and Sunday from 9am to 3:30pm; and the **Snack-A-Rama** in the Mandell Center lobby, open daily from 11am to shortly before museum closing, serving beer and wine. Vendors outside sell Philadelphia soft pretzels with plenty of mustard.

Logan Circle, 20th St. and Benjamin Franklin Pkwy. ✆ 215/448-1200. www.fi.edu. Admission charges are confusing and depend on what you want to do. Basic admission to exhibitions, Fels Planetarium, and 3D Theater $12 adults, $9 children; with IMAX Theater included, $16 adults, $13 children. Sun–Thurs 9:30am–5pm; Fri and Sat 9:30am–9pm. CoreStates Science Park May–Oct daily 10am–4pm. Bus: 33, 76, PHLASH.

3 More Attractions

Reading Terminal Market is an attraction in itself, as is the Italian Market if you're exploring South Philadelphia. Both are described in detail in chapter 6, "Dining."

ARCHITECTURAL HIGHLIGHTS

Benjamin Franklin Bridge ★   Great cities have signature bridges, and this is Philadelphia's. The Benjamin Franklin Bridge, designed by Paul Cret (one of the architects of the Parkway across town) was the largest single-span suspension bridge in the world (1⅓ miles) when it was finished in 1926. The bridge carries cars and commuter trains and also has a foot/bicycle path along its south side, more reachable than ever since Independence Mall has been expanded to the edge of the bridge. For the bicentennial of the U.S. Constitution, a Philadelphia team including Steven Izenour, a leading American architect and planner, created a computer-driven system for illuminating each and every cable. At night, Philadelphians are treated to the largest lighting effects show since Ben Franklin's kite.

Entrance to free bicycle/pedestrian walkway at 5th and Vine sts. 6am–dusk. Bus: 50.

City Hall ★   When construction of City Hall began in 1871, it was planned to be the tallest structure in the world. But plans were scaled back, other buildings surpassed it, and the elaborate 1901 wedding cake by John McArthur Jr., with an inner courtyard straight out of a French château, immediately seemed dated. It still arouses wildly differing reactions, although Philadelphians generally love the crowning 37-foot statue of William Penn by A. M. Calder. The northeast quadrant should look brand new by 2003, after repainting, new cast iron work, and cleaning.

You may wish to wander inside the vast floors, which range from the breathtaking to the bureaucratically forlorn. Both inside and out, City Hall boasts the richest sculptural decoration of any American building. The Mayor's Reception Room (room no. 202) and the City Council Chamber (room no. 400) are especially rich.

The highlight of City Hall is the **tower view.** The Juniper Street entrance is most convenient, but you can take any corner elevator to the seventh floor and follow the red tape (always indicative of city government). In this case, it leads to two escalators and a waiting area for the tower elevator. The elevator up to Penn statue's recently cleaned shoestrings, at 548 feet, can hold only eight people, and the outdoor cupola cannot hold many more. On the way, notice how thick the walls are — City Hall is the tallest building ever constructed without a skeleton of steel girders, so that its white stone is 6 feet thick at the top and 22 feet thick at ground level. The simply stupefying view from the top encompasses not only the city but also the upper and lower Delaware Valley and port, western New Jersey, and suburban Philadelphia. It's windy up there, though. If you look straight down, you can see more of the hundreds of sculptures designed by Calder, the works of whose descendants — Alexander Sterling Calder (1870–1945) and Alexander Calder (1898–1976) — beautify Logan Circle and the Philadelphia Museum of Art. You could spend hours, although 45 minutes should do it for the highlights.

Broad and Market sts. ✆ 215/686-2840. Free admission. Tower tours weekdays 9:30am–4:30pm. During school year, Mon–Fri 10am–noon reserved for school groups. Last tour at 2:45pm. Interior tours daily from the East Portal courtyard at 12:30pm. Bus/Subway: Most lines converge beside or underneath the building.

Fisher Fine Arts (Furness) Library   Like the Pennsylvania Academy of the Fine Arts building (see above), this citadel of learning has the characteristic chiseled thistle of Frank Furness, although it was built a decade later from 1888 to 1890. The use of 1890s leaded glass here is even richer than on the Pennsylvania Academy of Fine Arts building. Originally the University's library, the building now houses, appropriately, the fine arts library of the University of Pennsylvania. It's best viewed in a quick look while on the U. Penn quadrangle.

220 S. 34th St. (at Locust Walk on the U. Penn. campus). © **215/898-8325.** Free admission. During academic year Mon–Fri 9am–10pm; summer hours Mon–Fri 9am–5pm. Bus: 44.

Pennsylvania Convention Center ⭐   With the July 1993 opening of the Philadelphia Convention Center (PCC), Philadelphia made it clear that the future of the area depends on its ability to welcome tens of thousands of visitors weekly. The statistics are staggering: With 440,000 square feet of exhibit space, the center is larger than 30th Street Station. But what's really great about the $522 million Convention Center is how solid, and elegant it is, and how nicely it fits in with its surroundings. Architects Thompson, Ventulett, Stainback & Associates shoehorned blocks of brick and limestone between I-76 in the back and Market Street in the front.

Unless you're one of the millions the PCC hopes to lure in for a meeting, you'll need to take the public tour for a peek inside, though a walkway between wings of the adjoining Marriott does overlook a section. The highlight is a stupendous Grand Hall on the second level, evoking the train shed and headhouse of the Reading Terminal, which was the first incarnation of this building. Gray and black Mexican marble alternates with waterfalls, steel, and terrazzo, plus huge granite pylons for heating and cooling the mammoth space. Judy Pfaff's vast, kaleidoscopic *Cirque* extends airy steel and aluminum tubes over 70,000 square feet of space. Esplanades and corridors contain a veritable museum of 52 living artists (35 from Philadelphia) in one of the most successful public art projects of our time. In 1995, the Market Street entrance, the original Reading Railroad facade, was restored, with an escalator up to the Train Shed. The Marriott next door has a skywalk into the Great Hall. The 37-foot rotating electric guitar, tucked into the southwest corner outside, signals the popular Hard Rock Cafe. If you don't want to dine at Hard Rock, head for the beers and burgers of the Dock Street Brew Pub. And don't forget that the incomparable Reading Terminal Market is downstairs.

Between 11th and 13th sts. and Market and Race sts. © **215/418-4728.** Public tours are free; most shows charge admission. Public tours Tues and Thurs at 11:30am, 12:30pm, 1:30pm, and 2:15pm. Enter at the northwest corner of 12th and Arch sts. Subway: Rail lines (including Airport Express) stop at Market East Station; SEPTA at 11th and Market and 13th and Market. Bus: 12, 17, 33, 44, PHLASH. Car: Separate exit from I-676, between I-95 and I-76.

CEMETERIES

Christ Church Burial Ground   This 1719 expansion of the original graveyard of Christ Church (see below) contains the graves of Benjamin Franklin and his wife, Deborah, along with those of four other signers of the Declaration of Independence and many Revolutionary War heroes. There are always pennies on Ben's grave; tossing them there is a local tradition that is supposed to bring good luck.

5th and Arch sts. © **215/922-1695.** Closed to the public. Bus: 48, 50, PHLASH.

Laurel Hill Cemetery ⭐ *(Finds*   How come you find Benjamin Franklin buried in a small, flat plot next to a church (see above), while Civil War General George Meade is buried in a bucolic meadow? Basically, the view of death and contemplation of nature changed as the 19th-century Romantic movement grew, and Laurel Hill reflects that romanticism. Laurel Hill, designated a National Historic Landmark in 1998, was the second American cemetery (after Mount Auburn in Cambridge) to use funerary monuments — some are like small Victorian palaces. Set amid the rolling, landscaped hills overlooking the Schuylkill, its 100 acres also house plenty of tomb sculpture, pre-Raphaelite stained glass, and Art Nouveau sarcophagi. People picnicked here a century ago, but only walking is allowed now.

3822 Ridge Ave., East Fairmount Park. ✆ **215/228-8200.** Entrance may be restricted, since it's still in use as a private institution. Grounds open Mon–Fri 8am–4pm, Sat 9:30am–1:30pm. The Friends of Laurel Hill arranges tours (✆ 215/228-8817); $10 donation per person. Bus: 61. Car: Go north on East River Dr., make a right on Ferry Rd., go 1 block to Ridge Ave., and turn right. The entrance is a half mile down on the right. Free parking.

Mikveh Israel Cemetery   Philadelphia was an early center of American Jewish life, with the second-oldest synagogue (1740) organized by English and Sephardic Jews. While this congregation shifted location and is now adjacent to the Liberty Bell, the original cemetery — well outside the city at the time — was bought from the Penn family by Nathan Levy and later filled with the likes of Haym Solomon, a Polish immigrant who helped finance the revolutionary government, and Rebecca Gratz, the daughter of a fine local family, who provided the model for Sir Walter Scott's Rebecca in *Ivanhoe*.

Spruce St. between 8th and 9th sts. ✆ **215/922-5446** (synagogue number). Summer Sun–Thurs 10am–3pm; off season, contact synagogue or park service. Bus: 47, 9.

CHURCHES

Arch Street Meeting House   This plain brick building dates from 1804, but William Penn gave the land to his Religious Society of Friends in 1693. In this capital city of Quakers, the Meeting House opens its doors to 12,000 local Friends for worship during the last week in March each year. Quakers believe in direct, unmediated guidance by the Holy Spirit; individuals publicly search their souls during "threshing sessions" in a spartan chamber with no pulpit, only hand-hewn benches that face one another. Other areas of the meetinghouse display Bibles, clothing, and implements of Quaker life past and present, along with a simple history of the growth of the religion and the life of William Penn.

4th and Arch sts. ✆ **215/627-2667.** Guided tours year-round. Mon–Sat 10am–4pm. Services Wed 7pm and Sun 10:30am. Suggested donation $2. Bus: 17, 33, 48, 50, PHLASH.

Christ Church ★★ *Moments*   The most beautiful colonial building north of Market Street has to be Christ Church (1727–54). Its spire gleams white from anywhere in the neighborhood, now that a grassy park and a subway stop have replaced the buildings to the south. The churchyard has benches, tucked under trees or beside brick walls.

Christ Church, dating from the apex of English Palladianism, follows the proud and graceful tradition of Christopher Wren's churches in London. As in many of them, the interior spans one large arch, with galleries above the sides as demanded by the Anglican church. Behind the altar, the massive Palladian window — a central columned arch flanked by proportional rectangles of glass — was the wonder of worshipers and probably the model for the one in Independence Hall. The main chandelier was brought over from England in 1744. As in King's Chapel in Boston, seating is by pew instead of on open benches — Washington's seat is marked with a plaque.

With all the stones, memorials, and plaques, it's impossible to ignore history here. William Penn was baptized at the font, sent over from All Hallows' Church in London. Penn left the Anglican church at age 23 (he spent most of his 20s in English jails because of it), but his charter included a clause that an Anglican church could be founded if 20 residents requested it, which they did. Socially conscious Philadelphians of the next generations adopted Anglicanism, then switched to Episcopalianism after the Revolution.

2nd St. ½ block north of Market St. ⓒ 215/922-1695. Donations welcome. Mon–Sat 9am–5pm; Sun 1–5pm. Sun services at 9am and 11am, Mon–Fri 8am, Wed noon. Closed Mon–Tues in Jan–Feb. Bus: 5, 17, 33, 48, PHLASH.

Gloria Dei (Old Swedes' Church) *Finds*

The National Park Service administers this church, the oldest in Pennsylvania (1700). Inside the enclosing walls, you'll think you're in the 18th century, with a miniature parish hall, a rectory, and a graveyard amid the greenery. The one-room museum directly across from the church has a map of the good old days. The simple church interior has plenty of wonderful details. Everybody loves the ship models suspended from the ceiling: The *Key of Kalmar* and *Flying Griffin* carried the first Swedish settlers to these shores in 1638. And note the silver crown in the vestry; any woman married here wears it during the ceremony.

916 Swanson St., near Christian and Delaware aves. ⓒ 215/389-1513. Apr–Oct daily 9am–5pm. By appointment in the off season. Bus: 5, 64, 79. By foot or car: Take Swanson St. under I-95 at Christian St. in Queen Village, opposite Pier 34, then a turn onto Water St.

Mother Bethel African Methodist Episcopal Church

This National Historic Landmark site is the oldest piece of land continuously owned by blacks in the United States. Richard Allen, born in 1760, was a slave in Germantown who bought his freedom in 1782, eventually walking out of St. George's down the street to found the African Methodist Episcopal order. The order today numbers some 2.5 million in 6,200 congregations, and this handsome, varnished-wood-and-stained-glass 1890 building is their mother church. Allen's tomb and a small museum, featuring his Bible and hand-hewn pulpit, are downstairs; open by appointment only.

419 S. 6th St. ⓒ 215/925-0616. Donations welcome. Tues–Sat 10am–3pm; Sun noon–1pm. Sun services 8am and 10:45am.

Old St. Joseph's Church *Finds*

When it was founded in 1733, St. Joseph's was the only place in the English-speaking world where Roman Catholics could celebrate Mass publicly. The story goes that Benjamin Franklin advised Father Greaton to protect the church, since religious bigotry wasn't unknown even in the Quaker city. That's why the building is so unassuming from the street, a fact that didn't save it from damage during the anti-Catholic riots of the 1830s. Such French allies as Lafayette worshipped here. The present interior (1838, and renovated in 1985 to its late-19th-century appearance) is Greek Revival merging into Victorian, with wooden pews and such unusual colors as mustard and pale yellow. The interior has also preserved a colonial style unusual in a Catholic church.

321 Willings Alley, near 4th and Walnut sts. ⓒ 215/923-1733. Mon–Fri 11am–3pm; Sat 11am–6:30pm; Sun 8:30am–3pm. Masses are held weekdays at 11:30am, Sat 11:30am, and 5:30pm, and Sun 7:30am, 9:30am, and 11:30am.

St. Peter's Episcopal

St. Peter's (1761) was originally established through the bishop of London, and has remained continuously open since. Like all pre-Revolutionary Episcopal churches, St. Peter's started out as an Anglican shrine. But what was wrong with Christ Church at 2nd and Market? In a word: mud. As a local historian put it, "the long tramp from Society Hill was more and more distasteful to fine gentlemen and beautiful belles."

Robert Smith, the builder of Carpenters' Hall, continued his penchant for red brick, pediments on ends of buildings, and keystoned arches for gallery win dows. The white box pews are evidence that not much has changed. Unlike most churches, the wineglass pulpit in St. Peter's is set into the west end and the chancel is at the east, so the minister had to do some walking during the service. George Washington and Mayor Samuel Powel sat in pew 41. The 1764 organ case blocks the east Palladian window. The steeple outside, constructed in 1842, was designed by William Strickland to house bells, which are still played.

Seven Native American chiefs lie in the graveyard, victims of the 1793 smallpox epidemic. Painter C. W. Peale, Stephen Decatur of naval fame, Nicholas Biddle of the Second Bank of the United States, and other notables are also interred here.

3rd and Pine sts. (C) 215/925-5968. Mon–Fri 9am–4pm; Sat 11am–3pm; Sun 1–3pm. Services Sun 9am and 11am. Bus: 50, 90, PHLASH.

HISTORIC BUILDINGS & MONUMENTS

Betsy Ross House *(Kids)* One colonial home everybody knows about is this one near Christ Church, restored in 1937, and distinguished by the Stars and Stripes outside. Elizabeth (Betsy) Ross was a Quaker needlewoman who, newly widowed in 1776, worked as a seamstress and upholsterer out of her home on Arch Street. Nobody is quite sure if no. 239 was hers, though. And nobody knows for sure if she did the original American flag of 13 stars set in a field of 13 red-and-white stripes, but she was commissioned to sew ship's flags for the American fleet to replace the earlier Continental banners.

The house takes only a minute or two to walk through. The wooden stairwell was designed for shorter colonial frames — certainly not Washington's! The house is set back from the street, and the city maintains the Atwater Kent Park in front, where Ross and her last husband are buried. The upholstery shop (now a gift shop renovated in 1998) opens into the period parlor. Other rooms include the cellar kitchen (standard placement for this room), tiny bedrooms, and model working areas for upholstering, making musket balls, and the like. Note such little touches as reusable note tablets made of ivory; pinecones used to help start hearth fires; and the prominent kitchen hourglass. Flag Day celebrations are held here on June 14 (see "Philadelphia Calendar of Events," in chapter 2).

239 Arch St. (C) 215/686-1252. www.betsyrosshouse.org. Suggested contribution $2 adults, $1 children. April–Oct daily 10am–5pm; Oct–March Tues–Sun 10am–5pm. Bus: 5, 17, 33, 48, PHLASH.

Carpenters' Hall *(★★)* Carpenters' Hall (1773) was the guildhall for — guess who? — carpenters. At the time, the city could use plenty of carpenters, since 18th-century Philadelphia was the fastest-growing urban area in all the colonies and perhaps in the British Empire outside of London. Robert Smith, a Scottish member of the Carpenters' Company, designed the building (like most carpenters, he did architecture and contracting as well). He also designed the steeple of Christ Church, with the same calm Georgian lines. The edifice is made of Flemish Bond brick in a checkerboard pattern, with stone windowsills, superb woodwork, and a cupola that resembles a saltshaker.

You'll be surprised at how small Carpenters' Hall is given the great events that transpired here. In 1774, the normal governmental channels to convey colonial complaints to the Crown were felt inadequate, and a popular Committee of Correspondence debated in Carpenters' Hall. The more radical delegates, led by Patrick Henry, had already expressed treasonous wishes for independence, but most wanted to exhaust possibilities of bettering their relationship with the Crown first.

What's here now isn't much — an exhibit of colonial building methods; some portraits; and Windsor chairs that seated the First Continental Congress. If some details seem to be from a later period, you're right: The fanlights above the north and south doors date from the 1790s, and the gilding dates from 1857. Hours are short because the Carpenters' Company still maintains the hall.

320 Chestnut St. (C) **215/925-0167**. Free admission. March–Dec Tues–Sun 10am–4pm; Jan–Feb Wed–Sun 10am–4pm. Bus: 9, 21, 42, 76, PHLASH.

Declaration House (Graff House) ⚐

Bricklayer Jacob Graff constructed a modest 3-story home in the 1770s, intending to rent out the second floor for added income. The Second Continental Congress soon brought to the house a thin, red-haired tenant named Thomas Jefferson, in search of a quiet room away from city noise. He must have found it, because he drafted the Declaration of Independence here between June 10 and June 18, 1776.

The 1975 reconstruction used the same Flemish Bond brick checkerboard pattern (only on visible walls), windows with paneled shutters, and knickknacks that would have been around the house in 1775. Compared to Society Hill homes, it's tiny and asymmetrical, with an off-center front door. You'll enter through a small garden and see a short film about Jefferson and a copy of Jefferson's draft (which would have forbidden slavery in the United States had that clause survived debate). The upstairs rooms are furnished as they would have been in Jefferson's time.

7th and Market sts. (C) **215/597-8974**. Free admission (part of Independence National Historical Park). Varies by season: daily 9am–5pm in summer, 10am–1pm off season. Bus: 17, 33, 48, 76, PHLASH.

Elfreth's Alley ⚐⚐

The modern Benjamin Franklin Bridge shadows Elfreth's Alley, the oldest continuously inhabited street in America. Most of colonial Philadelphia looked like this: cobblestone lanes between the major thoroughfares; small two-story homes; and pent eaves over doors and windows, a local trademark. Note the busybody mirrors that let residents see who was at their door (or someone else's) from the second-story bedroom. In 1700, most of the resident artisans and tradesmen worked in shipping, but 50 years later haberdashers, bakers, printers, and house carpenters set up shop. Families moved in and out rapidly, for noisy, dusty 2nd Street was the major north-south route in Philadelphia. Jews, blacks, Welsh, and Germans made it a miniature melting pot in the 18th and 19th centuries. The destruction of the street was prevented in 1937, thanks to the vigilant Elfreth's Alley Association and a good deal of luck. The minuscule, sober facades hide some ultramodern interiors, and there are some restful shady benches under a Kentucky Coffee Bean tree on Bladen Court, off the north side of the street.

Number 126, the 1755 **Mantua Maker's House** (cape maker), built by blacksmith Jeremiah Elfreth, now serves as a museum. An 18th-century garden in back has been restored, and the interior includes a dressmaker's shop and upstairs bedroom. You can also buy colonial candy and gifts and peek into some of the open windows on the street. On the first weekend in June all the houses are open for touring — don't miss this.

2nd St. between Arch and Race sts. (C) **215/574-0560**. Street is public; Visitor Center at #124 free; Mantua Maker's House at #126 admission: $2 adults, $1 children. Mar–Oct Mon–Sat 10am–5pm, Sun noon–5pm; Nov–Feb Thurs–Sat 10am–5pm, Sun noon–5pm. Bus: 5, 48, 76, PHLASH.

Masonic Temple

Quite apart from its Masonic lore, the temple — among the world's largest — is one of America's best on-site illustrations of the use of post–Civil War architecture and design — no expense was spared in the construction, and the halls are more or less frozen in time. There are seven lodge halls, designed to capture the seven "ideal" architectures: Renaissance, Ionic,

Oriental, Corinthian, Gothic, Egyptian, and Norman (notice that Renaissance was the newest style that architect James Windrim could come up with!). This is the preeminent Masonic Temple of American Freemasonry; many of the Founding Fathers, including Washington, were Masons, and the museum has preserved their letters and emblems.

1 N. Broad St. ✆ **215/988-1917.** Free admission. Tours Mon–Fri 10am, 11am, 1pm, 2pm, and 3pm, Sat 10am and 11am. Bus: 17, 33, 44, 48, 76.

Pennsylvania Hospital   Pennsylvania Hospital, like so much in civic Philadelphia, owes its presence to Benjamin Franklin. This was the first hospital in the colonies, and it seemed like a strange venture into social welfare at the time. Samuel Rhoads, a fine architect in the Carpenters' Company, designed the Georgian headquarters; the east wing, nearest 8th Street, was completed in 1755, and a west wing matched it in 1797. The grand Center Building by David Evans completed the ensemble in 1804. Instead of a dome, the hospital decided on a surgical amphitheater skylight. In spring, the garden's azaleas brighten the neighborhood. The beautifully designed herb garden (highlighting plants used as medicines in the 18th century) is very popular.

8th and Spruce sts. ✆ **215/829-3720.** Free admission. Mon–Fri 8:30am–4:30pm. Guided tours are no longer obligatory; copies of a walking tour itinerary available from the Marketing Department on the 2nd floor of the Pine St. building. Bus: 47, 90.

Powel House ★★   If Elfreth's Alley (see above) leaves you hungry for a taste of more well-to-do colonial Philadelphia, head for the Powel House. Mayor Samuel Powel and his wife, Elizabeth, hosted every founding father and foreign dignitary around. (John Adams called these feasts "sinful dinners," which shows how far Powel had come from his Quaker background.) He spent most of his 20s gallivanting around Europe, collecting wares for this 1765 mansion.

It's hard to believe that this most Georgian of houses was slated for demolition in 1930, because it had become a decrepit slum dwelling. Period rooms were removed to the Philadelphia Museum of Art and the Metropolitan Museum of Art in New York. But the Philadelphia Society for the Preservation of Landmarks saved it and has gradually refurnished the entire mansion as it was. The yellow satin Reception Room, off the entrance hall, has some gorgeous details, such as a wide-grain mahogany secretary. Upstairs, the magnificent ballroom features red damask drapes whose design is copied from a bolt of cloth found untouched in a colonial attic. There is also a 1790 Irish crystal chandelier and a letter from Benjamin Franklin's daughter referring to the lively dances held here. An 18th-century garden lies below.

244 S. 3rd St. ✆ **215/627-0364** or 215/925-2251. Admission $3 adults, $2 students and seniors; free for children under 6. Guided tours only. Thurs–Sat noon–5pm; Sun 1–5pm. Be sure to arrive at least 30 min. before closing. Bus: 50, 76, 90.

LIBRARIES & LITERARY SITES

Athenaeum of Philadelphia (Finds)   A 15-minute peek into the Athenaeum will show you one of America's finest collections of Victorian-period architectural design and also give you the flavor of private 19th-century life for the proper Philadelphian. The building, beautifully restored in 1975, houses almost one million library items for the serious researcher in American architecture. Visitors are welcome to the changing exhibitions of rare books, drawings, and photographs in the recently reconstructed first-floor gallery; tours of the entire building or collections require an appointment.

219 S. 6th St. (Washington Sq. E.). (℡) **215/925-2688.** www.philaAthenaeum.org. Free admission. Mon–Fri 9am–5pm. Permission to enter and guided tours given on request. Bus: 21, 42, 90.

Free Library of Philadelphia   Splendidly situated on the north side of Logan Circle, the Free Library of Philadelphia rivals the public libraries of Boston and New York for magnificence and diversity. The library and its twin, the Municipal Court, are copies of buildings in the Place de la Concorde in Paris (the library's on the left).

The main lobby and the gallery always have some of the institution's riches on display, from medieval manuscripts to exhibits of modern bookbinding. Greeting cards and stationery are sold for reasonable prices, too. The second floor houses the best local history, travel, and resource collection in the city. The local 130,000-item map collection is fascinating. The third-floor rare book room hosts visitors Monday through Friday from 9am to 5pm, with tours at 11am or by appointment. If you're interested in manuscripts, children's litera-ture, early printed books, and early American hornbooks, or you just want to see a stuffed raven, this is the place.

If you're hungry, the Skyline Cafe (Mon–Fri 9am–4pm) is a very nice loca-tion for a snack and one of the only dining options on the Parkway. There's also an active concert and film series.

Central Library, Logan Circle at 19th and Vine sts. (℡) **215/686-5322.** www.library.phila.gov. Free admission. Mon–Thurs 9am–9pm; Fri 9am–6pm; Sat 9am–5pm; Sun 1–5pm. Bus: 2, 7, 27, 32, 33, 76, PHLASH.

Edgar Allan Poe National Historical Site   The acclaimed American author, though more associated with Baltimore, Richmond, and New York City, lived here from 1843 to 1844. "The Black Cat," "The Gold Bug," and "The Tell-Tale Heart" were published while he was a resident. Just re-opened follow-ing structural work, it's a simple place — after all, Poe was poor most of his life — and the National Park Service keeps it unfurnished. An adjoining build-ing contains basic information on Poe's life and work, along with a reading room and slide presentation. The Park Service also runs intermittent discussions and candlelight tours on Saturday afternoon.

532 N. 7th St. (near Spring Garden St.). (℡) **215/597-8780.** Free admission. Daily 9am–5pm in summer; closed Mon–Tues Nov–May. Bus: 47, 63.

Rosenbach Museum and Library *(Finds*   The Rosenbach specializes in books: illuminated manuscripts, parchment, rough drafts, and first editions. If you love the variations and beauty of the printed word, they'll love your presence.

The opulent town-house galleries contain 30,000 rare books and 270,000 documents. Some rooms preserve the Rosenbachs' elegant living quarters, with antique furniture and Sully paintings. Others are devoted to authors and illus-trators: Marianne Moore's Greenwich Village study is reproduced in its entirety, and the Maurice Sendak drawings represent only the tip of his iceberg (or for-est). Holdings include the original manuscript of Joyce's *Ulysses* and first editions of Melville, in the author's own bookcase. Small special exhibitions are tucked in throughout the house, and don't miss the shop behind the entrance for bar-gains in greeting cards and a superb collection of Sendak.

You are welcome to wander around the rooms unaccompanied, but you are not allowed to sit down and leaf through the books. For access to the books, you need to call and arrange a special admission. For the most part, you will only be allowed to arrange to peruse the books if you are visiting with a specific schol-arly purpose.

Fun Fact **Philadelphia's Oddball Museums**

Philadelphia has an amazing assortment of small single-interest museums, built out of the passions of, or inspired by, a single individual. Maybe you and your family are ready for these!

- The Mummer's Parade on New Year's Day is uniquely Philadelphian; dozens of crews spend months practicing their musical and strutting skills with spectacular costumes. Talk about multicultural — mumming comes out of both Anglo-Saxon pagan celebrations and African dancing. The **Mummers Museum,** 2nd Street and Washington Avenue (© 215/336-3050), is devoted to the history and display of this phenomenon. It's open Tuesday through Saturday from 9:30am to 5pm and Sunday from noon to 5pm.

- In the northeast district of the city (we know, it's a schlep), Steve Kanya's **Insectarium,** 8046 Frankford Ave. (© **215/338-3000**), has taken off (mostly as a school-class destination) thanks to a write-up in the *Wall Street Journal.* Can you believe an admission of only $5 to watch more than 40,000 cockroaches, assorted bugs, and their predators (scorpions, tarantulas, and so on) scurry around? It's open Monday through Saturday from 10am to 4pm.

- Also not for the squeamish is the **Mutter Museum,** 19 S. 22nd St. (© **215/587-9919**), a collection of preserved human oddities assembled in the 1850s by a Philadelphia physician. Skeletons of giants and dwarves and row upon row of plaster casts of abnormalities inhabit this musty place. It's open daily from 10am to 5pm.

- What could belong more in South Philly than the **Mario Lanza Museum,** in the process of relocating to 712 Montrose St. (© **215/468-3623**)? This tribute to the actor/tenor is on the site of his first music lessons, with a life-size bust, clippings, and telegrams. It's open from September to June, Monday through Saturday from 10am to 3:30pm.

Expansion and renovations for disabled access are arriving in 2003, along with unaccompanied tours and a Maurice Sendak exhibition commemorating the 50th anniversary of "Where the Wild Things Are."

2010 Delancey Place (between Spruce and Pine sts). © 215/732-1600. www.rosenbach.org. Admission $5 adults, $3 children under 18, students, and seniors. Tues, Thurs, and Fri 11am–4pm; Wed 11am–8pm; Sat–Sun 10am–5pm. Bus: 17, 90.

MORE MUSEUMS & EXHIBITIONS

Academy of Natural Sciences *Kids* If you're looking for dinosaurs, the Academy is the best place to find them. Kids love the big diorama halls, with cases of various species mounted and posed in authentic settings. A permanent display, "Dinosaurs Galore," features more than a dozen specimens, including a huge *Tyrannosaurus rex* with jaws agape. The Dig (weekends only) gives you an opportunity to dig for fossils in a re-created field station. The North American Hall, on the first floor, has enormous moose, buffalo, and bears. A small marine exhibit shows how some fish look different in ultraviolet light and how the bed of the Delaware River has changed since Penn landed in 1682.

The second floor features groupings of Asian and African flora and fauna. Many of the cases have nearby headphones that tell you more about what you're seeing. Five or six live demonstrations are given here every day; the handlers are experts in conducting these sessions with rocks, birds, plants, and animals. The Egyptian mummy, a priest of a late dynasty, seems a bit out of place. Several daily demonstrations (called "Eco Shows") are given on the second floor and in the auditorium downstairs.

Upstairs, "Outside In" is a touchable museum designed for children under 12, with a model campsite, fossils, minerals, and shells. It stimulates almost every sense: Children can see, feel, hear, and smell live turtles, mice, bees in a beehive, and snakes (all caged), and wander around mock forests and deserts. An exhibit of live butterflies rounds out the picture, along with frequent films. There's a brown-bag lunchroom and vending area with drinks and snacks.

19th St. and Benjamin Franklin Pkwy. (C) 215/299-1000. www.acnatsci.org. Admission $9 adults, $8.25 seniors, $8 children 3–12, free for children under 3. Mon–Fri 10am–4:30pm; Sat–Sun and holidays 10am–5pm. Bus: 32, 33, 76, PHLASH.

The African-American Museum in Philadelphia   This museum, 3 blocks northwest of the Liberty Bell, is built in five split levels of ridged concrete (meant to evoke African mud housing) off a central atrium and ramp. As you ascend, you follow a path leading from the African roots of black Americans to the role they have played in U.S. history. Specific exhibitions change.

The ground floor contains the admissions office, the gift shop, and the African Heritage Gallery. The second level, concentrating on slavery and captivity, is the most dramatic and informed part of the museum. It emphasizes that the slave trade was hardly exclusive to, or even predominant in, North America, and that it persisted in South America until 1870.

The upper three levels, dealing with black history and culture after emancipation, lose some focus. Black cowboys, inventors, athletes, spokespeople, and business-people are all presented, along with the history of such organizations as the NAACP and CORE and the civil rights movements of the 1960s.

7th and Arch sts. (C) 215/574-0380. www.aampmuseum.org. Admission $6 adults, $4 children and seniors. Tues–Sat 10am–5pm; Sun noon–6pm. Bus: 47, 48, PHLASH.

American Swedish Historical Museum   Modeled after a 17th-century Swedish manor house, this small museum chronicles 350 years of the life and accomplishments of Swedish Americans. Traditional Swedish holidays are celebrated year round, including *Valborgsmässoafton* (Spring Festival) in April, *Midsommarfest* in June, and the procession of St. Lucia and her attendants in December.

1900 Pattison Ave. (C) 215/389-1776. www.libertynet.org/ashm. Admission $5 adults, $4 students and seniors, free for children under 12. Tues–Fri 10am–4pm; Sat–Sun noon–4pm. Bus: 17. Near the Naval Hospital and Veterans Stadium, at the southern edge of the city.

Atwater Kent Museum   The small and newly vitalized Atwater Kent Museum occupies an 1826 John Haviland building. The Atwater Kent shows you — with more artifacts than the Visitor Center — what Philadelphia was like from 1680 to today. Nothing, apparently, was too trivial to include in this collection, which jumps from dolls to dioramas, from cigar-store Indians to period toyshops. Sunbonnets, train tickets, rocking horses, ship models, and military uniforms all fill out the display. A hands on history laboratory opened in 2001.

15 S. 7th St. (C) 215/685-4830. www.philadelphiahistory.org. Admission $5 adults, $3 seniors and children 13–17, free for children under 12. Wed–Mon 9am–5pm. Bus: 17, 33, 42, 76, PHLASH.

Independence Seaport Museum ★★ *Kids*   Opposite Walnut Street, between the two dock areas, is this great new facility in the contemporary poured-concrete structure north of the Olympia jetty. The match between the 1981 state-owned building and the 1961 museum took several years to achieve, but was consummated in July 1995. Now the user-friendly maritime museum is the jewel in the crown of the city's waterfront.

The museum is beautifully laid out, blending a first-class maritime collection with interactive exhibits for a trip through time that engages all ages. The 11,000-square-foot main gallery is the centerpiece for exhibits, educational outreach, and activities that are jazzy and eye-catching without being noisy or obtrusive. Twelve sections mix the personal with the professional — call up interviews with river pilots, navy personnel, and shipbuilders. My family loves the stories of immigrants who flooded Philadelphia between 1920 and 1970, and the rich reminiscences and memorabilia that make the past come to life. I defy anyone to ace the computer-screen quiz.

One of the museum's most attractive features is the **Workshop on the Water,** where you can watch classes in traditional wooden boat building and restoration throughout the year.

Penn's Landing at 211 S. Columbus Blvd. ✆ 215/923-5439. www.phillyseaport.org. Combined admission to the museum and Historic Ship Zone (USS *Olympia* and USS *Becuna;* berthed at Penn's Landing) $8 adults, $6.50 seniors, $4 children. Daily 10am–5pm except for major holidays. RiverPass tickets, including admission to the museum, the Riverbus Ferry, and the New Jersey State Aquarium at Camden, $21.50 adults, $21 seniors, $15.50 children 3–11; this will take at least 5 hr. Ships Ticket including the museum, the Battleship *New Jersey* berthed in Camden, and round-trip ferry, $19 adults, $15 seniors, $13 children 3–11. Bus: 5, 21, 33, 76, PHLASH.

National Museum of American Jewish History   This is the only museum specifically dedicated to preserving and presenting Jewish participation in the development of the United States. The complex was built in the aftermath of the 1950s clearance for Independence Mall, although the congregation connected to it, Mikveh Israel, was established in Philadelphia in 1740 (p. 124). Enter close to 4th Street (passing Christ Church Cemetery, with Ben Franklin's grave) into a dark-brick lobby. The museum starts with a fascinating permanent exhibition, "Creating American Jews," combining reproductions of portraits and documents, actual diaries, letters, and oral histories from five diverse "snapshots" from today's six million American Jews and their predecessors. Smaller rotating exhibitions supplement this presentation. Attracting 40,000 visitors a year, the museum is usually cool and restful and makes a good break from a hot Independence Park tour. A small gift shop is attached.

55 N. 5th St. ✆ 215/923-8311. www.nmajh.org (a great website!). Admission $4 adults; $3 students, seniors, and children; free for children under 6. Mon–Thurs 10am–5pm; Fri 10am–3pm; Sun noon–5pm. Bus: 17, 33, 48, 50, PHLASH.

Physick House ★   Like the Powel house (discussed earlier in the chapter), the Physick (formerly Hill-Physick-Keith) House combines attractive design and historical interest. The house is the area's most impressive — freestanding but not boxy, gracious but solid. Built during the 1780s boom, with money from importing Madeira wine, it soon wound up housing the father of American surgery, Philip Syng Physick (a very propitious name for a physician). The usual pattern of neglect and renovation applies here, on an even grander scale.

All the fabric and wallpaper was fashioned expressly for use here, and the mansion as restored is an excellent illustration of the Federal style from about 1815. The drawing room opens onto a lovely 19th-century walled garden, and contains a Roman stool and 18th-century Italian art, collectibles that illustrate the excitement caused by the discovery of the buried city of Pompeii at that time. Look for an inkstand blessed by Ben Franklin's fingerprints. Dr. Physick treated Chief Justice Marshall, and Marshall's portrait and gift of wine testify to the doctor's powers.

321 S. 4th St. © **215/925-7866** or 215/925-2251. Admission $3. June–Aug Thurs–Sat noon–4pm, Sun 1pm–4pm; Sept–May Thurs–Sat 11am–2pm. Guided tours only. Bus: 50, 90, PHLASH.

Please Touch Museum ☆ *Kids*   This is one of the best indoor activities in town for a family with young kids, and the location is great — just off the Parkway, 2 blocks south of the Franklin Institute. Dedicated to a unique fun-filled educational, cultural, hands-on experience, the converted factories help bring out the creative, exuberant, and receptive in us all.

Once you're in, you can park strollers, check coats, and buy tickets at counters that cater to kids. Exciting hands-on exhibits like "Growing Up" encourage parent/child participation and focus on specific social, cognitive, and emotional areas of child development. "Me on TV," installed in 1993, allows children to experience being behind the camera and on stage in a television studio, including sound effects and camera angles. An exhibit of oversize settings and creatures comes from celebrated author/illustrator Maurice Sendak. The museum collaborates with the Franklin Institute to operate the 38,000-square-foot CoreStates Science Park between May and September, on the lawn between the two institutions. It's a great playground for the mind and body.

The Please Touch Museum is not a day-care center; you cannot simply drop the kids off, and you won't want to. Educational activities like storytelling and crafts are available daily from 11am to 3:30pm. It's also a great place to celebrate a child's birthday if you plan ahead.

210 N. 21st St. © **215/963-0667**. www.pleasetouchmuseum.org. Admission $8.95 adults and children. Voluntary donation Sun 9–11am. No strollers inside, but Snuglis available. Daily 9am–4:30pm. Bus: 7, 48, 76.

Rodin Museum *Moments*   The Rodin Museum exhibits the largest collection of the master's work (129 sculptures) outside the Musée Rodin in Paris. It has inherited a little of its sibling museum's romantic mystery, making a very French use of space inside and boasting much greenery outside. Entering from the Parkway, virtually across the street from the Franklin Institute (see above), you'll contemplate *The Thinker* contemplating other things, then pass through an imposing arch to a front garden of hardy shrubs and trees surrounding a fish pond. Before going into the museum, study the *Gates of Hell*. These gigantic doors reveal the artist's awesome power to mold metal with his tremendous imagination.

The galleries have just reopened after a 2000 top-to-bottom renovation, and the works look superb, with a cleaned-up exterior to boot. The main hall holds authorized casts of *John the Baptist, The Cathedral,* and *The Burghers of Calais.* Several of the side chambers and the library hold powerful erotic plaster models. Drawings, sketchbooks, and Steichen photographic portraits of Rodin are exhibited from time to time.

Benjamin Franklin Pkwy. between 21st and 22nd sts. © **215/763-8100**. $3 donation requested. Free with same-day admission ticket from the Philadelphia Museum of Art (see earlier in this chapter). Tues–Sun 10am–5pm. Bus: 7, 32, 38, 43, 48, 76, PHLASH.

U.S. Mint   The U.S. Mint was the first building authorized by the government, during Washington's first term. The present edifice, diagonally across from Liberty Bell Pavilion, turns out about 1.5 million coins every hour. As of

September 2002, tours must be arranged through your representative in Congress in advance; see the mint website for details, or call ℂ 202/354-6700.

5th and Arch sts. ℂ **215/408-0114**. www.usmint.gov. Free admission, but limited to Congressionally-sponsored groups of 6 or fewer. Call in advance to arrange a tour. Bus: 5, 48, 76.

University of Pennsylvania Museum of Archaeology and Anthropology ⓐ★

The 115-year-old Museum got started early and well, and is endowed with Benin bronzes, ancient cuneiform texts, Mesopotamian masterpieces, pre-Columbian gold, and artifacts of every continent, mostly brought back from the more than 350 expeditions it has sponsored over the years. The taller structures that surround this museum give its Romanesque brickwork and gardens a secluded feel. The museum has had spectacular special exhibitions recently, with forays into ancient Iran, Roman glass, and works from ancient Canaan and Israel.

Exhibits are intelligently explained. The basement Egyptian galleries, including colossal architectural remains from Memphis and "The Egyptian Mummy: Secrets and Science," are family favorites. Probably the most famous excavation display, located on the third floor, is a spectacular Sumerian trove of jewelry and household objects from the royal tombs of the ancient city of Ur. Adjoining this, huge cloisonné lions from Peking's (now Beijing's) Imperial Palace guard Chinese court treasures and tomb figures. The Ancient Greek Gallery in the classical world collection, renovated in 1994, has 400 superb objects such as red-figure pottery — a flower of Greek art — and an unusual lead sarcophagus from Tyre that looks like a miniature house. Other galleries display Native American and Polynesian art and a small but excellent African collection of bronze plaques and statues.

The glass-enclosed Museum Cafe, overlooking the museum's inner gardens, serves cafeteria-style snacks and light meals from 8:30am to 3:30pm on weekdays, from 10am to 3:30pm on Saturday, and from 1 to 5pm on Sunday. The Museum Shop has cards and jewelry and crafts from around the world, and the Pyramid Shop has children's items. There's a very active schedule of events throughout the year.

33rd and Spruce sts. ℂ **215/898-4000**. www.upenn.edu/museum. Admission $5 adults, $2.50 students and seniors, free for children under 6. Free on Sun. Tues–Sun 10am–4:30pm. Closed Mon, holidays, and Sun Memorial Day to Labor Day. Bus: 21, 30 (from 30th St. Station), 40, 42.

UNIVERSITY OF PENNSYLVANIA ⓐ★

You could call Philadelphia one big campus, with 27 degree-granting institutions within city limits and 50,000 annual college graduates. The oldest and most prestigious university is U. Penn. This private, coeducational Ivy League institution was founded by Benjamin Franklin and others in 1740. It boasts America's first medical (1765), law (1790), and business (1881) schools. Penn's liberal arts curriculum, dating from 1756, was the first to combine classical and practical subjects. The university has been revitalized in the last 30 years, thanks to extremely successful leadership, alumni, and fund-raising drives. Under President Judith Rodin, it's starting to reshape its neighborhood positively, with the successful Sansom Commons project across the street, including the wonderful Inn at Penn, retail stores, cinemas, and the massive Barnes & Noble–run university bookstore. A six-screen cinema on 40th and Walnut street is in the works.

The core campus, based in West Philadelphia since the 1870s, features serene Gothic-style buildings and specimen trees in a spacious quadrangle. Visitors can hang out comfortably on the lawns and benches. More modern buildings are results of the 20th-century expansion of the university to accommodate 22,000 students enrolled in 4 undergraduate and 12 graduate schools, in 100 academic departments. Sights of most interest to visitors include the University Museum of Archaeology and Anthropology, the Annenberg Center for the Performing Arts, and the Institute for Contemporary Art.

34th and Walnut sts. and surrounding neighborhood. ℭ 215/898-5000. www.upenn.edu. Bus: 21, 30, 40, 42, 90. Car: Market/Chestnut exit from I-76 (Schuylkill Expressway), 6 blocks west toward West Philadelphia.

A ZOO & AN AQUARIUM

Philadelphia Zoological Gardens ★★ *(Kids)*   The Philadelphia Zoo, opened in 1874, was the nation's first. By the late 1970s, the 42 acres tucked into West Fairmount Park had become run down, with few financial resources. The zoo has since become a national leader, with nearly 1,800 animals. The Zoo celebrated its 125th anniversary with the opening of the **PECO Primate Center,** a breathtaking pavilion that blurs the line between visitors and its 11 resident species. Note that the basic admission will not cover a lot of special attractions like the new Channel 6 **Zooballoon** ($16 per person), a 15-minute ride on a helium balloon that goes 400 feet high.

The 1½-acre **Carnivore Kingdom** houses snow leopards and jaguars, but the biggest attraction is the rare white lions. Feeding time is around 11am for smaller carnivores, 3pm for tigers and lions. The monkeys have a new home on four naturally planted islands, where a variety of primate species live together naturally.

In the **Jungle Bird Walk,** you can walk among free-flying birds. Glass enclosures have been replaced with wire mesh so that the birds' songs can now be heard from both sides. The **Treehouse** ($1), opened in 1985, contains six larger-than-life habitats for kids of all ages to explore — oversize eggs to hatch from, an oversize honeycomb to crawl through, and a four-story ficus tree to climb and see life from a bird's-eye view. The very popular Camel Rides start next to the Treehouse. A **Children's Zoo** portion of the gardens lets your kids pet and feed some baby zoo and farm animals; this closes 30 minutes before the rest of the zoo.

Other exhibits include polar bears; the renovated Reptile House, which bathes its snakes and tortoises with simulated tropical thunderstorms; and cavorting antelopes, zebras, and giraffes that coexist in the "African Plains" exhibit. The zoo has a McDonald's across from the lion house. There is a Fidelity Bank MAC ATM machine at the North Gate. Try to arrive early in the day; it's a long hike from the more distant lots if you don't.

34th St. and Girard Ave. ℭ 215/243-1100. www.phillyzoo.org. Admission $12.95 adults, $9.95 seniors and children 2–11, free for children under 2. Parking spaces for 1,800 cars, $6 per vehicle. Mon–Fri 9:30am–4:45pm; Sat–Sun 9:30am–5:45pm. Closed Thanksgiving, Christmas, and New Year's Day. Bus: 76. Car: Separate exit off I-76 north of Center City.

New Jersey State Aquarium ★ *(Kids)*   This aquarium opened in 1992 as a first step in reclaiming the once-vital (and now denuded) Camden waterfront. It filled the need for an aquarium in the Delaware Valley. The aquarium added the Camden Children's Garden in 2001, with carousel and train ride. Currently, the aquarium is moving into land-based exhibits on the South American rainforest.

Up to 4,000 aquatic animals live here. The main attraction is a 760,000-gallon tank, the second largest (next to Epcot Center's) in the country, with stepped seat/benches arranged in a Greek amphitheater on the first floor. Three times a day, a diver answers questions through a "scuba phone." The "Ocean Base Atlantic" tank contains sharks, rockfish, a shipwreck, and a mockup of the underwater Hudson canyon off the Jersey coast. Also on the first floor is a

Caribbean outpost with 1,000 tropical fish and beach birds. The second floor features interactive exhibits and strange ocean dwellers. Touch tanks are on both floors. The Riverview Café serves basic fast food; outdoor seating is frequently windy.

1 Riverside Dr., Camden, NJ 08103. © **856/365-3300**. www.njaquarium.org Admission $13.95 adults, $11.95 students and seniors, $10.95 children 3–11, free for children under 3. April 15–Sept 15 daily 9:30am–5:30pm; Sept 16–April 15 Mon–Fri 9:30am–4:30pm, Sat–Sun 10am–5pm. Closed Thanksgiving, Christmas, and New Year's Day. Ferry: The RiverLink Ferry from Independence Seaport Museum at Penn's Landing is $5 adults, $3 children, each way (see Independence Seaport Museum listing above for ferry/package admissions); hourly arrivals/departures. Car: From I-676 eastbound (Vine St. Expressway/Ben Franklin Bridge) or westbound from I-295/New Jersey Turnpike, take Mickle Blvd. exit and follow signs.

4 Parks, the Parkway & Penn's Landing 🌟

BENJAMIN FRANKLIN PARKWAY 🌟

The Parkway, a broad diagonal swath linking City Hall to Fairmount Park, wasn't included in Penn's original plan. In the 1920s, however, Philadelphians wanted a grand boulevard in the style of the Champs Elysées. In summer, a walk from the Visitors Center to the "Museum on the Hill" is a flower-bedecked and leafy stroll. And year round, various institutions, public art, and museums enrich the avenue with their handsome facades. Most of the city's parades and festivals pass this way.

Logan Circle, outside the Academy of Natural Sciences, Free Library of Philadelphia, and Franklin Institute, used to be Logan Square before the Parkway was built, and it was a burying ground before becoming a park. The designers of the avenue cleverly made it into a low-landscaped fountain, with graceful figures cast by Alexander Sterling Calder. In June, look for students from neighboring private schools, getting a traditional graduation dunking in their uniforms! From this point, you can see how the rows of trees follow the diagonal thoroughfare, although all the buildings along the Parkway are aligned with the grid plan. Under the terms of the city permit, the Four Seasons Hotel now landscapes and tends Logan Circle, to magnificent effect.

Bus route no. 76 goes both ways every 20 minutes, and the PHLASH bus goes up as far as Logan Circle every 10 minutes.

FAIRMOUNT PARK 🌟🌟

The northern end of the Benjamin Franklin Parkway leads into Fairmount Park, the world's largest landscaped city park, with 8,700 acres of winding creeks, rustic trails, and green meadows, plus 100 miles of jogging, bike, and bridle paths. In addition, this park (© **215/685-0000**) features more than a dozen historical and cultural attractions, including 29 of America's finest colonial mansions (most are open year-round, including weekends, and standard admission is $2.50), as well as gardens, boathouses, America's first zoo, a youth hostel, and a Japanese teahouse. Visitors can rent sailboats and canoes, play tennis and golf, swim, or hear free symphony concerts in the summer. See the Fairmount Park map on p. 137 to find your way around the park. See below for information on renting bikes and inline skates at Lloyd Hall (at the start of Boat House Row) for a couple of hours; they're cheap, and can get you in and out of the heart of the park quickly.

You can get here by taking bus no. 76 to the Museum of Art entrance, or no. 38 or 76 to the upper end. If you're driving, there are several entrances and exits off I-76; East and West River drives are local roads flanking the Schuylkill River.

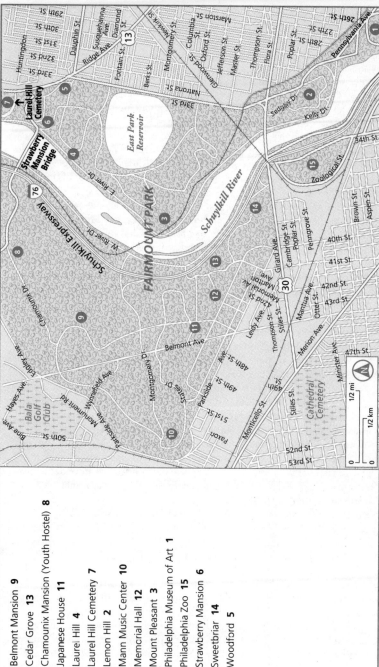

Belmont Mansion **9**

Cedar Grove **13**

Chamounix Mansion (Youth Hostel) **8**

Japanese House **11**

Laurel Hill **4**

Laurel Hill Cemetery **7**

Lemon Hill **2**

Mann Music Center **10**

Memcrial Hall **12**

Mount Pleasant **3**

Philadelphia Museum of Art **1**

Philadelphia Zoo **15**

Strawberry Mansion **6**

Sweetbriar **14**

Woodford **5**

The park is generally divided by the Schuylkill River into East and West Fairmount Park. Before beginning a tour of the mansions, stop by the **Waterworks** (© 215/236-5465). Philadelphia set the waterworks up here in 1812 to provide water for the city. They set aside a 5-acre space around the waterworks, which became a park in 1822.

The Greek Revival mill houses in back of the Art Museum and an ornamental post–Civil War pavilion connecting them are undergoing the end of a $23 million restoration. An upscale, year-round restaurant, open air market, summer stage, and new bike path will join the renovated houses in summer 2003. Also on the east bank, don't miss **Boat House Row,** home of the "Schuylkill Navy" and its member rowing clubs. Now you know where Thomas Eakins got the models for all those sculling scenes in the Art Museum. These gingerbread Tudors along the riverbank appear magical at night, with hundreds of tiny lights along their eaves.

The four most spectacular colonial houses are all in the lower east quadrant of the park. **Lemon Hill** (© 215/232-4337), just up the hill from Boat House Row, shows the influence of Robert Adam's architectural style, with its generous windows, curved archways and doors, and beautiful oval parlors. John Adams described **Mount Pleasant** (© 215/763-8100), built for a privateer in 1763 and once owned by Benedict Arnold, as "the most elegant seat in Pennsylvania" for its carved designs and inlays. **Woodford** (© 215/229-6115), the center of Tory occupation of the city in 1779, is not to be missed, both for its architecture and for the Naomi Wood Collection of colonial housewares. Along with Winterthur (see chapter 11), this is the best place to step into 18th-century home life, with all its ingenious gadgets and elegant objects. The next lawn over from Woodford is the park's largest mansion, **Strawberry Mansion** (© 215/ 228-8364), with a Federal-style center section and Greek Revival wings.

Just north of this mansion is bucolic **Laurel Hill Cemetery** (see "Cemeteries," earlier in this chapter, for a full description), but if you cross Strawberry Mansion Bridge, West Fairmount Park also has many charms. Located in West Fairmount Park, **Belmont Mansion** (© 215/878-8844), currently being restored, hosted all the leaders of the Revolutionary cause. South of this area, you'll enter the site occupied by the stupendous 1876 Centennial Exposition. Approximately 100 buildings were designed and constructed in under 2 years. Only two remain today: **Ohio House,** built out of stone from that state, and **Memorial Hall** (© 215/685-0000), now the park's headquarters and a recreation site. The **Japanese House and Gardens** (© 215/878-5097), on the grounds of the nearby Horticultural Center, is a typical 17th-century Japanese scholar's house, with sliding screens and paper doors in place of walls and glass. It was originally presented to the Museum of Modern Art in New York. Since the Centennial Exposition had featured a similar house, it wound up here. The waterfall, grounds, and house are serene and simple and were extensively refurbished in 1976 by a Japanese team as a bicentennial gift to the city. It's open during the summer only, Tuesday through Sunday from 11am to 4pm.

Two more major homes lie south of the Exposition's original concourses: **Cedar Grove** (© 215/763-8100), a Quaker farmhouse built as a country retreat in 1748 and moved here in 1928, and **Sweetbriar** (© 215/222-1333), a mixture of French Empire and English neoclassicism with wonderful river views. Continuing south past the Girard Avenue Bridge will bring you to the **Philadelphia Zoo** (see above), and then to Center City.

If you have some time and really want to get away from it all, Wissahickon and Pennsylvania Creeks lie north of the park and don't allow access by automobile — only pedestrians, bicycles, and horses can tread here. The primeval trees and slopes of these valleys completely block out buildings and noise — right within the limits of the fifth largest city in the United States! Search out attractions like the 340-year-old Valley Green Inn and the only covered bridge left in an American city.

PENN'S LANDING ⚔

Philadelphia started out as a major freshwater port, and its tourism and services are increasingly nudging it back to the water after 50 years of neglect (typified by the placement of the I-95 superhighway between the city and its port). In 1945, 155 "finger" piers jutted out into the river; today, only 14 remain. The Delaware waterfront is quite wide, and the esplanade along it has always had a pleasant spaciousness. The challenge has been to give it a unified, coherent sense of destination. Since 1976, the city has added on parts of a complete waterfront park at Penn's Landing (© **215/629-3200;** www.pennslandingcorp.com), on Columbus Boulevard (formerly Delaware Ave.) between Market and Lombard streets, with a seaport museum and an assembly of historic ships, performance and park areas, cruise facilities, and a marina. Further additions include more pedestrian bridges over I-95; a 1996 project to install wider sidewalks, lighting, and kiosks along Columbus Boulevard; and the new riverside Hyatt Penn's Landing hotel.

You can access the Penn's Landing waterfront by parking along the piers or by walking across several bridges spanning I-95 between Market Street, at the northern edge, and South Street to the south. There are pedestrian walkways across Front Street on Market, Chestnut, Walnut, Spruce, and South streets; Front Street connects directly at Spruce Street. Bus nos. 17, 21, 33, 76, and the purple PHLASH go directly to Penn's Landing; the stop for bus no. 42 is an easy walk from 2nd Street. If you're driving from I-95, use the Columbus Boulevard/Washington Street exit and turn left on to Columbus Boulevard. From I-76, take I-676 across Center City to I-95 south. There's ample parking available on-site.

Walking south from Market Street, you'll see an esplanade with pretty new blue guardrails and charts to help you identify the Camden shoreline opposite. The hill that connects the shoreline with the current Front Street level has been enhanced with the addition of the festive **Great Plaza,** a multitiered, tree-lined space. In the other direction is a jetty/marina complex, perfect for strolling and snacking, anchored by the **Independence Seaport Museum,** the Hyatt hotel, and the Chart House restaurant. The sober 1987 **Philadelphia Vietnam Veteran Memorial** lists 641 local casualties. Nearby, you'll find the **International Sculpture Garden** with its obelisk monument to Christopher Columbus.

There's also plenty to do in and near the water. Just north of the Great Plaza at Columbus Boulevard and Spring Garden Street is Festival Pier. The Penn's Landing Corporation coordinates more than 100 events here annually, all designed to attract crowds with high-quality entertainment. Even on a spontaneous visit you're likely to be greeted with sounds and performances. Festival Pier is also the location of the Blue Cross RiverRink, Philadelphia's only outdoor skating rink, open daily from late November to early March.

Several ships and museums are berthed around a long jetty at Spruce Street, and the Independence Seaport Museum is slowly consolidating management of these attractions as the **Historic Ship Zone.** Starting at the north end, these attractions are the brig *Niagara,* built for the War of 1812 and rededicated as the official flagship of Pennsylvania in 1990; the **USS** *Becuna,* a guppy-class submarine, commissioned in 1944 to serve in Admiral Halsey's South Pacific fleet; and the **USS** *Olympia,* Admiral Dewey's own flagship in the Spanish-American War, with a self-guided three-deck tour. (Separate admission to both the *Olympia* and the *Becuna* is $3.50 for adults, $1.75 for children under 12; both are open daily 10am–5pm.) The harbor cruise boats *Liberty Belle II* (✆ **215/629-1131**) and *Spirit of Philadelphia* (✆ **215/923-1419**), and the paddle-wheeler *Riverboat Queen* (✆ **215/923-BOAT**), are joined by private yachts. In fact, Queen Elizabeth docked her yacht *Britannia* here in 1976. Anchoring the southern end is the **Chart House** restaurant, open for lunch and dinner, and the restored **Moshulu** four-masted floating restaurant, in Penn's Landing marina since June 2002 (see "The Club & Music Scene" in chapter 10 for details).

Another group of boats occupies the landfill directly on the Delaware between Market and Walnut streets. The *Gazela Primiero,* a working three-masted, square-rigged wooden ship launched from Portugal in 1883 and in renovation until 2003, has visiting hours on Saturday and Sunday from 12:30 to 5:30pm when it's in port. Normally present, but now in drydock are the *Barnegat Lightship* and the tugboat *Jupiter.* All boasts mentioned in the paragraph are operated by the Philadelphia Ship Preservation Guild (✆ **215/923-9030**); admission $3 adults, $2 students.

If you want to get out onto the water, the *RiverLink* (✆ **215/925-5465**), at the river's edge in front of the Independence Seaport Museum at Walnut Street, plies a round-trip route to the Camden attractions including the New Jersey State Aquarium, the Camden Children's Garden, and the Battleship *New Jersey,* next to the Tweeter concert arena. The ferry crosses every hour on the hour between 9am and 5pm. The trip takes 10 minutes, and the fare without museum admission on either end is $5 adults, $3 children each way. Penn's Landing also runs a free **Waterfront Shuttle** on Friday, Saturday, and Sunday evenings between 9pm and 2am in the summer. This is meant to reduce drunk driving between the many Columbus Boulevard clubs to the north of Penn's Landing. It does stop here as well as at Pier 34 and the Moshulu. Call ✆ **215/629-3200** for more information.

5 Especially for Kids

Philadelphia is one of the country's great family destinations. It has a variety of attractions for different ages, and because it's so walkable and neighborhood-based, a snack, a rest, or a new distraction is never far away. Since so many of the family attractions are explained in more detail elsewhere in this or other chapters, I'll restrict myself to a list of the basics. See "Fast Facts: Philadelphia," in chapter 4, for babysitting options.

The Independence Visitor Center, at 6th and Market streets, coordinates and sells several packages that combine free admission to many kid-friendly attractions with accommodations at hotels such as the Penn Tower, Sheraton Society Hill, and Embassy Suites Center City. Call the Family Friendly Funline at ✆ **800/770-5889** for information.

MUSEUMS & SIGHTS

In Center City, you'll find the **Please Touch Museum,** 210 N. 21st St. (until it moves to Penn's Landing); **Franklin Institute,** Benjamin Franklin Parkway and

20th Street; **CoreStates Science Park** between these two on 21st Street; and the **Academy of Natural Sciences,** the Parkway and 19th Street. The **Free Library of Philadelphia Children's Department,** across Logan Circle at Vine and 19th streets, is a joy, with a separate entrance, 100,000 books and computers in a playground-like space, with weekend hours. Around Independence Hall are the **Liberty Bell Pavilion** at Market and 5th streets; **Franklin Court,** between Market and Chestnut streets at 4th Street; the waterfront at **Penn's Landing,** off Front Street; the new **National Constitution Center** at Arch and 5th streets; and, of course, the guided tour of **Independence Hall.** You can also take the ferry from Penn's Landing and the great new **Independence Seaport Museum** to the **aquarium, children's garden,** and **battleship** in Camden, New Jersey. In West Fairmount Park you'll find the **zoo.**

PLAYGROUNDS

Rittenhouse Square at 18th and Walnut streets has a small playground and space in which to eat and relax. Other imaginative urban playgrounds on this side of Center City are **Schuylkill River Park** at Pine and 26th streets, and at 26th Street and the Benjamin Franklin Parkway, opposite the art museum. Nearest Independence Hall, try **Delancey Park** at Delancey between 3rd and 4th streets (with lots of fountains and animal sculptures to climb on) or **Starr Garden** at 6th and Lombard streets. The best park in Fairmount Park is the **Smith Memorial** (head north on 33rd St., then take a left into the park at Oxford Ave., near Woodford).

ENTERTAINMENT

There is lots of children's theater in Philadelphia. **The Arden Theatre** at 40 N. 2nd St. (© 215/922-1122) is one of a dozen companies that produces children's theater year-round. **Mum Puppettheatre** at 115 Arch St. presents a season of thought-provoking and enjoyable plays for all ages; call © **215/925-8686** for schedule and details. **Penn's Landing** has free children's theater performances by American Family Theater on Fridays at 7pm in July and August; call © **215/629-3237** for details.

The **Philadelphia Museum of Art** has dedicated itself to producing Sunday-morning and early afternoon programs for children, at minimal or no charge. Your kids could wind up drawing pictures of armor or watching a puppet play about dragons, visiting a Chinese court, or exploring Cubism. Call © **215/763-8100,** or 215/684-7500 for 24-hour information.

OUTSIDE PHILADELPHIA

In Bucks County, there is **Sesame Place,** based on public TV's *Sesame Street,* in Langhorne, and the restored antique carousel at **Peddler's Village** in Lahaska. To the northwest, try the 20th-century entertainment areas connected with **Franklin Mills,** and **Ridley Creek State Park** and its 17th-century working farm in Montgomery County. For Revolutionary War history in action, try Valley Forge or Washington Crossing National Historical Parks. And for a fascinating experience, spend a couple of days in Lancaster County — you can even stay on a working Amish farm. See chapters 11 and 12 for directions and information.

6 Organized Tours

BOATING TOURS

Two choices are available at Penn's Landing. The *Spirit of Philadelphia* (© 215/923-1419) at the Great Plaza combines lunch, brunch, or dinner with a cruise on a 600-person passenger ship, fully climate-controlled, with two enclosed decks and two open-air decks. Trips, which require reservations, are $30 and up for 2 or 3 hours.

The newly redecorated *Liberty Belle II* (© 215/629-1131) boards from Lombard Street Circle, near the Chart House restaurant at the southern end of Penn's Landing, and can accommodate up to 475 passengers on three decks.

The *RiverLink* (© 215/925-5465) provides a 10-minute interstate crossing from landings just outside the Independence Seaport Museum and the New Jersey State Aquarium. The ferry is large inside, and the views of the Philadelphia skyline are great. Departures from Penn's Landing are on the hour, from Camden on the half-hour, from 9am to 5pm daily. One-way fares are $5 for adults, $3 for children and seniors. The packages including admission to various Camden attractions are a good deal. You can purchase the packages at the Independence Visitor Center, the Seaport Museum, or at any attraction along the Philadelphia or Camden waterfront.

BUS TOURS

Those trolleys clanging along the city streets are from **American Trolley Tours** (© 215/333-2119). Tours of historic areas, conducted by guides in the climate-controlled vehicles, leave every 30 minutes, with boarding and re-boarding privileges, across from the Liberty Bell on Market St. between 5th and 6th streets. The tours cost $15 for adults, $5 for children.

Gray Line (© 800/577-7745) has introduced year-round, 3-hour excursions of historic Philadelphia, Philadelphia at night, and Valley Forge: $22 adults and $16 children ages 3 to 11. All tours leave from 30th Street Station, but shuttles from hotels are available.

CANDLELIGHT STROLLS

From May to October, evening tours of the historic area, led by costumed guides, leave from Welcome Park at 2nd and Walnut streets at 6:30pm. Tours of Old City (Fri) and Society Hill (Sat) take 90 minutes; they cost $8 for adults, $6 for seniors and children. Call © 215/735-3123 for reservations with **Centipede Tours,** 1315 Walnut St. **Historic Philadelphia** (© 215/625-5801) offers programs such as the "Tippler's Tour" starting from the Visitor Center and the Powel House.

HORSE & CARRIAGE TOURS

To get the feel of Philadelphia as it was (well, almost — asphalt is a lot smoother than cobblestones), try a narrated horse-drawn carriage ride. Operated daily by the **76 Carriage Co.** (© 215/923-8516), tours begin at 5th and Chestnut streets in front of Independence Hall, from 10am to 5pm in fall, winter and spring, and from 10am to 8 pm in summer. Fares range from $18 for 15 minutes to $30 for 30 minutes, with a maximum of four per carriage; additional people $5 each. Reservations are not necessary.

WALKING TOURS

The next chapter will give you some guided walking tours to follow. The most spectacular, the "Lights of Liberty" show using Independence National Historic Park as a backdrop, is described earlier in this chapter. There are also many specific-interest tours, focusing on topics such as African-American Philadelphia, architecture, Jewish sights in Society Hill, and the Italian Market. Check with the Independence Visitor Center (© 215/965-7676; www.independence visitorcenter.com) for information.

7 Outdoor Activities

I can't begin to make a complete list of all that you can do outdoors while in Philadelphia, so the following is merely a sample. You may also want to contact the Department of Recreation (℃ **215/686-3600**).

BIKING/BLADING

Lloyd Hall in **Fairmount Park,** the most southerly Boathouse Row building along the Schuylkill, is the jumping-off spot for these activities, with its sports trailer (℃ **215/235-7368**) full of bikes and skates for rental. It's an ideal spot, almost in the Art Museum's backyard, and at the tip of Fairmount Park. You can rent all kinds of bikes, blades, and baby joggers at $8 per hour or $20 for 4 hours, helmets and gear included. Once you're on wheels, the paths along the Schuylkill on Kelly (East River) Drive, West River Drive, and off West River Drive to Belmont Avenue are pure pleasure. The lower half of West River Drive along the Schuylkill is closed to vehicular traffic most weekend hours in summer. You can rent mountain bikes or in-line skates for about $25 at **Via Bicycle** at 606 S. 9th St. (℃ **215/627-3370**), or the **Bike Lines** at 226 S. 40th in University City (℃ **215/243-2453**), or 1028 Arch near the Convention Center (℃ **215/923-1310**). The ground is flat near the Schuylkill on either side but loops up sharply near Laurel Hill Cemetery or Manayunk. Anyone who enjoys cycling will love the outlying countryside, and you can rent bicycles in Lumberville, 8 miles north of New Hope on the Delaware (℃ **215/297-5388**), and in Lancaster, the heart of Amish farmland (℃ **717/684-7226**). Bicycles may be taken free on all SEPTA and PATCO trains, so you're within easy range of some nice country rides.

Call the **Bicycle Club of Philadelphia** at ℃ **215/735-2453** or visit www. phillybikeclub.org for specific neighborhood recommendations.

BOATING

Outside of the city, try **Northbrook Canoe Co.,** north of Route 842 at 1810 Beagle Rd. W., in West Chester on Brandywine Creek (℃ **610/793-2279**), or **Point Pleasant,** on Route 32, 7 miles north of the New Hope exit on I-95, with canoeing, inner tubing, and rafting on the Delaware River (℃ **215/297-8823**).

FISHING

Pennypack Creek and **Wissahickon Creek** are stocked from mid-April to December with trout and muskie and provide good, even rustic, conditions. A required license of $17 for Pennsylvania residents, or $15 for 3 days, $30 for 7 days, and $35 for a season for out-of-staters, is available at sporting-goods stores such as **I. Goldberg,** 1300 Chestnut St. (℃ **215/925-9393**), or at the **Municipal Services Building,** located at 1401 John F. Kennedy Blvd., near the Visitors Center. Licenses are also available at the **Wal-Mart** at 1601 S. Columbus Blvd. (℃ **215/468-4220**). Outside the city, **Ridley Creek** and its **state park** (℃ **610/566-4800**) and **Brandywine Creek** at Hibernia Park of Chester County (℃ **610/383-3812**) are stocked with several kinds of trout.

GOLF

The quality and variety of public access golf is wonderful. The city of Philadelphia operates five municipal courses in the region. All have 18 holes, and current fees range from $15 to $25 Monday through Friday and $20 to $30 on Saturday and Sunday. Not everyone can get onto the legendary Pine Valley or Merion, but Hugh Wilson of Merion also designed the pretty and challenging

Cobbs Creek, 7800 Lansdowne Ave. at 72nd Street (✆ **215/877-8707**). Since Meadowbrook Golf Group took over in April 1999, course conditions have improved dramatically. **Karakung** is the shorter 18-hole course, and preferred for seniors and juniors. **John F. Byrne,** Frankford Avenue and Eden Street in North Philadelphia (✆ **215/632-8666**), has an Alex Findlay design with Torresdale Creek meandering through or beside 10 holes, and plenty of rolling fairways and elevations. **Walnut Lane,** Walnut Lane and Henry Avenue in Roxborough (✆ **215/482-3370**), places a premium on short game skills, with 10 par-3 holes and deep bunkers set into hills and valleys. There's also a driving range in East Fairmount Park.

Among the better township courses outside the city are **Montgomeryville Golf Club,** Route 202 (✆ **215/855-6112**); **Paxon Hollow Golf Club,** Paxon Hollow Road in Marple Township (✆ **610/353-0220**), under 6,000 yards and demanding accuracy; and **Valley Forge Golf Club,** 401 N. Gulph Rd., King of Prussia (✆ **215/337-1776**). Expect fees of $65 and up.

HEALTH CLUBS

The Philadelphia Marriott, Wyndham Franklin Plaza, Four Seasons, Rittenhouse, and Sheraton Society Hill have in-house facilities that are free for guests but open to nonguests at an additional charge. The spectacular **Sporting Club** (✆ **215/985-9876**) offers $10 day passes to guests of other hotels in Center City. Most other moderately priced hotels have at least a few Exercycles and an aerobics space; the Buttonwood Square Hotel, 4 blocks from Logan Circle, has a full gym room, pool, and tennis court. Alas, you'll only have access to the facilities if you stay at the hotel. Near Society Hill, the top health club that admits per-day guests is **Gold's Gym,** 834 Chestnut St. (✆ **215/592-9644**). It provides a great staff, large Universal weight machines, free weights, and several aerobics classes daily. The cost is $10 per guest, and it's open Monday through Friday from 6am to 10pm, Saturday and Sunday from 8am to 5pm. Another alternative closer to midtown is the **12th Street Gym,** 204 S. 12th St. (✆ **215/985-4092**), a restored 1930s men's club (women are welcome these days), with a pool, full basketball court, courts for squash and racquetball, and weights and aerobics rooms. It's open Monday through Friday from 5:30am to 11pm, Saturday from 8am to 8pm, and Sunday from 8am to 7pm. The basic rate is $10 per guest.

HIKING

Fairmount Park (✆ **215/686-3616**) has dozens of miles of paths, and the extensions of the park into the Wissahickon Creek area are quite unspoiled, with dirt roads and no auto traffic. Farther afield, **Horseshoe Trail** (✆ **215/664-0719**) starts at Routes 23 and 252 in Valley Forge State Park and winds 120 miles west marked by yellow horseshoes until it meets the Appalachian Trail.

HORSEBACK RIDING

There are riding trails in Fairmount Park, the Wissahickon, and Pennypack Park, all within city limits. Plus, Chester and Brandywine valleys are famous for horsemanship. However, the only riding stable within city limits that allows visitors to rent horses is **Harry's Riding Stables** (✆ **215/335-9975**), 2240 Holmesburg Ave., near Pennypack Park. It's open 7 days a week from 9am to 7pm, and seven or eight horses are always available, with rates of $20 per hour for guided trail rides with Western saddles. The easiest direction from Center City is via I-95 north. Take the Academy Road exit, following the exit ramp to the left onto Academy until the first light; then turn left onto Frankford Avenue and continue for 2 miles. After a hill, there's an intersection with a railroad trestle that passes above Frankford. Before going under it, take the dirt road on the left and follow 300 yards to the white barn building on the right.

ICE SKATING

One great improvement to the city is the new **Blue Cross RiverRink at Festival Pier,** open for public skating near the intersection of Columbus Boulevard and Spring Garden Street daily, from late November to early March. Admission for one 2-hour session is $4 to $6, with skate rental only $2. Call ✆ **215/925-RINK** for details; there's a nice food court, too.

RUNNING & JOGGING

Again, **Fairmount Park** has more trails than you could cover in a week. An 8¼-mile loop starts in front of the Museum of Art, up the east bank of the Schuylkill, across the river at Falls Bridge, and back down to the museum. At the north end, Forbidden Drive along the Wissahickon has loops of dirt/gravel of 5 miles and more, with no traffic. The Benjamin Franklin Bridge path from 5th and Vine streets is 1¾ miles each way.

SWIMMING

Philadelphia has 86 municipal swimming pools, and many hotels have small lap pools. Municipal pools are open daily from 11am to 7pm and are free. Two of the best are **Cobbs Creek,** 63rd and Spruce streets, and **FDR Pool,** Broad and Pattison in South Philadelphia. Call ✆ **215/686-1776** for details. Of the best indoor pools, try The Sporting Club at the Park Hyatt Philadelphia (p. 68).

TENNIS

Some 115 courts are scattered throughout **Fairmount Park,** and you can get a tourist permit to use them by calling ✆ **215/686-0152.** You might also try the University of Pennsylvania's indoor courts at the **Robert P. Levy Tennis Pavilion,** 3130 Walnut St. (✆ **215/898-4741**). Hours are limited, but guest fee and rates total $38 for two visitors until 4pm, $42 for two after 4pm.

8 Spectator Sports

Even in these days of nomadic professional teams, Philadelphia fields teams in every major sport and boasts a newly enhanced complex at the end of South Broad Street to house them all. **Veterans Stadium** (✆ 215/686-1776) is a bowl with undulating ramps that can seat 58,000 for the Phillies in baseball and 68,000 for the Eagles in football. It's becoming a parking lot in winter 2004, though. The city is developing a separate new football facility, **Lincoln Financial Field,** to seat 66,000 for Eagles games starting in the fall of 2003. The Phillies will occupy a more intimate 21st-century park, seating 43,000 on the north side of Pattison Avenue and 11th Street, by Opening Day in 2004. The new $230 million, 21,000-seat **First Union Center** houses the Philadelphia Flyers pro hockey team and the Philadelphia 76ers basketball team. It couples with the 17,000-seat **Spectrum,** which functions as one of the best rock-concert forums around and hosts the U.S. Pro Indoor Tennis Championships and other one-of-a-kind events.

All these facilities are next to each other and can be reached via a 10-minute subway ride straight down South Broad Street to Pattison Avenue ($1.60). The same fare will put you on the SEPTA bus C, which goes down Broad Street more slowly but is the safer choice late at night.

Professional sports aren't the only game in town, though. Philadelphia has a lot of colleges, and **Franklin Field** and the **Palestra** dominate West Philadelphia on 33rd below Walnut Street. The Penn Relays, the first intercollegiate and amateur track event in the nation, books Franklin Field on the last weekend in April. Regattas pull along the Schuylkill all spring, summer, and fall, within sight of Fairmount Park's mansions.

A call to Ticketmaster (© **212/507-7171** in New York, or 215/336-2000 in Philadelphia) can often get you a ticket to a game before you hit town.

BASEBALL

The **Philadelphia Phillies,** Box 7575, Philadelphia, PA 19101 (© **215/463-1000** for ticket information, or 215/463-5300 for daily game information), won the National League pennant in 1993 and made playoffs in 1995. While recent years have been thinner, they expect improvements under intense manager Larry Bowa. They play at Veterans Stadium, Broad Street and Pattison Avenue, until they move to new digs in 2004. Day games usually begin at 1:35pm, regular night games at 8:05pm on Friday, 7:35pm on other days. When there's a twilight doubleheader, it begins at 5:35pm.

Box seats overlooking the field at Veterans Stadium are $20, and the cheapest bleacher seats are $6 to $12 if you're over 14.

BASKETBALL

Energized by young superstar Allen Iverson, the **Philadelphia 76ers,** Box 25050, Philadelphia, PA 19147, play about 40 games at the First Union Center between early November and late April. Call © **215/339-7676** for ticket information, or charge at © **215/336-2000;** single tickets range $15 to $65. There's always a good halftime show, and the promotion department works overtime for the special event nights.

There are five major college basketball teams in the Philadelphia area, and the newspapers print schedules of their games. Most games are at the Palestra, with tickets going for $5 to $8. Call © **215/898-4747** to find out about ticket availability.

BIKING

The **CoreStates Pro Cycling Championship,** held each June, is a top event in the cycling world. The 156-mile race starts and finishes along the Benjamin Franklin Parkway. Watching the cyclists climb "The Wall" in Manayunk is terrifying.

BOATING

From April to September, you can watch regattas on the Schuylkill River, which have been held since the earliest days of the "Schuylkill Navy" a century ago. The **National Association of Amateur Oarsmen** (© **215/769-2068**) and the **Boathouse Association** (© **215/686-0052**) have a complete schedule of races, one of the best known being the Dad Vail Regatta.

FOOTBALL

Football is, without a doubt, Philadelphia's favorite sport, and current quarterback Donovan McNabb is especially popular. It will take all your ingenuity to get tickets, since 85% of tickets to **Philadelphia Eagles** games (at Veterans Stadium, Philadelphia, PA 19148 until 2003, and at Lincoln Financial Field thereafter) are sold to season ticket-holders. Call © **215/463-5500** for ticket advice. The games start at 1 or 4pm, and tickets cost up to $75.

HORSE RACING

Philadelphia Park (the old Keystone Track) is the only track left in the area, with races from June 15 to February 13, Saturday through Tuesday. (Post time is 12:35pm.) Admission, general parking, and a program are free. The park is at 3001 Street Rd. in Bensalem, half a mile from Exit 28 on the Pennsylvania Turnpike. Call 𝒞 **215/639-9000** for information.

Philadelphia Park Turf Club, 7 Penn Center, 1635 Market St., on the concourse and lower mezzanine levels (𝒞 **215/245-1556**), features 270 color video monitors and an ersatz Art Deco design; it brings the wagering to you in the comfort of Center City.

ICE HOCKEY

The First Union Center rocks to the **Philadelphia Flyers,** led by star Eric Lindros, from fall to spring. Tickets are even harder to get for the Flyers than for the Eagles — 80% of tickets are sold by the season, which starts in October. Call 𝒞 **215/465-5500** for ticket information; if you can get them, they'll cost between $23 and $85.

TRACK & FIELD

The city hosts the **Penn Relays,** the oldest and still the largest amateur track meet in the country, in late April at Franklin Field. There's an annual **Marathon** in November and a September **Philadelphia Distance Run,** a half-marathon; the latter is becoming a world-class event. Call 𝒞 **215/686-0053** for more details on any of these runs.

8

City Strolls

Philadelphia is probably the most compact, walkable major city in the United States, just as it was in 1776. Even on a random walk, you'll be fascinated by the physical illustration of the progress of the centuries, and the many unexpected juxtapositions between past and present. Keep in mind that the nearer you are to the Delaware, the older (and smaller) the buildings are likely to be. The walking tours mapped out below are specifically designed to cover the most worthwhile attractions. **Note:** It is important that you purchase tickets for Independence Hall, the Liberty Bell, Bishop White House, and Todd House (all on Tour 1) at the Independence Visitors Center. You will not be able to purchase tickets at the attractions themselves.

WALKING TOUR 1	HISTORIC HIGHLIGHTS & SOCIETY HILL

Start:	Independence Visitors Center, 6th and Market streets.
Finish:	City Tavern, 2nd and Walnut streets; optional extension to Penn's Landing.
Time:	From 6 to 7 hours.
Best Time:	Start between 9 and 11am to avoid hour-long waits for Independence Hall tours.
Worst Time:	Mid-afternoon

Start your tour at the:
❶ Visitor Center
The Visitor Center (open 8:30am–5pm) is located in Independence National Historical Park, on 6th and Market streets. This handsome brick building was built for the 21st-century renovation of Independence Mall. It maintains spotless rest rooms, a cafe for that jump-start-your-day coffee, and a plethora of information about the Park, the city, and the region. This is where you pick up tickets to get inside Independence Hall and the Liberty Bell Pavilion (whether you've reserved in advance or are counting on walk-up access). Tickets to the Bishop White and Todd Houses (see below), and information about special tours and

special daily events are also available here. The John Huston–directed film *Independence* is shown free of charge every half-hour. There is a handsome exhibition area and a substantial quality gift shop and bookstore.

Just north of the Visitor Center is the:
❷ National Constitution Center
This is a generous half-block long space that will be open as of July 2003. The center explores the history of the framing of the Constitution in 1787, and also challenges the visitor to think about the effect that this document has had on the lives of all Americans, from 1787 to the present day. Expectations are high, but the designers have a great track record with the Holocaust Museum in Washington,

Walking Tour: Historic Highlights & Society Hill

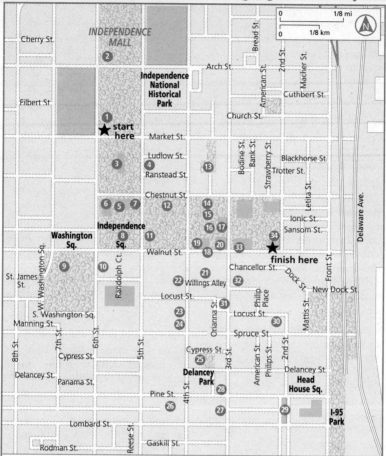

1 Independence Visitor Center
2 National Constitution Center
3 The Liberty Bell
4 The Bourse
5 Independence Hall
6 Congress Hall
7 Old City Hall
8 Independence Square
9 Washington Square
10 Athanaeum
11 Library Hall and Philosophical Hall
12 Second Bank of the United States
13 Franklin Court
14 Pemberton House
15 New Hall
16 Carpenters' Hall
17 First Bank of the United States
18 Row Houses
19 Todd House
20 Bishop White House
21 St. Joseph's Church
22 Philadelphia Contributionship
23 Episcopal Diocese of Philadelphia
24 Old St. Mary's Church
25 Hill-Physick-Keith House
26 Old Pine Presbyterian
27 St. Peter's Episcopal Church
28 Kosciusko National Memorial
29 Head House Square
30 Man Full of Troubles Tavern
31 Powel House
32 St. Paul's Episcopal Church
33 Philadelphia Exchange
34 City Tavern

the Rose Planetarium in New York, and Cleveland's Rock & Roll Hall of Fame. They've spared no expense in creating architecture and multi-media exhibits that are informative, entertaining, educational, and relevant. Families can split up during their visit to experience different parts of the center. Expect great spaces, and a crowded and electric environment.

Backtrack across the Visitor Center block with its new landscaping to:

❸ The Liberty Bell

Once located in Independence Hall, the Liberty Bell moved in 2003 to its new glass pavilion, between Market and Chestnut streets. This new location does justice to the colonial sights that make up the backdrop for the bell. Additional information panels have been added. See p. 116 for a full description.

Just to the east of the Liberty Bell is:

❹ The Bourse

This building is a superb example of late Victorian architecture. It has been renovated as a mall in the form of two arcades surrounding an expansive atrium with a skylight. Built from 1893 to 1895 as a merchants exchange, the Bourse handsomely combines a brick-and-sandstone exterior with a cool and colorful interior. You will probably not be allowed to explore upstairs (security concerns) but you can see a lot from the ground floor.

TAKE A BREAK
The Bourse's spacious, cool ground-floor **Food Court** is open Monday, Tuesday, and Thursday from 10am to 6pm; Wednesday, Friday, and Saturday from 10am to 8pm; and Sunday from 11am to 6pm.

Right ahead of you between 5th and 6th streets (the crowds and carriages will tip you off) is:

❺ Independence Hall

Independence Hall is grand, graceful, and one of democracy's true shrines (see p. 114 for a full description). Ranger-led 35-minute tours depart every 15 minutes or so. The two flanking buildings, **Old City Hall** (built to house the Supreme Court) and **Congress Hall,** were intended to balance each other, and their fanlight-adorned doors, keystone-decorated windows, and simple lines are appealing from any angle. They were used by a combination of federal, state, county, and city governments during a relatively short period.

Turn left as you exit Independence Hall and walk next door to:

❻ Congress Hall

Built in 1787, this building housed the U.S. Congress for 10 years and witnessed the inaugurations of Washington and Adams. The wall-to-wall carpeting and venetian blinds are disappointingly modern, but it's hard to get mahogany desks and leather armchairs of such workmanship nowadays. Look for the little corners where representatives could smoke, take snuff, and drink sherry during recess. Watching the House and Senate from the balconies was a popular social activity. If debate was boring, one could always admire the ceiling moldings.

Exit Congress Hall and turn right, passing Independence Hall, to reach:

❼ Old City Hall

Built in 1790, and located at the corner of 5th and Chestnut streets, Old City Hall was home to the third branch of the federal government, the U.S. Supreme Court, under Chief Justice John Jay, from 1790 to 1800. From 1800 to 1870 the building was used as the city hall. An exhibit here describes the first years of the judiciary branch of the U.S. government.

In back of this central trio of buildings is the shady and hallowed:

⑧ Independence Square

On July 8, 1776, John Nixon read the Declaration of Independence to the assembled city on this spot. At night, from April to October, the Lights of Liberty sound-and-light tour/show ends with projections on the back wall of Independence Hall.

Cut through Independence Square to the greenery at the southwest corner. This is:

⑨ Washington Square

This square is just as expansive and even leafier than when it was the town's pasture. In the 1840s, this was the center of fashionable Philadelphia. Many handsome structures have been razed to make room for chunky offices and apartment houses. Only the 1823 southwest corner Federals, the **Meredith-Penrose House** and its neighbors, give you a sense of what was lost. The square now houses the Tomb of the Unknown Soldier from the Revolutionary War, with its eternal flame. The square has also been the center of Philadelphia publishing for 150 years, with **Lea and Febiger** and **J. B. Lippincott** at no. 227. The massive white building on the north side of the square has been redeveloped, but the Curtis Publishing Co. (now the **Curtis Center**) once sent out the *Saturday Evening Post* and other magazines from here.

Turn to look east. The solid, Italianate Revival brownstone (1845–47) on Washington Square East is the:

⑩ Athenaeum

The Athenaeum is a virtually unchanged pocket of 19th-century society life (see p. 128 for a fuller description).

Returning to Independence Square, walk behind Old City Hall. Along 5th Street and opposite, you'll find the:

⑪ Library Hall and Philosophical Hall

Library Hall is the 1954 reconstruction of Benjamin Franklin's old Library Company, which was the first lending library in the colonies. The Library Company is now at 1314 Locust St., and this graceful Federal building now houses the library of the American Philosophical Society, across the street. The collection is fascinating, including Franklin's will, a copy of William Penn's 1701 Charter of Privileges, and Jefferson's own handwritten copy of the Declaration of Independence. The exhibits focus on the history of science in America. The library's hours follow the park schedule (daily 9am–5pm). **Philosophical Hall,** across the way, is the home of the American Philosophical Society. The society, founded by Ben Franklin, is made up of a prestigious honor roll of America's outstanding intellects and achievers. In Franklin's day, philosophers were more often than not industrious young men with scientific and learned interests. Current members of the society include former senator Ben Bradley, violinist Itzhak Perlman, poet Rita Dove, and commentator Bill Moyers. The building's interior is not open to the public, but look for traces of old Georgian springing into new Federal architecture, such as fan-shaped and larger windows and more elaborate doorsteps.

Next to Philosophical Hall is the:

⑫ Second Bank of the United States

Its strong Greek columns have worn away somewhat, but the bank still holds interest. The Second Bank was chartered by Congress in 1816 for a term of 20 years, again at a time when the country felt that it needed reliable circulating money. The building (1818–24), designed like the Philadelphia Exchange by William Strickland, is adapted from the Parthenon, and the Greeks would have been proud of its capable director, Nicholas Biddle. An elitist to the core, he was the man Andrew Jackson and his supporters had in mind when they complained about private individuals controlling

C Architectural ABCs

You'll enjoy your stroll around Society Hill and Queen Village even more if you know something about colonial and Federal architecture, especially since many homes aren't open for individual tours. Brick is the constant, clay being abundant by the Delaware's banks — but construction methods have varied over the past 150 years.

Generally, houses built before the 1750s, such as the **Trump House** at 214 Delancey St., are two and one-half stories, with two rooms per floor and a dormer window jutting out of a steep gambrel roof (a gambrel roof consists of a roof with two slopes on each of the two sides, with the lower slope steeper than the upper). An eave usually separates the simple door and its transom windows from the second level. Careful bricklayers liked to alternate the long and short sides of bricks (called "stretchers" and "headers," respectively), a style known as Flemish Bond. The headers were often glazed to create a checkerboard pattern. Wrought-iron boot scrapers flank the doorsteps.

Houses built in Philadelphia's colonial heyday soared to three or four stories — taller after the Revolution — and adopted heavy Georgian cornices (the underside of a roof overhang) and elaborate doorways. The homes of the truly wealthy, such as the **Powel House** at 244 S. 3rd St. and the **Morris House** at 235 S. 8th St., have fanlights above their arched brick doorways; the **Davis-Lenox House** at 217 Spruce St. has a simple raised pediment. Since the Georgian style demanded symmetry, the parlors were often given imaginary doors and windows to even things out. The less wealthy lived in "trinity" houses — one room on each of three floors, named for faith, hope, and charity. Few town houses were free-standing (most were row houses) — the **Hill-Physick-Keith House** at 321 S. 4th St. is an exception.

Federal architecture, which blew in from England and New England in the 1790s, is less heavy (no more Flemish Bond for bricks), generally more graceful (more glass, with delicate molding instead of wainscoting). Any house like the **Meredith House** at 700 S. Washington Sq., with a half story of marble stairs leading to a raised mahogany door, was surely constructed after 1800. Greek Revival elements such as rounded dormer windows and oval staircases became the fashion from the 1810s on. Three Victorian brownstones at 260 S. 3rd St. once belonged to Michel Bouvier, Jacqueline Kennedy Onassis's great-great-grandfather.

If you're here in May, don't pass up the **Philadelphia Open House** to view the interiors of dozens of homes (volunteered by proud owners). Call *©* **215/928-1188** for information.

public government. "Old Hickory" vetoed renewal of the bank's charter, increasing the money supply but ruining Biddle and the bank.

The building was used as a Customs House until 1934. Now the National Park Service uses it as a gallery of early Americans. The collection contains many of the oldest gallery portraits in the country, painted by Peale, Sully, Neagle, Stuart, and Allston. Admission is $2 for persons 17 or over. The building is open daily from 9am to 5pm.

Walk east on Chestnut Street one block. The southern side of the block is 18th-century all the way, passing New Hall Museum (we'll get back to that). Crossing the street brings you to a handsome collection of 19th-century banks and commercial facades, including the 1867 First National Bank at no. 315 and the Philadelphia National Bank at no. 323. Go into the marked alleyway to enter:

⑬ Franklin Court

See p. 117 for a full description of this wonderful tribute to Benjamin Franklin in his final home.

You can cross through to Market Street to the north to buy some stamps from Ben's own re-created post office, or return to Chestnut Street for more history at:

⑭ Pemberton House

Joseph Pemberton, a Quaker sugar and Madeira wine merchant, had just built this fine Georgian home when the Second Continental Congress, in the aftermath of the gunfire at Concord and Lexington, cut back on British imports. Pemberton went bankrupt, and the house was razed in 1862, only to be reconstructed a century later. The exhibit here shows the development of the fledgling U.S. Army and Navy. A film about the military history of the Revolutionary War plays continuously. The second floor's highlight is the model gun deck of a frigate, with instructions on maneuvering for a naval battle.

⑮ New Hall

This is a modern copy of a hall built in 1791 by the Carpenters' Company, who rented it out to various people. When the federal government was provisionally based in Philadelphia, this space was used as the headquarters for the first War (now Defense) Department. The building now houses the Marine Corps Museum.

(The Marine Corps was founded at nearby Tun Tavern.) You'll see lots of uniforms, swords, and medals.

Walk south upon exiting New Hall. In midblock sits the delicate:

⑯ Carpenters' Hall

This was a newly built guildhall when the First Continental Congress met here in 1774. See p. 126 for a more detailed description.

Walk to the east across the manicured walkways to find the:

⑰ First Bank of the United States (built in 1795)

This building is not open to the public but is a superb example of Federal architecture. This graceful edifice is the oldest surviving bank building in America. Initially, each of the new states issued their own currency. Dealing with 13 different currencies hampered commerce and travel among the states, so Alexander Hamilton proposed a single bank (originally in Carpenters' Hall) for loans and deposits. The classical facade, Hamilton's idea, is meant to recall the democracy and splendor of ancient Greece. The mahogany American eagle on the pediment over the Corinthian columns at the entrance is a famous and rare example of 18th-century sculpture.

The Park Service cleared many of the non-historic structures on the block behind the First Bank (and throughout the Historic Park area), creating 18th-century gardens and lawns.

You may be surprised to learn that Society Hill wasn't named after the upper crust who lived here in colonial times. Rather, the name refers to the Free Society of Traders, a group of businessmen and investors persuaded by William Penn to settle here with their families in 1683. The name applies to the area east of Washington Square between Walnut and Lombard streets. Many of Philadelphia's white-collar workers, clerics, teachers, importers, and politicos have lived and worked here over the years.

Despite the colonial facades, nobody would have considered walking through this decrepit and undesirable neighborhood a few decades ago. That's all changed now thanks to a massive urban-renewal project, which did a superb job of blending new housing developments in with their Georgian neighbors.

Of course, Society Hill isn't just residential. Georgian and Federal public buildings and churches, from **Head House Square** and **Pennsylvania Hospital** to **St. Peter's** and **St. Paul's**, may make you feel as if you've stumbled onto a movie set. But all of the buildings are used — and the area works as a living community today. A bit south of your present location fine restaurants and charming stores cluster south of Lombard, especially around Head House Square (1803) at 2nd and Lombard streets.

Continuing on your tour from the greenery in back of the First Bank, you'll see very typically restored row houses along the southern side of Walnut St. between 3rd and 4th Streets. Take some time to explore these:

⑱ Row Houses

These restored row houses will catch your eye with their paneled doors and shutters, bands of brick or stone between floors, and small diamonds of painted metal. These last are fire-insurance markers — all early American cities were terrible fire hazards, and Philadelphia, led by Benjamin Franklin, was the first to do anything about it. The plaques functioned as advertisements for the various companies and also helped firemen identify which houses they were responsible for saving. Now the houses belong to park offices and the Pennsylvania Horticultural Association, which maintains an 18th-century formal garden open to the public.

At the corner of Fourth and Walnut streets is the:

⑲ Todd House

Tours of the house (for 10 persons at a time) are required (you can't explore on your own), and tickets by advance reservation are required. They cost $2 at the Independence Visitors Center (you can't buy directly from Todd House). John Todd Jr. was a young Quaker lawyer of moderate means. His house, built in 1775, cannot compare to that of Bishop White (see below), but it is far grander than Betsy Ross's. Todd used the ground-floor parlor as his law office and the family lived and entertained on the second floor. When Todd died in the 1793 epidemic of yellow fever, his vivacious widow Dolley married a Virginia lawyer named James Madison, the future president.

Double back down Walnut toward 3rd Street, at no. 309, is the other park-run dwelling, the:

⑳ Bishop White House

Tours (for 10 persons at a time) are the only way to see the house; $2 tickets can *only* be obtained at the Independence Visitors Center. This house is on one of the loveliest row-house blocks in the city, and it's a splendid example of how a pillar of the community would have lived in Federal America. Bishop White (1748–1836) was the founder of Episcopalianism, breaking with the Anglican church. He was a good friend of Franklin, as you'll see from the upstairs library. Notice how well the painted cloth floor in the entrance hall survived muddy boots and 20 varnishings. In case you take indoor plumbing for granted, remember that outhouses provided the only relief on most colonial property. The library reveals the bishop's tastes, featuring Sir Walter Scott's Waverley novels, the *Encyclopaedia Britannica,* and the Koran alongside traditional religious texts.

Across the street, the park has purchased property and created a garden that exposes the side of:

㉑ Old St. Joseph's Church

This is the first Roman Catholic church in Philadelphia (see p. 125 for a description). It's much more intriguing if you enter through the iron gate and archway on Willing's Alley, off 4th Street between Walnut and Spruce.

The headquarters of the 18th-century fire-insurance companies are located in the heart of Society Hill and are open to the public. As mentioned above, in a neighborhood as moneyed and as crowded as this one was, fire was a constant danger. Before the days of fire departments, groups of subscribers pledged to help each other in case of fire. Many companies required a complete inventory of a house's possessions before they would set premiums, and these inventories have helped in the restoration of run-down town houses. You can see the insurance plaques on the upper facades of many homes.

Turn down Fourth Street, and walk to 212 S. 4th Street to find the:

㉒ Philadelphia Contributionship (1836)

This building has sported the "Hand-in-Hand" fire-insurance mark since it was built in 1836 as the headquarters of the Hand-in-Hand fire-insurance company (which was founded in 1752). The facade of the building is Greek Revival, with a gorgeous limestone entrance, columns, and balustrades leading to the front door. The architect, Thomas U. Walter, also designed the dome and the House and Senate wings of the U.S. Capitol. Entrance to the building is free, and it's open Monday through Friday from 10am to 3pm. The normal exhibition displays old leather fire-fighting equipment and the original policy statement and list of members. If you call ⓒ **215/627-1752** ahead of time, you'll get to view two meeting rooms and a dining room, with their veined

marble fireplaces and rare bird's-eye maple dining-room chairs.

Walk down 4th street until you reach no. 240, which is the is the:

㉓ Episcopal Diocese of Philadelphia

This building combines two splendid row houses built in 1750 and 1826 for the Cadwallader family. Both houses are closed to the public. Look opposite the Diocese to see **Bingham Court,** a 1967 adaptation of the Society Hill style of brick row houses.

Continue down 4th Street to 248 4th Street:

㉔ Old St. Mary's Church

The most important Roman Catholic church during the Revolution, this was the "Sunday" church, as opposed to St. Joseph's which functioned as a weekday chapel. The interior is fairly prosaic, but the paved graveyard is a picturesque spot for a breather, with some interesting headstones and memorials.

Walk a quarter of a block south of the church. The corner of Spruce and 4th streets is a good place to take a breath, with the town houses of **Girard Row** in front of you. Half a block to the west at 426 Spruce St., Thomas U. Walter, the architect of the Contributionship (see above), designed a Baptist church in 1830 that has been modified as the **Society Hill Synagogue,** run by Romanian immigrants at the turn of the century and by Conservative Jews more recently.

Continue down 4th Street to no. 321, the:

㉕ Physick House

This is possibly the finest residential structure in Society Hill (see p. 54 for a fuller description). Take a few steps east on adjoining Cypress Street to reach **Delancey Park,** a delightful playground with places to play and a group of stone bears that are perfect photo props.

Impressions

It is a handsome city, but distractingly regular. After walking about it for an hour or two, I felt that I would have given the world for a crooked street. The collar of my coat appeared to stiffen, and the brim of my hat to expand, beneath its Quakery influence. My hair shrunk into a sleek short crop, my hands folded themselves upon my breast of their own calm accord, and thoughts of taking lodgings in Mark Lane over against the Market Place, and of making a large fortune by speculations in corn, came over me involuntarily.

— Charles Dickens, *American Notes* (1842)

Continue south along 4th St. More Georgian and Federal church facades appear at the corners of 4th and Pine streets. Take a right down Pine St. At No. 412 Pine St. you'll find:

26 Old Pine Presbyterian

With its enormous raised facade and forbidding iron fence, this building didn't always look like a Greek temple. The Penns granted the Presbyterians this land in perpetuity, and the first sanctuary took shape in 1768. The double Corinthian columns, inside and out, were added in 1830, after the occupying British soldiers burned most of the interior. Everything is linear at Old Pine: The portico leads into a rectangle of pews, and slim pillars support a gallery with an elaborately carved rail of flowers and dentils. The altar will surprise you — it's just a dais backed by elaborate columns and entablature. You'll find it hard to believe that this filigree is of wood and not clay or plaster. Exploration of the building is free. It's open daily from 9am to 5pm.

If you like, take a detour and keep going south on 4th Street to Lombard and South St., until South Street's funky shopping and nightlife district. If you've taken this detour, double back up to Pine St. Walk east on Pine St. to:

27 St. Peter's Episcopal Church (1761)

This church is an example of classic Georgian simplicity (see p. 125 for a full description).

Farther north, at 301 Pine St., is the:

28 Kosciuszko National Memorial

This double 1775 Georgian building housed Kosciuszko, the Polish engineer and soldier who turned the tide for American forces at Saratoga and West Point. It's part of the Park system and open daily from 10am to 5pm.

Now follow Pine Street to 2nd Street, the major north-south route through Philadelphia in colonial days. Open markets were a big part of urban life. In fact, no colonial native would recognize Market Street today without the wooden sheds that covered stalls from Front to 6th streets and its narrow cart paths on both sides. One place that would be recognizable, though, is:

29 Head House Square

This square was built in 1803 in the middle of 2nd Street as a place where shoppers could congregate. Head House itself, a brick shed with a cupola that once held a fire bell, trails a simple brick arcade between Pine and South streets. The building used to house fire companies and stables. In those days, market took place at dawn on Tuesday and Friday. Butter and eggs were sold on the west side, meat under the eaves, and herbs and vegetables on the river side. Fish sellers were relegated to the far sidewalks (it isn't hard to imagine why). Now craftspeople spread out their goods here in summer, especially on weekends.

TAKE A BREAK
Dark Horse Inn, 421 S. 2nd St., and several other Head House Square restaurants make excellent lunch or snack stopovers; the Dark Horse (open from 11:30am daily) has an English afternoon tea, as well as a tempting ground-floor bakery. For great chocolate chip cookies or brownies, go to **Koffmeyer's Bakery** on 2nd near Lombard.

Now head up 2nd Street to Spruce Street. Across the street from the 1765 Abercrombie House (one of the tallest colonial dwellings in America), at no. 127 Spruce Street, is the:

⑳ Man Full of Trouble Tavern

This place re-creates the life of Capt. James Abercrombie. The Knauer Foundation has restored the tavern to its original appearance with Delft tiles, a cagelike bar, and tables with Windsor chairs and pewter candlesticks. The 1760 tavern bordered Little Dock Creek at the time, and sailors and dockworkers ate, drank, and roughhoused here nightly. Admission is now by group appointment only (call ☎ 215/922-4367 to schedule a tour).

Look just up the hill to see the **Society Hill Towers** (1964), the I. M. Pei twins, which seemed so modern at the time, yet stick out like 30-story sore thumbs today.

It's best to walk west back to 3rd Street, then north to a stunning block of row-house mansions including Bishop Stevens at no. 232, with its cast-iron balcony; Atkinson House at no. 236, which today conceals an indoor pool; and Penn-Chew House at no. 242, owned by the grandson of William Penn and the last colonial governor of Pennsylvania. The mansion that you can actually visit, at no. 244 S. 3rd St., is:

㉛ Powel House

This is the impressive home of Philadelphia's last colonial and first U.S. mayor. (See p. 128 for more details).

Across the street, at no. 225 S. 3rd St., is:

㉜ St. Paul's Episcopal Church (1761)

This is another church founded thanks to Philadelphia's religious tolerance. When the High Anglican Church refused to license the speech of William McClenachan, a young clergyman who preached such radical notions as the separation of church and state, St. Paul's was set up as his "bully pulpit." The money for the Georgian hall was raised through donations and lotteries. Now the building houses the headquarters of the denomination's community inside beautiful pre-Revolutionary wrought-iron gates and marble-topped enclosing walls. If you go up to the second floor (open Mon–Fri 9am–5pm), you can still see most of the original chancel.

Standing at the corner of 3rd and Walnut streets, you can't miss the:

㉝ Philadelphia Exchange (1832)

This building is a masterwork by William Strickland. It's not open to the public.

Head toward 2nd Street and the river, crossing one of my favorite spaces, a broad area of cobblestones covering Dock Street (Dock Creek in Penn's day) and the Delaware River beyond. The Ritz 5 movie house on your left shows fine independent movies. Soon you'll make a rear approach to the reconstructed restaurant and gardens of:

㉞ City Tavern

Built in 1773, this was the most opulent and genteel tavern and social hall in the colonies and the scene of many discussions among the founding fathers. Unlike most of the city's pubs, it was built with businessmen's subscriptions, to assure its quality. George Washington met with most delegates to the Constitutional Convention for a farewell dinner here in 1787. The park now operates the City Tavern as a concession, which serves continuously from 11am (see p. 85). The back garden seating is shady and cool — perfect for a mid-afternoon break in warm weather.

If you choose to continue toward the Delaware via the pleasant pedestrian extension of Walnut Street and the staircase at its end, you'll pass between the new **Sheraton Society Hill** hotel and the famed but overrated **Old Original Bookbinder's** restaurant, winding up more or less in front of the wonderful **Independence Seaport Museum** and the new Hyatt Regency on the waterfront. Consult the "Parks, the Parkway & Penn's Landing" section in chapter 7 for more details on this area.

WALKING TOUR 2   OLD CITY

Start: Welcome Park, 2nd and Walnut streets.

Finish: Market Place East, 7th and Market streets.

Time: From 3 to 5 hours.

Best Time: Start no later than 3pm to avoid museum closings. If contemporary art and socializing is your interest, the first Friday of every month brings special late hours for all galleries, all cafes, and many historic attractions.

Worst time: Afternoons

Old City is an intriguing blend of 17th and 18th-century artisan row houses, robust 19th-century commercial structures, and 20th-century rehabs of all of the above featuring artist lofts and galleries. See it while you can: Many property owners would rather demolish than rehab, and classics at 110–112 S. Front St., for example, were recently destroyed despite public outcry.

Across from the narrow lane adjoining City Tavern, on 2nd Street, near Walnut Street, is:

❶ Welcome Park

This is the site of the Slate Roof House, where William Penn granted the "Charter of Privileges" (now at the Library Hall off Independence Square) in 1701. The pavement bears a massive and whimsical map of Penn's City, with a time line of his life on the walls.

Next door is the **Thomas Bond House,** a restored 1769 Georgian row house that's now a bed-and-breakfast (see p. 66 for more information).

Walk along the block-long AMC Olde City 2 cinemas to:

❷ Front Street

Front Street actually butted up to the river's edge in colonial times. A walk north brings you to **Bonnie's Exceptional Ice Cream** at the corner of Chestnut Street and the possibility of exploring Penn's Landing (see chapter 7 for a description of the area) via a beautifully terraced park.

Perhaps deterred by the large, blocky Hyatt Regency between you and the water, head back to the florid Corn Exchange Bank at 2nd and Chestnut streets, then turn right onto one of the liveliest blocks in the historic area. Once you hit the newly widened sidewalks of Market Street (High St. in colonial times), you'll find a different world, where a burst of natural food stores and upgraded bistros like Fork, Novelty, and Continental are moving in on sharp discount clothing and wholesale toy stores. The many alleyways between Front and 5th streets, with names like Trotter Street, Black Horse Alley, Bank Street, and Strawberry Lane, testify to the activities and preoccupations of colonial residents.

TAKE A BREAK
The block of "Two Street" between Chestnut and Market contains lots of good restaurants such as **New Mexico Grille.** A nice cafe with full bar, called **Blue Martini,** boasts great food and quiet, cool seating for 40 at the rear. It's open Monday through Friday from 9am to 1am, Saturday and Sunday until 2am.

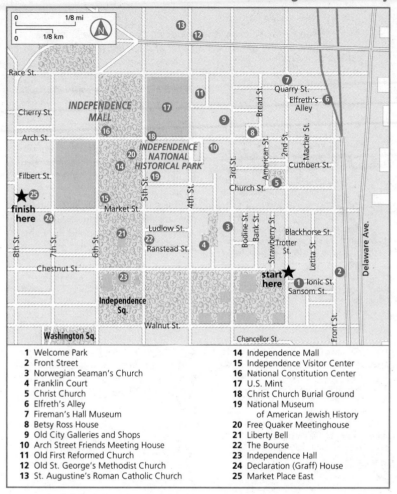

0   1/8 mi
0   1/8 km

Race St.

INDEPENDENCE MALL

Cherry St.

Arch St.

Filbert St.

finish here ⭐ ㉕

Market St.

Chestnut St.

Independence Sq.

Washington Sq.

Walnut St.

Chancellor St.

INDEPENDENCE NATIONAL HISTORICAL PARK

Church St.

Ludlow St.

Ranstead St.

Quarry St.

Elfreth's Alley

Cuthbert St.

Blackhorse St.

Trotter St.

Sansom St.

Ionic St.

start here ⭐ ①

Delaware Ave.

1 Welcome Park	**14** Independence Mall
2 Front Street	**15** Independence Visitor Center
3 Norwegian Seaman's Church	**16** National Constitution Center
4 Franklin Court	**17** U.S. Mint
5 Christ Church	**18** Christ Church Burial Ground
6 Elfreth's Alley	**19** National Museum
7 Fireman's Hall Museum	of American Jewish History
8 Betsy Ross House	**20** Free Quaker Meetinghouse
9 Old City Galleries and Shops	**21** Liberty Bell
10 Arch Street Friends Meeting House	**22** The Bourse
11 Old First Reformed Church	**23** Independence Hall
12 Old St. George's Methodist Church	**24** Declaration (Graff) House
13 St. Augustine's Roman Catholic Church	**25** Market Place East

A particular favorite facade of mine is at no. 22 S. 3rd St. This is the:

❸ Norwegian Seaman's Church

This William Strickland gem from 1837, with Corinthian columns and granite steps, is now a restaurant and club.

If you took the first walking tour, continue right through the Franklin Court stop (stop number 4) to Market Street and Christ Church. Otherwise continue on Market St. until you are between 3rd and 4th streets, where you will find:

❹ Franklin Court

This was Ben Franklin's final home, and is now a post office (see p. 117 for a full description).

Standing on Market Street, you can't miss the graceful spire of:

❺ Christ Church

Urban renewal removed the unsightly buildings that hid the church walls from Market Street. Christ Church, with its restful benches and adjoining cemetery, is Philadelphia's leading place of worship. See p. 124 for a full description.

Impressions

[With its] streets of small, low, yet snug-looking houses . . . Philadelphia must contain in comfort the largest number of small householders of any city in the world.

— London Times *reporter William Bussell,*
My Diary North and South *(1850)*

TAKE A BREAK
It may be a bit early for another refueling stop, but the block of Church Street directly to the west of the church contains **Old City Coffee** at no. 221, a favorite place for marvelous coffee and light lunches. I also like **Gianfranco Pizza Rustica** at 6 N. 3rd St. for lunch, with its delicious thin, crispy crust, along with innovative toppings such as broccoli rabe. If the end of the day is approaching by the time you get here, duck underneath the Market Street ramp to I-95 at Front Street to reach **Panorama's** wine bar and bistro.

Walk east down Church St. and take a left at Front Street. Walk north along Front Street for 4 short blocks to get the flavor of the 1830s warehouses, such as Girard at 18–30 N. Front St. and Smythe at 101 Arch St. If you continued north and east, you would come to the bustling clubs and restaurants on the water, such as Meiji-en, Rock Lobster, and The Beach Club. Instead, take a left onto:

❻ Elfreth's Alley

Since 1702, this has been the oldest continuously occupied group of homes in America. See p. 127 for a full description of these tiny houses. Several courts are perfect for wandering into, and you can enter the house at no. 126.

Walk to the end of Elfreth's Allety and make a right back onto 2nd Street, with its china and restaurant supply stores. Detour north for a minute to look at **2nd Street Art Building,** which houses the Clay Studio and NEXUS galleries, and stop when you reach Quarry Street to visit the:

❼ Fireman's Hall Museum

This restored century-old firehouse contains a hand pump used by Ben Franklin, who helped advance fire fighting beyond tossing water from rudimentary wooden buckets. On display are 19th- and 20th-century fire wagons, along with assorted fire-fighting tools and memorabilia.

Head south now and turn right on Arch Street, where you'll come to no. 239, the:

❽ Betsy Ross House

See p. 126 for full details on the house. The tour of the house is short, but there's a large garden to explore. Directly opposite the house, you'll find the **Mulberry Market,** an upscale deli with seating in the rear, and **Humphry Flags,** if you're feeling patriotic.

Continue west on Arch Street until you find 3rd Street. At the corner of 3rd Street, turn north (toward the Ben Franklin Bridge) to reach the:

❾ Old City galleries and shops

This block of North 3rd St. has some of the coolest Old City furniture, crafts, and art you can find. I love **Foster's Urban Homeware** at no. 124, and the **OLC** lighting store at no. 152.

Cross 3rd Street to the Hoop Skirt Factory at 309–313 Arch St., dating from 1875, and the charming Loxley Court just beyond, designed by carpenter Benjamin Loxley in 1741. (It stayed within the family until 1901.) On the south side of Arch Street is the:

❿ Arch Street Meeting House

This is the largest Quaker meeting-house in America, a simple 1805 structure with a substantial history (see p. 124 for details).

Walk west on Arch Street and make a right when you reach 4th Street. Walk north on 4th Street to no. 151, the:

⑪ Old First Reformed Church

Built in 1837 for a sect of German Protestants, the building survived a stint as a paint warehouse in the late 19th century. The church functions as a small and always full youth hostel during July and August.

Continuing on 4th Street and crossing under the gloomy piers of the Benjamin Franklin Bridge, you'll see no. 235 N. 4th Street, the:

⑫ Old St. George's Methodist Church

This was the cradle of American Methodism and the scene of fanatic religious revival meetings in the early 1770s.

Cross to the other side of 4th Street, below Vine, to find:

⑬ St. Augustine's Roman Catholic Church

This is another 18th-century building. This one was built for German and Irish Catholics who couldn't get to St. Joseph's, south of Market Street, because of muddy streets. Villanova University, and the Augustinian presence in the United States, started here. The building actually only dates from 1844; the original burned down during anti-Catholic riots.

Now, keep walking west along the bridge to 5th Street, then head south along:

⑭ Independence Mall

Independence Mall is a swath of urban renewal that has recently been graced with the new Independence Visitors Center, beautiful landscaping, and a new home for the Liberty Bell.

Walk over to the area between Market St. and Arch St. to visit the:

⑮ Independence Visitor Center

For a general rest stop, tickets to chief Independence National Historical Park sights, and information about the city and region, this new-in-2001 facility is superb. See p. 114 for a fuller description.

Walk one block north to:

⑯ National Constitution Center

This brand-new attraction is described in Walking Tour 1, above, and on p. 117.

At the upper end of the Mall (Florist St.) is the bicycle and pedestrian entrance to the Benjamin Franklin Bridge; cycling or walking across the bridge makes for a thrilling but time-consuming expedition.

Continuing on, head down 5th Street, stopping at the:

⑰ U.S. Mint

Of the three mints in the country (the others are in Denver and San Francisco), Philadelphia's is the oldest and the largest. (See p. 133 for hours and description, but note that with security concerns the Mint is generally closed to walk-up traffic.)

Just south of the Mint, on Arch Street, is:

⑱ Christ Church Burial Ground

This is the resting place of Benjamin and Deborah Franklin and other notables (toss a coin through the opening in the brick wall for luck).

Walk south down 5th Street to no. 55 N. 5th St. to find the:

⑲ National Museum of American Jewish History

The city of Philadelphia has a history of distinguished Jewish involvement in town affairs that's almost as long as the life of the city itself. This museum, connected to the city's oldest congregation, commemorates the history of Jews in America (see p. 132 for a fuller description). You'll notice how much lower street level used to be by looking at the statuary outside.

Turn up 5th Street, and look for a small building across from the Franklin graves, in Independence Mall. This is the:

⑳ Free Quaker Meetinghouse

"Fighting Quakers," such as Betsy Ross, were willing to support the Revolutionary War. But since this violated the tenets of pure Quakerism, they were forced to leave Arch Street

Friends and establish their own meetinghouse, which they did — right here. The building is now run by the Park Service.

Cross Market Street on Independence Mall to see the:

21 Liberty Bell

See p. 116 for a description and history of the bell.

Walk east from the Liberty Bell, to 5th Street where you'll find:

22 The Bourse

This was a 19th-century exchange that now contains a food court and pleasant urban mall (a "Take a Break" stop discussed in the "Historic Highlights" tour above).

Walk south on 5th Street and reenter Independence Mall via Chestnut Street, and you'll be in front of:

23 Independence Hall

Independence Hall is described, as are the two flanking buildings, **Congress Hall** and **Old City Hall,** on p. 114. Tour hours are also given on this page.

Continue west along Chestnut Street to 7th Street, and turn right onto a historic block containing the Atwater Kent Museum of city memorabilia and the:

24 Declaration (Graff) House

This is a reconstruction of the lodgings where Thomas Jefferson drafted the Declaration of Independence. It is run by the National Park Service, with free daily admission. You'll find a full description of the Declaration House on p. 127.

Right behind Graff House on Market Street is a huge McDonald's designed for children; directly opposite it on Market Street is:

25 Market Place East

This is the converted and rehabilitated former home of Lit Brothers Department Store, a wrought-iron palace that's a block long (see the full description on p. 165). The below-ground food area contains an **Au Bon Pain,** or you can pick up your own fixings at **Pagano's Market.**

9

Shopping

In colonial days, Philadelphia was one of the most interesting shopping cities in the world. Franklin's *Autobiography* tells of his surprise upon coming to breakfast one morning to find a china bowl and silver spoon in his very own kitchen: "Luxury will enter families and make a progress in spite of principle." Due in part to its proximity to New York City, Philadelphia still has plenty of goods to help luxury enter your life.

1 The Shopping Scene

In general, this chapter concentrates on Center City stores that carry unique, special, or unusual items. The best places to look for high fashion and international wares are the specialty shops around **Liberty Place** and **Rittenhouse Square.** You'll find SoHo-style cutting-edge fashion, art, and crafts in the **Old City** area just north of the historic landmarks. For more contemporary items, **Manayunk,** several miles up the Schuylkill River to the northwest of town, is also a hip Philadelphia shopping neighborhood. The new airport retail center carries a surprising number of national names, and the once-funky area on **South Street,** just south of Society Hill, has tuned into big business and hosts a clutch of conservative stores that are run more as businesses than as conduits for individual artistic expression. Because restaurants and nightlife now line South Street from Front to 8th streets, many of the 180 stores here are open well into the evening. Stores in this area offer goods ranging from the genteel to the somewhat grotesque.

It's useful to note that the outskirts (mainly the north) of Philadelphia contain prime examples of the enormous malls now ubiquitous at the interchanges of American superhighways — the 21st-century version of colonial village squares. You'll find all of the luxury chains and even some branches of downtown Philly's gems, at **King of Prussia** — a 450-store behemoth, second only to Minnesota's Mall of America — and at **Franklin Mills,** an outlet mall that draws four times the traffic of the Liberty Bell.

There is no sales tax on clothing; other items are taxed at 7%. Most stores stay open during regular business hours, from 10am to 6pm Monday through Saturday and later on Wednesday evening. Some are also open on Sunday.

MALLS & SHOPPING CENTERS

The Bellevue   The lower floors of the Park Hyatt/Bellevue Hotel have been turned into a upscale collection of the top names in retailing. Browsing here is a low-key affair — the space feels a little like a private club. The **Polo/Ralph Lauren** store here is the third largest in the world, boasting three floors of mahogany-and-brass splendor. Other tenants include **Tiffany & Co.,** with its extraordinary jewelry, silver, and accessories; **Williams Sonoma** for gourmet snacks and high end kitchen supplies; a just right fashionable **Nicole Miller; Hope Chest** for intimates and lingerie; **Suky Rosan** for women's fashion; **Vigant** luggage; and

---

> **Finds Food & Shops at the Airport**
>
> If you haven't seen the **Philadelphia International Airport** (✆ **215/937-1200**), in the past couple of years, you're in for a big surprise. They've added over 30 shops and eateries in the "Philadelphia Marketplace" between Terminals B and C, including a lively and spacious food court with seating for 400. Retail includes **GAP/GAP Kids, Discovery Channel Store, Brookstone,** and **Wilson's Leather,** while the **Dock Street Airport Brew Pub** headlines the food court operation. There are 70 other shopping and dining venues along the concourses near airline gates.

Origins cosmetics. Dining is at **Ciboulette** on the mezzanine, the **Palm Restaurant,** or the lower-level food court. Broad and Walnut sts. ✆ 215/875-8350.

Franklin Mills   Fifteen miles northeast of Center City, on the edge of Bucks County, the former Liberty Bell racetrack opened in mid-1989 as Franklin Mills, the city's largest single-story mall, with 1.8 million square feet devoted to 220 discount and outlet stores. It generates 18 million shoppers annually, and there's parking for more than 9,000 cars in four color-coded zones. Anchor stores are JCPenney, Boscov's, and Marshall's. More recently, Franklin Mills has become a discount shoppers' landmark, with last-call outlets from Saks Fifth Avenue, Neiman Marcus, Nordstrom, Bally Shoes, Burlington Coat Factory, and Kaspar. General Cinema has just opened a 14-screen multiplex with stadium seating. For other amusement, the **49th Street Galleria** has bowling, roller skating, miniature golf, batting cages, rides, and games (open Mon–Thurs 10am–11pm, Fri–Sat until midnight, and Sun until 9pm). Two ancillary malls nearby are a 61-checkout-lane (that's right, 61 lanes) **Carrefour** supermarket/department store, and a 30-store **Home and Design Centre.** Open Monday through Saturday from 10am to 9:30pm and Sunday from 11am to 6pm. 1455 Franklin Mills Circle. ✆ 800/336-6255 or 215/632-1500. Follow the signs from I-95 (take Exit 24 north) or from the Pa. Turnpike (take Exit 28 south). SEPTA trains go right to the complex.

The Gallery at Market East   The Gallery at Market East, next to the Pennsylvania Convention Center, features four levels accommodating more than 170 stores and restaurants around sunken arcades and a glass atrium. The JCPenney department store, at the 10th Street corner of Market Street, has replaced the Gimbel's that was formerly there, and a two-story Kmart is one of three in the city. The **food court** has more than 25 snack bars and takeout spots, and top stores include **The Gap** and **The Children's Place.** The **Hardshell Café,** at the street corner of 9th and Market, offers all-you-can-eat specials. Stores offer running shoes, books, pets, cameras, jewelry, fresh produce, toys, and all the clothing you could ever need. **Strawbridge's** connects over 9th Street with merchandise of slightly higher quality and prices. You can pick up a substantial coupon discount book at the Gallery's Information Center (located just within the main entrance), which also provides city maps and sells SEPTA day passes and PHLASH bus passes. Open Monday, Tuesday, Thursday, and Saturday from 10am to 7pm, Wednesday and Friday from 10am to 8pm, and Sunday from noon to 5pm. 8th to 11th and Market sts. ✆ 215/925-7162.

King of Prussia Court and Plaza *Value*   People have always been drawn to King of Prussia because of its name, though the mall is generally referred to as the "Court and Plaza." It's now the second largest mall in the country, impeccably designed and marketed, with 450 establishments in three connected tiers, grouped roughly by price range. The major stores include Bloomingdale's, JCPenney, Lord & Taylor, Neiman Marcus, Nordstrom, Strawbridge's, and Sears. Other top-quality boutiques include Hugo Boss, Versace, Williams-Sonoma, Hermes, Guess Home Collection, and Tiffany & Co. There's the expected food court in the Plaza, but the restaurant scene is hot, with lines at The Cheesecake Factory, Maggiano's Little Italy, Rock Bottom Brewpub, and Morton's of Chicago Steakhouse beyond mall hours. Kids love "Rock It, Man!" a 24-foot climbing wall with four routes to the summit, at $6 for two ascents. And with 126 acres of parking, don't forget where you left your car. Open Monday through Saturday from 10am to 9:30pm, Sunday from 11am to 6pm. Near junction of U.S. 202 and Pa. 363. ℂ 610/337-4752 or 610/265-5727. www.kingofprussia mall.com. ½ mile south of I-276; 3 miles south of Valley Forge National Historical Park via Rte. 422.

Market Place East   The century-old Lit Brothers Department Store was a sprawling assembly of wrought-iron facades that has been recently and beautifully resuscitated as the Market Place East. The ground floor has attracted tenants including **Ross Dress for Less** and **Dress Barn.** The lower level has a food court with atrium seating. There is garage space nearby. Open Monday through Thursday and Saturday from 10am to 6pm, until 8pm on Wednesday. Some stores are open from noon to 5pm on Sunday. 701 Market St., between 7th and 8th sts. ℂ 215/592-8905.

The Shops at Liberty Place *Kids*   The Liberty Place development is the real thing: It's a handsome 60-story tower that supplanted City Hall as the city's tallest spire, and it contains 70 stores and stalls that together achieve an ambience and a comfort level that are the finest in the city. It's beautifully designed, with many street exits and entrances that curve and converge on a soaring, glass-domed rotunda. Representative of the retailers are **Rand McNally** for maps and children's games, **Brentano's** for books, **The Coach Store** for luggage, **Country Road Australia** and **Warner Bros. Studio Store** for casual clothes, **Handblock** for high-quality Indian clothes and fabrics, a new **Ann Taylor Loft** and **J. Crew** for traditional clothes, and a new **Victoria's Secret.** The second floor houses a wonderfully convenient, reasonably-priced food court where you can eat on the run, with hundreds of well-kept tables and chairs around quality food stalls. There are two ATMs inside, near the 16th and 17th Street entrances, and the garage directly underneath holds 750 cars. Open Monday through Saturday from 9:30am to 7pm, Wednesday to 8pm, and Sunday from noon to 6pm. 1625 Chestnut St. between 16th and 17th sts. ℂ 215/851-9154.

The Shops at Penn and Sansom Commons   You'll find dozens of specialty, fashion, music, book and gift shops, and a nine-store food court, as part of U. Penn's urban redevelopment around the campus. Naturally, stores are geared to the collegiate and vital, with offerings such as **Steve Madden** for shoes and **Eastern Mountain Sports.** The Shops at Penn, 34th and Walnut sts; Sansom Commons, 36th and Sansom sts. ℂ 215/222-8595.

2 Shopping A to Z
ANTIQUES
Philadelphia sometimes seems like one big attic, full of the heirlooms and cast-offs of previous generations. Pine Street from 9th to 12th streets boasts some 25 antiques stores, many of which do their own refinishing. Old City stores may specialize in any decade from the 1850s through the 1970s, and Germantown

Avenue in Chestnut Hill also has a large concentration of antiques shops. As in any antiques market, you'll have to bring your own expertise to the store, and you'll have to trust your dealer. There are usually dozens of antiques markets every week in the Delaware Valley. Consult the "Weekend" section of the *Philadelphia Inquirer* for details.

Calderwood Gallery This is an international resource for French Art Nouveau and Art Deco furnishings, which are beautifully displayed in a recently renovated Rittenhouse Square town house. The prices are reasonable compared to those in New York City. 1622 Spruce St. ℂ 215/546-5357.

First Loyalty Antiques The displays of Victorian and Art Deco furnishings and jewelry here are remarkably uncluttered compared to the other stores in the neighborhood. 1042 Pine St. ℂ 215/922-5594.

Freeman/Fine Arts of Philadelphia The dean of the nation's auction houses since 1805, Freeman stages a full auction every Wednesday (previews on Mon and Tues), specializing in Americana, which eBay has started streaming in real time for online antiques lovers. Special fully cataloged auctions for jewelry and fine furniture are held about once a month. Regular auctions include standard home furnishings and some fine silver, rugs, jewelry, and decorative arts. 1808 Chestnut St. ℂ 215/563-9275.

Gargoyles *Value* Among Society Hill antiques shops, my personal favorite is Gargoyles, which has everything from toothpick holders to mantels and bars. Although much of the stock is American, there's also a delightful selection of English pub signs, dart boards, top hats, polo mallets, and the like. Several large items have been salvaged from 19th-century buildings and businesses. 512 S. 3rd St. ℂ 215/629-1700.

M. Finkel and Daughters Finkel is one of the true anchors of Pine Street Look here for folk art, furniture, and painting. And if you're looking for antique needlework samplers, this is the place — they publish the scholarly journal *Samplings* twice a year. Appointments are advised. 936 Pine St. ℂ 215/627-7797.

W. Graham Arader III Gallery *Finds* Arader has become one of the country's leading rare book, map, and print dealers in the past 20 years thanks to its aggressive purchasing techniques (which translates into high prices). You'll find a variety of interesting items here. 1308 Walnut St. ℂ 215/735-8811.

ART GALLERIES

The line between museums that exhibit studio artists, and galleries that promote sales is more blurred here than in many cities. The line between art and crafts is also a fine one (see "Crafts," below, for more listings). Many of the less traditional galleries are in Old City or on South Street.

The Eyes Gallery Isaiah and Julia Zagar have presented a cheerful assortment of Latin American folk art, including *santos* and *retablos* (portable religious shrine panels and sculptures), for 30 years now, in the same location. One-of-a-kind articles of clothing and sterling silver jewelry are also spread over three floors. Open every day of the week. 402 South St. ℂ 215/925-0193.

Fleisher/Ollman Gallery This gallery is known for carrying fine works by emerging contemporary and self-taught American artists such as Martin Ramirez. Style is variable. 211 S. 17th St. ℂ 215/545-7562.

Gross-McCleaf Gallery Now in its 29th year, Jay Gross's gallery features regional painting, as well as exhibits of any medium that can be hung. The focus is on painterly realism, including landscape, still life, and figurative work. 127 S. 16th St. ℭ **215/665-8138.**

Locks   This is a powerhouse gallery for paintings, sculptures, and mixed-media works, hard to beat for its serenity and elegance. Gallery 1 is frequently devoted to group theme shows, while the smaller Gallery 2 usually focuses on a single artist — Ena Swansea, Warren Rohrer, and Jennifer Bartlett are scheduled for 2003–2004. Sueyun Locks aims "to help collectors get savvy," and there's more for the beginner than you might think. 600 Washington Sq. South. ℭ **215/629-1000.**

Moderne Gallery   Moderne is unique, specializing in vintage craft furniture. Owner Robert Aibel offers a very good selection of American and French iron-works — both furniture and decorative items. He's added inventory from the 1940s and 1950s, and features the world's largest selection of vintage pieces by renowned woodworkers such as George Nakashima. You'll also find books and fabrics with 20th-century designs. 111 N. 3rd St. ℭ **215/923-8536.**

Newman Galleries *Finds*   The oldest gallery in Philadelphia (founded in 1865), Newman Galleries has a strong representation of Bucks County artists, American sculptors, and painters in general. Custom framing and art conserva-tion work is also available. Signed, limited edition prints start at $200. 1625 Wal-nut St. ℭ **215/563-1779.**

Paul Cava Fine Arts   This Old City stalwart has wonderful vintage and con-temporary photographs along with modern art. 54 N. 3rd St. ℭ **215/922-2126.**

Philadelphia Art Alliance *Finds*   Founded in 1915 in a striking mansion on Rittenhouse Square, the Alliance now boasts exhibition space along with 30 per-forming/literary programs annually and the acclaimed OPUS 251 restaurant. The alliance's committee of laypersons and artists chooses the three floors of local talent displayed here. There's a new satellite gallery on the third floor of the Rittenhouse Hotel across the square. Open Tuesday through Sunday from 9am to 5pm. Rittenhouse Square, 251 S. 18th St. ℭ **215/545-4302.**

The School Gallery of the Pennsylvania Academy of Fine Arts   The first art school in the country has student and faculty exhibits that change fre-quently during the year. Housed in a gorgeous rehab near the Convention Cen-ter, it's open daily from 9am to 7pm. Admission is free. Note that with the completion of PAFA's renovation of its North Broad St. neighbor 2 blocks north of City Hall, this location's days are numbered. 1301 Cherry St. ℭ **215/972-7600.**

University of the Arts Rosenwald-Wolf Gallery   This gallery in the heart of the Avenue of the Arts presents works by faculty and students, along with dis-tinguished art from outside locals like SEI's fine corporate collection of Western photography. Look for cutting-edge, sometimes distressing presentations. 333 S. Broad St. (Avenue of the Arts). ℭ **215/717-6480.**

BOOKSTORES

AIA Bookstore and Design Center   This bookstore has expanded to include gardening and gadgets books along with architecture and design litera-ture. It also offers an excellent downstairs gallery of architectural renderings, watercolors, and drawings (see below, under "Crafts"). It's a triple "Best of Philly" award winner. And the bookshelves are gorgeous! 117 S. 17th St. at Sansom St. ℭ **215/569-3188.**

Barnes & Noble   Going head to head with archrival Borders (see below) but open one hour later (until 11pm nightly), B&N opened this massive store, with a cafe, right on Rittenhouse Square next to Anthropologie. The neighborhood seems to be able to sustain both bookstores. Visiting authors and guest speakers abound, and top sellers are discounted to 40%. 1805 Walnut St. ✆ 215/656-0716.

Big Jar Books *Finds* In Old City, you'd expect a bookstore to have a sizable collection of trendy and substantive fiction and nonfiction, both new and used, supplemented by mouth-watering cookies, pastries, and espresso at the counter. It's all here. 55 N. 2nd St. ✆ 215/574-1650.

Book Trader If you're on South Street and feel like browsing or just resting, Book Trader has a fine paperback and fiction collection, along with benches and a resident cat. It's open until midnight every night. You can also find a good selection of out-of-print books and used LPs, tapes, and CDs. 501 South St. ✆ 215/925-0219.

Borders Started by the Borders brothers in Minneapolis, this was the first superstore of its kind in town, and it remains a cultural center. The stores has just moved into a massive three-story space at the top of the Avenue of the Arts, 1 block south of City Hall and across from the Ritz-Carlton. Borders features a great staff, and a more thoughtful atmosphere and greater selection than B&N (see above). It has an active reading series in the evening that pays attention to local writers. Musical events may be added in this new location. There's a fine children's book section with toys and there are storytelling hours on most Saturdays. There is also a second-floor espresso bar with newspapers. 1 S. Broad St. (corner of S. Broad and Chestnut). ✆ 215/568-7400 (phone may change).

The University of Pennsylvania Bookstore A 50,000-square-foot collaboration between U. Penn and Barnes & Noble, this store opened in 2000. It's a great academic bookstore, but you'll also find excellent selections of quality fiction and nonfiction and children's books; a 100-seat Starbucks cafe; a comprehensive music department with listening stations; and even clothes and accessories suitable for that hastily scheduled job interview. Open Monday through Saturday from 8:30am to 11pm, Sunday from 10am to 6pm. Sansom Commons, 3601 Walnut St. ✆ 215/898-7595.

COLONIAL REPRODUCTIONS

Ball and Ball Antique Hardware Reproductions It's suburban, about 1¼ miles west of the junction of Routes 100 and 30, but the quality of the reproductions, from Colonial to Victorian, is so superb that it makes the trip worth it. The staff is an excellent resource for information on similar shops concentrating on all aspects of things past, from furniture and fireplaces to clocks and silver. 463 W. Lincoln Highway (Rte. 30), Exton, PA. ✆ 610/257-3711.

Fried Brothers Near the Edgar Allan Poe National Historical Site, Fried Brothers specializes in hardware and furnishings suitable for colonial buildings, with a complete line of door hardware and home security. If you've admired the doorknobs in Society Hill, you can purchase similar ones here. 467 N. 7th St. ✆ 800/523-2924 or 215/627-3205.

CRAFTS

Philadelphia artisanship has always commanded respect. The tradition lingers on, both in small individual workshops and in cooperative stores. The Old City section, north of Society Hill, has seen a mushrooming of contemporary craft and design stores. The Craft Show held every November at the Convention Center is one of the best in the country.

For outdoor crafts vendors, the re-landscaped **Independence Mall** will probably continue its summer weekend schedule in some form. **Head House Square** becomes a bustling bunch of booths from April to September, all day Saturday and Sunday afternoon. And while it's enclosed, the **Reading Terminal Market** has a bunch of booths devoted to tableware, wearable art, and South American and African crafts.

AIA Bookstore and Design Center   This recently renovated lower-level gallery specializes in small home furnishings, lighting, and drawings. They've also added custom framing to their list of services. In the fall, it becomes a gorgeous holiday shop and each spring, the center features Inuit sculpture and textiles. Connected to it is an excellent bookstore (see above, under "Bookstores"). 117 S. 17th St. ℂ 215/569-3188.

The Black Cat *(Finds*   Next door to the White Dog Cafe, Judy Wicks has set up a charming arts-and-crafts store that's open Monday through Wednesday until 9pm, Thursday through Sunday until 11pm. Offerings include weaving, frames, clocks, and silverware among other crafts. There's a small collection of antiques and items that are contemporary but look antique. 3424 Sansom St. ℂ 215/386-6664.

The Fabric Workshop and Museum   This is the only nonprofit arts organization in the United States devoted to creating, displaying, and selling new work in fabric and other materials. You'll find an abundance of finished fabric crafts on sale. The store also operates as a workshop center and collaborates with both emerging and recognized artists. Don't miss the Venturi and Red Grooms-designed bags, scarves, ties, and umbrellas. The store is close to the Convention Center. 1315 Cherry St., 5th floor. ℂ 215/568-1111.

OLC *(Finds*   OLC, in the Old City, has 6,000 feet of sophisticated lighting and furnishings displayed in a museum-quality setting that's been lauded by the American Institute of Architects. It represents 30 European lighting lines and classic furniture by LeCorbusier, Bertoia, Breuer, and hard-to-get contemporaries like B&B Italia. 152–154 N. 3rd St. ℂ 215/923-6085.

Snyderman/The Works Gallery   This Old City veteran, where dramatic light pours through tall windows onto polished wood floors, is one of my neighborhood favorites. The recently merged gallery now focuses primarily on painting, sculpture, and studio artists working in wood, clay, and glass. Photography is also tucked in between rooms. 303 Cherry St. ℂ 215/922-7775 or 215/238-9576.

DEPARTMENT STORES

Lord & Taylor   As Wanamaker's, this was one of the first of the great department stores in the country — a real city institution. Several owners later, it's a subdivision of May Department Stores, and it looks like Lord & Taylor is making this glorious building a destination again. The style of much of the apparel is "updated American classic." The present building (1902–10), which fills a city block, is ingeniously modeled on Renaissance motifs, giving its 12 stories proportion and grace.

On the first floor, there's an Adrien Arpel salon, a chiropodist on call at the shoe salon, and an estate-jewelry counter. On the mezzanine, you'll find a service center with a post office, film developer, travel bureau, dry cleaner, and optometrist. The retail area has shrunk from eight to five floors, with three stories of commercial offices on top. You'll see Ralph Lauren, DKNY, and the rest of the designer gang on deep discount near the end of a season — watch the

Manayunk Shopping

This neighborhood, 8 miles up the Schuylkill from the Art Museum and Center City, soared in popularity in the 1990s. It houses some of Philadelphia's hippest restaurants and shops (see chapter 6 for the former). A wonderful hour-long stroll along the spine of Main Street will put you in touch with contemporary crafts, clothing, antiques, and galleries. Getting there is easy: From the Belmont Avenue exit (north, crossing the Schuylkill River) off I-76 or from 1 block south of the Green Lane SEPTA stop, just follow Main Street east alongside the river from the 4400 to the 3900 addresses. A cohesive local development group runs a continuous series of weekend festivals and events to attract business. Parking is plentiful, and store hours tend to run late to match dinner reservations.

ARTS, CRAFTS & GIFTS   In recent years, quality branches of national brands like **Restoration Hardware,** 4130 Main St. ((C) **215/930-0300**), selling everything from tea strainers to leather couches, have moved in. Among specialty stores, I like **Xcessories Inc. by Design,** 4321 Main St. ((C) **215/483-9665**), for its elegant candlesticks, updated Tiffany-style lamps, and contemporary frames. **Owen Patrick Gallery,** 4345 Main St. ((C) **215/482-9395**), has interesting glass and ceramics, as well as bigger furniture and sculptural art, and carries American West/Urbana upholstered pieces from California. **Artistes en Fleurs,** 4363 Main St. ((C) **215/ 508-9908**), specializes in hand-painted furnishings and uncommon pieces perfect for gardeners. If you're in the market for a modern watch or clock, you should definitely check out **Timeworks,** 4386 Main St. ((C) **215/482-5959**), with a large selection in every price range.

FASHION   In 6 years, **Nicole Miller,** 4249 Main St. ((C) **215/930-0307**), has become the high priestess of high fashion, with little black dresses, cool

Inquirer for ads with coupons that can shave a further 20% to 30%. A five-story court presents Christmas shows with a massive 30,000-pipe organ; this court also hosts daily organ concerts at 11:15am and 5:15pm. Café Americanstyle overlooks the scene from a third floor terrace. Between Market and Chestnut and 13th and Juniper sts. (C) 215/241-9000.

Strawbridge's   Formerly Strawbridge & Clothier, this store, which was formerly family-run, quietly anchors the Market East neighborhood. Now connected to the Gallery Mall, it covers three stories. Prices and boutiques are moderately scaled, with frequent sales. It contains an underrated but excellent food hall. 8th and Market sts. (C) 215/629-6000.

DISCOUNT SHOPPING

Daffy's   Daffy's offers excellent value on name and house brands for men, women, and children in a beautiful 1920s Art Deco building. Prices are 40% to 75% off regular retail, and men's and women's Italian suits, fine leather items (on the third floor), and lingerie are particular bargains. What you see is what you get — it's all out on the floor for the taking. 17th and Chestnut sts. (C) 215/963-9996.

sportswear, and whimsical men's neckties, formal wear, and boxers. Three delightful Boston sisters run **Ma Jolie Atelier,** 4340 Main St. (✆ **215/483-8850**), in a handsome 2-story cross between a boutique and a mansion. It's primarily aimed at the fashionable woman, carrying both elegant and casual wear, but they've also added an adorable kids' fashion area and an upstairs cappuccino bar. **Public Image,** 4390 Main St. (✆ **215/482-4008**), has two stories of hip designer labels such as Product, Vivienne Tam, Diesel, and Freelance; and **Touchables,** 4309 Main St. (✆ **215/487-7988**), has a very extensive selection of lingerie and night wear, including Swiss cotton and silk loungewear and peignoirs. **Neo Deco,** 4409 Main St. (✆ **215/487-7757**), sounds dated, but has a very well chosen selection of chic men's and women's fashions at reasonable prices.

FOOD It's impossible to walk through Manayunk without being seduced, storefront after storefront, by tempting baked goods, sandwiches, coffee bars, sweets, and full-scale restaurants. If you're purchasing for future consumption, go to the **Manayunk Farmer's Market,** 4120 Main St. (✆ **215/483-0100**), a former factory near the eastern edge of the chic part of Manayunk, with a wonderful deck overlooking the river. It's got some true farm stand booths such as **Casey's Farm Fresh Rotisserie** and the wonderfully named **Hel's Kitchen** (selling excellent takeout sandwiches), and it also sells elegantly packaged processed goods of all sorts. **Manayunk Brewing Company & Harry's Pub** (✆ **215/482-8220**) serves regional American cuisine alongside the brewing vats. For full-fledged restaurants like **Kansas City Prime** and **Sonoma** — probably the two best-known — see chapter 6.

House of Bargains   This South Philly institution for children's clothes stocks a remarkable assembly of brand names with discounts of anywhere from 40% to 80% off retail prices. It's located at the intersection of South Broad Street and Passyunk Avenue, where post-shopping treats abound. 1939–1943 S. Juniper St. ✆ **215/465-8841.**

Night Dressing   Locations in Rittenhouse Square and Society Hill carry Lily of France, Olga, Warners, and other lingerie lines, almost all at half price. New arrivals come in almost daily. There's a big selection of sleepwear and robes. 2100 Walnut St. ✆ **215/563-2828.** Also at 724 S. 4th St. (✆ **215/627-5244**).

Ron Friedman Co.   Umbrellas of all sorts are the main selling point, but you can also save 40% to 60% on American and imported leather handbags, wallets, and briefcases. 14 S. 3rd St. ✆ **215/922-4877.**

FASHION

Although there are exceptions, look for conservative styles in the stores around Rittenhouse Square and in department stores. For more sharply styled or contemporary fashions, try Old City. Remember, there is no state sales tax on clothing

Anthropologie   A 1992 offshoot of Urban Outfitters, this exclusive chain was founded to bring the best of other cultures into our own, with party-style funky flair. You may not like everything — but what you like, you'll love. The store's buyers troll bazaars and artisan shops in Europe, India, and the Far East for inspiration, and they adapt or reproduce apparel, accessories, home decor (think platters and comforters, for example) and gifts exclusively in their 20 U.S. stores. This one's a gorgeous turn-of-the-century mansion on the corner of Rittenhouse Square, and shopper's consorts will welcome the overstuffed sofas. 235 S. 17th St. ✆ 215/564-2313.

Burburrys Limited   The rejuvenated Burberrys has the traditional suits, raincoats, and accessories you'd expect for both men and women, but it also offers renaissance additions, from bikinis to skateboards. 1705 Walnut St. ✆ 215/557-7400.

J. Crew   This store offers a nice mix of casual and formal clothes, all brightly colored and softly styled. A highlight is the beautiful cable-knit sweaters. It's a popular rendezvous spot for high-school and college-aged students. Liberty Place, 1625 Chestnut St. ✆ 215/977-7335.

The Original I. Goldberg *Value*   An army-navy paradise for three generations, I. Goldberg has just relocated to a better three-story location a block from the Avenue of the Arts. I. Goldberg provides, at excellent prices, the basic goods you'll need for anything outdoors, with styles ranging from the determinedly antifashion to the up-to-the-minute. The selection is very large, but the staff is harried. 1300 Chestnut St. ✆ 215/925-9393.

Polo/Ralph Lauren   Polo and RL typify American luxury style. The local outpost is in the Bellevue. The Bellevue, Broad and Walnut sts. ✆ 215/985-2800.

CHILDREN'S FASHION

Born Yesterday   Right on Rittenhouse Square, this store outfits babies, boys to size 8, and girls to size 10 in current, stylish fashions. You'll find a selection of classics (overalls, for example) in addition to more "trendy" items. This is a "Best of Philly" store for unique baby gifts and tapes of classical music for kids. Attentive staff. 1901 Walnut St. ✆ 215/568-6556.

Children's Boutique   This place features many all-cotton, color-coordinated outfits by local designers, plus a good selection of top-of-the-line traditional children's clothes. The store has a large infant's department and stocks some toys. 1717 Walnut St. ✆ 215/732-2661.

Gap Kids   The ubiquitous children's clothing store is right here, in the heart of shopping central. 1510 Walnut St. ✆ 215/546-7010.

Kamikaze Kids   You'll find stylish, up-to-the-minute kid's fashion here. The stock ranges from tights to hair ornaments — everything the urban chic child needs. The store also stocks incredible Halloween costumes. Nothing is cheap, except for the 25¢ carnival rides. 527 S. 4th St. ✆ 215/574-9800.

MEN'S FASHION

Black Tie *Finds*   If you find yourself suddenly in need of formal wear, sales and rentals can be found at Black Tie. They carry Perry Ellis, Ralph Lauren, Oscar de la Renta, Lord West, After Six, and other suave styles, and offer custom tailoring as well as accessories from top hats to cuff links to shirts. 1120 Walnut St. ✆ 215/925-4404.

Boyd's *Finds*   Under the Gushner family's ownership, Boyd's has moved "uptown" to a beautifully restored blue-and-white commercial palace. The store sells everything from shoes to formal coats to ties. Boyd's has 65 tailors on site, and boasts European and American lines of all types, as well as alterations for a variety of fine designers such as Ermenegildo Zegna. Boyd's still has its valet and has added a cafe. The sales staff is relaxing and helpful. Sale periods are January and July. 1818 Chestnut St. ℂ **215/564-9000.**

Brooks Brothers   Even in conservative Philadelphia, this is not your father's Brooks. They won't steer you wrong on perfectly acceptable items for business and casual wear, but the whole store is infused with pizzazz and a playful conservative-but-fashionable style. Women are also covered here, but the styles are more hit-or-miss. 1513 Walnut St. ℂ **215/564-4100.**

Wayne Edwards   This stretch of Walnut Street is *the* block for fashion. Wayne Edwards sports a slightly larger selection of contemporary styles than the other stores, including Prada, Vestimenta, Loro Piana, Brioni, and Ralph Lauren Purple Label collections of clothes, sportswear, and shoes. The store also carries some of the finest handmade shoes in the world. 1521 Walnut St. ℂ **215/563-6801.**

WOMEN'S FASHION

Boyd's *(Finds*   Boyd's, a superb men's fashion mansion (see above), doubled the size of its women's department in 2001 and moved it to the center of the first floor. Look for the largest Armani collection in town, featuring classic suits, dresses, and casual wear, as well as hip names such as Philosophy, Genny, Sonia Rykiel, Isaac Mizrahi, and Krizia. The store provides free custom alterations and incorporates a cafe. 1818 Chestnut St. ℂ **215/564-9000.**

Joan Shepp Boutique   The presentation is elegant, with an eclectic mix of accessories, antique jewelry, cosmetics, and home furnishings. Among the Yohji Yamamatos, Rifbat Ozbeks, Prada, and Robert Clergeries, you'll occasionally find spectacular bargains. Joan has moved back with the times, opening the Glamour Girls Salon in 2001, a dynamite balcony full of impeccable vintage by the likes of Trigere and Givenchy. 1616 Walnut St. ℂ **215/735-2666.**

Knit Wit *(Value*   Now in a chic new location, Ann Gitter's Knit Wit specializes in the latest in contemporary fashions and accessories for women, from designers such as Miu Miu, Paul Smith, and Bluemarine. Sales come in March and September. 1721 Walnut St. ℂ **215/564-4760.**

Plage Tahiti   A tiny, selective store and a frequent "Best of Philly" winner, Plage Tahiti has original separates with an artistic slant from Theory, Ghost, and Garfield + Marks. The second floor sale racks have some real steals in Betsey Johnson dresses and the like. As the name suggests, French bathing suits are a constant. 128 S. 17th St. ℂ **215/569-9139.**

Rescue 138   The closest thing to SoHo in Old City, this stores features a mix of consignments, new designers like Kim Montenegro, and standards like Chanel, grouped by colors for simplified browsing. 138 N. 3rd St. ℂ **215/873-0214.**

Rodier   This expensive, fashion-forward retailer is now back in Rittenhouse Square. The sophisticated clothing offered is designed and manufactured in France. 1737 Walnut St. ℂ **215/496-0447.**

Toby Lerner *(Value*   This store is in one of the most affluent neighborhoods in town, and prices match the location. An intimate setting houses clothes, accessories, and shoes. Selections include the best: Armani, Calvin Klein, Versus by Versace, Jimmy Choo Shoes, Celine, TSE Cashmere, and Moschino, with lower-priced lines from Jenne Maag, Votre Nom, and others. 117 S. 17th St. ℂ **215/ 568-5760.** Also in Suburban Square, Ardmore ℂ **610/642-8370.**

FOOD

Also see the review of the **Reading Terminal Market** at 12th and Market streets, with its dozens of individual booths and cafes, on p. 96. In addition, see the "Local Favorites: Cheesesteaks, Hoagies & More" section on p. 106.

Caviar Assouline   An astonishing selection of oils, chocolates, caviar, and other delicacies greets you at this superb gourmet market. There's an excellent selection of gift baskets. Open daily. 505 Vine St. ℂ **215/627-3511** and at Liberty Place, 1625 Chestnut St. ℂ **215/972-1616.** Also at Marketplace at the Airport.

Chef's Market *(Finds)*   The premier gourmet store in Society Hill is Chef's Market, offering a staggering array of charcuterie, cookbooks, and condiments. Would you believe this place stocks breads and cakes supplied by 20 bakeries? 231 South St. ℂ **215/925-8360.**

Fresh Fields Whole Food Market   I know, I know — a supermarket? Fresh Fields, however, has a wonderful selection of the finest natural and organic foods, including a great assortment of prepared dishes and oven-baked goods. Just north of the Ben Franklin Parkway, they are open from 8am to 10pm daily, and they offer seating with a relaxing view of the Philadelphia skyline at no extra charge. Generous samples in every aisle, too. 2001 Pennsylvania Ave. ℂ **215/557-0015.**

Italian Market *(Finds)*   The Italian Market feels like it's straight out of another era, with pushcarts and open stalls selling fresh goods, produce, and cheese Tuesday through Saturday (the end of the week is better). Many shops are open until noon on Sunday. Particular favorites are **DiBruno's** at 930 S. 9th St. (ℂ **888/322-4337** or 215/922-2876) for cheese, **Sarcone and Sons** at 758 S 9th St. (ℂ **215/922-0445**) for bread, **Pasticceria** at 9th and Federal streets (no phone) for pound cake, and **Fante's** at 1006 S. 9th St. (ℂ **215/922-5557**) for kitchenware. The Italian Market is also a great place to pick up cheap clothes: Try **Evantash** lingerie at 1022 S. 9th St. (ℂ **215/413-3433**) or **Irv's** endless racks at 1118 S. 9th St. (ℂ **215/468-8204**). You can always snack on fried dough or pastries as you shop. To reach the market, head 5 blocks south of South Street; SEPTA bus no. 47 goes south on 8th Street from Market. 9th St. between Christian and Wharton sts.

GIFTS & SOUVENIRS

You will run into your basic historic Philadelphia memorabilia all over Society Hill and Independence National Historical Park, beginning with the gift shop at Independence Visitor Center at 6th and Market streets.

Amy & Friends   You'll have to put up with a fair amount of disorder to enjoy this place, but you'll be rewarded with a truly eclectic assortment of antiques and bric-a-brac, including a boutique specializing in top-quality fountain pens. 2124 Walnut St. ℂ **215/496-1778** or 215/232-3714.

Country Elegance   Unique gifts and home accessories, along with a great selection of fine and antique linens, are sold here. 269 S. 20th St. ℂ **215/545-2992.**

Details   Sumptuous gifts, such as invitation cards, high-end desktop accessories, picture frames, and the largest selection of fine stationery in town, are sold in this turn-of-the-century town house. 131 S. 18th St. ℂ **215/977-9559.**

Touches This upscale boutique stocks goods from three broad areas: contemporary jewelry; home accessories such as leather goods, boxes, perfume bottles, frames, and baby gifts; and tableware. Open daily. 225 S. 15th St. ✆ 215/546-1221.

Urban Outfitters Urban Outfitters was actually founded in 1970 right here in town as the People's Free Store. The chain has grown to 40 stores nationwide, all selling casual clothing, gift items, and apartment and home accessories geared to Generation Xers. They have some nice tech toys like digital camera watches, too, but watch the service attitude. 1809 Walnut St. ✆ 215/564-2313.

Xenos Candy and Gifts Miniature Liberty Bells? Snow globes featuring Independence Hall? Tea towels illustrated with the Betsy Ross story? All this and much more is available just around the corner from the sights themselves. 231 Chestnut St. ✆ 215/922-1445.

JEWELRY & SILVER

Philadelphia is known for all types of jewelry — traditional, one of a kind, heirloom, and contemporary. Most of the city's jewelers can be found within a couple of city blocks at **Jeweler's Row,** centering on Sansom and Walnut streets and 7th and 8th streets, which touts itself as offering 30% to 50% off the retail price (though I can't vouch for this). This area contains more than 350 retailers, wholesalers, and craftspeople. Particularly notable is **Sydney Rosen** at 714 Sansom St. (✆ **215/922-3500**). **Robinson Jewelers,** 730 Chestnut St. (✆ **215/627-3066**), specializes in Masonic jewelry and watch repair.

Bailey, Banks & Biddle Established in 1832, Bailey, Banks & Biddle has extraordinary silverware and stationery as well as jewelry. It's a huge store (or museum, if you're not looking to spend). 16th and Chestnut sts. ✆ 215/564-6200.

Jack Kellmer Kellmer imports diamonds by the dozen and sells unusual gold and diamond jewelry out of a magnificent marble showroom. This is an official Rolex jeweler, and carries almost all top watch brands. 717 Chestnut St. ✆ 215/627-8350.

J.E. Caldwell & Co. This is a big, traditional store, founded in 1839. It stocks watches and silver as well as jewelry, carrying such lines as Waterford, Orrefors, Kosta Boda, Lalique, and Reed and Barton. It also does repairs. The building has been magnificently renovated. 1339 Chestnut at Juniper St. ✆ 215/864-7800.

Lagos Lagos is known for its striking fashion-forward settings and unusual colored gems, like evergreen topaz. Oprah is a fan, and you may have spotted the store's wares on TV's *Will & Grace.* 1735 Walnut St. ✆ 215/864-7800.

Linde Meyer Gold & Silver (Value) This nook on the ground floor passage to the central atrium of Liberty Place presents contemporary designer jewelry from Niessing, Georg Jensen, and Henrich+Denzel in precious metals, along with an adjoining collection of estate jewelry and giftware. Meyer's taste in jewelry is impeccable. Liberty Place, 1625 Chestnut St. ✆ 215/851-8555.

Niederkorn Silver Antique baby items, dressing-table adornments, napkin rings, picture frames, and Judaica are featured here. Also on display is Philadelphia's largest selection of period silver, including works of such fine crafters as Jensen, Tiffany, and Spratling. 2005 Locust St. ✆ 215/567-2606.

Spiros Doulis Browsing through this small shop is like looking through your grandmother's jewelry and watch collection — there's a combination of unusual and antique settings and new pieces. They will happily customize pieces and repair watches. 136 S. 11th St. ✆ 215/922-1199.

Tiffany & Co. *(Finds)* Tiffany & Co. is an American institution with an international reputation for quality, craftsmanship, and design. Today, the store has an extensive collection of sterling silver jewelry, but also offers china, crystal, timepieces, writing instruments, and fragrance. Though many items are very expensive here, there are plenty of attractive articles under $100. The Bellevue, 1414 Walnut St. ⊘ 215/735-1919.

LUGGAGE

Bon Voyage From airplane roll-ons to backpacks, adventure wear, and accessories, this Rittenhouse Square store offers a combination of outdoor necessities and the luggage you need to get where you're going. Liberty Place, 1625 Chestnut St. ⊘ 215/567-1677.

Robinson Luggage Company At this flagship of six regional locations, you'll find a great selection of leather gear, along with discounted travel accessories and briefcases. Broad and Walnut sts. ⊘ 215/735-9859.

MUSIC

Watch for the **Borders** coming to the corner of Broad and Chestnut in 2003.

HMV *(Value)* How they got zoning approval for a gleaming, two-story, double-width cube of a building on Rittenhouse Row's best block is a question best left unasked. But it's huge, with a wonderful CD selection that cuts across a range of genres and prices. 1510 Walnut St. ⊘ 215/875-5100.

Theodore Presser Music Store Known primarily as a piano store (since 1900), this store (formerly known as Jacobs Music Co.) is Center City's best source of sheet music for classical and pop musicians alike. 1718 Chestnut St. ⊘ 215/568-0964.

Tower Records *(Value)* The Los Angeles–based Tower Records, careening near bankruptcy but somehow always managing to stay afloat, stocks virtually all current recordings at low prices, and the Tower Records Classical Annex across the street at no. 537 (⊘ **215/925-0422**) is even cheaper. You'll also find videos and books. Open daily. 610 South St. ⊘ 215/574-9888.

SHOES

Aldo Aldo has zoomed into prominence as a hip urban chain, with the latest styles for both sexes (though most of the inventory is geared to women). Most shoes are priced under $100. You'll also find handbags and jewelry here. This new shoe store in Liberty Place has classics and up-to-date fashions and great, high-energy service. Liberty Place, 1625 Chestnut St. ⊘ 215/564-5736; also Gallery at Market East, 901 Market St., ⊘ 215/625-9854, and at Franklin Mills Outlet Center.

Bottino Shoes Look here for sharp, avant-garde European (particularly Italian) men's and women's shoes. 121 S. 18th St. ⊘ 215/854-0907.

Dan's Cancellation Shoes *(Value)* Fully guaranteed and tremendously discounted designer shoes are found here. It's more like a bazaar than a full-service store. Don't expect much service. You won't find loads of funky, trendy, or get-noticed shoes here, but there are some real finds hiding among the regular stuff. 1733 Chestnut St. ⊘ 215/922-6622.

Sherman Brothers At this location for more than 35 years, and recently expanded into the suburbs, Sherman Brothers has the city's best collection of fine men's shoes like Cole Haan, Allen Edmonds, Clarks, and Rockport, as well as difficult sizes. Everything is discounted 10% to 25% all the time. 1520 Sansom St. ⊘ 215/561-4550.

SPORTING GOODS

City Sports   This well-designed, full-service store for those who "do it" rather than dress the part (the urban runner, in-line skater, baseball or hockey player, swimmer, or racquet player) has captured the Center City market. You can buy a second pair of athletic shoes for only $25. 1608 Walnut St. ℭ 215/985-5860.

Eastern Mountain Sports   This superstore adjoining U. Penn. has a complete line for hiking, trekking, and camping. Brands include Timberland, Patagonia, Woolrich, and the excellent house EMS brand. Clothing and equipment are only the start; EMS has an extensive book and magazine selection. 130 S. 36th St. ℭ 215/386-1020.

TOBACCO/CIGARS

Harry's Smoke Shop   Harry's has been puffing along since 1938 and retro-cool has caught up with its historic location. Premium cigars like Arturo Fuente, Macanudo, and Partegas are the specialty. You'll find shaving accessories here also. 15 S. 3rd St. ℭ 215/925-4770.

Holt's   Holt's is renowned throughout the country for its selection of pipes and tobaccos. There are enough fresh cigars here to fill every humidor on Wall Street, plus an excellent pen selection. The opulent relocation and late hours fit perfectly with the neighborhood. 1522 Walnut St. ℭ 215/732-8500.

TOYS

Chestnut Toybox   This store offers a diverse selection of specialty toys for all ages, including Brio, Gund, Playmobil, Carolle, and others. It has an old-fashioned atmosphere of fun and friendly service. 1316 Chestnut St. ℭ 215/545-0455.

WINE & LIQUOR

After the repeal of Prohibition, Pennsylvania decided not to license private liquor retailing but to establish a government monopoly on alcohol sales. You can only buy wine and spirits in state stores (or at a vineyard), which are usually open Monday and Tuesday from 11am to 7pm, Wednesday through Saturday from 9am to 9pm. The selection has improved greatly in recent years, but the system is widely regarded as an anti-consumer nuisance. Beer, champagne, wine coolers, and hard cider are exempt from the system; pick them up at a delicatessen, distributor, or licensed supermarket.

Near Independence Hall, **Old City Liquor,** 32 S. 2nd St. (ℭ 215/625-0906), looks and acts almost like a nonstate store. It's open Monday and Tuesday from 11am to 7pm and Wednesday through Saturday from 9am to 9pm. Also in the Independence Hall area, try the **Bourse Building,** 5th and Chestnut streets (ℭ 215/560-5504) or **Society Hill Shopping Center** (ℭ 215/560-7064).

In the City Hall/Convention Center area, there is a Center City "super store," one of a few extra-large stores featuring up to 5,000 varieties of liquor, open from 9am to 9pm Monday through Saturday at 1218 Chestnut St. (ℭ 215/560-4381). A regular state store is close by at 1318 Walnut St. (ℭ 215/560-4295).

Around Rittenhouse Square, you might try **The Wine Reserve,** at 205 S. 18th St. (ℭ 215/560-4529), a more upscale store where consumers can browse freely amid mahogany counters and shelves. In University City there's a state store at 4049 Walnut St. (ℭ 215/823-4709).

10

Philadelphia After Dark

Most cultural attractions keep their box offices open until curtain time. Also check out **UPSTAGES** (© 215/569-9700), the city's premier non-profit box-office service. They take phone orders Monday through Saturday from 9am to 5pm, and the principal walk-up location is 1412 Chestnut St.; hours are from 10am to 6pm Monday through Friday, from 10am to 5pm Saturday, and from noon to 5pm Sunday. You can buy tickets from UPSTAGES at the Arts Bank, 601 S. Broad St.; Plays and Players Theater, 1714 Delancey St.; and at the top of the escalators at Liberty Place, 1625 Chestnut St., which also offers half-price tickets on the day of the show. There's a small service charge. Hours vary at each of these venues.

For commercial attractions from theater to pop shows, an advance call to Tele-Charge (© 800/833-0080) or Ticketmaster (© 215/336-2000) is your best bet. Local ticket brokers such as the **Philadelphia Ticket Office,** 1500 Locust St. (© 215/735-1903), or **Ticket Warehouse** (© 800/252-8499 or 856/786-7700) are also reliable, since they are limited to selling at 25% above face value. Out-of-state brokers have no limit, so while they may have better selections, the prices could be exorbitant. Many of the fine performing arts have assigned their telephone box office to **Ticket Philadelphia,** at © 215/893-1999.

Seniors can receive discounts of about 10% or $5 per ticket or more at many theaters, including the Annenberg Center, American Music Theater Festival, and Wilma Theater. Concert halls generally make rush or last-minute seats available to students at prices under $10; these programs sometimes extend to adults as well. Groups can generally get discounts of 20% to 50% by calling well in advance.

1 The Performing Arts

Music, theater, and dance are presented regularly all over the city. I have restricted the venues below to those located in Center City and West Philadelphia, where you'll be most of the time, and where the quality of entertainment tends to be highest. There's really no off-season for the performing arts in Philadelphia; when the regular seasons of the Philadelphia Orchestra or Pennsylvania Ballet finish at the end of May, the outdoor activities that make Philadelphia so pleasant take over.

PERFORMING ARTS COMPANIES & GROUPS
CLASSICAL MUSIC GROUPS

The Chamber Orchestra of Philadelphia   This excellent orchestra, made up mostly of homegrown Curtis graduates and talent from New York, performs chamber music at the **Perelman Theater,** the smaller hall within the **Kimmel Center.** 338 S. 15th St. © 215/545-5451 office, or 215/893-9700 box office through Upstages. www.concertosoloists.org. Tickets $15–$35.

Encore Series, Inc.   Soloists, chamber groups, dance troupes, and occasionally theater groups presented by this non-profit umbrella organization perform at the Academy of Music weekday nights at 8pm or Sunday at 3pm. The talent is world class. The Encores Series, Inc. also presents the **Philadelphia Pops** at the Academy of Music some 12 times per year. Bridging symphonic and popular music under acclaimed pianist Peter Nero, the Pops sells out for most performances. 1530 Locust St. ℂ **215735-7506.** Tickets $15–$51.

Philadelphia Chamber Music Society *(Value)*   This series is the best: director Tony Cecchia knows all of the classical music greats from his Marlboro Music Festival time, and brings renowned international soloists, chamber musicians, and jazz and popular artists to the city. Most concerts take place at the Pennsylvania Convention Center's 600-seat hall, or the Perelman Theater of the Kimmel Center. Ticket prices are exceptionally low for the quality of the performances. 135 S. 18th St. ℂ **215/569-8587.** www.pcmsnet.org. Tickets $18–$20.

The Philadelphia Orchestra   For many people, a visit to Philadelphia isn't complete without hearing a concert given by the smooth, powerful Philadelphia Orchestra, under the direction of the dynamic Christoph Eschenbach as of fall 2003. Eschenbach follows an incredible string of 20th-century leaders: Leopold Stokowski, Eugene Ormandy (for 44 legendary years), Riccardo Muti, and Wolfgang Sawallisch. The ensemble has built a reputation for virtuosity and balance that only a handful of the world's orchestras can match. They're still adjusting to their new hall (and vice versa), but Verizon Hall itself is like sitting inside a cello — warm, dark woods, curved spaces, and plush seats ringing the stage.

Concerts are Tuesday, Thursday, Friday, and Saturday evenings and Friday and Sunday afternoons. More tickets to individual performances are available than in the past, with certain dress rehearsals open and fewer subscriptions sold. Try to buy tickets well in advance for the best seats.

In summer the orchestra moves to Mann Music Center for 4 weeks of free concerts (see "Mann Music Center" review below). Regular season Sept–May at Verizon Hall in the Kimmel Center, Broad and Spruce sts. ℂ **215/893-1999** Ticket Philadelphia to charge tickets, or 215/893-1900. www.philorch.org. Tickets $27–$122 for subscription concerts, $10–$42 family concerts. Student rush seats are $8 ½ hr. before concert time for subscription concerts. Community Rush tickets at $10 available 5:30–6:30pm for same day 8pm concerts, 11:30–12:30pm for same day 2pm concerts.

Relâche Ensemble   This contemporary music group, with a particular affinity for young composers, strikes a refreshing balance between the interesting and the intellectual. Made up of a dozen or so instrumentalists, the group performs at the Arts Bank on South Broad Street (p. 182), the Painted Bride Art Center (p. 184), and Villanova University (located on the Main Line). If you're driving it's at the intersection of Rte. 30 and Rte. 476. One public transportation, it's a 25-minute ride to Villanova's station on the R5 commuter line from Suburban Station. Office only at 715 S. 3rd St. ℂ **215/574-8246.** Tickets $10–$20.

DANCE COMPANIES

Local troupes perform successfully alongside such distinguished visitors as Alwin Nikolais, Pilobolus, and the Dance Theater of Harlem. Contact the **Philadelphia Dance Alliance,** 1429 Walnut St., Philadelphia, PA 19102 (ℂ **215/564-5270;** or www.libertynet.org/dance), whose members include most of the performing dance companies in the city.

Movement Theatre International   MTI goes well beyond modern dance to present vaudeville, clown theater, mime, circus acts, and classical dance-drama under the "Penn Presents" umbrella. Productions are held at a tabernacle temple near the University of Pennsylvania campus. MTI produces an annual festival and rents its space out to outside presenters as well. 3700 Chestnut St. ℂ 215/382-0600. www.pennpresents.org. Tickets $15.

Pennsylvania Ballet   Founded in 1963, this nationally renowned company almost went under in 1991 but was rejuvenated by young director Christopher d'Amboise, son of dancer/choreographer Jacques d'Amboise, and later by Roy Kaiser. The company is known for diverse classical dance with a Balanchine backbone. They perform at the Academy of Music and the Merriam Theater during the annual season. The Christmas-season performances of Tchaikovsky's *Nutcracker,* with the complete Balanchine choreography, are a new city tradition. Each of the company's dozens of performances, held from September to June, offers something old, something new, and always something interesting. 1101 S. Broad St. at Washington Ave., ℂ 215/551-7014; box office at Academy of Music, ℂ 215/893-1930; at the Merriam Theater, ℂ 215/875-4829. www.paballet.org. Tickets $20–$75; Nutcracker holiday tickets $19–$92.

Philadanco   Around since 1970, this company is now the Kimmel Center's dance world resident. The company has grown from a community arts group to 17 crack dancers blending African-American styles with ballet, jazz, and cutting edge styles. They tour frequently, but show off at home in November and May. Kimmel Center, S. Broad and Spruce sts. ℂ 215/387-8200. www.philadanco.org. Tickets $27–$37; limited $10 rush seats.

OPERA COMPANIES

The Curtis Opera Theater   This company presents full-scale productions, either at home or out in beautiful Haverford College's Centennial Hall. 1726 Locust St. ℂ 215/893-5252. Opera theater in-house or at suburban Haverford campus; tickets $25.

Opera Company of Philadelphia   The opera company, which is the star tenant of the Academy of Music, presents five fully staged operas per year. Performances take place Monday, Tuesday, Thursday, or Friday evenings, with Sunday matinees; seating preference is given to season subscribers. Advance tickets are sold at the Kimmel Center 3 blocks south. Such international opera stars as Benita Valente (who lives down the street), Ruxandra Donose, and Nathan Gunn appear in about half of the productions. 510 Walnut St., Suite 1600 ℂ 215/928-2110. www.operaphilly.com. Tickets $25–$150; half-price amphitheater tickets available on day of performance.

THEATER COMPANIES

At any given time there will be at least one Broadway show in Philadelphia, on its way into or out of New York. There are also student repertory productions, professional performances by casts connected with the University of Pennsylvania, small-theater offerings in the various neighborhoods of Center City, and cabaret or dinner theater in the suburbs.

Arden Theatre Company   One of the city's most popular professional theaters, the Arden has recently relocated among the trendy galleries and restaurants of Old City. The Arden performs in an intimate 175-seat space and has mounted 34 diverse productions over the past 8 years, including 11 world premieres. 40 N. 2nd St. ℂ 215/922-8900, or UPSTAGES at 215/569-9700. www.ardentheatre.org. Tickets $20–$30.

InterAct Theatre Company   InterAct was founded in 1988 as a theater with a social conscience, mirroring today's world. All plays are new to Philadelphia audiences, with three contemporary productions mounted annually between September and May. 2030 Sansom St. ℂ **215/568-8077**. www.interacttheatre.org. Tickets $33–$60.

Philadelphia Theater Company   This company combines fine regional talent with Tony Award–winning actors and directors. They've produced the local premieres of plays such as *King Hedley II* and *Glengarry Glen Ross,* and Broadway-bound productions like *Master Class* and *Side Man.* Their "Plays and Players Theater" is a slightly antiquated but charming hall just off Rittenhouse Square. 1714 Delancey Place. ℂ **215/735-0631** or 215/568-1920. www.phillytheatreco.com. Tickets $30–$45.

Walnut Street Theatre   This theater has been in business, incredibly, since 1809. The regional Walnut Street Company plays in this 1,052-seat theater, along with numerous local and touring groups. The resident company presents five plays from September to June; both subscriptions and single tickets are available. Wednesday is singles night, with half-price tickets and a mixer. The company's Studio Theater Season presents new and more experimental works in the 75- and 90-seat studio spaces at 825 Walnut St., adjoining the theater. Barrymore's Café is a welcome downstairs addition. 9th and Walnut sts. ℂ **215/574-3550**. www.wstonline.org. Tickets $30–$55, with $10 student rush. Same-day tickets (if available) are sold for half price between 6 and 6:30pm every day.

Wilma Theater   The premier modern theater company in town has to be the Wilma, which has grown to receive national acclaim. Recent seasons featured new plays by Athol Fugard, Tom Stoppard, Martin McDonagh, and Tina Howe, along with a new dance series. They've left their old quarters for a new, state-of-the-art 300-seat theater designed by Hugh Hardy in the heart of the "Avenue of the Arts" district. Broad and Spruce sts. ℂ **215/546-7824**. www.wilmatheater.org. Tickets $29–$41.

PERFORMING ARTS VENUES

In addition to musical performances held at the following major institutions, look for the many concerts presented in churches, especially around Rittenhouse Square.

Academy of Music   In the early 19th century, building an Academy of Music was a proposal much discussed by the cultural movers and shakers in Philadelphia. At the time, opera was the hallmark of culture, and in the 1852, Philadelphia followed New York and Boston in constructing of a hall specifically equipped to handle opera. Modeled on La Scala in Milan, the Academy of Music is grand, ornate, and acoustically problematic. The academy underwent a major multimillion-dollar overhaul from 1997 to 2001, with construction of a level extended stage, replacement of an old bowl-shaped floor with a raked one, and better seating and lighting. It remains a symphony of Victorian crimson and gold, with original gaslights still flaming at the Broad Street entrance. The marble planned for the facade has never been added, but the brick and glass seem to suit Philadelphia far better.

The Philadelphia Orchestra, the owner of the building and chief resident since 1900, moved to the Kimmel Center (see below), 1 block south, in 2001. So the calendar's now a patchwork of touring orchestras and local groups such as the Pennsylvania Ballet and the Opera Company of Philadelphia. Tours of the academy (reservations required) are $5 (reserve at ℂ **215/893-1935**). Broad and Locust sts. ℂ **215/893-1935** for general information, or Ticket Philadelphia (ℂ 215/893-1000) for ticket availability and purchase. www.academyofmusic.org. Advance sales are through the

Kimmel Center Box Office, S. Broad and Spruce sts. 10am–6pm daily. Academy of Music Box Office open only 1 hr. before performances to ½ hr. after performance begins. Discounted $10 student tickets available. Prices vary.

Annenberg Center at the University of Pennsylvania Located on the beautiful University of Pennsylvania campus and easily reached by bus or subway, the Annenberg Center presents a wide variety of performances by American and international companies from September to June. Of the two stages, the Harold Prince Theater generally has more intimate, and usually more avant-garde, productions. The Zellerbach Theater can handle the most demanding lighting and staging needs.

Since U. Penn established its own Penn Presents in 1999 as the professional performing arm of the campus, they've expanded the programming mix to include classical, world, and jazz music; Philadelphia's leading contemporary dance series, Dance Celebration; and the Philadelphia International Theatre Festival for Children, a 5-day event that attracts a regional audience. 3680 Walnut St. ✆ **215/898-6791** (also the number for Penn Presents), or TDD 215/898-4939. Tickets through Penn Presents, www.pennpresents.org. Box office open noon–6pm weekdays. Tickets $18–$50 depending upon event. Discounted tickets available for students and seniors.

Arts Bank One of the cornerstones of the new Avenue of the Arts project, the Arts Bank is a gift of the William Penn Foundation, which realized that there wasn't enough quality, affordable performance space in Center City. The 230-seat theater is owned and operated by the nearby University of the Arts and serves a large, diverse constituency. The stage has a sprung (bouncy) wood floor and state-of-the-art computerized lighting and sound. This is the place for excellent, cheap student and professional theater. Relâche and University of the Arts students are just a few of the performing artists. 601 S. Broad St. at South St. ✆ **215/545-0590,** 215/567-0670 for box office, or 215/875-4800 for telecharge. Box office is open noon–6pm. Tickets $10–$25.

Curtis Institute of Music Philadelphia has a surfeit of excellent musicians and music instruction programs, many of them springing from the world-famous Curtis Institute, led for many years by Rudolf Serkin and now headed by Gary Graffman. Curtis itself has a small hall just off Rittenhouse Square that's good for chamber works; call ✆ **215/893-5261** for a schedule of the mostly free concerts, operas, and recitals. Student recitals are Monday, Wednesday, and Friday evenings at 8pm. As mentioned above, The Curtis Opera Theater presents full-scale productions, either at home or out in beautiful Haverford College's Centennial Hall. 1726 Locust St. ✆ **215/893-5252.** www.curtis.edu. Most in-house concerts free; faculty and guest artist recitals $15–$25. Curtis Orchestra performs at the Kimmel Center; tickets $25. Opera theater in-house or at suburban Haverford campus; tickets $25.

The Forrest Of the commercial Philadelphia theaters, The Forrest — owned by The Shubert Organization — is the best equipped to handle big musicals like *Phantom of the Opera,* and it hosts several of these during the year, along with other short-running plays and concerts. Performances are usually Tuesday through Saturday at 8pm (occasionally Sun night as well) and Wednesday, Saturday, and Sunday at 2pm. 11th and Walnut sts. ✆ **215/923-1515.** Tickets $25–$80.

Harold Prince Music Theater Founded in 1984 by visionary Marjorie Samoff, the old American Music Theater Festival has triumphantly renovated an old 450-seat picture palace. Musical theater is presented in all major forms — opera, musical comedy, cabaret, and experimental theater, along with film. *Time* magazine calls the Harold Prince Music Theater the foremost presenter of new

---

Tips **Blow Your Cover**

HMV, 1510 Walnut St. (📞 **215/875-5100**); the new **Borders,** 1 S. Broad St. at Chestnut St. (📞 **215/568-7400**); and **Tower Records,** 610 South St. (📞 **215/574-9888**), have stacks of coupons for reduced admission to clubs and music venues.

---

and adventurous music theater in the country. 1412 Chestnut St. 📞 **215/972-1000**. www.princemusictheater.org. Tickets $25–$45.

Kimmel Center for the Performing Arts   Opened with tremendous fanfare in December 2001, the dramatic glass and steel vault along the Avenue of the Arts encompasses two freestanding buildings within: **Verizon Hall**, a 2500-seat cello-shaped concert hall built specifically to house the Philadelphia Orchestra; and **Perelman Theater,** a 650-seat hall for chamber music, dance, and drama with a turntable stage. The irregular spaces between the two buildings becomes a sort of plaza, open through the day. Other features at Kimmel include an inter-active education center; "black box" theater space; a daytime cafe and gift shop in the plaza along Spruce St.; and parking and restaurant facilities. Above all, there is space, acres and acres of it; space designed to sparkle and amaze, unlike anything else in the area. The Kimmel Center took 15 years from conception to completion, and a seemingly endless saga of money, planning, and clashing egos continues even now. Initial verdicts? Verizon Hall is a pleasure, with its comfort-able mahogany interior and four levels of seating, and the acoustical match between the orchestra and the hall improves month by month. Perelman's design is also nice, with a metal-clad exterior and light woods and warm fabrics within. However, the physical logistics of entering the building, securing tickets, finding the restrooms, and getting to your seat are a bit convoluted.

Most of the jewels in Philadelphia's cultural crown — the city opera, orches-tra, ballet, and pops companies — perform either at Kimmel or at the historic Academy of Music (which is affiliated with Kimmel and located 1 block north). Prestigious visiting talent in music and dance (either renting the spaces them-selves, or presented by the Kimmel Center) also use the Kimmel Center fre-quently. Tickets for *both* locations are sold during the day only at the Kimmel Center box office. Broad and Spruce sts. 📞 **215/790-5800** for general information, or ticket purchase from Ticket Philadelphia, 📞 215/893-1999 9am–8pm daily. Fax 215/790-5801. www. kimmelcenter.org. Advance sales at the box office, open 10am–6pm daily. Ticket prices depend upon performance event.

Mann Music Center   The Mann Music Center, traditionally specializing in summer presentations of the Philadelphia Orchestra in the 4-week PNC Bank Summer Concert Series, has recently been presenting artists such as Tony Ben-nett, Garrison Keillor, and Bernadette Peters, and series such as Symphonic Pops, Jazz at the Mann, a Family Series, and rock 'n' roll concerts.

A Mann concert is one of the delights of summer. Special SEPTA buses travel from Center City and there's plenty of paid parking available in lots around the Mann. Concerts are Monday, Wednesday, and Thursday at 8pm. Tickets for the covered amphitheater seats may be purchased at the box office there, if available, or by calling ahead.

If you prefer, you can enjoy music under the stars, on the grassy slopes above the orchestra, for free. Seating is unassigned, but tickets are required. The food stall choices range from fine and ethnic to fast, and wine and beer are available. Send a request along with a self-addressed, stamped envelope to the Department of Recreation, P.O. Box 1000, Philadelphia, PA 19105. There's a limit of two tickets per request, and requests made too far in advance (more than 2 months or so) will be returned. Don't forget the blankets and insect repellent. George's Hill near 52nd St. and Parkside Ave. ✆ **215/893-1999.** Tickets from Ticket Philadelphia at ✆ 215/893-1999, or the box office at ✆ 215/567-0707. www.manncenter.org. Amphitheater (covered) seats $18–$68; free lawn seating.

Merriam Theater　The Merriam, belonging to the newly rejuvenated University of the Arts, hosts many of Broadway's top touring shows such as *Annie Get Your Gun* and *Cats,* in addition to popular artists like Patti LaBelle and Barbara Cook. Comedians, magicians, and the Pennsylvania Ballet also perform here. The Merriam is an ornate turn-of-the-century hall with 1,668 seats. The theater is renovated to some degree for uses never foreseen during the vaudeville era. 250 S. Broad St. at Locust St. ✆ **215/732-5446,** or call Ticketmaster (✆ 215/336-1234). Tickets $25–$80.

Painted Bride Art Center　It's hard to know what to call the Painted Bride Art Center, located near the entrance to the Benjamin Franklin Bridge. It's an art gallery catering to contemporary tastes, but it also hosts folk, electronic, and new music, plus jazz, dance, and theater events. Although its director claims that the room can hold 300, the official seat count for the main hall is 60. 230 Vine St. ✆ **215/925-9914.** Tickets $10–$20.

2 The Club & Music Scene

Club kids of all ages (and interested onlookers) will be happy to learn that Philadelphia has plenty of homegrown DJ talent and enjoys frequent visits from New York artists and DJs. Most of the clubs mentioned below are within blocks of the Delaware waterfront. The minimum legal drinking age in Pennsylvania is 21. Bars may stay open until 2am; establishments that operate as private clubs can serve until 3am.

NIGHTLIFE CENTERS
DELAWARE WATERFRONT

With its huge, open spaces and lights shimmering off the water, the Delaware Waterfront — the unused piers and warehouses of Delaware Avenue (aka Christopher Columbus Blvd.), both north and south of the Ben Franklin Bridge — exploded as a social scene in the early 1990s. Although many waterfront spots serve passable food (I recommend **Meiji-en, Moshulu, Rock Lobster,** and **The Chart House**), they are known primarily for their nightlife.

If you're driving, park at Pier 24 at Callowhill Street, between **Rock Lobster** and **KatManDu,** 3 blocks north of the bridge ($5), or at Pier 31 ($3) well to the south. To help reduce drunk driving, club owners have subsidized water shuttle taxis (summer only) that run between waterfront venues every 30 minutes. Prices and exact schedule are still unclear as of press time. Most clubs charge admissions of $10 to $15 during peak hours and accept major credit cards.

The clubs are constantly changing; I've included the current favorites. Start about 3 blocks north of the intersection of Delaware Avenue and Spring Garden Street and work your way south.

Spurred by the Delaware riverfront boom, a number of new clubs have opened in the Old City, in the shadow of the Ben Franklin Bridge.

Tips **Sleepless in Philadelphia: Where the Nightlife Is**

Philadelphia has the reputation of rolling up the sidewalks after 10pm. It seems that way only because there are so many sidewalks and so many diverse little pockets of late-night activity. The best places to start looking for entertainment after the sun goes down include:

- The Delaware Avenue pier clubs (watch the traffic, though, because these clubs get very, very crowded, and muscle cars routinely break the speed limits and traffic laws).
- The neighborhoods next to the waterfront, west along either Spring Garden Street to the north (rehabbed industrial warehouse clubs and restaurants, edging into smaller bistros in Old City to the south) or into South Street's funky/tawdry vibrancy.
- For sophisticated clubbing, the 1500 block of Walnut, between 15th and 16th streets, with Circa, Le Bar Lyonnais, and the nearby bars of the Park Hyatt at the Bellevue.
- The fringes of the University of Pennsylvania, west of the Schuylkill, especially on Walnut and Sansom streets.
- South Philly, for those craving cheesesteak or pasta.

The South Street Area, the Rittenhouse Square area, and the City Line/Manayunk area are other hot spots for nightlife.

A COMEDY CLUB

The Laff House   This Abbott Square lounge hosts writers and performers from Comedy Central, among other comedy breeding grounds. Shows are Wednesday through Sunday evenings. 211 South St. ℂ **215/440-4242.** Admission $10–$25.

DANCE CLUBS

Also see the **Monte Carlo Living Room** on p. 192 and **Dave & Busters** (p. 194).

Baja Beach Club   The former testosterone-fueled summer party scene with live music has gotten a lot classier recently. There's a complimentary 50-foot hot and cold dinner buffet and no cover — so guess what the drinks cost? 939 N. Delaware Ave. ℂ **215/928-9979.** No cover.

Brasil's   Brasil's offers warm feasts of *feijoada* or steak, and Thursday brings a famed all-you-can-eat grilled meat extravaganza for $16. But people also rave about the spirited salsa moves upstairs on the small, mirrored dance floor on weekends. The music is irresistible, and the crowd of South Americans in Lycra is awesome. Salsa instruction given on Wednesday and Saturday is devoted to torrid Brazilian music and dance. 112 Chestnut St. ℂ **215/413-1700.** Cover $5 weekdays, $10 weekends.

Chemistry Nightspot   This Manayunk complex, housed in a former mill, with a deck overlooking the Schuylkill, mixes a great dance floor (laser lights, bubble tubes, Saturday Night Ladies night with no cover before 11pm) with a fine restaurant. The music tends toward current commercial hits, and the crowd is collegiate plus. 4100 Main St., Manayunk. ℂ **215/483-4100.** Cover $5 Thurs–Sat, $10 Sun

Circa   I love this club: It tastes like the Mediterranean, looks like Paris, and feels like Manhattan. Thursday through Saturday, after the excellent dinner (see p. 94), the main room is cleared to accommodate stylish throngs on a wooden dance floor until 2am. Music is DJ-spun house, pop, and 1970s disco. 1518 Walnut St. ℂ 215/545-6800. Cover $5 Fri–Sat after 9pm, $8 after 10pm. Free admission for 2 if you use valet parking.

The District   The District plays the loudest, hottest house music in this part of town. It offers one of the city's largest dance floors, situated in a shabby yet chic renovated 1872 Frank Furness–designed bank. The Thursday open bar and buffet, from 9pm to 2am, is a steal at $10. 600 Spring Garden St. ℂ 215/351-9404. Cover $10 Thurs, $7 Fri, and $5 Sat.

Egypt   Located on the west side of Delaware Avenue, this is probably the city's most popular nightclub. The music is still great though the ambience has slipped a notch. A bi-level dance floor features concert light and sound systems in a campy "oasis" setting in the main room, with different DJs (Q102 broadcasts on Sat) and atmospheres in two different areas. 520 N. Delaware Ave. at Spring Garden St. ℂ 215/922-6500. **Cover around $10.**

Fighth Floor/Ciao   This very upscale spot attracts a style-conscious 30s and 40s crowd. The wraparound waterfront view, with rooftop summer dining to boot, is terrific. With 15,000 square feet, it's usually not overwhelmingly crowded, and it's easier to get a drink than at most clubs. Ciao Restaurant (ℂ 215/925-2700) offers serious fresh fish, veal, and steaks. 800 N. Delaware Ave. ℂ 215/922-1000. Fri Latin night, with a happy hour cover $5 until 8pm, $12 thereafter. On-site parking $6–$10.

Five Spot   Just south of Market St. in Old City, the Five Spot is very popular with singles. They do a combination of lessons and dance sessions most nights. Tuesday brings jazz music, Thursday Latin, and Friday and Saturday a nightclub scene. There is plenty of room on two floors to move or talk. 5 S. Bank St. ℂ 215/574-0070. Tues–Sun 8pm–2am. Cover $5.

Fluid   This is a great dance club in a cool space with blue wood floors. Depending on the night, you'll encounter hip-hop, swing, drum and bass, or house. The scene is always high energy. The entrance is an unmarked door in the alley just off 4th Street, above The Latest Dish. 613 S. 4th St. ℂ 215/629-0565. Cover $3–$10.

KatManDu   Club Med in Philadelphia. KatManDu was the first and remains the most pleasant outdoor island getaway, complete with palm trees, white-sand beaches, world dance music, daiquiris, and an island "mall" with a travel agency. An enclosed two-story addition allows it to stay open year-round, with a music stage and room for 400. There's a reasonably priced outdoor pit barbecue, plenty of secluded nooks, and dancing to classic rock or artists like Buju Banton. Pier 25, 417 N. Delaware Ave. ℂ 215/629-7400. Cover $8.

Maui Entertainment Complex   You'll find 9 acres of lush tropical foliage like something out of *Gilligan's Island,* an outdoor beach grill and volleyball court, the city's biggest dance floor, and hot Nigerian musician King Sunny Ade playing live music, or a live radio broadcast at deafening levels. The crowd, up to 3,000 people, is in its 20s and 30s. Pier 53, 1143 N. Delaware Ave. ℂ 215/423-8116. No cover for ladies on Thurs $5, Fri–Sat $10.

Polly Esther's Culture Club   A blast from the past, Polly Esther's has two dance floors, one for '70s disco, one for '80s retro. Lots of singles of both

genders feel comfortable here, and bartenders get good marks. 1201 Race St.
© 215/851-0776. Thurs–Sat 8pm–2am.

Quincy's   The top choice in this flashy suburban-mall area is Quincy's.
Smooth sounds emanate from good bands, there's lots of wood paneling and old
brass, and there are backgammon tables galore. Quincy's also provides one of the
best happy hours anywhere, with incredible buffet tables. There's dancing most
nights and a singles dance on Sunday from 5 to 10pm. City Line Ave. at Monument
Rd., at the Adam's Mark. © 215/581-5000. No cover on Sun, $10 most nights.

Rock Lobster   At the corner of Race Street, just north of Ben Franklin Bridge
and on the Marina, Marty and Joanne Kennan run this blend of top night-
club/disco and restaurant, which was greatly improved over the winter of 2001.
From May to mid-September, it serves hundreds of moderately priced lunches
and dinners daily in a 4,000-square-foot tent or an alfresco area designed to look
like a Maine yacht club. The restaurant opens for lunch at 11:30am and stays
open until 2am for dancing. The crowd is in its 30s, 40s, and 50s. 221 N. Delaware
Ave. © 215/627-7625. There's no cover until 9pm, then it's usually $5 Wed–Thurs, $10 Fri–Sat.
The cover is higher when national acts appear. Valet parking $8.

Shampoo   This spot, the former Milkbar, spreads progressive music and
trendy retro chic decor over two floors with eight bars and three dance floors.
It's popular with a mixed gay and straight crowd, and summer brings a tent-
covered Groove Garden with patio furniture, Jacuzzi, and an extra DJ. 417 N. 8th
St. © 215/922-7500. Wed, Fri, and Sat from 9pm. Cover charges vary; usually $10 on a non-event
night.

FOLK & COUNTRY VENUES

Grape Street Pub   Manayunk's best live music. A small second-floor stage
featuring everything from singer-songwriter folk to hip-hop supplements a very
popular watering hole on the ground floor. Bands every night but Monday, and
Y-100 broadcasts on Tuesdays. 105 Grape St., Manayunk. © 215/483-7084. No cover
most nights.

The Khyber   Stars like Joe Pernice and My Morning Jacket have a local home
here. See p. 189 for more details. 56 S. 2nd St. © 215/238-5888. Cover $5–12.

Tin Angel Acoustic Café   This very conveniently located 105-seat club above
Serrano restaurant/bar (p. 190) is riding the unplugged wave with artists like

---

(*Moments* **That's Amore: Italian Crooning in South Philly**

There's a tremendous history of Italian crooning in South Philadelphia.
This style developed when operatic training was applied to American
popular singing. Frank Sinatra in the 1940s and 1950s led to other jazz-
influenced singers like Vic Damone, who in turn led to the smooth har-
monics of singers like Frankie Avalon and groups like the Persuasions. Of
the dwindling number of places where you can get a good handle on Italian singing, I like **The Saloon,** deep in the heart of South Philly at 7th and
Catharine streets (© 215/627-1811). It features a fine Italian restaurant
decorated with Victorian antiques. But the real star is the glossy
mahogany bar upstairs where you can take in this mellow music. The
Saloon bar is open from Wednesday to Saturday until 12:30am. The drinks
average $3 and admission is free.

John Wesley Harding, Livingston Taylor, and Maria Muldaur. Open Wednesday through Saturday. 20 S. 2nd St. ✆ 215/928-0770. No cover for Wed open-mike evenings; other nights run $8–$15.

JAZZ & BLUES CLUBS

Philadelphia is one of the great American hot spots for jazz, boasting performances from everyone from John Coltrane to current sax phenomenon Grover Washington Jr., who still lives in the city, to bassist Christian McBride. May brings Jam on the River, and the Mellon PSFS Jazz Festival is held in June (see "Philadelphia Calendar of Events," in chapter 2). The new Philadelphia Clef Club on the Avenue of the Arts has given jazz a legitimate performance home. Major cultural venues like the Philadelphia Museum of Art are beginning to present jazz performances. For specific information, write or call **Mill Creek Jazz and Cultural Society,** 4624 Lancaster Ave., Philadelphia, PA 19131 (✆ 215/473-2880).

Chris' Jazz Club   This three room bar puts the stage in the corner of the front section of the bar, and the front and middle rooms get a fine show nightly. There are four beers on tap. 1421 Sansom St. ✆ 215/568-3131. Cover $5.

Ortlieb's Jazzhaus   The entrance looks like a Home Depot reject, but the expansion of Delaware riverfront life has caught up with this longtime jazz hangout. Quartets headed by Shirley Scott and Mickey Roker are regulars here. There's a terrific seven-piece house band that performs nightly at 9:30pm, and there's no cover charge to enjoy the smoky, down-home ambience. You can park in the small strip mall across the street for free. 847 N. 3rd St. at Poplar St. ✆ 215/922-1035. Cover $5.

Philadelphia Clef Club of Jazz & Performing Arts   The nonprofit Clef Club is dedicated solely to the preservation and promotion of jazz. In its handsome building on the Avenue of the Arts, it presents jazz workshops and instrumental training as well as concerts in a 250-seat performance hall. 736–738 S. Broad St. ✆ 215/893-9912. Ticket prices vary.

Warmdaddy's   Run by the Bynum brothers, who made jazz club Zanzibar Blue (see below) a success, this wine-colored, sophisticated addition to the historic district features authentic live blues from Koko Taylor, Murali Coryell, and the like, and excellent traditional Southern cuisine, with entrees ranging $11 to $17. The stage and sound system are first rate, and the ambience is simultaneously sexy and familial. Front and Market sts. ✆ 215/627-2500. Cover $8 after 8pm waived with dinner. Closed Mon. Cover $10–$12.

Zanzibar Blue   This place, down the escalator at the Bellevue, features the best of the city's — and increasingly the nation's — jazz bands. The ambience is elegant, so you may want to dress up for a visit. 200 S. Broad St. ✆ 215/732-5200. Open until 2am nightly; Sun jazz brunch $24. Cover $10–$12.

ROCK CLUBS & ROCK CONCERT VENUES

Two firms control the presentation of large rock concerts in town, and advance tickets are almost obligatory. The long-established local firm is **Electric Factory Concerts** (✆ 215/569-9416 or 215/568-3222; www.electricfactory.com), which usually books major talent into the **First Union Spectrum** (box office ✆ 215/336-3600), the city's major indoor arena, in South Philly. Other venues include **The Electric Factory,** 421 N. 7th St., a plain industrial rehab with questionable acoustics; the **Tower Theatre,** at 69th and Market streets in West Philadelphia (scene of recent Elvis Costello and Rolling Stones concerts); and, in the summer, the **Mann Music Center** in Fairmount Park. The **Theater of Living Arts** at 334 South St. (℃ **215/922-1011**), now bereft of all seating, is used for smaller shows like Mary Chapin Carpenter.

The 500-pound gorilla of national presenters, Clear Channel Entertainment (www.cc.com) has begun muscling national acts such as Diana Ross, Barry Manilow, and Kenny Rogers into **Tower Theatre** and **Theater of Living Arts** in Center City, the **First Union Spectrum,** and the beautiful 25,000-seat outdoor amphitheater or 1,600-seat concert hall of the **Tweeter Center at the Waterfront** in Camden, New Jersey (local box office ℃ **856/365-1300**). Tickets are available in advance through **Tele-Charge** (℃ **800/833-0800**) for most venues.

Abilene   Abilene opened way back in 1997 with a Southwestern menu and blues to match; more recently it's gone into straight-ahead American R&B and rock. Three dining rooms to choose from, including one nonsmoking. Call to see what band is playing when you're in town. 429 South St. ℃ 215/922-2583. Cover $5–$10.

The Khyber   This is one of the most popular spots to hear jazz, funk, and rock nightly. There's live entertainment from 9:30pm until 1 or 2am, depending on the crowd and the day. Khyber Pass is named after the route the British took to get through Pakistan, and this is somebody's version of what a British overseas officers' club would look like. It does have a certain attic-like charm. English ales and Irish stout are served. 56 S. 2nd St. ℃ 215/238-5888. Cover is usually $5.

North Star Bar   North Star, located near the Philadelphia Museum of Art, hosts photo exhibits and poetry readings in addition to the rock groups that perform 5 nights a week in a glassed-in courtyard. This old bar is a comfortable place to drink, and the spicy chicken wings are very tasty. 27th and Poplar sts. ℃ 215/235-7827. Cover $3–$10.

Pontiac Grille   The Pontiac and its predecessor have featured rock bands, both crude and smooth, every night until 2am since the 1970s. The upstairs serves food until 1am. It's a hard-drinking, hard-smoking place, with lots of energy when the band is good. Both floors are now hooked into a closed-circuit live feed of the main stage. 304 South St. ℃ 215/925-4053. Cover $5 or less.

3 The Bar Scene

Bars are everywhere in Philadelphia and they run from neighborhood bars, to after-work blue-collar hangouts, to yuppie social centers, to temples of hipness. The hottest bars in town now are in that bastion of propriety, **Rittenhouse Square**. Rittenhouse Square has always been a place where residents walk dogs, artists set up easels, and children play in fountains. But the area used to roll up the sidewalks at night. Now, however, thanks to some smart entrepreneurs, the stretch along the entire east side (18th St.) now glows with heat lamps and candles, and resounds with murmurs of conversation and the clink of glasses. Neil Stein initiated the alfresco movement with his 1920s-style parlor bistro **Rouge,** at 205 S. 18th St. in April 1998. It's a Mobil Travel four-star awardee, and it serves a great $12 burger. In 2000, he followed Rouge with **Bleu** at 227 S. 18th St., where whimsical murals enliven a great $29 3-course prix-fixe dinner. Also present are **Devon Seafood Grill,** and **Potcheen** around the corner on Locust St. All are active until 11pm Sunday through Thursday, and until 1am Friday and Saturday.

BREWERIES & PUBS

Bridgid's This tiny, very friendly horseshoe-shaped bar near the Philadelphia Museum of Art stocks a superb collection of Belgian beers, including an array of fruit-to-hops-originated brews. A varied menu is also available at the bar. No smoking allowed is allowed, except for the smoke that billows out of the warm fireplace. 726 N. 24th St. ✆ 215/232-3232.

Dock Street Brewpub at the Terminal If you don't want to venture far from the Convention Center, you can't do better than this huge, attractive space with a great selection of freshly brewed beers and late-night munchies. 1150 Filbert St. ✆ 215/922-4292. Open to 2am daily.

Fado Fado, an Atlanta-based chain that sells more Guinness than anyone else in the United States, is Kieran McGill's personal vision of Victorian-era Dublin, with carved mahogany, cast iron, cozy fireplaces, displays of antique china, and the finest Irish and European draft beers. Intimate nooks seat up to a dozen. Stop by for the Irish music on Tuesdays and Thursdays. 1500 Locust St. ✆ 215/893-9700.

Irish Pub This Rittenhouse Square stalwart packs in hundreds of good-natured professionals, both men and women of all ages. There is Irish and American folk music in the front, and a quieter area in the back. Open until 2am nightly. 2007 Walnut St. ✆ 215/568-5603.

Monk's Café This small brewpub wins "Best of Philly" awards as the first and premier local importer of kegs of flavorful Belgian ales like Chimay. The back bar is more "authentically drafty," while the front bar is more decorous. Both serve from an extensive wine list and furnish a simple menu, with great mussels. 264 S. 16th St. ✆ 215/545-7005.

Nodding Head Brewery and Restaurant This place is close to perfect. The brew house was opened in the late 1980s as an offshoot of the Sansom Street Oyster House downstairs, but now has its own identity. Three beers are regularly brewed right here: a light ale, an amber ale, and a dark porter. The restaurant menu features burgers, tuna steak, and chicken sandwiches as well as vegetarian choices. Try to secure one of the spacious booths in a semicircle opposite the bar. 1516 Sansom St. ✆ 215/569-9525.

Saint Jack's Fascinating, friendly and funky: Think two floors of exotic comfort in the heart of the historic district, with deep reds and beads and a long bar. Owner Louis DeMaise hosts a mixed clientele of college students, club-hoppers, artists, and professionals. The restaurant/bar menu is Asian-American and reasonable (I like the vegetarian dumplings), there is no cover charge, and there are weekday $2 drink specials. 45 S. 3rd St. ✆ 215/238-9353.

Serrano Serrano, along with the Tin Angel Acoustic Café (p. 187), offers a wonderful collection of brews, along with eclectic world cuisine, in an intimate setting. It's located on one of the Historic District's nicest blocks. The old wooden bar has antique stained glass behind it, and a spiced wood fire burns in the fireplace. If you can't get out to Stoudt's own brewpub in Adamstown (p. 230), try their unpasteurized beer here ($5.95 per bottle). 20 S. 2nd St. ✆ 215/928-0770.

XandO XandO — as in "hugs and kisses" — started right here in Philadelphia and now operates bustling cafes serving coffee throughout the day and drinks starting at 4:30pm, in 11 states and 7 Philadelphia locations. In the evenings, the signature sliding bar front lifts to reveal a full liquor bar, table service begins, and lighting and music levels gradually shift for a hopping nightlife scene. Service is variable. Historic area: 325 Chestnut St. ✆ **215/399-0214;** 215 Lombard St. ✆ 215/925-4910. Center City: 1128 Walnut St. ✆ 215/413-1608; 15th and Locust sts. ✆ 215/893-9696; 1700 Market St. ✆ 215/569-2833; 201 S. 18th St. ✆ 215/735-2004; University City: Sansom Commons, 3601 Walnut St. ✆ 215/222-4545.

LOUNGES & PIANO BARS

Alma de Cuba   The wonderful fusion–South American creation of Stephen Staff and Douglas Rodriguez houses swanky, evocative lounges on both floors. Mambo classes once a week. 1623 Walnut St. ✆ **215/988-1799.**

Avenue B   The 100-year-old Steinway sitting in the lounge gives an idea of the quality of this lounge. This is an ideal place to observe the cosmopolitan atmosphere of the Avenue of the Arts, since the lounge is located right across the street from the Kimmel Center for the Performing Arts' sparkle. The late night menu is wonderful. 260 S. Broad St. ✆ **215/790-0705.**

Bridget Foy's South Street Grill   Newly renovated and featuring a fine open-style grill at reasonable prices, Bridget Foy's offers a nice, mellow atmosphere. There's no pressure to socialize if you don't feel like it, but plenty of company to keep you entertained if you do. Situated at the lower corner of Head House Square, the establishment features a lively sidewalk cafe in summer. It's open every evening until 1am. 200 South St. ✆ **215/922-1813.**

Continental Restaurant and Martini Bar   This Old City vintage diner, aluminum siding and all, has been turned into bar that is one of the coolest spots of the moment for over-30s. The martinis deserve the *Food and Wine* magazine's "Best Chef Hangout" award that they won. Tapas from all over the world include filet mignon brochettes and miniature spring rolls. 138 Market St. ✆ **215/923-6069.**

Cutters   This is the quintessential 1990s bar: long, high, massively stocked, with businesslike high-tech systems. If you're upwardly mobile and comfortable in the canyons of commerce, it's friendly and elegant; if not, it's too stuffy. The location, in the IBM building at Commerce Square, makes it a fine postbusiness meeting place. 2005 Market St. ✆ **215/851-6262.**

Downey's   Downey's is a terrific Irish pub with a contemporary flair. Many local professional athletes head here to relax after a game. There's a piano upstairs and a piano player performs, sometimes with other instrumentalists, Friday and Saturday from 8pm to 1am. At Sunday brunch (11:30am–3pm), a strolling string quartet adds to the relaxed atmosphere. A beautiful wraparound second-floor deck offers waterfront views for dining or cocktails. Earthy, comfortable Irish and American fare is served until late. Front and South sts. ✆ **215/625-9500.**

Le Bar Lyonnais   Downstairs from the famed Le Bec-Fin Restaurant (p. 90), you'll find this crowded, intimate, smoky bar, a favorite hangout of those with high bank balances, hormones, or hopes. 1523 Walnut St. ✆ **215/567-1000.**

Lounge at the Omni   This lounge is a very posh spot, with dark woods and Oriental carpets, a crackling fireplace, a piano trio, and large picture windows surveying Independence National Historical Park across the street. Good if you're looking for a quiet, sophisticated backdrop to conversation. It stays open past midnight on weekends. 4th and Chestnut sts. ✆ 215/925-0000.

Impressions

*I have never observed such a wealth of taverns and drinking establish-
ments as are in Philadelphia. . . . There is hardly a street without several
and hardly a man here who does not fancy one his second home.*

— Thomas Jefferson, letter to a Virginia friend (1790)

Love Lounge & Knave of Hearts   The Knave of Hearts has been a long-time
South Street standby for its continental menu and Art Deco bar. The Love
Lounge downstairs attracts an artsy, sophisticated crowd in its 40s, and sports
rosy lighting, plush couches, and informal ambience. 232 South St. ✆ 215/922-3956.

Marmont   Marmont is a swanky narrow bar and restaurant, serving excellent
tapas and more for dinner, followed by live jazz on Wednesday and great DJs
Thursday through Sunday. It's almost all candle-lit; summer brings a few street-
side cafe tables. A great date location. 222 Market St. ✆ 215/923-1100.

Monte Carlo Living Room   The way to do the Monte Carlo is to dine
romantically and well, then dance the night away at the piano bar and a disco
upstairs, which falls somewhere between timeless and time-warp in decor, complete with sentimental artwork and a tinkling fountain illuminated in alternat-
ing reds and blues, all reflected in lots of mirrors. The Living Room is open
Monday through Saturday from 6pm to 2am. Dancing to continental crooners
starts at 9:30pm, with a DJ playing Top 40 between sets. 2nd and South sts.
✆ 215/925-2220. Proper attire required (coats and ties for men, dresses for women). Cover $10
Fri–Sat, unless you've dined downstairs or are a member.

Silk City Lounge   With lava lamps and a young, ultrahip crowd, this is what
would have been called a dive before the postmodern era. Occasional nights are
devoted to music of the Sinatra era, although the owner likes to change themes
every six months or so. Live bands play about once a week. The attached American Diner is open all night Friday through Sunday. 5th and Spring Garden sts.
✆ 215/592-8838.

Society Hill Hotel   The Society Hill Hotel, renovated from the 1832 shell of
the building, has a dozen rooms upstairs, but it's the bar below that has all of
Society Hill excited. It's one of the few modern bars in town that's sophisticated
but not glitzy, and the outdoor cafe is truly charming on a summer eve. (Why
don't more places follow their lead and screw hooks into the undersides of tables
and counters so that women can hang their purses safely but conveniently?) 3rd
and Chestnut sts. ✆ 215/925-1919.

Sugar Mom's Church Street Lounge   This basement lounge, next door to
Christ Church, draws a diverse and hip crowd in its 20s and early 30s, with
plenty of friendly chatter. The jukebox is one of the best in town. 225 Church St.
✆ 215/925-8219.

TGI Friday's   TGI Friday's has become a favorite of the younger crowd that
populates Logan Circle's new office towers. There's standing room only at the
outdoor terrace on summer evenings for the happy-hour buffet and socializing.
18th St. and the Parkway. ✆ 215/665-8443.

A WINE BAR

Panorama   Panorama is at the rear of Penn's View Hotel but separate from the
moderately priced Italian restaurant. Its curving wine bar features 120 different

selections by the glass, most around $6, or you can order flights of five tasting-sized glasses, which makes for a convivial learning experience. There's piano entertainment to accompany your tasting. 14 N. Front St. at Market St. ℭ 215/922-7800. Sun–Thurs until midnight, Fri–Sat to 1am.

4 The Gay & Lesbian Scene

The area between Walnut and Locust streets south of the Convention Center — roughly from 9th Street to 13th Street — is the heart of gay and lesbian Philadelphia, and it's filled with social services, bookstores, clubs, bars, and restaurants. You can leaf through a copy of *Philadelphia Gay News* for suggestions of places that cater to a variety of niches and sub-niches. What follows is a brief selection of the most mainstream nightlife spots.

Bump   This 2002 deluxe gay bar has a cozy feel, titillating artwork, and trendy cocktails including $2 martinis during happy hour. Sundays bring a "Beef and Drag Brunch," which is basically brunch . . . in drag. 1234 Locust St. ℭ 215/732-1800. Open until dawn Fri–Sat.

Judy's Café   I've mentioned Judy's as a simple, very affordable Queen Village neighborhood restaurant (p. 87). If you're looking for a friendly place just to hang out, it's a hot spot for gay and lesbian singles and couples in the front bar area. 627 S. 3rd St. at Bainbridge. ℭ 215/928-1968.

Rodz   Rodz has a cute piano bar along with excellent, affordable eclectic American cuisine for a primarily gay male clientele. 1418 Rodman St. ℭ 215/546-1900.

Sisters   This excellent lesbian center, featuring three bars over three floors, covering over 5000 square feet, is close to City Hall and the Convention Center. It features Saturday "Liquid Sex" events (where the drink creations are supposed to be as good as sex, hence the name), Sunday vinyl dance parties, and Thursday karaoke. 1320 Chancellor St. ℭ 215/735-0735.

12th Air Command   This place caters to a primarily male clientele nightly until 2am. Crowds tend to spill outside on nice nights. Downstairs there's a lounge bar and game room. Italian cuisine is served Wednesday through Saturday and there's a Sunday brunch. There's another bar and a crowded disco upstairs. 254 S. 12th St. ℭ 215/545-8088. Cover $5 for dancing only Fri–Sat. No credit cards.

The 2-4 Club   The Weiss family, who transformed the Eighth Street Lounge in Old City and Grape Street Pub in Manayunk, cleaned up this cavernous after-hours gay bar and dance club in 1999. Fabrics abound, from neon zebra fake fur to baroque red velvet and chandeliers. It's got three floors, and the top floor is filled with couches and multimedia screens. Altogether the space holds nearly 1,000 people and hosts top-name DJs and drag hostesses. 1221 St. James St. ℭ 215/735-5772.

Woody's   The party atmosphere at Woody's attracts both a gay and straight clientele. The original bar is downstairs, and a sandwich counter with cyberbar (and free Internet access) has been added alongside. The disco adjoining the upstairs lounge features trompe l'oeil Atlases holding up a roof of stars. Line dancing, with free two-step lessons, is featured Thursday nights. 202 S. 13th St. ℭ 215/545-1893. Cover Fri–Sat $5–$10.

5 Other Nighttime Entertainment

BOWLING

Philadelphia is not much of a bowling town; no lanes are found in Center City, but there are lanes out along the northern routes leading out of the city, or across the Delaware in New Jersey. Many lanes have adapted to a younger social crowd by offering special "cosmic" or "extreme" bowling nights on the weekends — same lanes but spiced up with loud music and black lights.

Boulevard Lanes   These lanes hold "Cosmic" evenings on Fridays and Saturdays. 8011 Roosevelt Ave. ✆ **215/332-9200.**

Thunderbird Lanes   Thunderbird gets high marks from devotees and daters alike. Saturday evenings are "cosmic bowling," and the wait for a lane can be up to an hour unless you're there early. The lanes host karaoke on Friday nights from 12:30 to 3:30am. There is no bar, but there are video games to entertain while you wait for a lane. 3081 Holme Ave. ✆ **215/464-7171.**

CINEMA

Center City is not as hospitable to modern movie-going as the suburbs are. **United Artist Riverview,** 1400 S. Columbus Blvd, along the Delaware River waterfront (✆ **215/755-2219**), features stadium seating and 17 screens, but it's a considerable taxi ride from anywhere.

In the historic district, **Ritz 5 Movies,** 214 Walnut St. (✆ **215/925-7900**), is the best choice for independent releases. It has five comfortable screening rooms and shows sophisticated, often foreign, fare. The first daily matinee performance is $4.

The five-screen **Ritz at the Bourse,** 4th and Ranstead streets (✆ **215/925-7900**), behind The Bourse and the new Omni Hotel, has the advantage of a superb espresso/cappuccino bar replete with long leather sofas.

In Center City, standard studio releases only are offered at the four-screen **United Artists Sameric,** 1908 Chestnut St. (✆ **215/567-0604**).

In University City, there's a six-plex coming to 40th and Walnut streets, through a U. Penn development. **International House,** 3701 Chestnut St. (✆ **215/387-5125**), presents a fine series of foreign films, political documentaries, and work from independent filmmakers. Admission is $4. **Cinemagic 3 at Penn,** 3925 Walnut St. (✆ **215/222-5555**), screens intelligent releases from the U.S. and abroad. The popcorn here is outstanding.

READINGS

Borders, 1 S. Broad St. at Chestnut St. (✆ **215/568-7400**), runs one of the country's top series of author readings in an elegant setting across the Avenue of the Arts from the Ritz-Carlton. Readings are usually at 7:30pm weekdays and 2pm weekends.

Going head to head with Borders is the **Barnes & Noble** in Rittenhouse Square, 1805 Walnut St. (✆ **215/665-0716**), with 7pm readings. **City Book Shop,** 1129 Pine St. (✆ **215/592-1992**), features poetry readings in a comfortable setting every Friday night. Call the bookstores directly to see who is reading while you're in town.

A VIDEO ARCADE

Traffic is huge for **Dave & Busters**, Pier 19, 325 N. Delaware Ave. (✆ **215/413-1951**) an urban country club with video arcades, virtual reality headsets, electronic golf, billiards, and blackjack. Downsides: Service to redeem coupons from prizes can be slow, and the burgers from the Bridgeside Grill get a mixed reaction. The cover is $5 Friday and Saturday after 10pm.

SALONS

Several spots around town have started catering to the large pool of intellectually curious singles in Philadelphia. Judy Wicks at the **White Dog Café,** 3420 Sansom St. (© **215/386-9224**), has instituted "salon meals," calling on local academics, artists, and her own contacts to address issues such as domestic and foreign policy, the arts, and social movements. The salon talks include a three-course dinner for $30 per person, and reservations are recommended.

SPECTACLES

The **Benjamin Franklin Bridge** has been outfitted with special lighting effects by the noted architectural firm Venturi, Rauch, and Scott Brown. The lights are triggered into mesmerizing patterns by the auto and train traffic along the span. As of 2000, permanent lighting was installed to play on most of the major monuments and bridges leading in and out of Center City and on City Hall as well.

May through October, from dusk until 11:15pm, Independence Historic National Park becomes the backdrop for the mesmerizing **Lights of Liberty** show. Wearing special headsets you hear stereophonic sound and see 50-foot projections and surprising special effects that illustrate the struggle toward America's independence. See p. 118 for details.

6 Late-Night Bites

Twenty years ago, this section wouldn't have existed; the fact is, Philadelphia does stay up late, but until recently the city was private about it. As the city becomes more oriented to tourism and service professions, hours are adapting to fit the clientele.

Bleu   Bleu, the Rittenhouse Square creation of notable Neil Stein, has simple, contemporary food with a modern twist, and the location is perfect for a summer evening. 227 S. 18th St. © **215/545-0342**. AE, DC, DISC, MC, V. Dinner served to 1am Mon–Sat and midnight Sun.

Melrose Diner   The Melrose's logo of a coffee cup with a clock face and knife-and-fork hands, like the place in general, is somewhere between kitsch and postmodern. The Melrose dishes out scrapple (a local fried combination of pork, herbs, and cornmeal) and eggs, creamed chipped beef, and the like 10 blocks north of the sporting stadiums in South Philly. If you hanker for the type of place where you'll be called "Hon," this is for you. They bake pies three times a day to ensure freshness and turn out wonderful butter cookies and a great buttercream layer cake. 1501 Snyder St. (intersection of 15th St., Passyunk Ave., and Snyder St., 1 block west of S. Broad St.). © **215/467-6644**. Reservations not accepted. No credit cards. Always open.

Silk City American Diner   This is what happens when a 1950s diner is given a real postmodern twist; in particular, the pastel pinks and grays in the decor combine with an eclectic song selection and the hip couture that patrons sport. The menu aspires to be gourmet, with dishes such as spicy jerk chicken with grilled plantains, chocolate bread pudding, and huevos rancheros. Adjoins Shampoo nightclub. 435 Spring Garden St. © **215/592-8838**. No credit cards. Open to midnight Sun–Thurs, 24 hr. Fri–Sat. Daily specials.

Tangerine   This is the closest you'll come to playing out a sophisticated fantasy of entering the Casbah for swank, exotic Moroccan fusion cuisine. The over-the-top, low-wattage decor varies from room to room. This place is somewhat pricey but service is excellent. 232 Market St. © 215/627-5116. AE, DISC, MC, V. Sun–Thurs 5pm–10pm, Fri–Sat 5pm–midnight.

11

Side Trips from Philadelphia

The same boats that brought Penn's Quakers to Pennsylvania also brought the pioneers that fanned out into the Delaware Valley to the south, Bucks County to the north, and what is now Pennsylvania Dutch Country to the west. This chapter covers Bucks and Brandywine counties; the next chapter guides you through the Amish heartland of Lancaster County.

Much of this area remains lush and unspoiled, although development-versus-environment struggles are becoming more frequent and more pointed. The major attractions of the Bucks and Brandywine countryside are historical: colonial mansions and inns, early American factories and businesses, and Revolutionary War battlegrounds.

1 Bucks County & Nearby New Jersey

Bucks County, at most an hour by car from Philadelphia, is bordered by the Delaware River to the east and Montgomery County to the west. Historic estates and sights, antiques stores, and country inns abound. The natural beauty here, which has survived major development so far, has inspired many artists and authors, including Oscar Hammerstein II, Pearl Buck, and James Michener. A new interest in this area is ecotourism — the landscape is great for gentle outdoor activities. Nearby New Jersey offers scenic routes for bicycling and walking, plus enjoyable restaurants.

ESSENTIALS
GETTING THERE The best automobile route into Bucks County from Center City is I-95 (north). Pa. 32 (which intersects I-95 in Yardley) runs along the Delaware past Washington Crossing State Park to New Hope, which connects to Doylestown by U.S. 202. By train, the R5 SEPTA commuter rail ends at Doylestown, with connections to New Hope and Lahaska.

From New York, take the New Jersey Turnpike to I-78 west; follow to Exit 29 and pick up Route 287 south to Route 202, which crosses the Delaware River at Lambertville, straight into New Hope. To stay a bit more north and rural, depart I-78 at Exit 15 in Clinton, and take Route 513 south 12 tranquil miles, crossing the Delaware at Frenchtown, New Jersey.

VISITOR INFORMATION To find out more about the hundreds of historic sites, camping facilities, and accommodations here, contact the **Bucks County Tourist Commission,** 152 Swamp Rd., Doylestown, PA 18901 (© **800/ 836-2825** or 215/345-4552; www.bctc.org). You can also write to or stop by the **New Hope Information Center,** South Main and Mechanic streets, Box 141, New Hope, PA 18938 (© **215/862-5880**); open Monday through Friday from 9am to 5pm, Saturday and Sunday from 10am to 6pm.

Along with the specific accommodations listed below, you might want to contact the **Association of Bed & Breakfasts,** P.O. Box 562, Valley Forge, PA 19481

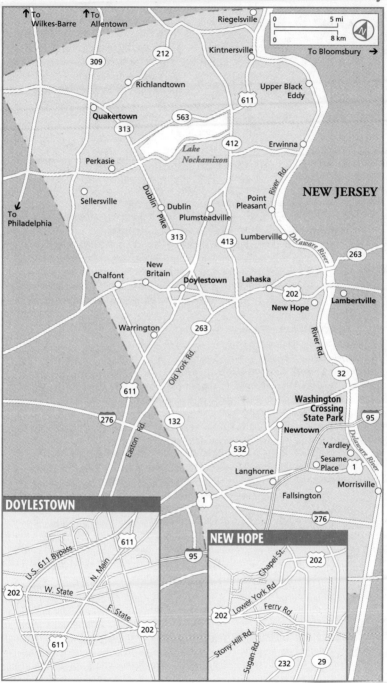

To Wilkes-Barre

To Allentown

Riegelsville

Kintnersville

309

212

Richlandtown

Upper Black Eddy

611

Quakertown

563

313

Lake Nockamixon

412

Erwinna

Perkasie

NEW JERSEY

Sellersville

Dublin Pike

Dublin

Point Pleasant

To Philadelphia

Plumsteadville

313

413

Lumberville

Delaware River

River Rd.

263

Chalfont

New Britain

Doylestown

Lahaska

263

202

New Hope

Lambertville

Warrington

263

River Rd.

611

Old York Rd.

132

32

276

Easton Rd.

Washington Crossing State Park

95

Newtown

Yardley

Delaware River

532

Sesame Place

1

Langhorne

Fallsington

Morrisville

1

276

DOYLESTOWN

U.S. 611 Bypass

611

N. Main

202

W. State

E. State

202

611

95

NEW HOPE

202

Chapel St.

Lower York Rd.

202

Ferry Rd.

Stony Hill Rd.

Sugan Rd.

232

29

To Bloomsbury →

0   5 mi
0   8 km

Fun Fact Where Washington Crossed the Delaware

A trip along the Delaware via Route 32 through Morrisville and Yardley will bring you to **Washington Crossing State Park** in New Jersey, 500 acres that are open year-round (there are another 400 acres of parkland east of the Delaware in Pennsylvania). Most people know that Washington crossed a big river in a small boat on Christmas Eve of 1776, and many people are familiar with the heroic painting depicting this event, with Washington standing in the boat, his eyes on the farther shore (the painting is by Emanuel Leutze, a German, who trained as an artist in Philadelphia). This was the spot, and an annual reenactment of the historic crossing takes place here at Christmas. The Durham boats that Washington and his troops used, which are on display in the boat barn, were hardly tiny — they held 30 soldiers each.

The Pennsylvania side of the park is divided into upper and lower sections separated by 3 miles; Washington left from the site that is now the lower park. You can sip a glass of punch at the low-ceilinged **Old (McKonkey's) Ferry Inn** (1752) where Washington ate before he crossed the river, and tour the bird sanctuary and the Memorial Building at the point of embarkation. The 30-minute film in the Visitors Center (closed Mon) is dated and not worth sitting through — just start exploring on your own.

The **Wild Flower Preserve** in the upper park is really an 100-acre arboretum, flower garden, and botanical preserve rolled into one; it contains 15 different paths, each emphasizing different botanical wonders. The **Thompson-Neely House** was intact when General Washington, Brigadier General Stirling, and Lt. James Monroe decided on the year-end push into New Jersey. Next to the Wild Flower Preserve is the stone **Bowman's Hill Tower;** it will reward you with a stunning view of this part of the Delaware Valley, which would probably still belong to the British Commonwealth if Washington's troops hadn't conquered the Hessians (German soldiers who fought with the British) in 1776. Washington Crossing State Park is located at Rte. 32, P.O. Box 103, Washington Crossing, PA 18977 (© **215/493-4076;** www.field trip.com/pa). A combination ticket, including a walking tour, Thompson-Neely House, Bowman's Hill and Tower, costs $5 for adults, $3 for seniors, and $2 for children ages 4 to 12. Buildings are open Monday through Saturday from 9am to 5pm, Sunday from noon to 5pm. Grounds open daily from 8:30am to 8pm or sunset. Parking is free. Located at the intersection of Pa. 532 and Pa. 32 (River Rd.), 3 miles north of I-95 from Exit 31.

(© **800/344-0123** or 610/783-7838; fax 610/783-7783; open 9am–9pm). They have dozens of charming rooms in Philadelphia, Bucks and Lancaster counties, and in the Valley Forge and Brandywine Valley areas from $60 to $100. Most of the B&Bs that they represent have fewer than five rooms and don't advertise.

ATTRACTIONS IN BUCKS COUNTY

Sesame Place ⭐⭐ *Kids*　　The nation's only theme park based on the award-winning television show *Sesame Street* is located 30 minutes from Center City and 90 minutes from New York City. My kids and millions of others spent a day totally involved in exploring this place — climbing through three stories of sloping, swaying fun on the Nets and Climbs, crawling through tubes and tunnels amid splashing fountains and showers of spray at Mumford's Water Maze, and enjoying the daily fun-filled, interactive musical parade and celebration starring Big Bird, Elmo, Zoe, Bert and Ernie, and the rest. Kids and parents will want their swimsuits for 13 age-safe water rides including Sky Splash, the five-story water adventure in Twiddlebug Land; Rubber Duckie; Slimey's Chutes; and Big Bird's Rambling River. Changing rooms are provided. Older kids will love *Vapor Trail*, the park's roller coaster. All of the best-loved *Sesame Street* characters perform in shows at Big Bird Theater and stroll around Sesame Neighborhood for photo opportunities. Indoors, you'll find air-conditioned game rooms and attractions. Altogether, the more than 60 physical play stations and water rides are perfect for any family with 3- to 15-year-olds.

100 Sesame Rd., Langhorne, PA 19047. ℂ **215/752-7070**. www.sesameplace.com. Admission $37 ages 3–55, $32 seniors over 55, twilight admission $20. Second-day tickets free with validated first-day ticket. Parking $8 per day. Lockers, wheelchair/ECV, and stroller rentals available. *Note:* Many hotels in the area offer discount tickets in their package rates. May to mid-June Mon–Fri 10am–5pm, Sat–Sun 10am–7pm; late June to Aug daily 9am–8pm; Sept–Oct Sat–Sun 10am–5pm. Junction of Rte. 1 and I-95.

Pennsbury Manor　　William Penn planned and lived in this very English plantation and manor at Pennsbury Manor, along the Delaware, 24 miles north of Philadelphia on Route 32 (River Rd.). He designed a self-sustaining, pre-Georgian estate of 8,400 acres, replete with smokehouse, icehouse, barn, herb garden, plantation office, and boathouse. The various dependencies and the manor itself were demolished but were rebuilt to the finest detail in 1939. Taking a tour, given four times daily, is mandatory if you want to see inside the buildings.

Pennsbury Manor boasts the largest collection of 17th-century antiques in Pennsylvania, spread over four floors of the house. On a sunny day, it's a treat to inspect the carefully labeled herb garden, step inside the icehouse for a cool respite, and watch the guinea fowl (more popular than chickens in the 1600s) wandering along the golden brick paths. Sundays frequently bring events such as a period Quaker wedding or a farm festival. Other special events are scheduled throughout the year. Call or check the website to see what's going on when you're visiting.

Morrisville, PA 19067. ℂ **215/946-0400**. www.pennsburymanor.org. Admission to buildings (by guided tour only) $5 adults, $4.50 seniors, $3 children 6–12, free for children under 6. Admission to grounds alone $4.50. Tues–Sat 9am–5pm; Sun noon–5pm. Mar 15–Nov 30 tours are Tues–Fri 10am, 11:30am, 1:30pm, and 3:30pm; Sat 11am, 12:30pm, 2pm, and 3:30pm; Sun 12:30pm, 1:30pm, 2:30pm, and 3:30pm. Take Pa. 9 (Tyburn Rd.) from U.S. 1 (intersects I-95) or U.S. 13.

Fallsington　　When Penn was in residence at Pennsbury Manor (see above) and wished to worship, he'd go to Fallsington, 6 miles north of his estate. This colonial village, grouped around the Quaker meetinghouse, has been preserved virtually intact. Again, tours, given hourly, are mandatory to enter the buildings.

Tyburn Rd., Fallsington, PA 19054. ℂ **215/295-6567**. www.bucksnet.com/hisfalls. Admission $3.50 adults, $2.50 seniors, $1 students 6–18. Mon–Sat 10am–4pm; Sun 1–4pm. Special open-house days on the second Sat in May and Oct. Take Pa. 13 north to Tyburn Rd. (Pa. 9), then turn right and follow the road, or south off U.S. 1 at Tyburn Rd.

NEW HOPE & LAMBERTVILLE

Four miles from Washington Crossing along River Road (Pa. 32), which is punctuated by lovely farmland (as opposed to U.S. 202's factory outlets), you'll come upon New Hope, a former colonial town turned artists' colony. Although it's somewhat commercial and heavily visited now — the weekend crowds can get fierce and parking is cramped — once you're there you'll enjoy the specialty stores, restaurants, and galleries. Lambertville, across the Delaware in New Jersey, has rather pedestrian architecture but boasts more scenic routes along the river than New Hope and, many say, better restaurants.

NEW HOPE AREA ATTRACTIONS

Bucks County Playhouse   This is the center of New Hope entertainment, with a summer theater that features Broadway hits and musical revivals. It's a former gristmill with a seating capacity of almost 500.

70 S. Main St. (P.O. Box 313), New Hope, PA 18938. ℭ 215/862-2041. www.buckscountyplayhouse.com. Tickets $20–$22. Apr–Dec Thurs–Sun evenings and Thurs and weekend matinees.

New Hope Mule Barge   For a while in the early 1800s, canals were thought to be the ultimate transport revolution in England and the eastern United States. Coal was floated down New Hope's canal in the 1830s from mines in the Lehigh Valley, with barges pulled by mules. The barges, still pulled by mules, run from April to November and leave from New Street.

New and S. Main sts., New Hope, PA 18938. ℭ 215/862-2842. Admission $7.50 adults, $6.75 seniors, $5.50 students, $4.75 children under 12. May 1–Oct 15 6 launchings daily; Apr and Oct 16–Nov 15 launchings on Wed, Sat–Sun.

Parry Mansion Museum   One of the loveliest old homes in town, this mansion was erected in 1784 by the elite of New Hope. The Parry family lived in this 11-room Georgian until 1966, and the rooms are decorated in different period styles ranging from 1775 (whitewash and candles) to 1900 (wallpaper and oil lamps).

Main and Ferry sts., New Hope, PA 18938. ℭ 215/862-5652. www.parrymansion.org. Admission $5 adults, $4 seniors, $1 children under 12. May–Dec Fri–Sun 1–5pm.

Peddler's Village   Five miles south of New Hope, on Route 202, Peddler's Village looks antique, but only the heavy commercial marketing is classic — most of the merchandise in over 70 specialty shops is contemporary. The village synergy kicks in with eight restaurants, an inn, and **Giggleberry Fair,** a new family entertainment corner with a restored 1922 carousel (rides $1.50 each) and three-story obstacle course. Among the restaurants, **Jenny's** on Route 202 at Street Road (ℭ **215/794-4020**), offers elegant continental dining in a room decorated with brass and stained glass. The specialties of the **Cock 'n' Bull** (ℭ **215/794-4010**), include a massive buffet on Thursday, an unlimited Sunday brunch, and beef burgundy served in a loaf of bread baked in the hearth. The 66 rooms in the **Golden Plough Inn** (ℭ **215/794-4063**) are scattered throughout the village — all with private bathrooms and complimentary champagne. Rates start at $125 per night.

U.S. 202 and Rte. 263, Lahaska, PA 18931. ℭ **215/794-4000**. www.peddlersvillage.com. Most stores Mon–Thurs 10am–6pm; Fri–Sat 10am–9pm; Sun 11am–6pm. Year-round festivals and events.

OUTDOOR ACTIVITIES IN THE NEW HOPE & LAMBERTVILLE AREA

BIKING & COUNTRY WALKING   Walking or riding along the Delaware River or along the canals built for coal hauling on either side of the river can be the highlight of a summer. The following two routes are particularly convenient: The first is between Lumberville and the point, 3 miles south, where Route 263 crosses the Delaware into New Jersey. The towpath along the canal on the Pennsylvania side is charming, and Lumberville has a quaint general store.

The second route, also just south of Lumberville, follows River Road (Rte. 32) south and west to Cuttalossa Road, which winds past an alpine chalet, creeks, ponds, and grazing sheep clanking their antique Swiss bells. **Cuttalossa Inn,** Cuttalossa Road, Lumberville, PA 18933 (✆ **215/297-5082**), offers high-class cuisine in a spectacular setting.

The **Lumberville Store Bicycle Rental Co.** (Rte. 32, Lumberville, PA 18933; ✆ **215/297-5388**) has all kinds of bicycles for rent at moderate day rates. It's open daily from 8am to 5pm and has wonderful sandwiches for the road.

CANOEING & TUBING   The award for relaxing family fun goes to canoeing and tubing from **Point Pleasant Canoe and Tube,** P.O. Box 6, Point Pleasant, PA 18950 (✆ **215/297-5000;** www.rivercountry.net). The ride lets you drift down the Delaware from Upper Black Eddy and Riegelsville back to their headquarters 8 miles north of New Hope. The water is 80° all summer, and the Delaware moves at 1½ mph, so it's pretty painless. Tube rates are $16 to $18 per person; canoe rates are $22 for a 2-hour stint for two people.

COVERED-BRIDGE TOUR   Call ✆ **215/639-0300** for information about this self-guided free tour of the area's covered bridges.

STEAM RAILWAY TOUR   A **steam railway** chuffs a 45-minute loop between New Hope and Lahaska (✆ **215/862-2707;** www.newhoperail road.com).

SHOPPING

Penn's Purchase Factory Outlet Stores   This pleasant faux village, straddling Route 202 between Doylestown and New Hope, contains 45 outlets for stores such as **Coach, Etienne Aigner, Jones New York,** and **Nautica.** For those immediate travel needs, there are clean restrooms, an ATM, and a Dairy Queen. You won't find too many other stores that are open on a Sunday morning around here.

Rte. 202, Lahaska, PA 18931. ((✆ **215/794-0300**). Mon–Fri 10am–8pm; Sat 9am–8pm; Sun 9am–6pm.

Rice's Sale & Country Market   Rice's Market is the real thing — a quality market that has been selling country goods and crafts since 1860. Amish wares are sold in the main building, along with antiques and collectibles. Plus, more than 1,000 outdoor stalls have vendors. New features include indoor bathrooms and paved walkways for strollers and wheelchairs. There's an ATM on the premises. Get there early.

6326 Greenhill Rd., New Hope, PA 18938. ✆ **215/297-5993.** www.ricesmarket.com. Admission $1 Tues, free on Sat. Tues and Sat 6am–1pm. Go 1 mile north of Peddler's Village on Rte. 263, then turn left by the Victorian gazebo onto Greenhill Rd.; Rice's is 1 mile ahead on the right.

WHERE TO STAY
COUNTRY INNS

New Hope and its New Jersey neighbor across the Delaware River, Lambertville, have well-deserved reputations for their country inns and restaurants. All used to require 2-day stays and frown on children, but the economic downturn and Sesame Place's success have changed all that. The listings here only scratch the surface; other choices include the romantic **Inn at Phillips Mill** in New

Hope (② **215/862-2984**); the beautifully restored 1812 **Lambertville House** (② **609/397-0200**), where virtually all the rooms boast original fireplaces; or the tranquil mansion rooms or carriage house cottages at Stockton's **Woolverton Inn,** complete with pet sheep (② **609/397-0802**).

Centre Bridge Inn ⭐ Situated beside the Delaware River 3½ miles north of New Hope, the current building is the third since the early 18th century. Many of the elegant guest rooms have canopy, four-poster, or brass beds; wall-high armoires; modern private bathrooms; outside decks; and views of the river or countryside. The inn also has a pretty restaurant overlooking the river and the adjoining canal (and the mule-drawn barges coasting on it) serving lunch, dinner, and a $23 fixed-price Sunday brunch.

P.O. Box 74, Intersection of Rte. 32 and Rte. 263, New Hope, PA 18938. ② **215/862-2048** or 215/862-9139. www.centrebridgeinn.com. 9 units. $135–$200 weekend, less weekdays. Rates include continental breakfast. DISC, MC, V. **Amenities:** Restaurant; riverside terrace; lounge with fireplace. *In room:* A/C, TV in 5 rooms, no phone.

Evermay on the Delaware Thirteen miles north of New Hope, on River Road in Erwinna, lies this gracious historic inn, now under the ownership of William and Danielle Moffley. Evermay once hosted the Barrymores for croquet weekends. Combining privacy with a romantic setting overlooking the Delaware, the inn offers rooms with luxurious antique furnishings. The formal dining room offers a wonderful restraint-to-the-winds $68 fixed-price six-course dinner at a 7:30pm seating on Friday, Saturday, Sunday, and holidays; it's open to the public as well as guests, so reserve well in advance.

River Rd., Erwinna, PA 18920. ② **610/294-9100.** Fax 610/294-8249. 16 units, 1 carriage house suite. $170–$235 double; $275 suite. Rates include continental breakfast and 4pm tea. AE, MC, V. **Amenities:** Restaurant; lounge. *In room:* A/C, dataport, iron.

Whitehall Inn ⭐ Four miles outside New Hope is this 18th-century manor house on a former horse farm, complete with a pool. Mike and Suella Wass serve magnificent four-course breakfasts, and their "innsmanship" is nationally known, with such touches as fresh fruit bowls, a bottle of mineral water in every room, and afternoon tea concerts.

1370 Pineville Rd., New Hope, PA 18938. ② **215/598-7945.** 5 units. $150–$200 single or double; $220 suite. Rates include 4-course breakfast and 4pm high tea. 2-night minimum. AE, DC, DISC, MC, V. **Amenities:** Restaurant; outdoor pool; rose garden. *In room:* A/C.

HOTELS & MOTELS

Comfort Inn Bensalem For moderate lodgings in Bucks County, this is one of the best choices, off I-95 about 20 miles from Washington Crossing and 5 miles from Sesame Place. This is a bright, modern three-story property; each room has two double beds, a queen-size bed plus sofa bed, or a king-size bed. There's only one elevator, so get used to the stairs.

3660 Street Rd., Bensalem, PA 19020. ② **800/228-5150** or 215/245-0100. 141 units. $79–$135. Rates include continental breakfast. Children under 18 free in parent's room. AE, DC, DISC, MC, V. **Amenities:** Exercise room; laundry service and dry cleaning. *In room:* A/C, TV.

New Hope Motel in the Woods ⭐ Just a mile west of town, off Route 179, you'll find this motel tucked in a peaceful woodland setting. For more than 30 years it has offered modern ground-level rooms with private bathrooms and standard motel amenities.

400 W. Bridge St., New Hope, PA 18938. ② **215/862-2800.** 28 units. $79–$99 double. AE, DISC, MC, V. **Amenities:** Outdoor pool. *In room:* A/C, TV, dataport.

Sheraton Bucks County Hotel *Kids*   This festive, modern, 14-story hotel is right across the street from Sesame Place. The soundproof guest rooms have oversize beds and quilted fabrics, and they can put a cot in the room for kids for $10. Facilities include a health club, an indoor swimming pool and sauna, and a full-service restaurant.

400 Oxford Valley Rd., Langhorne, PA 19047. ✆ **800/325-3535** or 215/547-4100. 167 units. $155–$165 double. Sesame Street packages $129–$159 including free shuttle and free room and board for children. AE, DC, DISC, MC, V. **Amenities:** Restaurant; lounge; indoor pool; fitness facility; sauna; laundry service and dry cleaning. *In room:* A/C, TV w/pay movies, dataport, coffeemaker, hair dryer.

WHERE TO DINE

Karla's INTERNATIONAL   In the heart of New Hope, next door to the Information Center, this lively and informal restaurant offers three settings: a sunlit conservatory with ceiling fans, stained glass, and plants; a gallery room with local artists' works; and a bistro with marble tabletops. The eclectic menu offers standards like Caesar salad and grilled rib-eye steak, but also veal à la française, and chicken breast with Thai ginger sauce. Lunch items are tamer. You can get very-late-night (or very-early-morning, depending how you look at it) weekend breakfast.

5 W. Mechanic St., New Hope, PA 18938. ✆ **215/862-2612.** Reservations recommended for dinner. Main courses $16–$23; lunch $4.95–$11. AE, DC, MC, V. Sun–Thurs 11am–10pm; Fri–Sat 11am–4am.

Moonlight INTERNATIONAL   This all-white confection of a restaurant arouses various strong emotions, but its nonchalant self-assurance and the classic New American cuisine from chef Matthew Levin have gotten an overwhelmingly positive buzz since the restaurant's fall 2000 opening. Escargots simmered in champagne and Maine lobster "macaroni and cheese" are followed by sashimi of yellowfin with pink grapefuit, or a veal chop with trumpet mushrooms. As befits an alum of Center City's famous Le Bec-Fin, desserts are extravagant. The recently opened Downstairs at Moonlight (Bar Lyonnais, anyone?) dishes up less pricey and more family-friendly bistro-type fare during the day, and transforms to a colorful club with live entertainment nightly.

36 W. Mechanic St., New Hope, PA 18938. ✆ **215/862-3100.** Main courses $17–$23; lunch $10–$15. AE, DC, MC, V. Fri–Sat 12–3pm; Mon–Sun 5:30pm (no specific closing time).

Odette's Fine Country Dining INTERNATIONAL   Surrounded by the river and the canal on the southern edge of town, this elegant restaurant has been an inn since 1794. The previous owner, Odette Myrtil, was a Ziegfeld Follies girl whose memorabilia adorns the place, and the spirited weekend cabaret blends in to the surroundings and honors Odette perfectly. The menus are seasonal and change three times a year, providing nice twists on steak, seafood, duck, and veal.

S. River Rd. and Rte. 32, New Hope, PA 18938. ✆ **215/862-2432.** Reservations recommended. Main courses $16–$26; lunch $8–$12. AE, DC, MC, V. Mon–Sat 11:30am–3pm and 5–10pm; Sun 4–10pm; brunch Sun 10:30am–1:30pm.

DOYLESTOWN

The intersection of U.S. 202 (west of New Hope), Pa. 313 (south of Scranton), and U.S. 611 (N. Broad St. in Philadelphia) defines Doylestown, the county seat. The R5 commuter rail from Center City ends here. It's a pleasant town just to walk around, but three interesting collections invite you indoors. All were endowed by Dr. Henry Chapman Mercer (1856–1930), a collector, local archaeologist, and master of pottery techniques. Motorists should exit the

Pennsylvania Turnpike at the Willow Grove Interchange (Exit 27) and follow Route 611 north to the Doylestown exit. Drive through scenic Doylestown and turn right onto Route 313 (Swamp Rd.).

DOYLESTOWN AREA ATTRACTIONS

Fonthill Museum 🏛 Everyone can call their home a castle, but Dr. Mercer could say it and mean it. The core of his castle, built from reinforced concrete in Mercer's own design, is a 19th-century farmhouse, with towers, turrets, and tiles piled on beyond belief. All the rooms are different shapes, each with tiles from Mercer's collection set into the floors and walls.

E. Court St., off Swamp Rd. (Rte. 313), Doylestown, PA 18901. ☎ **215/348-9461.** Admission $7 adults, $6.50 seniors, $2.50 children. Mon–Sat 10am–5pm; Sun noon–5pm. Closed Thanksgiving, Christmas, and New Year's Day. Guided tours only; reservations recommended.

Mercer Museum 🏛🏛 Mercer Museum displays thousands of early American tools, vehicles, cooking pieces, looms, and even weather vanes. Mercer had the collecting bug in a big way, and you can't help being impressed with the breadth of his collection and the castle that houses it. It rivals the Shelburne, Vermont, complex for Americana — and that's 35 buildings on 100 acres! The open atrium rises five stories, suspending a Conestoga wagon, chairs, and sleighs as if they were Christmas-tree ornaments. During the summer, a log cabin, schoolhouse, and other large bits of colonial American life are open for inspection. The museum recently added six hands-on stations, where children can build a log house, try on period clothes, and drive a buggy, among other activities. The old library is a functional reading room.

Pine St. at Ashland St., Doylestown, PA 18901. ☎ **215/345-0210.** www.mercermuseum.org. Admission to the museum and library $6 adults, $5.50 seniors, $2.50 children 6–17, free for children under 6. Mon–Sat 10am–5pm; Sun noon 5pm; Tues 10am–9pm. Spruance Library (Bucks County history): Tues 1–9pm; Wed–Sat 10am–5pm. Closed Thanksgiving, Christmas, and New Year's Day.

Moravian Pottery and Tile Works Down the road on Pa. 313, the Moravian Pottery and Tile Works was Dr. Mercer's next big project. If you go to the State Capitol in Harrisburg, you can see more than 400 mosaics illustrating the history of Pennsylvania — they originated here. The ceramists working at the pottery turn out tiles and mosaics available through the museum shop; prices range from $5 to $1,800.

Swamp Rd., Doylestown, PA 18901. ☎ **215/345-6722.** Admission $3 adults, $1.50 youths, $2.50 seniors. Daily 10am–4:45pm. Tours available every 30 min. until 4pm. Closed major holidays.

WHERE TO DINE

The Inn on Blueberry Hill AMERICAN Sounds quaint and country, but the restaurant here is a fresh creation from Bill Kim — one of the top young chefs in the region — and manager Mark Dombkowski, who are both alums of the hot Philadelphia restaurant Susanna Foo. It's a converted Victorian house with a glassed-in porch and stone-walled living room. The cuisine is superb American with Asian touches: think thyme-herbed duck breast with a sauce of kumquats candied with anise, or flounder baked in parchment with fingerling potatoes and baby bok choy. Customers yodel over the baked Alaska.

1715 S. Easton Rd., Doylestown, PA 18901. ☎ **215/491-1777.** Jackets recommended for men. Main courses $18–$28. AE, DISC, MC, V Tues–Thurs 5–9pm; Fri–Sat 5–10pm; Sun 4–8pm.

2 Exploring the Brandywine Valley

The Brandywine Valley, bridging Pennsylvania and Delaware, makes a great 1- or 2-day excursion into rolling country filled with Americana from colonial days through the Gilded Age.

Many of the farms that kept the Revolutionary troops fed have survived to this day. There are 15 covered bridges and 100 antique stores in Chester County alone, with miles of country roads and horse trails between them. Spring and fall are particularly colorful seasons, and don't forget Delaware's tax-free shopping.

The valley is rich in history. Without the defeat at Brandywine, Washington would never have ended up at Valley Forge, from which he emerged with a competent army. When the Du Pont de Nemours family fled post-Revolutionary France, they wound up owning powder mills on the Brandywine Creek. Every pioneer needed gunpowder and iron, and the business grew astronomically, expanding into chemicals and textiles. The Du Ponts controlled upper Delaware as a virtual fiefdom, building splendid estates and gardens. Most of these, along with the original mills, are open to visitors. On the art front, Winterthur houses the finest collection of American decorative arts ever assembled, and artists like Pyle and Wyeth left rich collections that are now on public view.

ESSENTIALS

GETTING THERE   I-95 South from Philadelphia has various exits north of Wilmington marked for specific sites, most of which are off Exit 7 to Pa. 52 North. If you have time, Pa. 100 off Pa. 52 North, linking West Chester to Wilmington, passes through picturesque pastureland, forest, and cropland. From New York, take Exit 2 off the New Jersey Turnpike onto Route 322 West over the Commodore Barry Bridge into Pennsylvania, and continue on Route 322 to Route 452; take Route 452 north 4 miles to Route 1, the main artery of the valley.

VISITOR INFORMATION   For more information, call the **Brandywine Valley Tourist Information Center,** located just outside the gates of **Longwood Gardens,** at *℃* **800/228-9933** or 610/388-2900. For motorists on I-95, Delaware maintains a visitor center just south of Wilmington, between routes 272 and 896. It operates from 8am to 8pm.

BRANDYWINE VALLEY AREA ATTRACTIONS

Brandywine Battlefield State Park   This picturesque park, 2 miles east of Chadds Ford on Route 1, has no monuments, since the British General Howe snuck north outside present Park borders to outflank Washington and eventually take Philadelphia. But Washington's and Lafayette's reconstructed headquarters mark the site, which in September 1777 saw one of the few full-army clashes between the Continentals and the British troops and mercenaries. The fields are excellent for picnicking and hiking.

Rte. 1, east of Chadds Ford. (Mailing address: P.O. Box 302, Chadds Ford, PA 19317). *℃* 610/459-3342. Grounds and visitor center open free Memorial Day to Labor Day until 8pm. House tour admission $8.50 family, or $3.50 adults, $2.50 seniors, $1.50 children ages 6–17, free for children under 6. Tues–Sat 9am–5pm; Sun noon–5pm; last house tours at 3pm.

Brandywine River Museum   Across the road from the Brandywine Battlefield State Park, a 19th-century gristmill has been restored and joined by a dramatic spiral of brick and glass. The museum showcases American painters from the Brandywine school and other schools. A newer wing contains a gallery devoted to paintings by Andrew Wyeth. Howard Pyle, painter and illustrator of adventure tales in the late 19th century, established a school nearby; his students included N. C. Wyeth, Frank Schoonover, and Harvey Dunn. Three generations of Wyeths, including N. C., Carolyn, Andrew, and Jamie, have remained here, and the museum is particularly strong in their works. Many of the museum's exhibits display the art of book and magazine illustration at its pre-television zenith.

Rte. 1 and Rte. 100, Chadds Ford, PA 19317. ℭ 610/388-2700. www.brandywinemuseum.org. Admission $6 adults, $3 seniors and children 6–12, free for children under 6. Daily 9:30am–4:30pm. Self-service restaurant open 11am–3pm.

Chadds Ford   This town is the site where a Native American trail (now U.S. 1) that forded the Brandywine Creek was purchased from William Penn by Francis Chadsey, an early Quaker immigrant. The present **Chadds Ford Inn,** at the junction of U.S. 1 and U.S. 100 (ℭ **610/388-7361**), filled one of the village's first needs — a tavern. For small villages in the middle colonies, taverns served as mail depots, law courts, election hustings (hosting speechmaking, voting and other campaign-related activities), and occasionally prisons. Before the Battle of Brandywine, Washington's officers stayed at the inn; afterward, British troops slaughtered the cattle before marching on Philadelphia. There's a small shopping area next to the premises.

Hagley Museum ★★   Since the early 1800s this has been Du Pont country, and the Hagley Museum shows how and when the family got their start. It's a wonderful illustration of early American industrialism and manufacturing.

Hagley has three parts: the museum building, the reconstructed grounds, and the Upper Residence. The museum building explains the harnessing of the Brandywine River's power, which was originally used to operate flour mills. The Du Ponts, who made their first fortune in gunpowder, needed waterpower and willow charcoal as their raw materials, and both were just a barge ride away. E. Irénée Du Pont, the founder of the gunpowder company, lived in the Upper Residence. He had experience in France with gunpowder and supervised the delicate production process. Nonetheless, explosions happened every decade or so.

On Blacksmith Hill, part of the workers' community has been restored. A visit through the Gibbons House reveals the lifestyle of a typical family, from food to furniture. Nearby is the school the children attended, complete with lesson demonstrations. At the base of Blacksmith Hill a restored 1880s machine shop offers an exciting illustration of change in the workplace. Volunteers demonstrate how the din of power tools with whirring belts and grinding metal replaced the quiet, painstaking hand-tooling of the earlier artisans.

Jitneys traverse the powder yard, but it's just as easy to walk the part of the 240 acres lying between the private family roads on the Upper Residence and the burbling Brandywine. A restored New Century Power House (1880) generates electricity here. Next to the electrical generator, a waterwheel, steam engine, and water turbine show improvements in power through the decades.

The wisteria-covered Georgian residence of the Du Ponts was renovated by a member of the fourth generation, Mrs. Louis Crowninshield, who lived here until her death in 1958. Empire, Federal, and Victorian styles of furniture are highlighted in various room settings. As with all Du Pont residences, the gardens and espaliered trees are superb, and there are flowers throughout the year.

The Belin House on Blacksmith Hill offers light lunches and drinks.

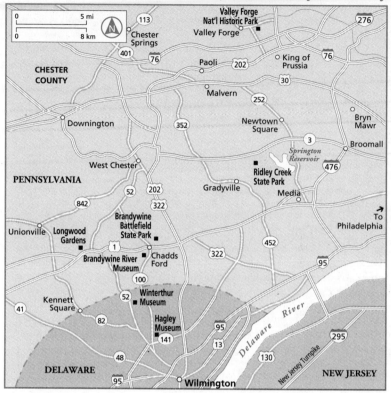

P.O. Box 3630, Rte. 141, Wilmington, DE 19807. ✆ **302/658-2400**. www.hagley.lib.de.us. Mar 15–Dec daily 9:30am–4:30pm; Jan–Mar 14 Sat–Sun only 9:30am–4:30pm. Upper Eleutherian Mills Residence is open seasonally in spring and fall; last jitney leaves at 3:30pm. Admission $30 per family, or $11 adults, $9 seniors and students ages 14–20, $4 children 6–14, free for children under 6. From Pennsylvania, take Rte. 52 to Rte. 100, go to the junction of Rte. 100 and Rte. 141, then follow directions on Rte. 141.

Longwood Gardens ✸✸✸   Longwood Gardens is simply one of the world's great garden displays. Pierre S. Du Pont devoted his life to horticulture. He bought a 19th-century arboretum and created the ultimate estate garden on 1,050 acres. You should plan at least half a day here.

The visitor center has a multimedia briefing on the gardens. Most people head to the left, toward the Main Fountain Garden, which has special water shows on Tuesday, Thursday, and Saturday evenings from June to September and fireworks shows on Friday and Saturday nights, usually preceded by hour-long garden concerts. Wrought-iron chairs and clipped trees and shrubs overlook the jets of water that rise up to 130 feet from the fountains. Near here, a topiary garden of closely pruned shrubs surrounds a 37-foot sundial.

The 4 acres of massive bronze-and-glass conservatories, renovated in 1996 and 1997, are among the finest and largest in the United States. The orangery displays are breathtaking. African violets, bonsai trees up to 400 years old, hibiscus, orchids, and tropical plants are among the specialties, but expect anything from Easter lilies to scarlet begonias. Special collections present silver desert plants, plants of the Mediterranean, and roses, among other types of plants and flowers. The plants are exhibited only at their peak and are constantly replaced from the extensive growing houses.

A parquet-floor ballroom was added later, connected to the greenhouses, along with a 10,000-pipe organ, a magnificent instrument played during the year (although it's under renovation right now).

Ahead and to the right of the visitor center, more gardens and fountains await, along with the Longwood Heritage Exhibit inside the Peirce–Du Pont House, the founder's residence. This exhibit, opened in 1995, illustrates the history of the property with artifacts from 2,000-year-old Native American spear points to Du Pont family movies. The restaurant offers cafeteria-style dining year-round and full-service dining from mid-April to December, with surprisingly good meals.

Route 1, Kennett Square, PA 19348. 30 miles west of Philadelphia and just west of the junction with Pa. 52. © 610/388-1000. www.longwoodgardens.org. Admission $14 for adults ($10 Tues), $6 for ages 16–20, $2 for ages 6–15, free for children under 6. Apr–Oct daily 9am–6pm (conservatories 10am–6pm); Nov–Mar daily 9am–5pm. The grounds and conservatories are frequently open late for special events and holiday displays.

Winterthur Museum, Garden and Library ★★★ The later home of the Du Ponts now provides the setting for America's best collection of native decorative arts. Henry Francis Du Pont, a great-grandson of E. I. Du Pont, was a connoisseur of European antiques. But when he turned his attention to a simple Pennsylvania Dutch chest in 1923, he realized no one had explored how American pieces are related to European crafts or how the concepts of beauty and taste differed on the two continents. Du Pont first collected American furniture, then decorative objects, then the interior woodwork of entire homes built between 1640 and 1840. Finally, he added to his home more than 200 rooms for the display of his collection. Because the museum started out as a private home, the rooms have a unique richness and intimacy.

In 1992, Winterthur opened the Galleries, a new building adjacent to the existing period rooms. On the first floor, the exhibition *Perspectives on the Decorative Arts in Early America* focuses on the social, practical, and other functions of objects in everyday life. The second floor features three areas displaying various aspects of American craftsmanship, with changing exhibitions. The Main Museum, which offers in-depth guided tours, displays the bulk of the collection and includes complete interiors from every eastern seaboard colony. Special landmarks include the famous Montmorenci Stair Hall, two Shaker Rooms, fine examples of Pennsylvania Dutch decorative art, and the Du Pont dining room. The Campbell Soup Tureen collection, with 125 items currently on display, is housed in the Dorrance Gallery, between the museum and the research building.

In spring, the extensive Winterthur Garden explodes into an abundance of cherry and crabapple blossoms, rhododendrons, Virginia bluebells, and azaleas. The lush, carefully planned garden is well worth viewing any season. Garden tram rides through the grounds are available when weather permits. There are two superb gift shops selling a selection of licensed reproductions, gifts, books, jewelry, and plants. The Visitor Pavilion Restaurant cooks breakfast, lunch, brunch, and tea to order and seats 350; the Cappuccino Cafe next to the museum offers lighter fare.

6 miles northwest of Wilmington, Delaware, on Rte. 52, Winterthur, DE 19735. © 800/448-3883 or 302/888-4600. www.winterthur.org. Mon–Sat 9:30am–5pm; Sun noon–5pm. Closed on major holidays. Three admission options: The **Estate Passport** ($10 adults, $8 seniors and students, $6 children 5–11), available year-round, is honored for 2 consecutive days and includes the Galleries, the Dorrance Gallery, a self-guided

garden walk, and the garden tram. The **Discovery Tours: the Mansion and More** tours (an additional $5 for each) are 45- to 60-min. guided tours of a selection of 175 period rooms or outdoor landscapes. Reservations are required for some tours. **Study Visas: Discovering World-Class Collections** (an additional $15 for each) offer a selection of conservation or specialized "connoisseur" tours for ages 12 and up. Reservations required. **Guided Garden Walk** passes are $5 in addition to general admission (the Estate Passport).

WHERE TO STAY

Abbey Green Motor Lodge
This excellent budget choice is close to the battlefield site at scenic routes 52 and 100. The family-run motel has a courtyard with its own picnic tables, gazebo, and outdoor fireplace, all set back from the road. All rooms have double beds and six units have individual fireplaces.

1036 Wilmington Pike (Rte. 202), West Chester, PA 19382. ✆ 610/692-3310. 18 units. $49–$52 double. AE, DISC, MC, V. Pets allowed. **Amenities:** 24-hr. coffee. *In room:* A/C, TV, fridge.

Brandywine River Hotel ✫
Built in 1988 and completely renovated by its new owners in 1995, this hotel, with a facade of brick and cedar shingle, blends into a hillside steps away from Chadds Ford Inn. Several rooms have working fireplaces and Jacuzzis. The lobby has a huge open stone fireplace and friendly service, and guest rooms are decorated with Queen Anne cherrywood furnishings, brass fixtures, chintz fabrics, and local paintings. Breakfast is served in an attractive hospitality room with a fireplace.

Rte. 1 and Rte. 100, P.O. Box 1058, Chadds Ford, PA 19317-1058. ✆ 610/388-1200. Fax 610/388-1200, ext. 301. 41 units. $130 double; $159–$179 suite; frequent specials. Rates include full continental breakfast and afternoon tea. Children under 12 stay free in parent's room. AE, DC, DISC, MC, V. **Amenities:** Fitness room. *In room:* A/C, TV, dataport, fridge, coffeemaker, hair dryer.

Hammanasett ✫
Built in 1856, this farmhouse now functions as one of the most impressive bed-and-breakfasts in the state. The house itself has been in the hands of Evelene Dohan's family since 1870. Mrs. Dohan's mother was director of the University of Pennsylvania Museum, and her father was a Philadelphia lawyer. The inn and its 48 acres reflect these ties to the world-class travels and achievements of the local "aristocracy." All rooms are beautifully furnished with family antiques; the first floor has a conservatory, 2,000-book and 500-video library, and magnificent foyer stairway. There is also a garden. Breakfast is opulent; afternoon tea and evening coffee are available. Mrs. Dohan has an encyclopedic knowledge of the history and attractions of the county — in her youth she covered it all on horseback.

P.O. Box 129, Lima, PA 19037. ✆ and fax 610/459-3000. 9 units, 7 with private bathroom. $100–$130 double. MC, V only through reservation service. No children under 14. No smoking. **Amenities:** Game room. *In room:* A/C, TV/VCR (video library on premises), access to fridge with complimentary beverages, access to microwave, coffeemaker, hair dryer.

Meadow Spring Farm
Anne Hicks operates this working 1936 farmhouse, situated on 125 acres traversed by walking paths. Rooms come with Amish quilts, and common areas display family antiques and dolls. Families are welcome; children may collect eggs, feed the animals, swim in the outdoor pool, or fish in the pond. Countryside carriage rides and picnic lunches are easily arranged.

201 E. Street Rd., Kennett Square, PA 19348. ✆ 610/444-3903. 7 units, 5 with private bathroom. $80–$90 double. No credit cards. Rates include full country breakfast. $10 per child in parent's room. 2-night minimum on weekends; reservations recommended. **Amenities:** Jacuzzi; game room. *In room:* A/C, TV.

WHERE TO DINE

Chadds Ford Inn CONTINENTAL
For Wyeth fans or Revolutionary War buffs, this is extremely sacred ground, since it's got prime examples of Wyeth art (reputedly bartered for meals) amid tin lanterns and candlesticks that have been

in use since the 1730s. The change to Brandywine Heritage management in 2000 has improved the kitchen, which now sticks to simpler staples of veal and seafood. The wine list is now substantial and varied.

Rte. 1 and Rte. 100, Chadds Ford, PA 19317 ℂ **610/388-7361.** Main courses $8–$12 at lunch, $17–$24 at dinner. Tavern menu $6–$12. AE, MC, V. Mon–Fri 11:30am–2:30pm; Sat 11:30am–4pm; Mon–Thurs 5:30–9:30pm; Fri–Sat 5–9pm; Sun 2:30–9pm.

Dilworthtown Inn CONTINENTAL   Another old inn, this 1754 tavern saw the last phase of the Battle of Brandywine (specifically, the British victory). It has as cozy a mood and decor as you'll find this side of the Revolutionary War, with a roaring fireplace that you could stand up in and candlelit tables amid thick plaster walls. Under Jim Barnes and Bob Rafetto, the food in the ultra-modern kitchen now stretches toward higher quality and consistency, with plenty of local mushrooms, and imports such as New Zealand lamb and tiger shrimp. Interesting wines by the glass or bottle. Some readers complain of slow service, however.

1390 Old Wilmington Pike, West Chester, PA 19382. ℂ **610/399-1390.** Reservations recommended. Main courses $23–$32 at dinner. AE, MC, V. Mon–Sat 5:30–10pm; Sun 3–9pm.

12

Lancaster County:
The Amish Country

Drive about 50 miles west of Philadelphia along Route 30, and you will happen upon a quietly beautiful region of rolling hills, winding creeks, neatly cultivated farms, covered bridges, and towns with picturesque names like Paradise and Bird-in-Hand. Amish, or Pennsylvania Dutch, Country is an area of 7,100 square miles centered around Lancaster County in the heart of the state. Pennsylvania Dutch Amish, Mennonites, and Brethren (see "Meet the Amish," below, for an explanation of the differences) represent 70,000 of Lancaster County's 475,000 residents. It's a small group that quietly and steadfastly continues to live a life of agrarian simplicity centered around religious worship and family cohesiveness. The preservation of the world of the Pennsylvania Dutch evokes feelings of curiosity, nostalgia, amazement, and respect. The Pennsylvania Dutch are a rare yardstick for us to measure the distance that our own "outside" world has come over the last 2 centuries. It is important to note that the Pennsylvania Dutch do not always greet the curiosity that many visitors feel towards their world with enthusiasm.

Pennsylvania Dutch Country has many special qualities that attract visitors. The area is relatively small, with good roads for motorists and bicyclists alike. There are opportunities to get to know the Amish, and tourism has, perhaps surprisingly, promoted continued excellence in quilt making, antiques, and farm-based crafts. There are historical sites, pretzel and chocolate factories, covered bridges, and wonderful farmer's markets, as well as modern diversions such as movie theaters, amusement parks, and great outlet mall shopping. And, of course, the family style, smorgasbord, all-you-can-eat, or gourmet Pennsylvania Dutch restaurants are experiences in themselves.

1 Introducing the Pennsylvania Dutch Country

This area has been a major farming region since German settlers came across its limestone-rich soil and rolling hills 3 centuries ago. Lancaster County boasts the most productive nonirrigated farmland in the United States, and it's the country's fifth-largest dairy-producing county. The natural abundance of the region, the ease of getting goods to market in Philadelphia, and the strong work ethic of the area's residents have preserved major portions of the land for farming, although manufacturing in Lancaster, York, and other towns is also important. In its day, Lancaster was a major center of commerce, culture, and politics. It was the largest inland city in the United States from 1760 to 1810, and was even a contender in the choice of the new nation's capital. The balance between factory and farm has been threatened in this century by the development of the automobile and the construction of such major roads as the Pennsylvania

Turnpike, which turned farmland into suburbs of Harrisburg and Philadelphia. The buildup of housing developments and attendant schools, services, and strip malls for an exploding population competes with the lovely, placid fields dotted with farmhouses, barns, silos, and small creeks crossed by covered bridges.

TOURIST DOLLARS VERSUS STRIP MALLS: THE AMISH TODAY

Until about 50 years ago, the Amish were not especially a "tourist attraction." But starting in the mid-1950s, with the growing presence of technology in all areas of life for the rest of the country, the Amish tenacity in maintaining their traditional customs and values made them seem both unusual and alluring. For better or worse, the Amish have spawned a major tourist industry over the last several decades.

As this process began, most people, including many Amish, saw tourism as a positive development. Money flowed into the county, and the Amish found a growing market for such goods as quilts, metalwork, crafts, and foodstuff — with customers literally appearing at their doors. But the less benign consequences of this development are becoming more and more apparent. The Amish population is about 25,000 and growing, but as outsiders move to Lancaster County, the non-Amish population has grown to 450,000. Their need for affordable housing is driving up land prices and attracting strip developers. In past years when Amish families looked for land to buy for their children's farms, they turned to other, non-Amish farmers. Today, those non-Amish farmers can get better prices by selling to developers.

This means that many Amish have been forced to leave their farms and set up nonfarming businesses. The local construction business in Lancaster County includes many Amish workers who have to travel to Delaware and Maryland to work. Women who traditionally worked in the home and on the farm are increasingly running restaurants and shops or overseeing quilting and craft enterprises. Despite the injunction to remain separate from wider society, many families offer "Amish-style" dinners at their homes, and aggressively exploit the cachet that "Amish-made" gives to foods, craft objects, clothing, hex signs, and other souvenirs and products.

MEET THE AMISH

William Penn's "holy experiment" of religious tolerance, together with word of mouth about the region's fertile farmland, drew thousands of German-speaking immigrants to Pennsylvania in the early 18th century. They were lumped together as Pennsylvania "Dutch" — a corruption of *Deutsch,* which is the German word meaning German. The Mennonite sects, particularly the Amish, stayed put in Pennsylvania and became the most famous of the immigrants, but the colonial period also saw a mixture of Scotch-Irish Presbyterians, French Protestants, English from Maryland, and Jews from Iberia settling in the region. The ethnic makeup in this part of the country has changed very little since 1796.

The religions of the Pennsylvania Dutch are part of the Anabaptist strand of the Protestant Reformation. A Christian faith that emerged during the 16th century, Anabaptists believe in the literal interpretation of the Bible, in baptism only for people adult enough to choose this rite of transformation, and in remaining separate from larger society. Menno Simons, a Catholic priest from Holland, joined the Anabaptists in 1536 and united the various groups, who began to be called Mennonites. In 1693, Jacob Amman, a Mennonite bishop

Lancaster & the Pennsylvania Dutch Country

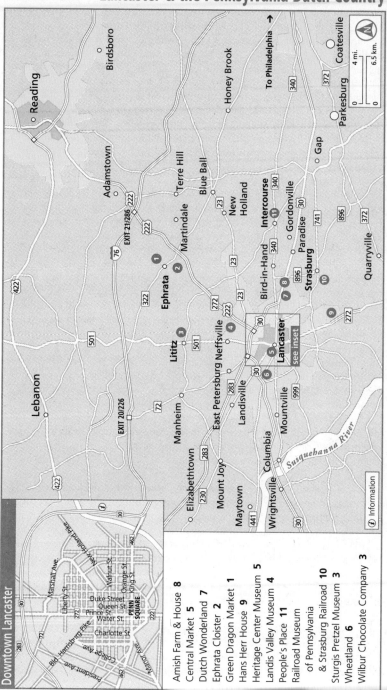

4 mi.
6.5 km.

To Philadelphia →

Coatesville
Parkesburg
Gap
Quarryville
Strasburg
Paradise
Gordonville
Intercourse
Bird-in-Hand
New Holland
Blue Ball
Terre Hill
Honey Brook
Reading
Birdsboro
Adamstown
Martindale
Ephrata
Lititz
East Petersburg Neffsville
Lancaster
see inset
Landisville
Mountville
Columbia
Wrightsville
Maytown
Mount Joy
Elizabethtown
Manheim
Lebanon

Susquehanna River

EXIT 21/286
EXIT 20/226

ⓘ Information

Downtown Lancaster

New Holland Pike
Marshall Ave.
Liberty St.
Walnut St.
Orange St.
King St.
Duke Street
Queen St.
Prince St.
Water St.
Charlotte St.
PENN SQUARE
College Ave.
President Ave.
Manor Ave.
Old Harrisburg Pike

Amish Farm & House **8**
Central Market **5**
Dutch Wonderland **7**
Ephrata Cloister **2**
Green Dragon Market **1**
Hans Herr House **9**
Heritage Center Museum **5**
Landis Valley Museum **4**
People's Place **11**
Railroad Museum
of Pennsylvania
& Strasburg Railroad **10**
Sturgis Pretzel Museum **3**
Wheatland **6**
Wilbur Chocolate Company **3**

who found the Mennonite Church too tolerant of lax sinners, broke with his followers to establish the Old Order Amish church.

The three major sects in Lancaster County, the Amish, the Mennonites, and the Brethren, as well as another sect, the Schwenkfelders, share many beliefs, including those concerning baptism, nonresistance, and basic Bible doctrine. They differ in matters of dress, use or avoidance of technology, degree of literal interpretation of the Bible, and form of worship. For example, the Amish worship in services at home, while the Mennonites hold services in churches. The Amish do not proselytize, while Mennonites have a strong tradition of missionary work.

Today, the Amish live in settlements in 20 states and in Ontario, Canada. In Lancaster County, they center around Intercourse, Bird-in-Hand, and Lancaster. Mennonites center around Terre Hill and Martindale, a few miles to the northeast. The majority of Amish live and work on farms growing corn, wheat, tobacco (though most will not smoke it and some won't grow it), and alfalfa. But an increasing number earn their incomes at other jobs, either in crafts, in a sideline business out of the home, or in the nonfarm economy of the region. They are a trilingual people, speaking Pennsylvania Dutch (essentially a dialect of German) at home, High German at worship services (the German of Luther's Bible translation), and English with members of the larger society.

The family is the most important social unit among the Amish, and large families with 7 to 10 children are the norm. Not surprisingly, the Amish population is growing — it has more than doubled since the 1980s — and more than half the Amish in Lancaster County are under the age of 18. You will see dozens of mailboxes marked with the names Zook, Stoltzfus, and Zinn — a testimony to the proliferation of extended families. The Old Testament–sounding practice of "shunning" — complete excommunication from family relations for Amish who marry outsiders or violate basic tenets — has relaxed in recent decades. Even so, about 80% of the Amish end up spending their entire lives within the community — many dying in the same house in which they were born.

Children attend school in one-room schoolhouses, built and maintained by the Amish, through the eighth grade. There are approximately 150 such schools in Lancaster County, and new ones are still being built. Amish schools teach only the basics; students have special exemptions from the standard state curriculum and are allowed to leave school at the age of 16 if they choose. There is no formal religious instruction in school; this is kept within the family.

To the visitor, the two most distinctive characteristics of the Amish are their clothing and their use of horse and buggies rather than cars. Both these features are linked to their religious beliefs. The distinctive clothing worn by about 35,000 "Plain People" in Lancaster County is meant to encourage humility and modesty as well as separation from larger society. Amish men and boys wear dark-colored suits, straight-cut coats without lapels, broadcloth trousers, suspenders, solid-colored shirts, black socks and shoes, and black or straw broad-brimmed hats. Men wait to grow beards until they are married, and do not grow mustaches. Women and girls wear modest, solid-colored dresses with long sleeves and long full skirts, covered by a cape and an apron. They never cut their hair, but gather it in a bun on the back of the head, concealed by a white prayer covering. Amish women do not wear jewelry or printed fabric. Single women in their teens and 20s wear black prayer coverings for church services. After marriage, a white covering is worn.

The Amish are reluctant to accept technology, which they believe could weaken the family structure. Their horse-drawn buggies help keep them close to home by limiting distances that can be traveled in a day. Most use no electricity or telephones. As new ideas emerge, each district congregation of about 100 families evaluates them and decides what to accept and what to reject. The fundamental criterion is that an innovation should not jeopardize the simplicity of their lives and the strength of the family unit. The 1998 arrest of two young Amish for drug trafficking, while hardly an everyday occurrence, has prompted wide reexamination of how much "outside" exposure is too much.

There are a number of excellent books on the Amish way of life. The classic is John Hostetler's *Amish Society.* A more impassioned, ideological, New Age take is *After the Fire: The Destruction of the Lancaster County Amish* by Randy-Michael Testa. Children's books include *Growing Up Amish* by Richard Ammon, and Raymond Bial's *Amish Home,* with wonderful photographs. Since Amish do not permit photography, any film depiction is bound to be compromised; this is unfortunately the case with *Witness* (1985), in which Harrison Ford goes undercover in the region as a Philadelphia cop.

2 Essentials

The heart of Pennsylvania Dutch Country centers on wedges of land to the east and (to a lesser extent) west of Lancaster. The Susquehanna River to the west, and the Maryland border and Mason-Dixon line to the south, form the borders of the area.

GETTING THERE

Lancaster County is 57 miles and 90 minutes west of Philadelphia, directly on Route 30. From the northeast, the easiest route is to take I-95 south from New York City onto the New Jersey Turnpike, then take Exit 6 onto the Pennsylvania Turnpike (I-76), following this to Exit 21 or 20 on either side of Lancaster. You'll still be about 10 miles north of the town: From Exit 21, you'll follow Route 222 into the city; from Exit 20, Route 72. Travel time is 2¼ hours, and tolls amount to $9 from New York City. From the south, follow I-83 north for 90 minutes from Baltimore, then head east on Route 30 from York into the county. If you're in Brandywine County or Longwood Gardens, you're only minutes from Amish farms in Gap, via routes 41 and 741.

By train, Amtrak (© **800/872-7245**) takes 70 minutes from 30th Street Station in Philadelphia to the great old Lancaster station, 53 McGovern Ave. (© **717/291-5080**), 10 blocks from Penn Square. The adult fare is $16 one way, and nine trains run daily. Three buses run daily from Philadelphia ($13) and take 2 hours from the Convention Center Trailways Terminal to Greyhound Bus Lines, at the train station in Lancaster (© **800/231-2222** or 717/397-4861).

VISITOR INFORMATION

Before you set out, you should get in touch with the **Pennsylvania Dutch Convention & Visitors Bureau,** 501 Greenfield Rd., Lancaster, PA 17601 (© **800/ PA-DUTCH,** ext. 2405, or 717/299-8901). The website **www.800padutch. com** has links to most of the attractions listed below. The office itself is off the Route 30 bypass east of Lancaster, Greenfield Road exit. They provide an excellent detailed map and visitors' guide to the region, along with answers to specific questions and help with special interests. They also have a wealth of brochures, direct telephone links to many local hotels, and a multi-image slide show, a good 14-minute overview of the county. The bureau is open June through October from 8am to 6pm (Sun 9am–6pm), and off season from 8:30am to 5pm (Sun 9am–5pm).

The **Mennonite Information Center,** 2209 Millstream Rd., Lancaster, PA 17602 (© **800/858-8320** or 717/299-0954), has a lot of the same information but specializes in linking you with Mennonite guest houses and church worship. Every half-hour they show a film featuring a Mennonite family at home on their farm. They will also provide Mennonite tour guides who can accompany you to otherwise hidden farm stands or the home workshops of local crafters and quilters — expect some gentle religious dialogue from guides. The center is open April through October, Monday through Saturday from 8am to 5pm, and Monday through Saturday from 8:30am to 4:30pm November through March.

Many towns such as Intercourse, Strasburg, and Lancaster have local information centers, and the **Exit 21 Tourist Information Center** (© **717/336-7482**), on Route 272 just south of I-76, is open from 10am to 2pm daily. It's next to **Zinn's Diner** (© **717/336-2210;** www.zinnsdiner.com), which looks suspect with its statue of "Big Amos," and its batting cages, and miniature golf, but the menu, portions, and clientele are very typically Pennsylvania Dutch. The diner is open daily from 6am to 11pm.

GETTING AROUND

Lancaster County's principal artery is Route 30, which runs from Philadelphia to York and Gettysburg. But beware: Major roads like Route 30 and Route 222 at Lancaster, and Route 340 from Intercourse to Lancaster, can be crowded, especially in the summer with the onslaught of bus tours. The 25,000 horse-drawn vehicles in the county tend to stick to quieter back roads, but some highways cannot be avoided. Traffic is much lighter in spring and autumn. And please be careful; the past few years have seen several horrible rear-end crashes in which tourists killed Amish families in buggies. If you're in a jam, you can reach AAA service at © **717/397-6135.**

Red Rose Transit Authority, 45 Erick St. (© **717/397-4246;** www.redrose transit.com), serves Lancaster County, with a base fare of $1.15 to $2.05 depending on distance. The Route no. 13 bus leaves from the Old Courthouse on Duke Street in Lancaster and goes through Bird-in-Hand and Intercourse.

ORGANIZED TOURS

Amish Country Tours, Route 340 in Intercourse (© **717/768-3800**), offers guided back-road bus and minivan tours during high season at 10:30am and 1, 2, and 2:30pm daily (10:30am and 2pm only on Sun), which last 2 hours and include stops at Amish farms and one-room schoolhouses. In the company's minibuses, the fare is $11 for adults and $5 for children 6 to 12; in your own vehicle, it's a flat $25 for up to three people, $5 per additional body. A 4-hour version of the tour is offered Monday through Saturday at 9am and costs $25 for adults and $15 for children. Tours leave from Plain and Fancy Farm on Route 340 in Intercourse, and you can buy tickets at local hotels or at the farm. The visitor center can recommend several tours with private guides who will take you in their vans or ride in your car. They generally run in the range of $30 per hour with a 2-hour minimum. Among the best are **Brunswick Tours,** at the National Wax Museum, 2249 Lincoln Highway, Route 30 East (© **717/397-7451**), and **Red Rose Excursions** (© **717/397-3175**), which provides guides Monday through Saturday from 9am to 9pm to any Lancaster County location. The **Mennonite Information Center** (see above) can also provide local guides; the basic fee is $7, plus $9.50 per hour with a 2-hour minimum. Finally, **Lancaster County Bicycle Tours** (© **717/393-7600**), offers maps and an active schedule of guided tours.

A NOTE ON ETIQUETTE

There aren't too many settings in the world where an entire native population is a tourist attraction. Pennsylvania Dutch country is one of them, but that doesn't mean that the Amish are there as theme park characters. They are hardworking people leading busy lives. Your courtesy and respect are especially vital because their lifestyle is designed to remove them as much as possible from your fast-paced 20th-century focus.

First, *do not trespass* onto Amish farms, homesteads, or schools in session. We've listed several settings where you can visit a working farm, take a carriage ride, or even stay on a farm. Although these are not operated by the most orthodox Amish, you will certainly get a taste of the Amish lifestyle.

Second, if you're dealing with Pennsylvania Dutch directly, *don't even think of photographing them, and ask before taking any photographs at all.* The Amish have a strongly held belief that photographic images violate the biblical injunction against graven images and promote the sins of personal vanity and pride. Taking pictures of their land and animals is permissible; taking pictures of them is not.

Third, *watch the road.* What passes for moderate suburban speed in a car can be life-threatening in this area. Roads in Lancaster County have especially wide shoulders to accommodate horses, carriages, and farm tractors, and these are marked with red reflective triangles and lights at night. It's preferable, if only to better see the sights, to slow down to Amish paces. And honking disturbs the horses. If you have the time, this is superb walking and bicycling country, punctuated by farm stands for refreshment and quiet conversations with Amish families.

3 Exploring Amish Country

LANCASTER

While Lancaster (pronounced *lank*-uh-stir) is still the most important city in the region, it hit its peak in the colonial era and as an early-20th-century urban beehive; this is reflected in the architecture and attractions. The basic street grid layout, copied from Philadelphia's, centers at Penn Square: the intersection of King (east-west) and Queen (north-south) streets. You won't see too many Plain People venturing into town anymore, since they can buy provisions and equipment more easily at regional stores, but they still sell at the **Central Market.** Erected just off Penn Square in 1889 but operating since the 1730s, this is the nation's oldest farmer's market, with more than 80 stalls. You can savor and select regional produce and foods, from sweet bologna and scrapple to breads, cheeses, egg noodles, shoofly pie (a concoction of molasses and sweet dough), and *schnitzel* or dried apple. The market is open Tuesday and Friday from 6am to 4:30pm and Saturday from 6am to 2pm.

Beside the Market is a **Heritage Center Museum** (© 717/299-6440) in the old City Hall, with a moderately interesting collection of Lancaster County crafts and historical artifacts. It's free and open Tuesday through Saturday from 10am to 5pm; closed from January to March. On the western edge of town is **Wheatland,** 1120 Marietta Ave., Rte. 23 (© 717/392-8721), the gracious Federal mansion and 4 garden acres of the 15th U.S. president, James Buchanan. It features costumed guides and is open April through November, daily from 10am to 4pm; admission is $5.50 for adults, $4.50 for seniors, $3.50 for students, and $1.75 for children 6 to 12.

Five miles south of town near Willow Street rests the 1719 **Hans Herr House,** 1849 Hans Herr Dr., off Route 222 (© 717/464-4438), the oldest

> _Tips_ **The Bridges of Lancaster County**
>
> Forget about the Midwest and Clint Eastwood — Pennsylvania is the birthplace of the covered bridge, with some 1,500 built between the 1820s and 1900. Today, 219 bridges remain, mostly on small country roads, and you can actually drive (slowly!) through most of them. Lancaster County has the largest concentration, with 28, including one on the way to Paradise, a small village east of Lancaster City (see information on Paradise later in this chapter). Bridges were covered to protect the trusses from the weather. Does kissing inside one bring good luck? Well, they're protected from rain, and their one-lane width means a certain amount of privacy — not to mention those evocative wooden planks. The Lancaster County Visitors Bureau map indicates all covered bridge locations; call ✆ **800/723-8824,** extension 2435, for a copy of the map.
>
> Of the 28 county bridges, the following three are interesting and relatively easy to get to:
>
> • **Hunsecker Bridge:** This is the largest covered bridge in the county, built in 1975 to replace the original, which was washed away in Hurricane Agnes. From Lancaster, drive 5 miles north on Route 272. After you pass Landis Valley Farm Museum, turn right on Hunsecker Road and drive 2 miles.
> • **Paradise/Leaman Place Bridge:** This bridge is in the midst of Amish cornfields and farms. An oversize truck put it out of commission in the 1980s, but it has been restored. Drive north 1 mile on Belmont Road from Route 30, just east of the center of Paradise.
> • **Kauffman's Distillery Bridge:** Drive west on Route 772 from Manheim, and make a left onto West Sunhill Road. The bridge will be in front of you, along with horses grazing nearby.

building in the county. Now owned by the Lancaster Mennonite Historical Society, it's been restored and furnished to illustrate early Mennonite life, with a historic orchard and outdoor exhibit of agricultural tools. You can visit from April to December, Monday through Saturday from 9am to 4pm; admission is $4 for adults and $1.50 for children 7 to 12.

The eastern side of town peters into a welter of faux Amish attractions and amusements like Dutch Wonderland and Running Pump Mini-Golf, fast-food restaurants, and outlet stores on Route 30 near where Route 340 splits to the north toward Intercourse. The **Amish Farm and House,** 2395 Lincoln Hwy. (✆ **717/394-6185**), offers guided tours of a 10-room Amish house, with live animals and exhibits including a waterwheel outside. A Dutch Food Pavilion provides local treats. It's open June through September daily from 8:30am to 6pm; November through March from 8:30am to 4pm; and from 8:30am to 5pm other months. Admission is $6.75 for adults and $4 for children 5 to 11.

INTERCOURSE

Intercourse's suggestive name refers to the intersection of two old highways, the King's Highway (now Rte. 340 or Old Philadelphia Pike) and Newport Road (now Rte. 772). The Conestoga wagons invented a few miles south — these are unusually broad and deep wagons that became famous for transporting home-steaders all the way west to the Pacific coast — were used on The King's Highway.

The town, in the midst of the wedge of country east of Lancaster, is now the center of Amish life in the county. There are about as many commercial attrac-tions, which range from the schlocky to good quality, as there are places of gen-uine interest along Route 340. One thing not to miss is **The People's Place,** 3513 Old Philadelphia Pike (© 717/768-7171; www.thepeoplesplace.com), an inter-pretive center with a 30-minute documentary on the Amish, an excellent hands-on museum exhibit, an exhibit of antique quilts, and a bookshop/gallery. It's open April through October, Monday through Saturday from 9:30am to 9pm; Novem-ber through March, from 9:30am to 5pm; admission to all exhibits is $8 for adults and $5 for children. Of the commercial developments, try **Kitchen Kettle Vil-lage,** also on the Old Philadelphia Pike, Route 340 (© 800/732-3538 or 717/768-8261; www.kitchenkettle.com). You'll find 32 stores selling crafts and homemade edibles, from decoys to fudge, grouped around Pat and Bob Burnley's 1954 jam and relish kitchen. Their Lapp Family Farms ice-cream store, with 20 all-natural flavors, is much more convenient than the original farm stand near New Holland.

EPHRATA

Ephrata, near Exit 21 off I-76 northeast of Lancaster, combines a historic 18th-century Moravian religious site with a pleasant country landscape and the area's largest farmer's market and auction center. **Ephrata Cloister,** 633 W. Main St. (© 717/733-6600), near the junction of routes 272 and 322, housed one of America's earliest communal societies, which was known for its *fraktur* — an ornate, medieval German lettering you'll see on inscribed pottery and official documents. Ten austere wooden 18th-century buildings (put together without nails) remain in a grassy park setting. The cloister is open Monday through Sat-urday from 9am to 5pm and Sunday from noon to 5pm; admission is $6 for adults, $5.50 for seniors, and $4 for children 6 to 17. Saturday evenings in sum-mer bring "Vorspiel" performances that feel like Bach live.

The main street of Ephrata is pleasant for strolling and features an old rail car on the place where the train line used to run. **Doneckers** (see below) has expanded from a single inn north of town into a farmer's market, gourmet restaurant, and shopping complex. On North State Street, 4 miles north of town, is the wonderful **Green Dragon Market & Auction** (© 717/738-1117), open Friday from 9am to 9pm. Two auction houses make up the heart of Green Dragon — one for antiques and bric-a-brac, one for farm animals. You'll see goats and cows changing hands in the most elemental way, and children are allowed total petting access in the process. Summer brings fresh corn, fruit, and melons. A flea market and arcade have sprung up around the auctions, with plenty of cotton candy, clams on the half shell, and fresh corn.

LITITZ

Founded in 1756, this town, 6 miles north of Lancaster on Route 501, is one of the state's most charming. The cottage facades along East Main Street (Rte. 772) haven't changed much in the past 2 centuries. One of the most interesting sights is the **Linden Hall Academy,** founded in 1794 as the first school for girls in the United States. There are several Revolutionary War–era churches and buildings on the grounds of the school. Lititz was once known as "the Pretzel Town," and

> **Fun Fact Some Facts About Pennsylvania Dutch Country**
>
> - The Pennsylvania Dutch Country hosts three to four million visitors a year.
> - Lancaster was the nation's capital for a day, when Congress fled from Philadelphia on September 27, 1777.
> - In-line skating is considered an acceptable form of transportation among the Amish.

across the street from Linden Hall is the **Julius Sturgis Pretzel House,** 219 E. Main St. (© **717/626-4354**). Founded in 1861, it's the oldest such bakery in the country. At the conclusion of the 20-minute guided tours you can try your hand at rolling, twisting, and sprinkling the dough with coarse salt. Summer tours are given Monday through Saturday from 9am to 5pm for $2.

At the junction of Route 501 and Main Street is **Wilbur Chocolate Company's Candy Americana Museum & Store,** 48 N. Broad St. (© **717/626-3249**). Famous for its "Wilbur buds" (Hershey Kiss–style bite-size chocolates in milk and dark varieties), the factory offers a look at the process and history of chocolate-making, with samples, plus a store selling cooking or gift chocolate in a turn-of-the-20th-century atmosphere. Next door is the **Lititz Springs Park,** with a lovely duck-filled brook flowing from the 1756 spring, in addition to fields, playgrounds, and the historic **General Sutter Inn** (call © **717/626-2115** for lodging reservations at the inn).

STRASBURG

This little town, named by French Huguenots, is located southeast of Lancaster on Route 896 and is a paradise for rail buffs. Until the invention of the auto, railroads were the major mode of fast transport, and Pennsylvania was a leader in building and servicing thousands of engines. The **Strasburg Rail Road** (© **717/687-7522**), winds over 9 miles of preserved track from Strasburg to Paradise and back, as it has since 1832; wooden coaches and a Victorian parlor car are pulled by an iron steam locomotive. The railroad head is on Route 741 east of town and is open from April to October daily, and on weekends only from November to March. The fare is $9 to $13 for adults and $4 to $5.50 for children, depending on whether you go coach, dining car, or deluxe; toddlers are $1. Other attractions include the **Railroad Museum of Pennsylvania** (© **717/687-8628**), displaying dozens of stationary engines right across from the Strasburg Rail Road; the **National Toy Train Museum** (© **717/687-8976**), on Paradise Lane off Route 741, with five huge push-button operating layouts; and **Choo Choo Barn–Traintown USA** (© **717/687-7911**), a 1,700-square-foot miniature Amish Country landscape filled with animated trains and figures, which enact activities such as parades and circuses. It's linked up with the inevitable authorized Thomas Trackside Station store.

4 Especially for Kids

With the exception of beaches, Pennsylvania Dutch Country has everything for families, including rainy-day entertainment. In addition to the suggestions below, try the above-mentioned **Julius Sturgis Pretzel House** in Lititz, **People's Place** in Intercourse, and the various **railroad attractions** in Strasburg.

BUGGY RIDES

Driving for a couple of miles along a country lane in a horse-drawn carriage not only sounds irresistible but fits right in with the speed of Amish life. Of the half-dozen outfits, the most reliable are **Abe's Buggy Ride** (© 717/295-5410 or 717/392-1794), located at Route 340 in Bird-in-Hand, one-half mile east of the Route 896 junction, which offers 20-minute, 2-mile jaunts, and **Ed's Buggy Rides** (© 717/687-0360), on Route 896, 1½ miles south of Route 30 in Strasburg, which has 3-mile rides leaving from the Red Caboose Motel. Abe's is slightly more expensive ($10 for adults and $5 for children versus $8 and $4, respectively for Ed's); both are open Monday through Saturday until dusk, and Ed's is now doing Sunday business too. Abe's owner Jack Meyer, his wife, Dee Dee, and their six children are Mennonite and are open to inviting guests to their home for dinner; the meal is $15 for adults and $7.50 for children. Call them at © 717/664-4888 for reservations or information.

DUTCH WONDERLAND

Dutch Wonderland (© 717/291-1888; www.dutchwonderland.com), that ersatz castle you see heading east on 2249 Lincoln Hwy. (Rte. 30) out of Lancaster, is the headquarters for a 44-acre amusement park with gardens and entertainment such as storytelling. There's a moderately wild roller coaster and a road rally, but most of the 30 rides are perfect for young families. Unlimited rides cost $25 for adults, $20 for children 3 to 5 and $18 for seniors. The park is open from May to mid-October, with peak hours of 10am to 7pm daily during high season and weekends only in the spring and fall. In late fall (usually Thanksgiving–Christmas), there is a Winter Wonderland opening of limited rides and other holiday attractions each weekend (weekends include Fri).

BALLOON TOURS

Amish country is spectacular from the air, with its rural landscapes and generally clear weather. It's undeniably pricey at $169 per person for a 1-hour flight, but the **U.S. Hot Air Balloon Team** (© 800/763-5987 or 717/299-2274; www.balloonflights.com) lifts off for the first and last 2-hour stretches of daylight. The local departure pad is at Lancaster Host Resort, near the intersection of routes 30 and 896.

HERSHEY

Hershey is technically outside the county, 30 minutes northwest of Lancaster on Route 422, but the assembly of rides, amusements, and natural scenery in a storybook setting makes the sweetest town on earth worth the trip. Milton Hershey set up his town at the turn of the 20th century to reflect his business and philanthropy; in 1998 alone the company poured $50 million into local attractions and lodgings. Start with the website (www.hersheypa.com) or in person with **Hershey's Chocolate World,** Park Boulevard (© 717/534-4900), a free tour that takes you from cacao beans to wrapped samples.

Hersheypark is a huge theme park at the junction of routes 743 and 422 (© 800/HERSHEY or 717/534-3090), with more than 50 rides and attractions including water rides, 4 roller coasters, 5 theaters with music, and 20 kiddie rides. The park also includes the 11-acre **ZooAmerica,** with more than 200 animals native to this continent. Hersheypark is open from mid-May to September, and all summer until 10pm Monday through Thursday, and until 11pm Friday through Sunday. ZooAmerica is open year-round except for Thanksgiving, Christmas, and New Year's Day. Admission to everything at Hersheypark is

$35 for adults (defined as ages 9–54), $20 for children 3 to 8 (free for kids 2 and under) and seniors 55 to 69, and $16 for seniors over 69; admission to just ZooAmerica is at $7 for adults, $6.50 for seniors, and $5.75 for kids (the Hersheypark age ranges mentioned above apply here too).

The logical place to stay is the **Hershey Lodge,** West Chocolate Avenue and University Drive (© **717/534-8600**), with miniature golf, tennis courts, and its own movie theater. And if you're tempted to sneak away without the kids, Hershey does have superb gardens, 72 holes of championship golf, and the palace-like **Hotel Hershey** (© **717/533-2176**) up the mountain, which offers a luxurious spa.

LANDIS VALLEY MUSEUM

Following Oregon Pike (Rte. 272) north from Lancaster for 5 miles, you'll come to Landis Valley, 2451 Kissel Hill Rd. (© **717/569-0401**), a large outdoor museum of Pennsylvania German culture, folk traditions, decorative arts, and language. George and Henry Landis established a small museum here to exhibit family heirlooms in the 1920s; when the state acquired it in the 1950s it mushroomed into a 21-building "living arts" complex. The costumed practitioners — clock makers and clergymen, tavern keepers and tinsmiths, storekeepers, teachers, printers, weavers, and farmers — are experts in their fields and are generous with samples, which are also for sale in the shop. The museum is open Monday through Saturday from 9am to 5pm and Sunday from noon to 5pm; admission is $9 for adults and $6 for children 6 to 17.

5 Shopping

There are many reasons to keep that credit card handy in Lancaster County. Quilts and other craft products unique to the area are sold in dozens of small stores and out of individual farms. The thrifty Pennsylvania Dutch have been keeping old furniture and objects in their barns and attics for 300 years, so antiquing is plentiful here. Fine pieces tend to migrate toward New Hope and Bucks County for resale, where you compete directly with dealers at the many fairs and shows. If antiques aren't your bag, a dozen outlet centers provide name-brand items at discounts of 30% to 70% along Route 30 east of Lancaster and in central Reading.

QUILTS

Quilts occupy a special place in Lancaster County life. Quilting is a time for fun and socializing, but it also affords an opportunity for young girls to learn the values and expectations of Amish life from their elders. German immigrant women started the tradition of reworking strips of used fabric into an ever-expanding series of pleasant, folkloric designs. Popular designs include "Wedding Ring", interlocking sets of four circles; the eight-pointed *Lone Star* radiating out with bursts of colors; "Sunshine and Shadow", virtuoso displays of diamonded color; and herringbone "Log Cabin" squares with multicolored strips. More contemporary quilters have added free-form picture designs to these traditional patterns. The process is laborious and technically astounding — involving choosing, cutting, and affixing thousands of pieces of fabric, then filling in the design with intricate needlework patterns on the white "ground" that holds the layers of the quilt together. Expect to pay $500 or more for a good-quality quilt, and $25 and up for pot holders, bags, and throw pillows.

The People's Place in Intercourse, 3513 Old Philadelphia Pike, is a good place to start looking for quilts; their Old Country Store (© **717/768-7171**) has a knowledgeable sales staff and excellent inventory. **The Quilt Shop at Miller's,** located at the famed smorgasbord on Route 30 1 mile east of Route 896 (☎ **717/687-8480, ext. 49**) has hundreds of handmade examples from local artisans, and is open daily. Emma Witmer's mother was one of the first women to hang out a shingle to sell quilts 30 years ago, and she continues the business with more than 100 patterns at **Witmer Quilt Shop,** 1070 W. Main St. in New Holland (☎ **717/656-9526**). The shop is open from 8am to 6pm Tuesday through Thursday and Saturday, and until 8pm Monday and Friday.

Most of the county's back roads will have simple signs indicating places where quilts are sold; selections tend to be more limited but prices are slightly lower. Rosa Stoltzfus operates **Hand Made Quilts** at 102 N. Ronks Rd. in Ronks (no telephone) out of a room in her Amish home in the middle of cornfields. **Hannah Stoltzfoos** has a similar selection on 216 Witmer Rd. (☎ **717/392-4254**), just south of Route 340 near Smoketown.

OTHER CRAFTS

Amish and Mennonites have created their own baskets, dolls, furniture, pillows, toys, wall hangings, and hex designs for centuries, and tourism has led to a healthy growth in their production. Much of this output is channeled into the stores lining Route 340 in Intercourse and Bird-in-Hand, such as the Amish-owned **Country Barn Quilts and Crafts,** 2808 Old Philadelphia Pike (☎ **717/768-0338**), and **Dutchland Quilt Patch,** 4361 Old Philadelphia Pike (☎ **800/411-3221** or 717/687-0534). The **Weathervane Shop** at Landis Valley Museum (see "Especially for Kids," above) has a fine collection produced by their own craftspeople, from tin and pottery to caned chairs. On the contemporary side, no one works harder than **The Artworks at Doneckers,** 100 N. State St., Ephrata (☎ **717/738-9503**), which combines crafts with designer clothing and contemporary needs.

ANTIQUES

Two miles east of Exit 21 off I-76, Route 272 in Adamstown, just before it crosses into Berks County to the northeast, is the undisputed local center of Sunday fairs, with six or seven competitors within 5 miles. The largest are **Stoudt's Black Angus Antique Mall,** with more than 350 permanent dealers, and **Renninger's Antique and Collectors Market,** with 370 dealers. At Renninger's, check out stall 52½A for Tiffany glass, 89 for children's clothes, or 32A for antique linens and hooked rugs. For weekday stocks, try the 125 dealers at **White Horses Antiques Market,** 973 W. Main St. (Rte. 230; ☎ **717/653-6338**), in Mount Joy, a pleasant town north of some covered bridges.

FARMER'S MARKETS

Most farmer's markets in Lancaster County today are stable shedlike buildings with stalls at which local farmers, butchers, and bakers vend their fruits and vegetables, eggs and cheese, baked goods and pastries, and meat products like turkey sausage and scrapple. Since farmers can only afford to get away once or twice a week (to sell at Germantown and at Reading Terminal in Philadelphia, for example), the more commercial markets tend to augment the local goods with gourmet stalls selling everything from deerskin to candy and souvenirs. And the low-ceilinged, air-conditioned spaces you'll find at the commercial markets lack the flavor of, say, **Central Market** in Lancaster (p. 217), with its swirling fans and 1000 tiles and hitching posts, or Friday at **Green Dragon Market** (p. 219), on North State Street in Ephrata.

A notable contemporary market is the **Bird-in-Hand Farmers Market** at Route 340 and Maple Avenue (© **717/393-9674**). It's open from 8:30am to 5:30pm Friday and Saturday year-round, as well as Wednesday and Thursday during the summer. They have homemade ice cream and are linked to the Good 'n' Plenty Restaurant nearby. I also like **Meadowbrook Farmers Market,** 345 Main St. (Rte. 23) in Leola (© **717/656-2226**), open Friday from 8am to 7pm and Saturday and Sunday from 8am to 5pm, with 180 stands. **Root's Country Market and Auction** (no phone), just south of Manheim on Route 72, is a very complete market on Tuesday.

Among the treats at the dozens of roadside stands that you'll pass, try the home-made root beer, breads, and pies at **Countryside Stand,** on Stumptown Road. Take a right turn from Route 772 heading west out of Intercourse and follow Stumptown for ½ mile. **Fisher's Produce,** on Route 741 between Strasburg and Gap, sells delicious baked goods along with fresh corn and melons in the summer.

OUTLET CENTERS

With over 120 stores, **Rockvale Square Outlets,** Route 30 East at the intersection with Route 896 (© **717/293-9595**), is Lancaster's largest outlet mall. Evan-Picone, Nautica, Izod, Jockey, London Fog, and Bass Shoes are represented, with Oneida, Lenox, Dansk, and Pfaltzgraff for housewares. Hours are Monday through Saturday from 9:30am to 9pm, Sunday from noon to 6pm. I prefer the newer **Tanger Outlet Center at Millstream,** 311 Tanger Drive, Route 30 East (© **717/392-7260**), for shops like Donna Karan, Reebok, J. Crew, Guess?, London Fog, and Brooks Brothers. It's slightly closer to Lancaster and more compact. The complex also includes a 125-seat bakery and deli run by Miller's, of Miller's Smorgasbord fame. My children love the selection of leggings (and movies) at So Fun, Kids! Tanger is open Monday through Saturday from 9am to 9pm, and Sunday from 10am to 6pm.

Manufacturers Outlet Mall, at the junction of Exit 22 off the Pennsylvania Turnpike and Route 23 in Morgantown (© **610/286-2000**), has more than 50 stores, including Levi Strauss, Munsingwear, and Van Heusen, in an entirely enclosed mall with a food court. A Holiday Inn with indoor recreation for guests rounds out the premises. It's open Monday through Saturday from 10am to 9pm and Sunday from 11am to 5pm.

I don't have the space or the adjectives to fully describe the self-described "Outlet Capital of the World" in **Reading,** built out of former textile mills along the Schuylkill. Some six million shoppers are drawn here annually to 260 separate outlet centers. It's 30 minutes from Lancaster or 75 from Philadelphia, via I-76 to I-176 north to Route 422. The two largest destinations are **VF Factory Outlet Complex,** just west of the city in Wyomissing, and **Reading Outlet Center,** a multistory rehab in the heart of the city.

6 Where to Stay

From campsites, to bedrooms in working Amish farmhouses, to exquisite inns and luxury conference resorts, you'll find a wide variety of places to stay in Lancaster County. The higher the price level, the more advance notice is recommended; this also goes for some farms that only have two or three rooms.

HOTELS & RESORTS

Best Western Eden Resort Inn and Suites ⭐   The amenities of this hotel are incongruous with the region that surrounds it; that is, the hotel provides comforts you'd almost forgotten about, including plush, if bland, rooms (request poolside), coffeemakers, and a tropically landscaped atrium and pool. If you want a respite from the minimalist style of Amish life, this is a great, very casual place to hang out.

222 Eden Rd., Rte. 30 and Rte. 272, Lancaster, PA 17601. ✆ **800/528-1234** or 717/569-6444. Fax 717/569-4208. www.edenresort.com. 274 units. $119 double; $185 suite. Up to 2 children under age 18 stay free in parent's room. 10% AAA/AARP discount. AE, DC, DISC, MC, V. Free parking. Some packages include breakfast. **Amenities:** 2 restaurants; lounge; indoor and outdoor pool, tennis and basketball courts; health club; Jacuzzi; shuffleboard; 2 movie theaters; business center; laundry service and dry cleaning. *In room:* A/C, TV w/pay movies, dataport, kitchenettes (Club Suites only), fridge, coffeemaker, hair dryer.

The Inns at Doneckers ⭐   Bill Donecker started building his customer service empire on Ephrata's north side in the early 1960s, beginning with a complex of stores featuring gifts, accessories, fashions, and collectibles. He's since added the fine Restaurant at Doneckers serving all meals (see "Where to Dine," below), the Artworks loft spaces for contemporary artists to work in and market their crafts, the Farmer's Market (a store that sells jams and other edibles), and four inns, and he spices things up with frequent events and festivals. Of the four inns, the 1777 House, built by a clock-maker member of Ephrata Cloister, is the most stately and distinguished; I also like the Gerhart House for its small size and removal from main streets. All rooms have hand stenciling, and local antiques and objects, and each site has a parlor with TV and library. The staff is outstanding.

322 N. State St. (near junction of Rte. 322 and Rte. 222), Ephrata, PA 17522. ✆ **717/738-9502.** Fax 717/738-9554. www.doneckers.com. 40 units in 4 houses. $69–$99 double; $150–$210 suite. Rates include full buffet breakfast. AE, DC, DISC, MC, V. Free parking. **Amenities:** Restaurant; Jacuzzi in suites only; shopping complex includes fashion store, flower shop, artworks gallery, furniture gallery, and local crafts. *In room:* A/C, TV.

Willow Valley Family Resort   This Mennonite-owned resort (no drinking or smoking is permitted on premises) started out as a farm stand in 1943 and now combines a very complete set of modern comforts — a 9-hole golf course, lighted tennis courts, and indoor and outdoor pools — with local touches such as a bakery specializing in apple dumplings and fresh-baked pies (shoofly, among others). A skylit atrium is home to two smorgasbords and a restaurant. Free bus tours of the Amish country are offered Monday through Saturday.

2416 Willow St. Pike (3 miles south of Lancaster on Rte. 222), Lancaster, PA 17602. ✆ **800/444-1714** or 717/464-2711. www.willowvalley.com. 352 units. $135 double; add $17 per person for all-you-can-eat dinner and breakfast smorgasbord. Children under 12 stay free in parent's room. Special packages available. AE, DC, MC, V. Free parking. **Amenities:** Restaurant; 2 indoor pools and an outdoor pool; 9-hole golf course; lighted tennis and basketball courts; fitness center; sauna; duck pond with gazebo; children's playground room. *In room:* A/C, TV, VCRs in premium rooms, fridge, coffeemaker, hair dryer, iron.

INNS

General Sutter Inn ⭐   The General Sutter has operated continuously since 1764 at the charming intersection of routes 501 and 772. The inn boasts such niceties as verandas overlooking a fountain, and marble-topped tables. While wings have been added and the lobby and restaurant renovated, most of the rooms occupy the original building and are decorated in Victorian style with folk art touches. There is a coffee shop for breakfast, lunch, and a notable Sunday brunch; the dining room offers a solid continental gourmet menu.

14 E. Main St. (junction of Rte. 501 and Rte. 772), Lititz, PA 17543. ✆ **717/626-2115.** Fax 717/626-0992. www.generalsutterinn.com. 16 units. $83–$110 double; $120–$140 suite. Additional guests $10. Rates include full breakfast. AE, DISC, MC, V. Free parking. **Amenities:** 2 restaurants; lounge. *In room:* A/C, TV, dataport.

Historic Strasburg Inn ⭐ This country inn, set on 58 acres, is completely surrounded by Amish farms. I like it because, with 102 units, it still feels like an inn, but it has a good-size pool, a newly renovated fitness center, and a triple-diamond rated three-room restaurant. Rooms are colonial-themed, with poster beds, handmade floral wreaths, and handsome chair rails. A full breakfast is served in the adjacent ice-cream parlor.

1 Historic Dr., Strasburg, PA 17579. ✆ **800/872-0201** or 717/687-7691. www.historicstrasburginn.com. 102 units. $90–$170 double. Frequent packages and AARP discount. AE, DISC, MC, V. Free parking. Rates include full breakfast. **Amenities:** Restaurant, tavern; heated outdoor pool; exercise room; Jacuzzi; sauna; children's playground; concierge; laundry service and dry cleaning. *In room:* A/C, TV/VCR, dataport, coffeemaker, hair dryer, iron.

BED & BREAKFASTS

Alden House ⭐ This 1850 brick Victorian house is at the center of the town's historic district. It was completely renovated recently, with private bathrooms installed in all rooms. Two suites can be accessed either through the house or via an outdoor spiral staircase to the second-floor porch. The owners may soon renovate the carriage house for more quarters. The morning brings a full breakfast with waffles or cinnamon-chip pancakes served in the dining room or overlooking the charming gardens outside. Be warned: The two cats have the run of the house.

62 E. Main St. (Rte. 772), Lititz, PA 17543. ✆ **800/584-0753** or 717/627-3363. www.aldenhouse.com. 5 units. $90–$120 double and suite. Rates include full breakfast. MC, V. Free parking. The inn is nonsmoking. *In room:* A/C, TV/VCR, dataport.

Churchtown Inn Bed and Breakfast This completely restored 1735 stone inn, written up in *The New York Times* in May 2002, has evening cocktail hours in the Victorian parlor, and an opulent breakfast is served in a glassed-in porch overlooking the garden. Guest rooms all have private bathrooms, and innkeepers Diane and Michael Franco have a standing arrangement for Saturday night dinner with nearby Mennonite or Amish families if you wish it. The Cornwall iron forge nearby, still functioning as a working historic site, supplied Revolutionary War troops with cannonballs and musket shot.

Main St. (Rte. 23), Churchtown, PA 17555. ✆ **800/637-4446** or 717/445-7794. Fax 717/445-0962. www.churchtowninn.com. 8 units. $75–$145 double. Rates include full breakfast. 2-night weekend minimum. MC, V. Free parking. Children under 12 not accepted. *In room:* A/C, TV.

Historic Smithton Inn This inn, near Ephrata Cloister, is a pre–Revolutionary War stagecoach stop. Dorothy Graybill, the owner, painstakingly decorates each room with canopy feather beds and collector-quality quilts, working fireplaces, sitting areas, and leather upholstered chairs. Triple-pane windows for quiet, magazines, and fresh flowers are typical thoughtful touches; the grounds have lovely gardens and a gazebo. There is a restaurant on the premises. Smoking is not permitted.

900 W. Main St., Ephrata, PA 17522. ✆ **717/733-6094.** www.historicsmithtoninn.com. 8 units. $85–$140 double; $150–$180 suite. Rates include full breakfast. Children welcome: under 12, $20 additional; over 12, $35 additional. 2-night minimum on holiday weekends. MC, V. Free parking. Nonsmoking. **Amenities:** Golf nearby; Jacuzzi in some rooms. *In room:* A/C, fridge, hair dryer and iron available.

MOTELS

Best Western Revere Inn and Suites ⭐ Eight miles east of Lancaster, the original inn is built off a historic 1740 post house now used as a restaurant and lounge. A 1999 new main building houses 65 oversize rooms and suites. Recently installed room amenities include coffeemakers, hair dryers, and refrigerators, as well as fireplaces and Jacuzzis in suites. It's close to the outlet malls and has both indoor and outdoor pools.

3063 Lincoln Hwy (Rte. 30), Paradise, PA 17562. ℂ **800/429-7383** or 717/687-7683. Fax 717/687-6141. www.revereinn.com. 95 units. $69–$119 double. Rates include continental breakfast. Children under 12 free in parents' room. AE, MC, V. Free parking. **Amenities:** Restaurant, lounge; 1 indoor and 1 outdoor pool; exercise room; Jacuzzi; coin-op laundry. *In room:* A/C, TV, dataport, fridge, coffeemaker, hair dryer, iron.

Bird-in-Hand Family Inn & Restaurant

This motel's location puts you directly in the heart of Amish country. It has a three-diamond AAA rating, and 70% of the guests are repeat customers or came through word of mouth. I prefer the back building, with rooms off an indoor hallway, to the front building's motel setup. The simple, utilitarian rooms were recently renovated, with 25 new rooms and a pool and mini-golf added in 2000. The hotel restaurant serves all meals buffet style and is a popular stop for tours. Grandma Smucker's Bakery offers wet-bottom shoofly pie and apple dumplings.

Rte. 340, Bird-in-Hand, PA 17505. ℂ **800/537-2535.** Fax 717/768-1117. www.bird-in-hand.com/familyinn. 125 units. $52–$109 double. Packages available. Children under 16 stay free in parent's room. AE, DC, DISC, MC, V. Free parking. **Amenities:** Restaurant; 1 indoor and 1 outdoor pool; 2 lighted tennis courts; mini-golf; bike rentals; game room; playground; free 2-hr. bus tour of country roads; coin-op laundry service. *In room:* A/C, TV, dataport, fridge, coffeemaker, hair dryer.

Country Inn of Lancaster ★

Thomas Dommel's inn is very convenient to Lancaster, just east of the Route 30 bypass. More to the point, its back building overlooks beautiful Amish farmland, the decor is unusually charming, and the amenities — elevators for all second-floor guests and a large heated pool, open from 9am to 9pm — are impeccably maintained. Most furnishings are handmade locally, from Amish quilts to branch wreaths, and all rooms have porches or balconies with wooden rocking chairs. The complex includes two buildings, each with several complimentary breakfast stations, an adjoining restaurant (you can get discount coupons for any meal there), and an extensive gift shop.

2133 Lincoln Hwy. E. (Rte. 30), Lancaster, PA 17602. ℂ **717/393-3413.** Fax 717/393-2889. www.country innoflancaster.com. 125 units. $64–$139 double. Rates include Continental breakfast. Packages available. Children under 12 stay free in parent's room. AE, DISC, MC, V. Free parking. **Amenities:** Restaurant; indoor/ outdoor pool; Jacuzzi; 24-hr. coffee and juice. *In room:* A/C, TV.

Harvest Drive Family Motel & Restaurant

Good farmland was converted to create this family-owned motel, and it's surrounded by corn and alfalfa fields on a quiet back road next to the family farm. The motel building has rooms with one to three double beds and pleasant but utilitarian decor. The simple restaurant features Dutch home cooking all day, and there's a gift shop in the barn.

Box 498, Intercourse, PA 17534. ℂ **800/233-0176** or 717/768-7186. Fax 717/768-4513. www.harvest drive.com. 50 units. $75–$85 double. 2-night minimum on holiday weekends. $5 for children over 14 in parent's room. AE, MC, V. Free parking. Take Clearview Rd. south off Rte. 340 just west of Intercourse, then bear right to 3370 Harvest Dr. **Amenities:** Restaurant; children's playground. *In room:* A/C, TV, dataport.

Mill Stream Country Inn

Of the dozens of motor lodges in the vicinity, this more modest sister of the Willow Valley Family Resort in Lancaster (see above) is one of the most popular, with three floors of simple rooms. The rear rooms are away from the road and overlook a stream. It's owned by Mennonites, and most rooms are nonsmoking. The restaurant serves breakfast and lunch (no alcohol).

Rte. 896 (between Rte. 30 and Rte. 340), Smoketown, PA 17576. ℂ **800/355-1143** or 717/299-0931. www.millstreamcountryinn.com. 52 units. $59–$139 double. 2-night minimum on weekends. Children under 6 stay free in parent's room, additional $5 for ages 6–11. AE, DISC, MC, V. Free parking. **Amenities:** Outdoor pool; golf course nearby. *In room:* AC, TV, dataport, hair dryer, iron.

FARM VACATION BED & BREAKFASTS

What better way to get the flavor of Amish life than by staying with a farm family? The **Pennsylvania Dutch Country Convention & Visitors Bureau** (© **800/PA-DUTCH;** www.padutchcountry.com) has a complete listing of about 40 working farms that take guests. Reservations are recommended since most offer only three to five rooms. Expect simple lodgings, hall bathrooms, and filling, family-style breakfasts, all at less than motel rates. Dinners with the family are sometimes offered at an additional charge. You'll be able to chat with the women in the family (the men start and end their days with the sun) and get suggestions on local routes, walks, and crafts producers. One tip: Stay away from dairy and poultry farms if you have a sensitive nose!

Green Acres Farm   Wayne and Yvonne Miller can sleep 26 people in this 150-year-old farmhouse, with private bathrooms in all rooms. It's a corn and soybean farm but also offers hay wagon rides, farm pets, a playhouse, and swings and major-league trampoline for kids. All rooms have one double or queen-size bed plus bunk beds. There's no smoking, but you're allowed to bring your own alcohol.

1382 Pinkerton Rd., Mount Joy, PA 17552. © **717/653-4028.** Fax 717/653-2840. www.thegreenacres farm.com. 7 units. $75 double. Additional child $5. Rates include family-style breakfast served at 8am. In summer, reservations are recommended. MC, V. Pinkerton Rd. is south of Rte. 772 just west of Mt. Joy's town center. You'll wind past Groff's Farm Resort and a creek before you get to the farm. In room: A/C.

Rayba Acres Farm   Ray and Reba Ranck offer clean, quiet rooms on a working fifth-generation dairy farm. (You're welcome to try milking.) Rooms are in a modernized 1863 farmhouse with a private entrance, or with private bathroom and TV in two motel-like units. A common room has a microwave and refrigerator. There's complimentary coffee in your room, but no smoking. Outside features a pretty pergola and gardens.

183 Black Horse Rd., Paradise, PA 17562. © **717/687-6729.** Fax 717/687-8386. www.800padutch.com/ rayba.html. 9 units, 6 with private bathroom. $62–$68 double. DISC, MC, V. From Paradise center, south from Rte. 30 onto Black Horse, follow 2 miles. In room: A/C, TV, coffeemaker.

7 Where to Dine

While Ben Franklin would probably be staggered at the size of a modern Pennsylvania Dutch meal or smorgasbord, he'd recognize everything in it — you'll still find the same baked goods, meat and poultry, and fruits and vegetables that have been offered here since colonial times. The Amish way of life calls for substantial, wholesome, long-cooking dishes, rich in butter and cream. Don't look for crunchy vegetables — if they're not creamed, they're marinated or thoroughly boiled. The baked goods are renowned, and even the main courses tend to the sweet. Shoofly pie, a concoction of molasses and sweet dough (hence its attraction to flies), is probably the most famous. Decor tends to take a back seat to large quantities of food at low prices.

Included here are the most representative family style and smorgasbord dining spots, as well as restaurants that update local ingredients and traditions. Family style means that you'll be part of a group of 10 or 12, ushered to long tables and brought heaping platters of food, course after course. At a smorgasbord, you construct your own plate at central food stations, with unlimited refills. Prices are fixed per person at both.

And when looking for a meal, don't neglect the signs along the road, or "Community Event" listings in the Thursday "Weekend" section of the

Lancaster New Era, for church or firehouse pancake breakfasts, corn roasts, or barbecue or game suppers. These generally charge a minimal amount for all the food you can eat and all the iced tea or soda you can drink; and they're great chances to meet the locals. You can also catch annual festivals, such as the rhubarb fair in Intercourse and the Sertoma Club's enormous chicken barbecues at Long's Park in Lancaster, both in May. The Dutch Food and Folk Fair is held in Bird-in-Hand each June.

FAMILY STYLE/SMORGASBORD

Good 'N' Plenty Restaurant PENNSYLVANIA DUTCH   They've added the 500-seat Dutch Room to the original 110-seat farmhouse here. The location is very convenient, and tables seat 10 to 12. Expect waits at peak dining hours: I wish they wouldn't wait for a 'full 12' before seating anybody at a table and filling it with platters. You can purchase baked goods and other gift items.

Rte. 896, ½ mile south of its intersection with Rte. 340 and north of intersection with Rte. 30, Smoketown. ℂ 717/394-7111. Reservations not accepted. Adults $17, children $7.50 for ages 4–12, free for children under 4; tax included. MC, V. Mon–Sat 11:30am–8pm.

Miller's Smorgasbord PENNSYLVANIA DUTCH/SMORGASBORD   In 1929, Anna Miller prepared chicken and waffles for truckers while Enos Miller repaired their vehicles. For millions since then, Miller's has been the definitive, if increasingly pricey, Pennsylvania Dutch smorgasbord. Homemade chicken corn soup, slow-roasted carved beef, turkey, and ham, chicken potpies, and a rich apple pie are just the tip of the iceberg. The breakfast smorgasbord, now offered only on Sunday, has made-to-order eggs and omelets, along with local sausage and pastries. The health-conscious diner will find plenty of choices here too.

Rte. 30 at Ronks Rd., 5 miles east of Lancaster and 1 mile east of Rte. 896. ℂ 800/669-3568 or 717/687-6621. Reservations accepted. Dinner $22 adults, $6.95 for children 3–8, $7.95 for children 9–12; breakfast $9.95 adults, $5.95 for children 3–12; tax included. AE, DISC, MC, V. Mon–Sat noon–8pm; Sun 8am–8pm year-round.

Plain & Fancy Farm & Dining Room PENNSYLVANIA DUTCH   This 40-year-old family style restaurant started out as a barn, as you can see by the posts that still support the front dining room. A back addition gives it a capacity of 260. They are less intent on filling full tables and more quick with service here. The fried chicken is crisp and flavorful. The newly renovated complex now includes a village of craft shops and a bakery. Smoking is not permitted.

Rte. 340, 7 miles east of Lancaster, Bird-in-Hand, PA. ℂ 717/768-4400. Reservations recommended. Adults $17, $6.50 for children 4–11; tax included. AE, DISC, MC, V. Noon–8pm year-round.

Shady Maple *Value* SMORGASBORD   This is somewhat north of most of the attractions, but it does an enormous business, with waits of up to 30 minutes on Saturday for one of the 600 seats. Tourist buses have their own entrance and seating. The Pennsylvania Dutch buffet is a mind-boggling 140-feet long, with 46 salads, 14 vegetables, 8 meats, 8 breads, 27 desserts, and a make-your-own-sundae station. Breakfast includes everything you've ever imagined eating at that hour. There's a touristy gift shop and a fast food version (why bother?) downstairs. The cheapest days are Monday, Wednesday, and Friday; the dinner price of $14 includes tax, tip, and all nonalcoholic beverages. Smoking is not permitted.

Rte. 23, East Earl, PA (1 mile east of Blue Ball, at intersection with Rte. 897). ℂ 800/238-7365 or 717/354-8222. Reservations not accepted. Dinner $13.50–$20; breakfast $6.50–$7.50, lunch $8.50. Children 4–10 half-price; 10% discount for seniors. AE, DC, DISC, MC, V. Mon–Sat 5am–8pm.

MORE DINING CHOICES

Alois CONTINENTAL   A surprise hides inside the former brewery and historic Bube's Hotel in downtown Mt. Joy. Chef Ophelia Horn has created a deluxe 6-course prix-fixe feast at Alois (*Al*-oh-weese), inside the Victorian hotel's old and very pretty dining room with hand-stenciled walls and ceilings. You should be prepared to devote almost 3 hours to the procession of courses (several choices available for the major courses). A brewpub, which started the taps flowing again in late 2001, and the excellent Catacomb tavern/bar are also on premises, in sections of the old brewery; a tour of the entire facility is a nice finish to the evening

102 N. Market St., Mt. Joy. ℭ 717/653-2056. Reservations recommended. Prix fixe dinner $32. AE, DC, DISC, MC, V. Tues–Thurs 5:30–9:30pm; Fri–Sat 5–10pm; to 9pm off-season. 12 miles from Lancaster on Rte. 30 west, then Rte. 283 west, then take 230 west; follow to Main St. in Mt. Joy and north on Market St. to Bube's Hotel.

The Restaurant at Doneckers CONTINENTAL   Chef Greg Gables presides over this haute cuisine menu. Prices are steep for the area, but quality is comparable to a Center City treat, though service is spottier. The menu features lobster ravioli or grilled dover sole in a citrus butter sauce, and mixes classic French dishes with contemporary American standards like infused oils, lighter ingredients, and healthier cooking. If you're in the mood for creamy sauces, though, they'll be more than happy to indulge you. Desserts are baked on the premises daily. For lighter fare, there's a bistro-style menu offered from 4 to 10pm. The wine list is extensive.

333 N. State St., Ephrata. ℭ 717/738-9501. Reservations recommended. Main courses $20–$30. AE, DC, DISC, MC, V. Mon–Sat 11am–10pm.

Stoudt's Black Angus Restaurant & Brew Pub STEAKHOUSE/BREW PUB   Stoudt's Golden Lager, Pilsner, and other German-style varieties are brewed here and make a perfect conclusion to a visit to the famed Sunday antiques market next door. The family has added a steakhouse specializing in aged prime beef, a clam and oyster bar, and an agreeable pub with Pennsylvania Dutch ham and chicken dishes alongside burgers, wursts, soups, and salads. The restaurant has a 1928 Packard in the lobby, and the pub offers country dancing Friday and Saturday. The complex also includes a medieval German-style village of shops and homes.

Rte. 272, 1 mile north of Exit 21 from I-76, Adamstown, PA. ℭ 717/484-4385. Reservations recommended. Main courses $17–$35; brewpub $6.95–$11.50. AE, DC, MC, V. Mon–Thurs 4:30–10pm; Fri–Sat noon–10pm; Sun 11:30am–8pm.

Appendix:
Philadelphia in Depth

Philadelphia in 2003–2004 will greet visitors with a new convention center, two new major sports arenas, improved theaters for the performing arts, a gleaming inner Center City core filled with new skyscrapers, and a revitalized cultural and street life.

History 101: The Philadelphia Story

Although Philadelphia may conjure up thoughts of William Penn and the Revolutionary period in the minds of most Americans, it was in fact a tiny group of Swedish settlers that first established a foothold here in the 1640s. Where does William Penn fit in? Well, his father had been an admiral and a courtier under Charles II of England. The king was in debt to Admiral Penn, and the younger Penn asked to collect the debt through a land grant on the west bank of the Delaware River, a grant that would eventually be named Pennsylvania, or "Penn's forest." Penn's Quaker religion, his anti-Anglicanism, and his contempt for authority had landed him in prison, and the chance for him to set up a Quaker utopia in the New World was too good to pass up. Since Swedish farmers owned most of the lower Delaware frontage, he settled upriver, where the Schuylkill met the Delaware, and named the settlement Philadelphia — City of Brotherly Love.

COLONIAL PHILADELPHIA When Philadelphia celebrated its 300th anniversary in 1982, Penn's original city plan still adequately described the Center City, down to the public parks and the site for City Hall. Penn, who had learned the dangers of narrow streets and semidetached wooden buildings from London's terrible 1666 fire, laid out the city along broad avenues and city blocks arranged in a grid. As he intended to treat Native Americans and fellow settlers equally, he planned no city walls or neighborhood borders. Front Street, naturally, faced the Delaware, as it still does, and parallel streets were numbered up to 24th Street and the Schuylkill. Streets running east to west were named after trees and plants (although Sassafras became Race Street, for the horse-and-buggy contests run along it). To attract prospective investors, Penn promised bonus land grants in the "Liberties" (outlying countryside) to anyone who bought a city lot; he took one of the largest for himself, now Pennsbury Manor (26 miles north of town). The Colonies were in the business of attracting settlers in those days, and Penn found that he had to wear a variety of hats — those of financier, politician, religious leader, salesman, and manufacturer.

Homes and public buildings filled in the map slowly. The colonial row houses of Society Hill and Elfreth's Alley (continuously inhabited since the 1690s), near the Delaware docks were the earliest homes. Thomas Jefferson, when he wrote the Declaration of Independence in 1776 almost a century later, could still say of his boardinghouse, on 7th and Market, that it was away from the city's noise and dirt!

Around 1800, the city spread west to Broad Street. Philadelphia grew along the river and not west as Penn had planned. Southwark, to the south, and the

C A Portrait of the Philadelphians

The first European settlers in Philadelphia, arriving in the 1640s, were from Sweden. (You can see models of the two ships that brought them over in Gloria Dei Church.) Unusual tolerance, epitomized by the Quakers, helped lead to two separate strains of immigration during the first centuries of the city's history. One was made up of large European families drawn to the new world by the promise of cheap farmland — English, Scottish, Sephardic Jews, and Germans (*Deutsch* in German — hence the term *Pennsylvania Dutch*). The other group included thousands of London-based craftsmen, servants, and sailors, including London-based French Huguenots. German immigrants specialized in linen and wool weaving and ironwork, French Huguenots in fine silver, and all immigrants from all ethnic groups farmed and built ships.

In general the quality of life was high, despite a disastrous 1793 yellow fever epidemic. Franklin's legacy flourished. The resources of the Library Company became available to the public, and both men and women received "modern" educations — that is, more emphasis on accounting and less on classics. The 1834 Free School Act established a democratic public school system. Private academies, such as Germantown Friends School and Friends Select, are still going strong today.

Culture flourished — the Walnut Street Theater, founded in 1809, is the oldest American theater still in constant use, and the Musical Fund Hall at 808 Locust St. (now apartments) hosted operas, symphony orchestras, and chamber ensembles. The 1805 Pennsylvania Academy of Fine Arts, now at Broad and Cherry streets, taught such painters as Washington Allston and the younger Peales. Charles Willson Peale, the eccentric patriarch, set up the first American museum in the Long Hall of Independence Hall; its exhibits included a portrait gallery and the first lifelike arrangements of full-size stuffed animals.

The 19th century saw the arrival of English commoners fleeing the industrialization of their countryside in the 1820s, Irish escaping from the 1840s potato famine, and waves of Germans and central Europeans seeking peace and stability during the 1870s. From the 1880s to the 1920s, Russians and Jews from eastern Europe, Italians, and free blacks from the American South all migrated in record numbers to the city. In recent years, Asian and Hispanic immigrants have filled in the gap left by the suburban exodus of earlier groups, creating a more multicultural Philadelphia than ever before.

Northern Liberties, to the north, housed the less affluent, including many sailors. These were Philadelphia's first slums — unpaved, without public services, filled with taverns set up in unofficial alleys, and populated by those without enough property or money to satisfy voting requirements.

Although Philadelphia was founded after Boston and New York, manufacturing, financial services, excellent docking facilities, and fine Pennsylvania farm produce soon propelled it into the first city of the colonies. It was the largest

English-speaking city in the British Empire after London. Colonial Philadelphia was a thriving city in virtually every way, boasting public hospitals and street-lights, cultural institutions and newspapers, stately Georgian architecture, imported tea and cloth, and, above all, commerce. The "triangle trade" shipping route between England, the Caribbean, and Philadelphia yielded estimated profits of 700% on each leg.

One man who will always be linked with Philadelphia is the multitalented, insatiably curious Benjamin Franklin. Inventor, printer, statesman, scientist, and diplomat, Franklin was an all-around genius. It sometimes seems that his influ-ence appears in every aspect of the city worth exploring! Colonial homes were protected by his fire-insurance company; the post office at 3rd and Market streets became his grandson's printing shop; and the Free Library of Philadel-phia, the University of Pennsylvania, Pennsylvania Hospital at 8th and Spruce streets, and the American Philosophical Society all came into being thanks to Franklin's inspiration.

FROM REVOLUTION TO CIVIL WAR   Like most important Philadelphi-ans, Franklin considered himself a loyal British subject until well into the 1770s, though he and the other colonists were increasingly subject to what they con-sidered capricious English policy. Colonists here weren't as radical as those in New England, but tremendous political debate erupted after Lexington and Concord and the meeting of the First and Second Continental Congresses. Moderates — wealthy citizens with friends and relatives in England — held out as long as they could. But with the April 1776 decision in Independence Hall to consider drafting a declaration of independence, revolutionary fervor gained a momentum that would become unstoppable.

"These are the times that try men's souls," wrote Thomas Paine, and they cer-tainly were for Philadelphians, who had much to lose in a war with Britain. Thomas Jefferson and John Adams talked over the situation with George Wash-ington, Robert Morris, and other delegates at City Tavern by night and at Car-penter's Hall and Independence Hall by day. On July 2, the general Congress passed their declaration; on July 8, it was read to a crowd of 8,000, who tumul-tuously approved.

Your visit to Independence National Historical Park will fill you in on the Revolution's effect on the City of Brotherly Love. Of the major colonial cities, Philadelphia had the fewest defenses. The war came to the city itself because British troops occupied patriot homes during the harsh winter of 1777 to 1778. Woodford, a country mansion in what is now Fairmount Park, was hosting Tory balls while Washington's troops drilled and shivered at Valley Forge. Washing-ton's attempt to crack the British line at Germantown ended in a confused retreat. The city later greatly benefited from the British departure and the Peace of Paris (1783), which ended the war.

Problems with the new federal government brought a Constitutional Con-vention to Philadelphia in 1787. This body crafted the Constitution that the United States still follows. In the years between the ratification of the Constitu-tion and the Civil War, the city prospered. For 10 of these years, 1790 to 1800, the U.S. government operated here while the District of Columbia was still marshland. George Washington lived in an executive mansion where the Liberty Bell is now; the Supreme Court met in Old City Hall; Congress met in Con-gress Hall; and everybody met at City Tavern for balls and festivals.

After the capital moved to Washington, Philadelphia retained the federal charter to mint money, build ships, and produce weapons. The city's shipyards, ironworks and locomotive works fueled the transportation revolution that made America's growth possible. Philadelphia vied with Baltimore and New York City for transport routes to agricultural production inland. New York eventually won out as a shipper, thanks to its natural harbor and the Erie Canal. Philadelphia, however, was the hands-down winner in becoming America's premier manufacturing city, and it ranked even with New York in finance. During the Civil War, Philadelphia's manufacturers weren't above supplying both Yankees and Confederates with guns and rail equipment. Fortunately for Philadelphians, the Southern offensive met with bloody defeat at Gettysburg before reaching the city. With the end of the Civil War in 1865, port activity rebounded, as Southern cotton was spun and shipped from city textile looms.

Philadelphia became the natural site for the first world's fair held on American soil: the Centennial Exposition. It's hard to imagine the excitement that filled Fairmount Park, with 200 pavilions and displays. There's a scale model in Memorial Hall, one of the few surviving structures in the park; it gives a good idea of how seriously the United States took this show of power and prestige. University City in West Philadelphia saw the establishment of campuses for Drexel University and the University of Pennsylvania, and public transport lines connected all the neighborhoods of the city.

INTO THE 21ST CENTURY   Philadelphia's 20th century has been checkered, and the city enters the 21st century with mixed fortunes. A new convention center, major sports arena, improved theaters for the performing arts, and selective Center City reclamation balance out many of the problems that plague urban centers throughout America — homelessness, drugs, crime, and inadequate resources for public services. Philadelphia's biggest challenge over the next few years is to create jobs through tourism in the urban core and to increase visitors from the current 5 million a year to 10 or even 15 million. This concept translates into investments that improve the city's attractiveness and quality of life for visitors.

If you go to the top of City Hall and look around, you'll see a panorama of factories, the old Navy Yard, warehouses, and docks. The places are virtually all shuttered or turned to other uses. You'll also see block after block of row houses built a century ago by new immigrants, whose more successful descendants have left for greener pastures. In terms of urban homeowners — an area in which Philadelphia led the world for decades — many successful citizens have left the city for more pleasant suburban areas, although the urban-renewal projects at Society Hill, the boom period of expansion along the northeast and Parkway, and the establishment of Independence National Historical Park have combated the migration somewhat. Although port and petroleum-refining operations bolstered the city's position as an industrial center until the 1980s, manufacturing in general has moved out of the city and the region. Half of the city's workforce was once employed in manufacturing. This figure has shrunk to 9% today. As industry moves out, the city must develop its service businesses to replace the revenue, and specifically aim at tourist business.

The opening of the $522 million Pennsylvania Convention Center in 1993, only minutes from both historic and business districts, has been a tremendous boon for the city. The hundreds of conventions, millions of visitors, and billions of dollars projected in revenues from the center over the next decade are crucial, after some lean years, to keep the restaurants, hotels, sights, and entertainment that we recommend afloat. Most convention managers have found the labor costs and operational frustrations at the Convention Center a turn-off for future business, so change is necessary although not assured.

Pennsylvania Convention Center dollars also tie into greater safety and great infrastructure improvements, with lots of repaving, new lighting, and curb cuts along lower Market Street, Columbus Boulevard and the waterfront, and the Italian Market. A dark blue "Direction Philadelphia" signage program that's clear and coherent can guide you on and off a reconstructed expressway system, now connecting I-95 and I-76 (along the two rivers), with plenty of easy entrances and exits. The burgeoning airport, now a US Airways hub, is undergoing a $1 billion capital improvement, with new terminals, a state-of-the-art shopping mall, and new runways. The nation's second busiest Amtrak stop, 30th Street Station, has completed a $100 million restoration, with a new bakery, charcuterie, and rejuvenated shops. Hot areas in town have radiated out from the city core. The Delaware River waterfront's piers and warehouses have been transformed into frenetic pleasure domes: bars, clubs, sports palaces, and beach resorts. On the other side, the once blue-collar terraced streets of Manayunk along the Schuylkill River host fashion — from high to funky — plus cuisine and shopping, along with a new farmer's market.

Corporate headquarters punctuate the northwest quadrant of Center City, and conventions throng Market Street east of City Hall. Major corporate headquarters in Philadelphia now include SmithKline Beecham (pharmaceuticals); Aramark (food and hospitality); Advanta (financial services); and CIGNA (insurance). With all those universities to train entrepreneurs and scientists, plenty of Internet and biogenetic firms are sprouting with local financing.

But tourism and hospitality are even more critical for revenue replacement, as evidenced by the coordination of public and private efforts in Center City under recent mayors Ed Rendell and John Street. The city looks ahead with a keen sense that visitors are the key to a vibrant urban core.

Index

See also Accommodations and Restaurant indexes, below.

ACCOMMODATIONS

RESTAURANTS

FROMMER'S® COMPLETE TRAVEL GUIDES

Alaska
Alaska Cruises & Ports of Call
Amsterdam
Argentina & Chile
Arizona
Atlanta
Australia
Austria
Bahamas
Barcelona, Madrid & Seville
Beijing
Belgium, Holland & Luxembourg
Bermuda
Boston
Brazil
British Columbia & the Canadian Rockies
Budapest & the Best of Hungary
California
Canada
Cancún, Cozumel & the Yucatán
Cape Cod, Nantucket & Martha's Vineyard
Caribbean
Caribbean Cruises & Ports of Call
Caribbean Ports of Call
Carolinas & Georgia
Chicago
China
Colorado
Costa Rica
Denmark
Denver, Boulder & Colorado Springs
England
Europe
European Cruises & Ports of Call
Florida

France
Germany
Great Britain
Greece
Greek Islands
Hawaii
Hong Kong
Honolulu, Waikiki & Oahu
Ireland
Israel
Italy
Jamaica
Japan
Las Vegas
London
Los Angeles
Maryland & Delaware
Maui
Mexico
Montana & Wyoming
Montréal & Québec City
Munich & the Bavarian Alps
Nashville & Memphis
Nepal
New England
New Mexico
New Orleans
New York City
New Zealand
Northern Italy
Nova Scotia, New Brunswick & Prince Edward Island
Oregon
Paris
Philadelphia & the Amish Country
Portugal
Prague & the Best of the Czech Republic

Provence & the Riviera
Puerto Rico
Rome
San Antonio & Austin
San Diego
San Francisco
Santa Fe, Taos & Albuquerque
Scandinavia
Scotland
Seattle & Portland
Shanghai
Singapore & Malaysia
South Africa
South America
South Florida
South Pacific
Southeast Asia
Spain
Sweden
Switzerland
Texas
Thailand
Tokyo
Toronto
Tuscany & Umbria
USA
Utah
Vancouver & Victoria
Vermont, New Hampshire & Maine
Vienna & the Danube Valley
Virgin Islands
Virginia
Walt Disney World® & Orlando
Washington, D.C.
Washington State

FROMMER'S® DOLLAR-A-DAY GUIDES

Australia from $50 a Day
California from $70 a Day
Caribbean from $70 a Day
England from $75 a Day
Europe from $70 a Day

Florida from $70 a Day
Hawaii from $80 a Day
Ireland from $60 a Day
Italy from $70 a Day
London from $85 a Day

New York from $90 a Day
Paris from $80 a Day
San Francisco from $70 a Day
Washington, D.C. from $80 a Day

FROMMER'S® PORTABLE GUIDES

Acapulco, Ixtapa & Zihuatanejo
Amsterdam
Aruba
Australia's Great Barrier Reef
Bahamas
Berlin
Big Island of Hawaii
Boston
California Wine Country
Cancún
Charleston & Savannah
Chicago
Disneyland®
Dublin
Florence

Frankfurt
Hong Kong
Houston
Las Vegas
London
Los Angeles
Los Cabos & Baja
Maine Coast
Maui
Miami
New Orleans
New York City
Paris
Phoenix & Scottsdale

Portland
Puerto Rico
Puerto Vallarta, Manzanillo & Guadalajara
Rio de Janeiro
San Diego
San Francisco
Seattle
Sydney
Tampa & St. Petersburg
Vancouver
Venice
Virgin Islands
Washington, D.C.

FROMMER'S® NATIONAL PARK GUIDES

Banff & Jasper
Family Vacations in the National Parks
Grand Canyon

National Parks of the American West
Rocky Mountain

Yellowstone & Grand Teton
Yosemite & Sequoia/ Kings Canyon
Zion & Bryce Canyon

FROMMER'S® MEMORABLE WALKS

Chicago	New York	San Francisco
London	Paris	Washington, D.C.

FROMMER'S® GREAT OUTDOOR GUIDES

Arizona & New Mexico	Northern California	Vermont & New Hampshire
New England	Southern New England	

SUZY GERSHMAN'S BORN TO SHOP GUIDES

Born to Shop: France	Born to Shop: Italy	Born to Shop: New York
Born to Shop: Hong Kong, Shanghai & Beijing	Born to Shop: London	Born to Shop: Paris

FROMMER'S® IRREVERENT GUIDES

Amsterdam	Los Angeles	San Francisco
Boston	Manhattan	Seattle & Portland
Chicago	New Orleans	Vancouver
Las Vegas	Paris	Walt Disney World®
London	Rome	Washington, D.C.

FROMMER'S® BEST-LOVED DRIVING TOURS

Britain	Germany	Northern Italy
California	Ireland	Scotland
Florida	Italy	Spain
France	New England	Tuscany & Umbria

HANGING OUT™ GUIDES

Hanging Out in England	Hanging Out in France	Hanging Out in Italy
Hanging Out in Europe	Hanging Out in Ireland	Hanging Out in Spain

THE UNOFFICIAL GUIDES®

Bed & Breakfasts and Country Inns in:	Southwest & South Central Plains	Mid-Atlantic with Kids
California	U.S.A.	Mini Las Vegas
Great Lakes States	Beyond Disney	Mini-Mickey
Mid-Atlantic	Branson, Missouri	New England and New York with Kids
New England	California with Kids	New Orleans
Northwest	Chicago	New York City
Rockies	Cruises	Paris
Southeast	Disneyland®	San Francisco
Southwest	Florida with Kids	Skiing in the West
Best RV & Tent Campgrounds in:	Golf Vacations in the Eastern U.S.	Southeast with Kids
California & the West	Great Smoky & Blue Ridge Region	Walt Disney World®
Florida & the Southeast	Inside Disney	Walt Disney World® for Grown-ups
Great Lakes States	Hawaii	Walt Disney World® with Kids
Mid-Atlantic	Las Vegas	Washington, D.C.
Northeast	London	World's Best Diving Vacations
Northwest & Central Plains		

SPECIAL-INTEREST TITLES

Frommer's Adventure Guide to Australia & New Zealand
Frommer's Adventure Guide to Central America
Frommer's Adventure Guide to India & Pakistan
Frommer's Adventure Guide to South America
Frommer's Adventure Guide to Southeast Asia
Frommer's Adventure Guide to Southern Africa
Frommer's Britain's Best Bed & Breakfasts and Country Inns
Frommer's Caribbean Hideaways
Frommer's Exploring America by RV
Frommer's Fly Safe, Fly Smart
Frommer's France's Best Bed & Breakfasts and Country Inns
Frommer's Gay & Lesbian Europe

Frommer's Italy's Best Bed & Breakfasts and Country Inns
Frommer's New York City with Kids
Frommer's Ottawa with Kids
Frommer's Road Atlas Britain
Frommer's Road Atlas Europe
Frommer's Road Atlas France
Frommer's Toronto with Kids
Frommer's Vancouver with Kids
Frommer's Washington, D.C., with Kids
Israel Past & Present
The New York Times' Guide to Unforgettable Weekends
Places Rated Almanac
Retirement Places Rated

America Online Keyword: Travel
Booked seat 6A, open return.
Rented red 4-wheel drive.
Reserved cabin, no running water.
Discovered space.